18,95

D0893905

POLITICS AND
PUBLIC POLICY IN
KENYA AND TANZANIA

POLITICS AND
PUBLIC POLICY IN
KENYA AND TANZANIA

edited by
JOEL D. BARKAN

with
JOHN J. OKUMU

PRAEGER PUBLISHERS
Praeger Special Studies

New York • London • Sydney • Toronto

Library of Congress Cataloging in Publication Data
Main entry under title:

Politics and public policy in Kenya and Tanzania.

Bibliography: p.
Includes index.
1. Kenya—Politics and government—Addresses,
essays, lectures. 2. Tanzania—Politics and government—
—Addresses, essays, lectures. 3. Kenya—Social policy
—Addresses, essays, lectures. 4. Tanzania—Social
policy—Addresses, essays, lectures. 5. Rural
development—Kenya—Addresses, essays, lectures.
6. Rural development—Tanzania—Addresses, essays,
lectures. I. Barkan, Joel D. II. Okumu, John.
JQ2947.A2P64   1979   309.1'676'204   78–19470
ISBN 0–03–023206–6
  pbk 0–03–052336–2

PRAEGER PUBLISHERS, PRAEGER SPECIAL STUDIES
383 Madison Avenue, New York, N.Y., 10017, U.S.A.

Published in the United States of America in 1979
by Praeger Publishers,
A Division of Holt, Rinehart and Winston, CBS Inc.

9 038 987654321

© 1979 by Praeger Publishers

To J.S.C.

PREFACE

DURING THE PAST DECADE, Kenya and Tanzania have attracted an unusual amount of attention because of the divergent conceptions of development each has chosen to pursue. As Kenya has sought to develop its political economy on the basis of *patron-client capitalism* and the continuation of strong ties with the West, while Tanzania has pursued the goal of *one-party socialism* combined with a foreign policy of "diversified dependence," these two East African neighbors have provided much fuel for the continuous debate over what constitutes development in a third-world society, and what are the most appropriate strategies for achieving it. In this context, Kenya and Tanzania are often perceived as a pair of case studies that approach the status of ideal types—virtually pure examples of the two most significant models of development (or, depending upon one's values, underdevelopment) pursued in the third world today.

To the extent that these perceptions are valid—and it is not always clear that they are—the experiences of Kenya and Tanzania raise many questions and provide numerous lessons for those concerned with developmental problems elsewhere in black Africa, and throughout the third world: To what extent have Kenya and Tanzania succeeded in carrying out their respective conceptions of development? Of the many policies they have attempted to implement since independence, which ones have been most effective for achieving their respective conception of development, and which ones have frustrated their goals? What factors, both domestic and foreign, have constituted the most significant opportunities and constraints for Kenyan and Tanzanian policy makers as they have attempted to operationalize the alternative models of development each has chosen to pursue? To what extent do the combined experiences of the two countries suggest that the two models of development they have followed constitute a meaningful, and especially a viable, set of choices and guidelines for policy makers charged with developing other third-world societies?

The purpose of this volume is to arrive at some tentative answers to these questions through a comparative analysis of the political institutions in the two countries, and the major policies each has followed to carry out its particular conception of development. This volume consequently departs from the usual formula of focusing on the developmental process in one political system, or of presenting a collection of diverse essays on some general theme, each of which deals with a different topic covering one or different locales. We shall therefore present a substantive review of the Kenyan and Tanzanian experience through mid-1977, via a series of comparative essays that explore different aspects of public policy as they have existed in both countries.* This volume thus purposely falls between two categories. On the one hand, it is not a research monograph that examines one particular problem or political system in depth. On the other hand, it is not the presentation of a loosely related collection of research papers by a random group of scholars. Instead, the volume is intended to be a discussion in which the participants attempt to speak, and argue with themselves and with each other, within the rubric of a single set of questions that pertain to their respective research interests. As such, it is the hope of the editors that this volume possesses a coherency of theme often missing in collected works, while at the same time maintaining a diversity of perspective in relation to that theme.

Given our objective, it is fitting that this book is basically a collegial effort by several members of the same generation of scholars, whose recent research activities have been of a comparative nature, and who have focused most of their work on the two countries considered herein. Since 1970, all of the contributors have conducted field research, and/or taught at the national universities, in both countries. Five of the eight contributors were colleagues in the Department of Political Science at the University of Dar es Salaam in 1973 and 1974, while another five have been, or are now, members of the Institute for Development Studies at the University of Nairobi. The backgrounds of the individual authors, however, and especially the opinions they hold about the developmental process in East Africa, vary greatly. It is therefore not surprising that they do not always agree in their assessments of the extent to which Kenya and Tanzania have moved toward their respective developmental objectives. Nor is there a consensus about what constitutes the most critical obstacle to development that each country must overcome, though all share a particular concern for the problem of inequality.

The essays presented in this volume are thus a continuation of many unresolved debates and informal discussions that the authors engaged in during their years together in Nairobi and Dar es Salaam in the early and mid-1970s. For this reason, the editors have thought it appropriate to dedicate this collection to a scholar/administrator of rare insight and integrity who, at one time or another, encouraged or facilitated the work of each of the editors and contributors: As the director of the Institute for Devel-

---

*Some of the essays in this volume also consider events that occurred in late 1977 and the first half of 1978. All were written, however, before the death of Kenya's first president, Jomo Kenyatta, on August 22, 1978.

opment Studies in the late 1960s, and the East African representative of the Rockefeller Foundation until 1973, James S. Coleman played a unique role in the establishment of the social sciences in East Africa. Unlike many men in similar positions, Jim Coleman actively encouraged the work of those who were among his most severe intellectual critics, as well as the work of those with whom he shared a commonality of views. As a catalyst for a wide spectrum of research efforts on the developmental process in East Africa, at a time when the meaning of development itself became the subject of intense debate, he contributed to the intellectual maturation of the contributors to this volume in ways that, at this juncture, can only be acknowledged, and not adequately measured or repaid.

The editors would also like to acknowledge the secretarial assistance provided by the Department of Political Science at the University of Iowa during the final preparation of the manuscript for publication, and the many months of patience on the part of Bruce Warshavsky of Praeger Publishers during which time the contributions appearing in this volume trickled in from various corners of the globe. Without this timely support, this volume would not have come to fruition.

CONTENTS

LIST OF TABLES AND FIGURE

PART I

Introduction

1

COMPARING POLITICS AND PUBLIC POLICY IN KENYA AND TANZANIA

Joel D. Barkan

THE SETTING

FOR MORE THAN A DECADE, students of African politics and development have followed events in Kenya and Tanzania* with special interest. Occupying adjacent territories in what was once a single colonial domain, the two countries have been the objects of continuous comparision since becoming independent in the early 1960s. Similar in population,[1] these two neighbors share a common and related history dating back to the precolonial era, a common culture and ethnic makeup, and a common set of geographical and natural conditions that bear on the day-to-day lives of their people.[2] These shared experiences gave rise to two states that, at the formal end of the colonial period, were fundamentally alike in terms of the structure of their political economies, and their capacity to become viable and independent national entities. Despite some important differences resulting from Kenya's history as a center of European settlement,[3] conditions in the two countries at the time of independence were basically the same. Given these conditions, the range of policy options available to the leaderships of the two countries were likewise similar. This was especially true in respect to questions concerning the meaning of national development, and the strategies by which development could be achieved.

---

*Tanzania has been known by several names. The country became independent as Tanganyika in 1961. Following the merger between Tanganyika and Zanzibar in 1964 the country became officially known as the United Republic of Tanzania. Throughout this volume the country shall be referred to as Tanzania, although the discussion pertains solely to events on the mainland.

That Kenya answered these questions with one set of policies, while Tanzania chose another, is well known to every reader of this book, and is the principal reason why the two countries together have attracted far more attention than either would have attracted alone, had they chosen to follow development strategies that were essentially the same. Although Kenya and Tanzania have been the objects of comparison since becoming independent states, these comparisions took on a special significance, and became more frequent, after 1965, and especially after 1967 when Tanzania turned away from the policies it had pursued since independence, to embark on a course of socialist development. Since that time the two countries have been perceived as prototypes of capitalist and socialist development and as such, have been viewed as a pair of concrete examples of what is likely to happen, and not happen, when an African country chooses one or the other of these two approaches to development. The many similarities in the basic conditions existing in Kenya and Tanzania have made their respective policies especially attractive objects of comparative study. In their attempts to assess the significance of the development strategies pursued by each country, students of comparative development can hold constant most variables other than the development strategies themselves, and thereby reach more accurate assessments of the impact of these strategies.

Given their common background and conditions, it is not surprising that in the years immediately after independence the domestic and foreign policies of Kenya and Tanzania were substantially alike. Prior to 1965 the leadership of both countries devoted much effort to increasing their ability to manage and contain political conflict, and thereby consolidate their position as the ruling elite.[4] Both countries commenced a rapid expansion and Africanization of the civil service by building upon the administrative framework established during the colonial period. Both sought to expand social welfare services for their citizens, especially education. Both sought to accelerate the rate of economic growth via heavy infusions of foreign aid and foreign private investment, and both sought to maintain relatively smooth relations with the United Kingdom, the former colonial overlord while at the same time professing a foreign policy of nonalignment.[5]

The policies pursued by Kenya and Tanzania in the early 1960s not only resembled each other, but were similar to those pursued by virtually every other African state, save Guinea and possibly Ghana, during this period. This similarity—indeed, duplication—in the basic thrust of public policy from one African country to the next was the result of similar conditions in these countries at the time of independence,[6] and of similarities in the backgrounds, interests, and perceptions of the nationalist political leaders to whom power was transferred by the outgoing colonial regimes.[7] Of the two, the interests and perceptions of the members of the nationalist elite were particularly important. Not until some leaders began to question the utility and cost of their initial policies did significant differences emerge between the policies pursued by different African states, and more fundamentally, between the conceptions of development the leaders of these states committed themselves to fulfill.

In Kenya and Tanzania, such questioning, and the differences in policy to which it gave rise, did not occur until 1965. The process of reassessment began in Tanzania as a result of a combination of circumstances over which neither country had control. Having obtained independence two years before Kenya did (1961 as against 1963), and having done so without experiencing severe divisions within the nationalist movement, Tanzania, by the end of 1965, had passed through four years of independent rule, during which time its leaders were able to devote an increasing amount of their attention to the country's problems of underdevelopment.[8] In contrast, Kenya's transition to self-rule was far more complex. During the first year of independence the country's leadership was preoccupied with resolving serious divisions within the ruling Kenya African National Union (KANU), containing and subsequently subduing an opposition party that represented the interests of roughly one-third of Kenya's population, reconverting the country's constitutional structure of government to that of a unitary state, and dealing with the ever-explosive issue of land shortages by resettling Africans on land formerly reserved for European farmers.[9] These pressing issues, and the mood of national crisis that accompanied them at the time, afforded the leadership few chances to reflect upon development policy, other than to endorse existing policies (of which land policy was probably the most significant) that had been set in place prior to independence.

A second, and probably the major, factor that prompted Tanzania to be the first to question its initial policies was the greater vulnerability of its policies to a variety of external pressures, both economic and political. Although the economies and the economic policies of Kenya and Tanzania were, and remain, highly dependent on the policies of industrialized countries, fluctuations in the world price for their respective agricultural exports, and the policies of foreign private investors, Tanzania has consistently been at a relative disadvantage compared to its northern neighbor. Because the Western enclave in Tanzania was always smaller,[10] and less developed than in Kenya, and because Dar es Salaam could not provide the range of external economies conducive to the establishment of new enterprises, Tanzania was unsuccessful from the start in attracting foreign private investors into the country, despite the passage of an act of Parliament guaranteeing their capital. Foreign aid from industrial nations was also less than expected at the time of independence, in part because of Tanzania's desire to pursue a foreign policy of nonalignment, and its uncompromising support for the liberation movements in southern Africa, particularly in Rhodesia and Mozambique. Thus while the country's first two development plans, for the periods of 1961–64 and 1964–69, were based on the expectation that roughly four-fifths of the country's development budget would be provided by external sources (both public and private), it was clear by the end of 1965 that these expectations were unrealistic.[11]

In addition, foreign exchange earnings from sisal, the country's major export, dropped in 1965 by 35 percent, compounding Tanzania's difficulties in fulfilling its goals. Squeezed by such pressures to a far greater extent than Kenya was, Tanzania began to search for alternative development strategies that were more in keeping with its limited resources. Thus by June 1966, President Julius K. Nyerere, in an address to the Tanzanian Parliament, set forth the outline of what was to become a new policy for development, based on self-reliance. Although Tanzania would continue to seek both foreign aid and foreign private investment, the country would no longer depend on such inputs. Development policy would henceforth be based on the resources the country could generate on its own.[12]

A third variable in the situation that led Tanzania to retreat from the policies of the immediate postindependence period was the reflective nature and capacity for self-criticism of the country's president, Nyerere. Writing almost a decade and a half after the events, one can only speculate as to whether Nyerere would have begun the reexamination of his government's policies in the manner that he did and when he did, had Tanzania not been subject to the opportunities and constraints noted above. Put differently, would Nyerere have initiated the reassessment of existing policies had he been in the shoes of his Kenyan counterpart, Jomo Kenyatta? Though no definitive answers can be given to these questions, one conclusion is clear: Given the conditions impinging on Tanzania at the time, Nyerere initiated a reassessment of his government's policies whereas other African leaders, when confronted with similar conditions, did not. Thus while some observers, such as Claude Ake, argue, as he does in Chapter 5, that Tanzania's socialist policies and ideological development of the late 1960s are primarily the result of the objective conditions that confronted Tanzania during this period, others, including this writer, would submit that the factor of individual leadership cannot be ignored.[13]

Although Nyerere's leadership provides only a partial explanation of why Tanzania embarked on a course of socialist construction, it is also obvious that he articulated a socialist response to the conditions confronting Tanzania with a clarity and comprehensiveness that others did not. One must distinguish, however, between Nyerere the socialist intellectual, and Nyerere the socialist policy maker. Nyerere's intellectual interest in socialism dates back to his student days in Edinburgh.[14] Like many other African leaders who became attracted to socialism while studying abroad,

Nyerere subordinated the goal of building socialism in his country to the goal of achieving independence, after he returned home and became involved in nationalist politics. Even after independence, Nyerere's commitment to socialism was more philosophical than substantive in terms of its impact on Tanzanian policy. In 1962, the year in which he turned over the prime ministership to Rashidi Kawawa so that he could devote his energies to revitalizing Tanzania's ruling party, the Tanganyika African National Union (TANU), Nyerere grappled with the meaning of socialism in the African context in an essay entitled "Ujamaa: The Basis of African Socialism."[15] Nyerere's primary concern in this discussion was to demonstrate the relevance, for Africa, of socialism's basic concern for equality and harmony in human relations. Socialism, Nyerere argued, was not a foreign ideology born out of the class conflicts of Western industrial societies and imported into Africa, but a set of universal principles relevant to all mankind. These principles, moreover, could only be realized through efforts at socialist construction that were sensitive to the unique conditions existing in different societies. Most important, socialism was indigenous to Africa, as evidenced by the equality of economic and social relations within the extended family system and the traditional local community. The challenge of socialist construction for African countries such as Tanzania was therefore that of extending principles already operative within the African family to the level of the nation-state.

Though interesting as a statement of political theory, Nyerere's essay appears to have had little effect on Tanzanian domestic policy prior to 1967, except, perhaps, in the decision to abolish the freehold system of land tenure instituted during the colonial period, and in the decision in 1964 to embark on a program of rural development modeled along the lines of the Israeli kibbutz. It is also interesting to note that, of the 58 published speeches that Nyerere gave between his essay on *ujamaa* in 1962 and the Arusha Declaration, in January 1967, in which he set forth the first policy guidelines for socialist construction, only five discuss or mention socialism as the framework for Tanzania's development.[16] Prior to the Arusha Declaration, Nyerere the socialist policy maker did not exist.

Tanzania's reassessment of its development policies thus began with a concern for the achievement of development through self-reliance rather than with a concern for socialist construction. As noted above, this reassessment was largely the result of world economic conditions that impinged upon the country, and considerations of foreign policy. Not until Arusha did the pressure of objective conditions combine with the philosophical principles of Tanzania's president to produce a set of policies and policy guidelines designed to develop the country within a socialist framework. It must also be remembered that the Arusha Declaration, as indicated by its subtitle—TANU's Policy on Socialism and Self-Reliance—placed equal weight on both socialism and self-reliance, and viewed the achievement of each as being dependent on the achievement of the other. The importance attributed to the goal of self-reliance underscores the decidedly nationalist context within which socialist construction was to occur.[17] What was at stake in the minds of Tanzania's leaders was not merely the development of Tanzania into a socialist society, but the transformation of the country into a truly independent state capable of pursuing its national interest as it defined it.

With the promulgation of the Arusha Declaration in January 1967, Tanzania made a dramatic departure from the policies it had pursued during its first five years of independence. The impact of Arusha was particularly great because of the comprehensiveness of the document, and the followup it generated in terms of substantive policies in a variety of fields. Included within the declaration itself was a decree nationalizing the banks and other major enterprises in the private sector, most of which were foreign owned. The declaration also contained a stringent leadership code, which forbids any government leaders, including civil servants, to own stock in private corporations, obtain rental income, or receive more than one salary. During the balance of 1967, guidelines were established to reorganize the national educational system, and to achieve rural development, in a manner consistent with the ethic of socialism and self-reliance.[18] Salaries of cabinet ministers and senior civil servants were subsequently frozen or reduced to lower the level of inequality within the public sector.

The flurry of pronouncements and activity that occurred in Tanzania during this period captured the imagination of many outside observers who were attracted by the eloquence and logic with which Nyerere articulated the need for his country to break with the past. In the words of one writer, students of African development became afflicted with "Tanzaphilia."[19] Nyerere's idealism and projected experiments were viewed by many as the solution to not only Tanzania's problems, but those of most other African states as well.[20] Whereas some African states, such as Kwame Nkrumah's Ghana, had tried and failed to build socialism on the basis of rapid industrialization, and were both authoritarian and corrupt in their rule, the Tanzanian experiment was directed toward the peasant, and was perceived as democratic and honest in its approach. Given these attributes, both real and ascribed, Tanzania soon attracted a large following of sympathetic supporters around the world, particularly liberals and intellectuals of the left of assorted hues.[21]

Tanzania's popularity in the wake of the Arusha Declaration also heightened the comparisons made between it and its northern neighbor. Whereas before Arusha, Kenya and Tanzania were perceived as two neighbors cut from the same cloth, after Arusha they were viewed as having chosen mutually exclusive conceptions of development, and incompatible strategies for achieving development. What was defined as development in Kenya was viewed as underdevelopment in Tanzania, and vice versa. That Tanzania had only just embarked on a course of socialist construction, and continued to have more in common with its neighbor than with those third-world states, such as North Vietnam and Cuba, that had undergone a socialist transformation, did not matter; the two countries were increasingly regarded as polar opposites insofar as their development strategies were concerned.

From roughly 1967 through 1975 the two countries were often viewed as something of a controlled experiment that would ultimately demonstrate which of the two strategies was most appropriate in the African context. After the fall of Nkrumah in Ghana in 1966, until the emergence of Marxist-oriented regimes in Angola, Ethiopia, Guinea-Bissau, and Mozambique in late 1974 and 1975, Tanzania was the only country in sub-Saharan Africa, except possibly Guinea, pursuing an avowedly socialist conception of development.

This period, which began with the Arusha Declaration and culminated in the forced villagization of up to 70 percent of the country's population, was a period of continuous experimentation and debate within Tanzania as the leadership searched, and in some cases groped, for policies to advance socialist construction in virtually every field. The period was also one in which Kenya, having dealt with the immediate problems that complicated her transition to self-rule, evolved her own conception of what development entailed, and a set of institutions and strategies by which it would be achieved. Though these policies were built upon the foundation of the colonial legacy and were less dramatic than the new departures undertaken by Tanzania, they were no less significant. The two countries together also gained a great deal of attention during this period as a result of the fact that, with the exception of the Nigerian civil war, no other sequence of events on the African continent continuously attracted so much attention from outside observers, or provided such important lessons for development. With the emergence of more radical regimes in Ethiopia and in the former Portuguese territories in the mid-1970s, and with events in southern Africa advancing to crisis stage, attention began to shift elsewhere. By then, Kenya and Tanzania had become known quantities. The short-term results of their efforts to realize their respective conceptions of development were visible to all.

THE MEANING OF DEVELOPMENT

The broad parameters of the strategies pursued by Kenya and Tanzania are well known to most readers, and need only be mentioned here. On the one hand, Kenya has defined development in terms of the continued growth and elaboration of the political and economic institutions established in the country during the colonial period. Chief among these has been (1) the expansion of the administrative state, particularly the provincial administration; (2) the establishment, in lieu of an effective political party, of a series of informal and regionally based patron-client hierarchies, composed of local, regional, and national leaders, that function as political machines to link the grass roots of the political system to the center; and (3) the expansion of an already developed private economic sector based in Nairobi and dependent on foreign capital for its growth. In contrast, Tanzania since 1967 has attempted a complete break with the institutional legacies it inherited at independence. Most important in this regard has been (1) the attempt to create an extensive, disciplined, and ideologically committed political party from the apex of the political system down to the grass roots for the purpose of mobilizing the country's population to achieve socialist development and increasing their participation in the governance of their society; (2) the subordination of all other institutions—especially the administrative agencies of the Tanzanian government—to the authority of the party;[22] and (3) the public takeover and constriction of the private sector of the economy.

In respect to economic policy, Kenya has concentrated on the achievement of rapid economic growth and a rise in the overall standard of living at the expense of increasing the levels of inequality between individuals of different socioeconomic status or class, between residents of the urban and rural areas, and between residents of those rural areas that are already moderately developed and integrated into the national economic system, and those that are not. Conversely, Tanzania has sought systematically to reduce and eventually eliminate the extent of all three of these forms of inequality to achieve a classless and nonexploitative society. Kenya and Tanzania thus pose the classic choice between concentration on the expansion of the national pie versus concentration on the distribution of the pie. As is shown below, that choice is not without costs.

Lastly, the two countries have pursued different strategies in respect to the conduct of their foreign affairs. Kenya has sought to maintain close ties with the major Western industrial nations, especially Britain, in order to build overseas markets for its products, expand tourism (Kenya's second largest source of foreign exchange), and maintain the flow of private and public foreign investment into the country. Tanzania, on the other hand, has made a concerted effort to pursue a policy of nonalignment by expanding trade and obtaining technical and military assistance from China, and from smaller Western countries such as Sweden and the Netherlands. Tanzania has also played an active role in providing support for the liberation movements in southern Africa, while Kenya has pursued a policy of noninvolvement on this issue.

At the risk of some oversimplification, we shall label Kenya's conception of development and the policies it has adopted as patron-client capitalism, and refer to the Tanzanian experiment as an example of one-party socialism. By affixing these labels we wish to draw attention to the contrasts between the conceptions of development each country is trying to pursue, and to the fact that these two examples are representative of the two major alternative roads to development traveled in the third world today. Having affixed these labels, however, we caution the reader to remember that, although Kenya and Tanzania have chosen different paths to development, the objective conditions existing in both countries remain basically the same. Neither of these countries has yet to realize its respective conception of development, nor will they do so for many years. To a great extent, these conceptions of development are just that—plans in the minds of the members of each country's governing elite, who comprise but a tiny proportion of the total population. One must not forget that the vast bulk of the population in both countries is made up of peasants, not elites, and that from their perspective, either conception of development represents an intrusion into their lives and institutions. Thus while the conceptions of development and the development strategies pursued by Kenya and Tanzania are very different in content, and are significant insofar as they are representative of what is happening in other countries, such distinctions are often not perceived or appreciated by the very people for whom they have been made. This extremely salient fact must be kept in mind when evaluating the degree of progress, or lack thereof, that Kenya and Tanzania have achieved toward their respective developmental goals. That both countries have encountered serious difficulties in their pursuit of development is not only a function of the strategies they have chosen, but of the magnitude of the task.[23]

Despite the fact that different countries such as Kenya and Tanzania define development in very different terms, most of the vast literature on development, both theoretical and empirical (and both liberal and socialist), has considered the developmental process in terms of the realization of a single set of specified conditions. While the particular conditions, and combinations thereof, often vary from one analysis to the next, as do the sequences of events by which these conditions can be achieved, each analyst invariably employs a single operational model to explain and measure the developmental process as that analyst defines it. Whether a given society is a "developed" society, and if so, how developed, thus becomes a question of measuring the extent to which the conditions specified by the analyst are present or absent in the society in question. The developmental process is similarly reduced to a search for those independent variables and/or contradictions that cause the conditions through which development is said to occur.

In this context, comparative discussions of the relative levels of development in two or more societies are discussions in which these societies are compared against some common standard. An obvious problem arises, however, when the societies in question are committed to achieving different conceptions of development, and therefore cannot be compared against the same set of criteria. In such cases, different societies making roughly the same progress in achieving their respective development goals may be regarded as relatively more or less developed simply because they are evaluated in the same terms. Conversely, different societies that have attained different levels of development in terms of their respective indexes of development, may be regarded as having made the same amount of progress when considered against a common standard.

The main point to be made here is that development is an inherently ethical phenomenon, a set of value judgments about what constitutes the good society and about the institutions and processes through which the good society can be achieved. Contrary to the positivist orientation of most behavioral scientists, development is not a value-neutral process or condition,[24] and attempts to treat it as such only muddy the conceptual waters. Attempts to formulate value-neutral systemic models of political and economic development either do not apply to societies pursuing conceptions of development that are inconsistent with these models,[25] or apply to all societies at such a general level of abstraction that they are of marginal utility for understanding the developmental process in specific locales.[26] Attempts to apply value-neutral models are especially useless when comparing and evaluating the policies of two or more countries committed to different development goals. While it is possible to formulate models of development that roughly classify all societies in terms of their relative levels of development, or, in the case of Marxist analysis, outline the historical process through which development occurs, it is virtually impossible to employ such theoretical constructs in evaluating the extent to which the specific policies of a given society advance or retard the realization of the particular conception of development that the society is trying to achieve.

It is at the level of policy making, however, that those concerned with the developmental process in its substantive—as distinct from its theoretical—properties act. To speak meaningfully to these people, social theorists concerned with development must consider the questions which weigh on the minds of policy makers. In most cases these are questions of how, and under what conditions, they might devise policies which are more effective for realizing the particular conception of development they are charged to achieve. They are not questions of whether their country is relatively more or less developed than some other country or set of countries with which their country might have something in common.

Because they tend to ask different questions, social scientists concerned with the theoretical aspects of development in a global context, and policy makers concerned with development in a specific society, frequently talk past each other. There is no logical necessity for this lack of communication to continue. A dialogue between social theorists and policy makers, however, is unlikely to occur until the former adjust their methods of evaluation to the fact that different groups of the latter subscribe to different values, and hence to different notions of what development entails.[27]

COMPARING COUNTRIES WITH DIFFERENT DEVELOPMENT GOALS

Because Kenya and Tanzania have chosen to follow such divergent paths to the good society, any attempt to measure their relative rates of progress against a single standard would be an exercise of marginal worth. We shall, instead, attempt to delineate the costs and benefits of each country's policies by employing multiple standards of evaluation. Because no standard of evaluation is neutral, we shall, for purposes of comparison, measure the appropriateness of each country's strategies against both its own development standards and those of the other country. Through this method we hope to call attention to both the intended and the unintended consequences of the policies pursued by the two countries, and thereby to specify the range of viable options open to the policy makers in each. As for a final decision on which are the most promising policies in each area of policy concern discussed in this book, we shall make no recommendation, for this depends on the overall conception of development one is committed to fulfill. We shall not refrain, however, from drawing attention to the lessons which the developmental experiences of Kenya and Tanzania provide for each other. Given the similar objective conditions in each, these lessons are many, despite the different conceptions of development each pursues.

Despite the great interest in Kenya and Tanzania as examples of capitalist and socialist development, relatively few comparisons of the two countries are found in the literature. As indicated by the Selected Bibliography, the literature on both countries is extensive, and probably exceeds that for any other independent African state except Nigeria. The great preponderance of this material, however, is concerned with only one of the two countries. Only a few works consider the development strategies of one in contrast to the strategies of the other. While in some analyses limited to an examination of one of the countries, that country's policies have been implicitly and explicitly contrasted with the policies of the other, these studies have merely assumed, rather than confirming by direct investigation, that the situation in the other country is the opposite of that in the country examined.[28]

Three reasons account for the dearth of comparative material on Kenya and Tanzania. First, and most important, is the relatively short period during which the two countries have pursued divergent development goals. The articulation of these goals by their respective leaders dates back only to the mid-1960s, while their respective policies to achieve these goals, especially in the case of Tanzania, are of more recent origin and are still in the process of being devised. The impact of these divergent strategies is thus only beginning to emerge, and their long-term significance can be discerned only in general terms. Any attempt to compare the developmental experiences of the two countries consequently runs the risk of being premature, and of being regarded by some observers—particularly policy makers in either country—as a rush to judgment. For this reason, the contributors to this volume regard their conclusions as tentative, and indeed speculative, when assessing the prognosis for the long term. We strongly submit, however, that it is far more enlightening to proceed with a comparative analysis that will later require some revision than to limit the discussion to one country or the other.

A second, and related, reason for the dearth of comparative literature on the developmental process in Kenya and Tanzania has been the shortage of available personnel to do the job. Although the essays that follow are but an overview of the development policies of the two countries, such an effort would not have been possible five years ago. Each essay summarizes the specialized research conducted by each author on a single aspect of policy formation in both countries, and the specialized literature on the same. Virtually all of these essays are of recent vintage. Any earlier effort to write a series of essays of the type presented here would have collapsed for lack of a sufficient empirical base.

Third, there are the inherent difficulties of comparing two systems that subscribe to such different concepts of what development entails. As discussed above, "development" is an ethical phenomenon, with the result that the choice between alternative development strategies is not simply a matter of measuring the performance of two or more systems against a common standard, but a choice of values. Comparative analyses between two systems that subscribe to different concepts of development consequently run the risk of degenerating into discussions where one system is praised and the other attacked simply because the former's development strategy is more or less consistent with the standard of evaluation employed by the analyst. On the other hand, it can be argued that a side-by-side presentation of the developmental experiences of two countries that does not attempt to compare these experiences against some standard is not a comparison at all. Analysts, in short, are damned by some if they make a direct comparison, and damned by others if they do not.

A PRELIMINARY ASSESSMENT

Since the purpose of this volume is to compare the institutions and policies of two countries that define development in different terms, it behooves us to make some preliminary assessment of the costs and benefits of each approach. For the reasons discussed above, we shall not attempt to make any final judgment as to which system is intrinsically superior to the other in terms of the concept of development each is trying to pursue. The perceptive reader will note, however, that some of the contributors have a marked preference for the goals of one system over those of the other. This is especially so for those who regard equality as a sine qua non of development, and who are consequently somewhat more predisposed to the Tanzanian experience. Our concern here, however, is primarily with performance: To what extent have Kenya and Tanzania fulfilled their conceptions of development? What have been the costs? What is the prognosis for the long term? What lessons have been learned?

To arrive at some tentative answers to these questions, one must return to the basic reality: that the objective conditions in Kenya and Tanzania have not changed dramatically since the mid-1960s, when the two countries embarked on different development paths. Like virtually every other African state, both countries remain underdeveloped and poor, with more than 90 percent of their respective populations deriving their livelihood from agriculture and related activities. Both are still marked by an essentially nodal and highly uneven pattern of development, which results in substantial differences between the quality of life in the urban areas and in the countryside, and between different rural areas. Both exhibit marked inequalities in the distribution of personal income between a tiny bureaucratic and, in the case of Kenya, commercial petty bourgeoisie on the one hand, and the mass of the population on the other. Both remain dependent on foreign capital, both public and private, to finance their development plans. Both remain extremely vulnerable to world economic conditions beyond their control, and both are limited in their capacity to pursue an independent course in foreign affairs.

Given the similarity, and especially the intractability, of these conditions, the differential impact of the development policies pursued by Kenya and Tanzania has been limited, relative to the objectives these policies are intended to attain. What impact these policies have had, however, has been significant in that the two countries have moved far enough in different directions to produce different results that are discernible for both the short and long term. These results, and the patterns of development they suggest, can be broadly assessed with respect to four groups of variables: (1) the overall and sectoral rates of economic growth; (2) the degree of inequality in the distribution of personal income, purchasing power, and government services; (3) the level and nature of participation in the political process; and (4) the extent to which the nation functions as an independent entity in a global context. Because Kenya and Tanzania have placed different emphasis on each of these dimensions, the performance of the two countries has not been the same on each. However, because these are the indexes on which both countries measure their own progress, we shall do the same for the purposes of our discussion.

Economic Growth and Production

That Kenya has placed a much greater emphasis on economic growth than has Tanzania is readily apparent from a comparison of the annual rates of growth of their gross domestic products between 1964 and 1977. As indicated in Table 1.1, the economies of the two countries grew at roughly the same rate between 1964 and 1967, the period when the development strategies of both were the same. However, since 1968, when the impact of Tanzania's socialist policies began to take effect, the growth of the Tanzanian economy has consistently lagged behind that of its northern neighbor except in 1975–76, when Kenya, with its larger manufacturing and tourist sectors, suffered disproportionately from the recession in the Western industrialized countries and Japan. A review of the growth rates of the manufacturing and commercial-agriculture sectors of the two economies, as presented in Table 1.2, indicates a similar pattern.

Kenya's advantage has been greatest in the manufacturing sector, the sector where the impact of the alternative development strategies pursued by the two countries has been most pronounced. Whereas virtually all of

TABLE 1.1: Annual Average Rates of Growth of Gross Domestic Product at Constant Prices (in percentages)

	1964–67	1968–72	1973–74	1975–76	1977
Kenya	6.8[a]	6.8[a]	5.3[b]	3.2[c]	7.3[d]
Tanzania	6.4[e]	4.6[e]	3.5[e]	4.4[f]	5.9[g]

[a] Economic Survey, 1973 (Nairobi: Government Printer, 1973), p. 5.

[b] Economic Survey, 1974 (Nairobi: Government Printer, 1974), p. 2.

[c] Economic Survey, 1977 (Nairobi: Government Printer, 1977), p. 13.

[d] "Kenya 1978: A Special Report," International Herald Tribune (Paris, September, 1978), p. s–1.

[e] Julius K. Nyerere, The Arusha Declaration: Ten Years After (Dar es Salaam: Government Printer, 1977), p. 32.

[f] Figure is an average of 3.5 percent estimated for 1975 from data presented in Nyerere, op. cit., and 5.2 percent for 1976 as cited in United Republic of Tanzania, Annual Plan for 1977/78 (Dar es Salaam: Government Printer, 1977), p. 1.

[g] Speech by Minister of Finance and Planning Introducing the Estimates of Public Revenue and Expenditure for 1978/79 (Dar es Salaam: Government Printer, 1978), p. 5.

TABLE 1.2: Annual Average Rates of Sectoral Growth at Constant Prices (in percentages)

	1964–67	1968–72	1973–74	1975–76	1977
	Manufacturing				
Kenya	7.6[a]	9.3[b]	9.3[c]	7.6[d]	15.0[e]
Tanzania	6.8[f]	4.0[f]	2.0[f]	3.3[g]	5.4[h]
	Commercial Agriculture				
Kenya	5.2[a]	6.7[b]	2.4[c]	3.5[d]	10.0[e]
Tanzania	4.1[i]	2.7[j]	1.8[k]	3.2[l]	5.6[m]
	Semimonetary Economy[n]				
Kenya	4.1[a]	3.6[b]	3.0[c]	.2[d]	n.a.[o]

[a]*Economic Survey, 1974* (Nairobi: Government Printer, 1974), pp. 4, 6.

[b]*Economic Survey, 1974*, op. cit., pp. 6–7.

[c]*Economic Survey, 1974*, op cit., p. 6 and *Economic Survey, 1977* (Naroibi: Government Printer, 1977), p. 13.

[d]*Economic Survey, 1977*, op. cit., p. 13.

[e]"Kenya 1978: A Special Report," *International Herald Tribune* (Paris, September, 1978), p. s–1.

[f]"Back to Back: A Survey of Kenya and Tanzania," *The Economist* (London: March 11, 1978), p. S–12.

[g]United Republic of Tanzania, *The Annual Plan for 1977/78* (Dar es Salaam: Government Printer, 1977), p. 1.

[h]*Speech by Minister of Finance and Planning Introducing the Estimates of Public Revenue and Expenditure for 1978/79* (Dar es Salaam: Government Printer, 1978), p. 6.

[i]*The Weekly Review* (Nairobi: October 31, 1977), p. 6.

[j]"Back to Back: A Survey of Kenya and Tanzania," op. cit., p. S–8.

[k]Estimated on the basis of a 30 percent drop in grain production from the levels of 1970–72. Because of the dramatic decline in agricultural production between 1973 and 1975 the Tanzanian government has published no official figures on the state of this crucial sector for these years.

[l]Estimated on the basis of a 1.8 percent rate of growth in 1975 and a 4.7 rate of growth as reported by the Tanzanian government in the *Annual Plan for 1977/78* op. cit., p. 1.

[m]*Speech by the Minister of Finance*, op. cit., p. 6.

[n]Data for Tanzania is unavailable, but given conditions of drought and the disruptions arising out of the villagization of the rural population between 1973 and 1976, it would be surprising if the rates of growth in Tanzania are higher than in Kenya. In Kenya, agriculture accounts for 78 percent of the income accruing to this sector.

[o]not available.

the manufacturing sector in Kenya remains in private hands, or—in cases where there is partial state ownership—under private management, the manufacturing sector in Tanzania has been almost totally state owned, and under state management since the early 1970s. Many parastatal enterprises in Tanzania have operated below capacity and at a loss.[29] Many are overstaffed, and since 1967 the output per worker in these organizations has steadily declined.[30]

Part of Kenya's advantage in manufacturing is, no doubt, due to a greater tendency among Kenyan firms to use capital-intensive over labor-intensive technology. Tanzania's parastatals are also undercapitalized compared to manufacturing firms in Kenya, where there has been a higher influx of foreign private investment. Tanzania's relatively poor performance, however, is in part due to the monopolistic position most parastatals enjoy over the type of goods they produce.

Another major factor affecting the performance of Tanzania's parastatals has been the misapplication of the TANU Party Guidelines of 1971 (Mwongozo) which, among other things, regulated the relationships between plant managers and supervisors on the one hand, and between managers and workers on the other. In an effort to raise the dignity of Tanzanian workers under Mwongozo, managers and supervisors were forbidden to treat subordinates in an arrogant manner, and workers were given the right to bring formal charges against managers who persisted, or who were perceived to persist, in such behavior. The result, in 1973 and 1974, was a series of work stoppages and lockouts of plant managers that in turn led to relatively loose supervision by managers, who feared further confrontation with their staffs.[31]

Although Kenya's margin of superior economic growth is greatest in the manufacturing sector, it is in agriculture where Tanzania's performance has been particularly disappointing. Recognizing that a strong agricultural base is a prerequisite to development in other fields, Tanzania vastly increased its expenditures on agricultural development following the Arusha Declaration. Whereas in 1967 the government invested $6.3 million in the agricultural sector, in 1976 the figure was in the neighborhood of $56 million.[32] Most of this investment, however, especially between 1973 and 1976, was not spent on activities or material inputs that would raise agricultural production, but on the relocation, into ujamaa villages, of roughly 70 percent of the country's rural population.[33] Although villagization was intended to facilitate the collective production and marketing of agricultural produce, and the provision of government services to the rural population, its initial impact has been one of mass dislocation, and declines in production. As indicated in Table 1.2, the rate of agricultural production in 1973–74 fell to 1.8 percent—a net decline on a per capita basis, given Tanzania's rate of population growth. Details of the ujamaa policy are discussed at length in Chapter 7, and to a lesser extent in Chapter 6. At this juncture it is sufficient to note that in 1974, Tanzania's production of food grains fell by more than 30 percent and the country experienced serious food shortages that necessitated substantial imports of maize and wheat. Though part of this decline may be attributed to severe drought conditions in parts of the country during this period, most of it was the result of government policies that sought to achieve goals other than growth alone.

It would thus appear that, while Tanzania's socialist policies may have achieved other development objectives, these policies, nonetheless, have been pursued at a cost of lower economic growth. Indeed, when one considers the annual rise of 2.7 percent in the country's population, there has been virtually no expansion of the Tanzanian economy since the Arusha Declaration. In contrast, Kenya's expansion, while not spectacular, has exceeded that of most other African states, and has been comparable to the growth rates of most Western industrial countries except Japan. Kenya's rise in productivity has also been undercut by a high population growth rate, of 3.3 percent, but except for the subsistence and semimonetary sector, which experienced a per capita decline between 1973 and 1976, the economy has moved forward on all fronts.

In his 1962 essay, "Ujamaa: The Basis of African Socialism," Nyerere declared that "the basic difference between a socialist society and a capitalist society does not lie in their methods of producing wealth, but in the way wealth is distributed."[34] Though valid for the purpose of classifying societies in general terms, Nyerere's distinction failed to consider whether the means for achieving the equal distribution of wealth that is basic to socialism requires any modification in the methods of producing that wealth. Given hard work, the expansion of production was assumed.

Ten years after the Arusha Declaration, in 1977, Nyerere, in a brutally candid review of his country's achievements and failures, acknowledged that Tanzania's rate of growth and productivity had lagged behind what was required for socialist development.[35] Although the president systematically identified the immediate causes of Tanzania's problems (for example, excessive management in state-owned enterprises, slackness, negligence), the relationships between the mechanisms for distributing wealth in an egalitarian manner—particularly, public ownership of the means of production—and the mechanisms of production were, once again, not examined. Other officials, however, have publicly acknowledged that in Tanzania there has been a conscious tradeoff between raising production and achieving the equal distribution of what is produced.[36] Socialist development is usually defined in terms of the achievement of both these objectives, while capitalist development concentrates on the former. The Tanzanian experience, however, suggests that the prospects for achieving both are limited.

Equality

Although the roads to socialist development are many, and Tanzania asserts that her route is, by necessity, unique, one concept dominates all variations of the socialist ideal—the notion of a classless society in which the members of that society live in harmony with each other because the society's wealth has been distributed equally and, hence, fairly to all. Despite Nyerere's assertion that socialism is thus indigenous to Africa, because traditional African societies were organized on the principle of equality, the fact remains that at the level of the nation-state, African societies rank among the most unequal in the world. As a result of the confrontation between Africa and the West, and the colonial experience that followed, the wealth of most African states is unequally distributed in at least three ways. First, and most pronounced, is the inequality in the distribution of personal income among the members of different and competing social classes. The maldistribution of personal wealth is especially great between members of the bureaucratic and commercial petty bourgeoisie on the one hand, and the remainder of the population, consisting mainly of peasants and, to a much lesser extent, workers, on the other. Inequality in the distribution of personal income is also significant across different strata of the rural population, that is, between the owners of large farms, owners of small farms, and those who own no land at all. A second dimension of inequality, and one which is of an aggregate nature is that which results from the maldistribution of personal income and the maldistribution of government services and opportunities for development between the urban areas and the countryside. Third are the aggregate inequalities that exist between different rural areas.

While it is an oversimplification to suggest, as Nyerere does, that all African traditional societies were organized on the principle of equality, it is, nonetheless, a fact that the colonial experience was the single most important source of the three forms of inequality existing in African states today. It was the colonial system that created a tiny Western-educated elite that, after independence, became the nucleus of a bureaucratic and commercial petty bourgeoisie. It was the colonial system that concentrated economic development and the development of social services (schools, health facilities, roads) around the towns it established to serve as sites for its administrative headquarters. And it was the colonial system that, when it attempted to develop the countryside, did so in a few selected areas that were established as centers for the production of export crops or were the location of other extractive industries. Thus while African societies may not have been perfectly egalitarian before the colonial intrusion, they experienced a marked increase in the level of inequality during the colonial era.

To the extent that independent African states have sought to develop their societies by building upon the institutions and centers of development created before independence, the level of inequality has continued to rise. The rapid Africanization of the civil service and the commercial sector after independence gave rise to a national petty bourgeoisie, which while not a bourgeoisie in the classic sense of owning the means of production, has controlled the distribution of their countries' wealth, and appropriated a disproportionate amount for its own use. Kenya and Tanzania have not been exceptions to this general pattern. But whereas this tendency has gone unchecked in Kenya (and, indeed, has been encouraged),[37] to the point that segments of the bureaucratic and commercial petty bourgeoisie are in the process of constituting a bourgeoisie proper, in Tanzania the process has been partially forestalled.

As only fragmentary data have been published on the distribution of personal incomes in both Kenya and Tanzania, it is exceedingly difficult to assess the degree of inequality in each. We cannot, for example, construct a series of yearly Gini indexes of inequality from 1967 to the present, to determine, with precision, the extent to which inequality in the two countries has become more or less pronounced as a result of the policies each has pursued. The broad outlines, however, are clear.

As in other African countries, rapid Africanization of the civil service and the commercial sector after independence in Kenya contributed to the emergence of a black middle class, and to an increasingly unequal distribution of the nation's wealth. In the absence of better data, the proportion of Kenya's national income accruing to this class can only be estimated in general terms. Results of a 1970 survey of households reported by the International Labour Office, in a critical review of employment and incomes, suggest that the wealthiest eighth of Kenya's population (consisting almost exclusively of civil servants, political leaders, and leading businessmen) accounted for approximately 57 percent of the country's annual income. Conversely, the poorest eighth earned only 2 percent, while the poorest three-fifths of the population accounted for 19 percent.[38]

It is also clear that the level of inequality in Kenya has become more pronounced since independence, and probably exceeds that in Tanzania. At the time of independence, Kenya's civil service was substantially larger than Tanzania's, with the result that a greater number of individuals began earning high salaries relative to the rest of the population, thereby accentuating the division between rich and poor. A similar development subsequently occurred in the commercial sector as a result of Nairobi's position as the commercial center of East Africa—a preeminence which has increased during the last decade as more and more multinational firms have set up operations in Kenya's capital, and have, in turn, hired recent Kenyan graduates from the University of Nairobi, and from institutions abroad. Further, salaries of Kenyan civil servants have been consistently higher than those of civil servants in Tanzania, where the ratio of the after-tax salary of the highest-paid government employee to the salary of the lowest-paid has been reduced from 20:1 to 9:1. Kenyan civil servants are also permitted to engage in private business ventures in addition to their services for the state,[39] while their Tanzanian counterparts are expressly forbidden from such activities by the country's leadership code. Also, the rate of taxation in Kenya is much less progressive than in Tanzania, and appears to have had minimal, if any, impact on the distribution of household income.[40] As noted previously, so great has been the level of accumulation of wealth by some members of the bureaucratic and commercial petty bourgeoisie that they are on the verge of constituting a bourgeoisie proper—a class that owns the means of production, and which seeks and has the capacity to create new wealth through the control thereof.[41]

A similar pattern of increasing inequality prevails in the agricultural sector, albeit at the middle- and lower-income levels. This situation is partly a result of the policy pursued by the Kenyan government, beginning in the early 1960s, to resettle African farmers on land formerly owned by Europeans. As discussed by S. E. Migot-Adholla in Chapter 7, the redistribution of land formerly in European hands was carried out on an unequal basis so as to exacerbate the already unequal distribution of land. The unequal distribution of income in the countryside has been compounded by Kenya's high rate of population growth, and by its limited supply of arable land. Whereas Tanzania possesses some 39,730 square kilometers of arable land, or .26 hectares per person, in Kenya, only 16,400 square kilometers of the land area are arable, or .12 hectares per person.[42] The result, quite simply, is that the problem of landlessness in Kenya has increased since independence, and now stands somewhere above 18 percent.[43]

The proportion of the population that is landless also continues to rise. As population pressure on land continues to build, more and more marginal farmers sell out their tiny holdings to those with large holdings, and offer their services as wage labor to the latter or in the towns. This process has been accelerated by the adverse terms of trade between the urban areas and the countryside—a burden that is borne disproportionately by marginal farmers and the landless, who do not reap the fruits of the commercial-agricultural sector. Increasing landlessness has also resulted in increasing numbers of unemployed within the urban areas and, consequently, in an increasing level of inequality within cities as well.

That the distribution of income in Kenya has become increasingly unequal at the lower reaches can be quickly seen by a review of the sectoral rates of economic growth in Table 1.2. Though not always high, the rates of growth in the manufacturing and commercial-agriculture sectors have been steady and positive, even after controlling for population rise. The rate of growth in the semimonetary sector, however, from which roughly two-thirds of the population derive their livelihood, has steadily declined over the last decade and is now negative, on a per capita basis.

Data on the distribution of personal income in Tanzania are even more fragmentary than those for Kenya. For the reasons noted above, however, the proportion of Tanzania's national income that accrues directly to the bureaucratic petty bourgeoisie is undoubtedly less than in Kenya—but how much less? Though Tanzania's civil servants, and the management of its parastatal enterprises, are paid less, taxed more, and forbidden to engage in private business ventures over and above their official duties, their indirect consumption of the gross domestic product, combined with their official emoluments, still leave them in a position of extraordinary privilege vis-a-vis the population as a whole. In addition to their basic salaries, members of the bureaucratic class in Tanzania receive a variety of "perks" including subsidized housing and access to state vehicles, which results in an overall pattern of inequality that is not substantially different from that in Kenya. One must also remember that per capita income in Tanzania ($170 per annum) is approximately 23 percent lower than that in Kenya ($220). The lower salaries paid to members of the bureaucratic class in Tanzania may thus constitute roughly the same proportion of the national income as that accruing to the members of the bureaucratic class in Kenya!

The key difference between the two countries is that the level of inequality in Tanzania is not increasing, as in Kenya, or, if it is increasing, is not rising at as fast a rate. The nationalization of Tanzania's manufacturing sector, and tight regulation of commerce following the Arusha Declaration, combined with the leadership code, have forestalled the emergence of a commercial petty bourgeoisie in Tanzania comparable to that in Kenya, and the emergence of a bourgeoisie proper. Tanzania has also succeeded in achieving what might best be termed "symbolic equality," to a degree undreamed of in Kenya. In Tanzania, because the salaries of the bureaucratic and political class are among the lowest in Africa, and because they are so severely taxed, the consumptive habits that typify this class elsewhere in Africa are minimal. Political leaders, civil servants, and managers of parastatal organizations are not perceived as "ripping off" the rest of Tanzanian society even though they consume a disproportionate amount of the national income.

It must also be acknowledged that the bureaucratic and managerial class in Tanzania has probably been squeezed to the point where any further attempt to reduce their share of the national income would be counterproductive. Most members of this class function almost totally within the monetary economy. Most also reside in the urban areas, where they must purchase virtually all of what they consume at high prices. As a result, many public servants in Tanzania can barely make ends meet. Morale within the civil service and the parastatals has consequently declined, and absenteeism has become a major problem.[44] Given the harsh egalitarian ethic that prevails in Tanzania, there are few rewards, and, hence, little incentive to perform beyond the minimum effort required to obtain one's monthly check. It was, no doubt, in recognition of this fact, and its relationship to Tanzania's mediocre rate of growth, that in 1976 the government retired 9,500 civil servants and officials in parastatal organizations, and, at the same time, raised salaries for those who remained. Equalization of income, in short, can be taken only so far.

The level of inequality that prevails in the countryside in Tanzania is also lower than that in Kenya, though it is difficult to estimate by how much. Population pressure has substantially reduced the size of land holdings in some areas, such as that around Mount Kilimanjaro, but there is no large segment of the population that is landless, as in Kenya. Land is available to those who are willing to move out of congested areas—an opportunity facilitated by the abolition of freehold land tenure soon after independence. The abolition of formal land ownership, combined with the availability, if not abundance, of land has eliminated land speculation, and has, in turn, reduced the probability of small holders selling out to large ones.[45]

The level of inequality within the rural areas has also been reduced, or prevented from increasing at a faster rate, by the lower prices Tanzanian farmers have been paid for their produce, compared to their counterparts in Kenya. While this has reduced the income differential between cash-crop farmers, and those in the subsistence and semimonetary sector (and for a time resulted in lower food prices for Tanzania's urban workers), the policy of low prices that was pursued until 1975 also resulted in periodic and, at times, severe food shortages. As with the low salaries paid to government bureaucrats, low prices have resulted in low production, and, in some cases, smuggling to neighboring countries, particularly Kenya, as well. Nyerere himself has acknowledged that the prices paid to farmers have been too low, and have been a major cause of Tanzania's crises in agricultural production.[46] Since 1975, prices have been selectively raised on a variety of agricultural products, but in the case of export crops such as coffee the amount paid to Tanzanian farmers still runs below that paid to their Kenyan colleagues.

With respect to the inequalities of income and government services prevailing in the urban and rural areas, the situation in the two countries is roughly the same. In both countries, the manufacturing sector has consistently outperformed the agricultural sector, with the result that those in the cities, despite the inequalities that exist within these areas, have enjoyed a relatively higher standard of living than those in the countryside. The terms of internal trade between the urban and rural areas of both countries have also moved steadily to the advantage of the former. The result has been a continuous net migration, from the countryside to the urban areas, especially to the capital cities, of the two countries, and a continued disproportionate amount of expenditures by government for services in the urban areas, to keep pace with their growth.

Once again, the degree of imbalance is probably higher in Kenya than in Tanzania, but only marginally. While the rates of growth in both the manufacturing and agricultural sectors in Kenya have exceeded those in Tanzania, the differential between the performances of the two sectors is greater as well (see Table 1.2). This differential is partly a function of the greater inflow of foreign private investment to Kenya, and to Nairobi in particular. The greater inequities existing within the rural areas in Kenya, combined with the scarcity of land, have also resulted in greater migration from the countryside. Despite these tendencies, the internal terms of trade between the rural and urban areas have turned against the farmer at roughly the same rate in both countries. Thus between 1965 and 1974 the terms of trade for Tanzanians declined by between 7.6 and 14.1 percent.[47]

That the terms of trade for Tanzanian farmers should be significantly less than for their Kenyan counterparts reveals another dilemma facing Tanzania in its quest for socialist development. Farmers are paid less for their crops to reduce the level of inequality in the countryside, and to lower food costs for those in the towns. The result, however, is not only reduced production but greater inequality between the purchasing power of those in the cities and those in the rural areas. Put differently, what has been gained on one dimension of the equality equation appears to have been lost on another. The seriousness of this dilemma is also underscored by the vast expenditures Tanzania has made on agriculture and social services in the rural areas. These expenditures, especially in the ujamaa villages, have been made to raise the standard of living, and the bargaining power, of those on the periphery vis-a-vis those at the center of the Tanzanian system. It is unclear, however, whether equality on this dimension can be bought.

Regional inequalities have likewise proven intractable in the two countries, though here again it is the Tanzanians who have made the greater effort to reduce the extent of the imbalance. In both countries, regions that became centers of cash-crop agriculture, particularly the production of crops for export (such as coffee and tea), developed more rapidly and became more fully integrated into the national political economy than those regions that did not. Natural conditions, as well as colonial policies that were designed to take advantage of these conditions, are both a major cause of unbalanced development and one reason why this imbalance is so difficult to overcome. In both countries the most developed regions are those consisting mainly of highland areas that contain the most fertile and sufficiently watered land; and given the scarcity of such land, it is not surprising that these areas maintain their advantage.

As centers of cash-crop production these regions have also developed a web of institutional structures that reinforce their dominant position.

These areas have historically had the most schools, with the result that they are disproportionately represented in the civil service and other positions of leadership in both countries. These regions were also the first to establish agricultural cooperatives, social welfare organizations, and, ultimately, political organizations to advance their interests. Where these regions have also been the homelands of the most populous and politically powerful ethnic groups, as in the case of the Central Province in Kenya, the dominance of the region has become further entrenched.

The extent to which regions in Kenya with these combinations of factors have been able to lay claim to a disproportionate amount of government resources and thereby maintain their dominant position has been documented by the International Labour Office in its review of incomes and employment cited above. In 1969–70 four of the top five of Kenya's 41 districts, in terms of the percentage of the population attending primary school, were located in the Central Province. Three of the top five, in respect to educational expenditures, were located in the Central Province; and two of the top five, in terms of kilometers of roads per 1,000 square kilometers, were located in the Central Province. Of the other districts that ranked in the top five on each of these dimensions, all were located in areas of cash-crop cultivation and had been centers of development since before the end of the colonial period. With the exception of the Machakos district, in the Eastern Province, all possess superior resources of high-potential agricultural land.[48]

Despite concerted efforts to channel resources for rural development (especially expenditures on ujamaa villages) to its poorest regions, a similar pattern of imbalance prevails in Tanzania, where the areas of Kilimanjaro, West Lake, and the Southern Highlands continue to be the most developed areas, as they were at the end of the colonial period. In addition to providing a greater proportion of new services (for example, schools, health clinics, water supplies, and agricultural extensions) to the poorest regions, Tanzania has sought to redress regional imbalance by lowering prices paid to producers of cash crops, and by manipulating access to educational opportunities at the secondary and postsecondary levels. As discussed by David Court in Chapter 9, recruitment for Tanzania's secondary schools is now done on a regional rather than a national basis to ensure that a greater proportion of the relatively smaller pool of applicants from disadvantaged regions continue their education. Recruitment for the university, and therefore the upper reaches of the civil service and parastatal organizations, is likewise now based on criteria such as ideological commitment or work experience, in addition to the applicants' scores on nationwide examinations. This has reduced the likelihood of recruiting offspring of the present educated elite, and students from regions that historically have had superior educational facilities. Efforts have also been made to reduce the position of privileged regions by disbanding the institutions through which they have previously exerted political pressure on the center, and gained access to the center's resources. Particularly noteworthy in this regard was the abolition of all agricultural cooperative unions in 1976.

Despite the policies implemented to reduce the level of regional inequality, the ability of the most developed regions to perpetuate their position of superiority has not been significantly reduced. Previous development in these regions has provided them with the resources they need to perpetuate their position in spite of their being deprived of the share of national resources they received in the past. Thus, while the Tanzanian government has reduced the rate at which it provides new educational facilities to the Kilimanjaro region, the residents of the region have overcome this cutback by establishing a network of private schools to educate their young. Once again, it would appear that although Tanzania has spent heavily to achieve equality, the results have been limited.

Citizen Participation and Control

Citizen participation in the governance of their society is a central component of the political dimension of development in both countries. The emphasis each country places on participation, however, the benefits it brings, and the means by which it is to be achieved are quite different. For Kenya, participatory government is democratic government in the Western sense of the term. As such, it is an abstract goal, which, while highly desirable, may need to be deferred or limited until the country possesses sufficient resources to sustain its operation. Above all, democracy as participatory government cannot be achieved at the risk of the breakdown of the political order.

Given this requirement, participatory government in Kenya has been operationalized in terms of representative government whereby the most significant, and therefore limited, form of political participation is voting. As discussed at length in Chapter 3, Kenyans have had the opportunity of participating in the electoral process with a regularity unmatched in most other African states, but participating in a way that does not demonstrably affect the content of public policy. Participation in Kenya exists for the purpose of selecting one's representatives to central political institutions so that one's community might be more effectively linked to the center and gain access to the resources the center commands. It does not occur for the purpose of changing the leadership or character of the system, and the goals—including the conception of development—to which the system is already committed to pursuing.

When defined in such limited terms, it is not surprising that participation in Kenya has been a "success" at least in the short term. As discussed in Chapter 3, a review of the electoral process in Kenya indicates that members of the general public, especially small farmers, have a clear set of expectations of what their elected representatives should do, and are capable of basing their voting decisions on their evaluations of their representatives' performance with respect to these goals. With increasing frequency, those elected to both local and national office, but especially to the Kenya National Assembly, are those who are most effective at obtaining central government resources for the communities they represent. With each successive election, more and more communities become more effectively linked to their government via a network of patron-client hierarchies, or machines, which serve as the main organizational mechanism through which those at the lower reaches of the political system, and on the periphery, gain access to those at the top. It is also clear, however, that as more and more communities make effective demands on the center, the amount of resources available for allocation to each community will be reduced and the intensity of political conflict between these communities will increase. Once this occurs, participation may result in a breakdown of the political order, and may subsequently be suppressed. Limited as participation may be in the short run, its long-term consequence, given the character of the Kenyan system, may thus be departicipation.

The objectives of political participation in Tanzania are both more ambitious, and more difficult to attain. As in Kenya, the purpose of participation is not to provide citizens with the opportunity to determine the character of the system or the developmental goals it is committed to pursuing. Participation, however, is intended to accomplish much more than the selection of representatives by local communities on the periphery of the political system, to link the periphery to the center.

As noted by Frank Holmquist at the beginning of Chapter 6, participation is viewed as a far more critical and immediate component of the developmental process in Tanzania than in Kenya. Whereas in Kenya, participation is to be limited until the conditions to sustain political order are set in place, in Tanzania participation, like equality, is regarded as a sine qua non of development that cannot be constrained or deferred. And whereas in Kenya participation is viewed as a means to political representation that will in turn result in a political system that is more responsive to popular demands, in Tanzania participation is viewed as an end in itself —the direct control by the people of their own affairs, regardless of what that control might bring. As stated succinctly in the TANU Party Guidelines of 1971 (Mwongozo): "Any action that gives them (the people) more control of their own affairs is an action for development, even if it does not offer them better health or more bread."[49] When defined in these terms, however, participation poses a serious dilemma for Tanzania's leaders. On the one hand, they are committed to the ideal of ceding political control to the mass population on the ground that such control is both democratic and just, and hence a requisite for socialist construction. Just as the unequal distribution of wealth must be eliminated to achieve a socialist society, so too must the unequal distribution of power be eliminated. Participation, in short, is the political corollary of material equality. On the other hand, participation must not lead to a retreat from the nation's development goal of socialist construction. While participation must enable the population to control their own affairs, such control must be maintained within the parameters of socialism. Put differently, if participation viewed as political equality is the corollary of material equality, participation must not lead to an unequal distribution of power or wealth. The result, as in other systems that have opted for a development strategy of one-party socialism, is to structure participation within the organizational framework of a disciplined and ideologically committed political party.

In this framework, political participation in Tanzania is both more extensive and frequent than in Kenya, but no less constrained. Whether Tanzanian citizens have more substantive (as distinct from symbolic) control over their day-to-day affairs is also an open question, especially if one is concerned with the control derived from participation within the institutions of the national political system, as opposed to the control derived from merely living on the periphery of society, beyond the system's reach.

Various dimensions of political participation are discussed in Chapters 3 and 6 of this volume, and need not be elaborated here. It would appear, however, that while Tanzanians are frequently and formally consulted on matters of public policy, while Kenyans are not, their impact on the content of specific policies is roughly the same. Through a hierarchy of party organs; affiliated organizations such as NUTA (National Union of Tanzanian Workers) and UWT (United Women of Tanzania); and especially, a hierarchy of ward, district, and regional development committees that are charged with formulating development plans for the rural areas, Tanzanians are presented with a myriad of opportunities to participate in the political process. However, because the leadership and participants at all levels of these organizations, except the lowest, are indirectly elected, direct control by the mass of participants is not possible. Thus, while the possibilities for participation are many, the discussions which follow suggest that it is doubtful whether effective control over the policy-making process has passed to the rank and file of Tanzanian society, nor is such control likely to pass to them in the foreseeable future.

Dependence and Independence

On the question of national independence, Kenya is invariably perceived as having entered into a neocolonial and therefore dependent relationship with the industrial countries of the West, while Tanzania is viewed as having actively tried to break out of the dependency syndrome that confronts most third-world states. Though substantially correct, this rough characterization of the foreign political and economic relations of the two countries is also more apparent than real. As two underdeveloped societies with small populations and a limited range of natural resources, both Kenya and Tanzania operate in an interdependent world, and more specifically within the institutional web of international capitalism, from which neither can withdraw. Both need to import commodities from other countries, especially the industrial societies of the West, to operate and develop their economies. Both in turn need to export their products abroad to pay for these imports. Neither is in the position of a country like China, of being populous enough and of having sufficient natural resources and internal markets to isolate itself from the rest of the world while it passes through the initial stages of the developmental process in the way in which it defines that process. As a result, the relevant question for both countries is not whether and how they can become truly independent entities in the international arena, for such an objective is an unfeasible one. Rather, the question is whether these countries can reduce their level of dependence to the point where they will be able to pursue long-term strategies (for example, of five to ten years' duration) to achieve their respective conceptions of development, without being subject to extreme external pressures, such as wars or another rise in the price of oil, that make the pursuit of such strategies impossible.

Posed in these terms, both countries have achieved a considerable measure of success, if not independence, at gaining control over the development process within their respective borders. Though both countries remain heavily dependent on foreign aid and investment to finance their development budgets, both have been able to regulate the character of that aid and investment to make it consistent with their respective developmental goals.

Given her capitalist orientation, Kenya has naturally been more accommodating and attractive to foreign investors than has Tanzania. Though critics of Kenya's policies have interpreted this as an indication of Kenya's dependency on the West, it can also be argued that such accommodation is but an enlightened policy to further Kenya's developmental goals. Foreign private investment has contributed greatly to the expansion of the manufacturing sector, and especially to the expansion of tourism. Whether one regards the penetration of Kenya by foreign capital as an exacerbation of the country's dependent condition, or as the establishment of a partnership that lessens that condition, is thus in large part a function of one's values. There can be no doubt, however, that Kenya's policies in this regard have at least partially achieved their intended results.

In a similar vein, as discussed by John Okumu in Chapter 10, Tanzania has been adept at diversifying its sources of foreign assistance, and at reducing the share of assistance provided by the major industrial countries, especially Britain and the United States. This diversification has reduced the vulnerability of Tanzania's strategies for socialist development to actions by the major capitalist powers, and, at the same time, permitted Tanzania to play a more active role than Kenya in the affairs of the region. This has been especially true with respect to both the support Tanzania has provided the liberation movements in Mozambique and Zimbabwe, and the leading role it has played in the attempts to negotiate a peaceful transition to black rule in Zimbabwe and Namibia.

Despite Tanzania's success at mitigating the negative consequences of dependency, the country has become more, rather than less, dependent on foreign donors since the Arusha Declaration. The record has been especially poor since 1974, when, as a result of falling agricultural production, Tanzania was forced to import massive amounts of grain, and seek emergency aid to feed its people.[50] Falling production has also resulted in a steady increase in the nation's trade deficits. As indicated by Table 1.3 (and by Tables 10.1 and 10.3), these deficits now exceed those of Kenya, and are increasing at a faster rate. Falling agricultural production has also

TABLE 1.3: Average Annual Balance-of-Trade Surpluses and Deficits Since Independence (in millions of dollars)

Period	Kenya	Tanzania
1961 to 1966[a]	−108.8	65.0
1967 to 1972	−154.7	−28.3
1973 to 1977[b]	−194.7	−255.2
Increase in average annual deficit from 1961–66[a] to 1967–72	−45.9	−93.3
Increase in average annual deficit from 1967–72 to 1973–77[b]	−39.7	−226.2

[a] Data for Kenya are for the period of 1963 through 1966 while the data for Tanzania are for the period of 1961 through 1966.
[b] Trade figures for 1977 were estimated from data for the first six months of the year.
Sources: International Monetary Fund, *Direction of Trade Annual* (Washington, D.C.: International Monetary Fund, 1961–65, 1964–68, and 1969–75), and *Direction of Trade Monthly*, December 1977.

resulted in a marked decline in Tanzania's reserves of foreign exchange, a condition which has in turn limited its ability to import the materials it needs, such as fertilizer, to raise production and reestablish a favorable balance of trade. On the vital question of self-sufficiency in food, Kenya, ironically, has achieved self-reliance while Tanzania has not.

Another facet of the dependency issue has been the extent to which the two countries have sought to develop their tourist industries, and thereby subject their societies to foreign cultural as well as financial influence. As discussed by Richard Stren in Chapter 8, Kenya has aggressively sought to enhance its position as the tourist center of East Africa by building new hotels financed by such major international chains as Hilton and Intercontinental, while Tanzania's tourism policies have been ambivalent and cautious. The result is that while tourism has become Kenya's second greatest source of foreign exchange, and often compensates for Kenya's deficits in foreign trade, Tanzania has yet to reap substantial benefits from this source of potential wealth. Given these results, it can be argued that both countries have become more dependent as a consequence of their policies on tourism, albeit in different ways. One, however, has become relatively rich while the other has had to measure the success of its policy in other terms.

In view of these developments, and because of the different conceptions of development pursued by the two countries, it is difficult to determine, with any precision, which has made the greatest progress at furthering its national independence. By becoming increasingly integrated into the international capitalist system, Kenya has achieved a significant measure of economic growth, at the price of tying its economic and political fortunes to those of the West. In contrast, Tanzania has achieved a measure of political independence, and maintained its course of development within a socialist framework, at a price of declining production. Put differently, Kenya has purchased a measure of economic health and, perhaps ultimately, a measure of economic power by surrendering a measure of its political and cultural sovereignty, while Tanzania has done the reverse.

SUMMARY AND CONCLUSIONS

In light of our preliminary assessment of the policies Kenya and Tanzania have followed to achieve their respective conceptions of development, what lessons do the experiences of the two countries offer to each other, and to other states of sub-Saharan Africa and the third world? To summarize our analysis, it would appear that the lessons are basically threefold.

First, as noted at the beginning of this introductory chapter and reiterated midway through our discussion, the objective conditions existing in the two countries at the time of independence, at present, and in the foreseeable future are, and will remain, the same. There are no easy roads to development, only different roads to different conceptions of what the good society entails. To the extent that the respective development strategies of both countries carry with them a series of attendant costs and trade offs, the prospects for any one strategy fully achieving its objectives are limited.

One measure of underdevelopment is the limited range of policy options available to those who direct the developmental process. Its significance lies in the fact that whatever policy is chosen to achieve a particular development objective, the costs of pursuing that policy are often such that the objective to which the policy is directed cannot be obtained. As suggested by the foregoing discussion, both Kenya and Tanzania are, to varying degrees, subject to this dilemma. The result is that while these two countries have pursued very different development strategies, the results, relative to the task as they have defined it, have been small.

The second lesson suggested by the experience of the two countries is that the degree of progress achieved by a country pursuing the development goal of socialist construction is likely to be less with respect to its standard of development, than the degree of progress achieved by a country pursuing capitalist development with respect to its standard.

The slower rates of progress that are likely to accrue to countries pursuing socialist, as opposed to capitalist, construction are largely a function of the nature of the development objectives these states pursue. Socialist construction is a holistic and therefore more ambitious conception of the good society than is capitalist development. In the context of the third world, capitalist development is primarily, and often exclusively, concerned with the achievement of economic expansion. It assumes that once expansion occurs, particularly if it becomes a self-sustaining process, progress on other dimensions, including the standard of living enjoyed by all members of society, the level of citizen participation in the political process, and the extent of national independence, will more or less automatically follow.[51] In contrast, socialism requires that progress occur on several dimensions at the same time, and makes no assumption that progress on one dimension will automatically result in progress on another, but rather that progress on all dimensions is a requisite for progress on the others. Thus, equality cannot be achieved without participation, and vice versa; nor can true independence be achieved without equality, and vice versa; nor can independence be achieved without participation, and vice versa.

Given these requirements, the task confronting policy makers committed to achieving development within a socialist framework is obviously far more difficult than the task confronting policy makers charged with achieving capitalism. This is particularly true in the third world among those countries which have not experienced a socialist revolution, such as China, Cuba, and Vietnam. In those third-world countries which have elected to pursue a model of patron-client capitalism the main tasks of development are those of maintaining and extending institutions and practices established during the colonial period. For countries such as Tanzania, however, which seek to systematically displace these institutions, the tasks are more complicated. Countries pursuing a model of patron-client capitalism, in short, have elected to pursue both a more modest set of development goals than the goals of those seeking socialist construction, and a set of goals that can be achieved within the institutional framework already existing in these countries. It is therefore hardly surprising that on their standard of development (as opposed to some absolute standard), these countries have achieved more than have countries which have chosen the socialist model.

A third, and related, lesson is that the goals of economic growth and equality are mutually exclusive, but that the country which opts for the goal of equality will not necessarily achieve its objective. Fragmentary as the data might be, there can be no doubt that Kenya's record on the dimension of growth has been superior to Tanzania's, but that this growth has been accompanied by increased inequities in the distribution of the country's wealth. It is equally true that Tanzania has made a more concerted effort to create an egalitarian society than has Kenya, but that the results have so far been limited. These findings suggest that in the context of the nonrevolutionary sector of the third world, any development strategy designed to achieve both growth and equality is unrealistic. They further suggest that any attempt to define development in terms of equality must take into account the different dimensions on which equality might be obtained. The distribution of personal income across social strata, as distinct from the distribution of aggregate income and government services between the urban and rural areas and between different rural areas, are very different dimensions of equality, and often require incompatible policies to be achieved.

Taken together, these lessons do not suggest an auspicious future for either Kenya or Tanzania over the long term. In Kenya, continued growth and inequality, combined with the demands of a more participative population, may ultimately result in a breakdown of what has been an unusually stable political order, and hence a breakdown of the economic system as well. Given Kenya's high rate of population growth and limited natural resources, especially arable land, the challenge to Kenya is one of bringing marginal land into production (which will require large capital expenditures for irrigation), and expanding the commercial and manufacturing sectors at a pace that is sufficiently rapid to absorb the growing numbers of landless and unemployed. Unemployment in Kenya is currently increasing at a rate of roughly 250,000 per year. Impressive as Kenya's economic record has been since independence, it is questionable whether the country's future rate of economic expansion will be equal to the task.[52]

For Tanzania, the problem is also one of economic expansion, a challenge increasingly acknowledged by the country's leaders, including President Nyerere, in light of current conditions in the country. Noble and interesting as the Tanzanian experiment has been, it is not unreasonable to suggest that it has both promised and attempted too much relative to its capacity to deliver. As suggested by Goran Hyden in Chapter 4, Tanzania's policy makers have often followed Nyerere's dictum of attempting to run while others walk. Though such an approach is, to some extent, necessary for a country attempting to make a dramatic break with its past, it would appear that the costs incurred may jeopardize the process of socialist construction itself, and perhaps the regime as well. Measured against its own criteria, the standard of living in Tanzania is not appreciably higher today, and on some indexes is lower on a per capita basis, than it was in 1967. Clearly, this situation cannot continue. For, while in the minds of some citizens, Tanzania's success at achieving symbolic equality may compensate for its limited progress in achieving economic growth, it is unlikely that symbolic outputs alone will prove to be a sufficient surrogate for material improvement over the long term. For both countries, in short, the critical challenge looms on the horizon.

NOTES

1. In 1978 Kenya's population was estimated to be 13.8 million people, and rising at an annual rate of 3.3 percent. Per capita income in Kenya was estimated at $220 per year. In the same year, Tanzania's population was estimated at 15.1 million people, and rising at an annual rate of 2.7 percent. Per capita income in Tanzania was estimated at $170 per year. Source: "Back to Back: A Survey of Kenya and Tanzania," *The Economist*, (London), March 11, 1978, p. S-2.

2. In terms of topography and climate, both countries share many features: Both are bordered on the east by the Indian Ocean, and have a ten to twenty mile strip of semitropical forest immediately behind the coast. Both consist mainly of semiarid plains bisected from north to south by the Rift Valley, and are studded with volcanic mountains. Both have their richest farmland in a number of highland areas between 4,000 and 7,000 feet above sea level which are most suitable for the cultivation of coffee and tea. Both border on Lake Victoria in the west, while Tanzania is also bordered by Lake Tanganyika and Lake Malawi. Both have no mineral deposits that contribute significantly to their national incomes although Tanzania does possess large deposits of iron ore and coal. In both countries, the bulk of the population

is concentrated along the coast, in the highlands, and along the lakes, the areas that contain virtually all of each country's arable land.

3. The most significant differences attributable to Kenya's history as a colony for European settlement were: a more extensive development of cash crop agriculture prior to independence, larger and more developed urban areas, more extensive commercial ties with the industrial nations of the West, particularly Britain, and a greater ability to attract foreign private investment. As a center for European settlement, Kenya was also the beneficiary of greater expenditures by the colonial government on schools, roads, and other public services, many of which were made at the direct and indirect expense of Tanzania.

4. In Kenya, President Jomo Kenyatta was preoccupied with resolving serious divisions within the ruling party, the Kenyan African National Union, containing a major opposition party, the Kenyan African Democratic Union, and changing the country's constitutional structure to that of a unitary state. In Tanzania, Julius Nyerere resigned his office of prime minister in 1962 to devote the year to the rebuilding of the country's governing party, the Tanganyika African National Union.

5. As discussed by John Okumu in Chapter 10, Kenya's relationship with the United Kingdom has remained close since independence. Tanzania's relationship with the United Kingdom was particularly close during the first year of independence as a result of Nyerere's belief that his country would need to rely on former members of the colonial civil service for many years until sufficient numbers of Tanzanians were trained to takeover the administration of the country. For details, see Cranford Pratt, *The Critical Phase in Tanzania, 1945–1968* (London: Cambridge University Press, 1976), chaps. 5 and 6.

6. At the time of their independence, virtually every African country was confronted by two fundamental problems, the problem of economic development and the problem of national integration. Though times of changed and new problems, such as the dependency of many African countries on the West, are now regarded with equal concern, the two basic problems of the 1960s still remain. For an early, and still relevant discussion of how these problems were perceived at the time, see James S. Coleman and Carl G. Rosberg, *Politics and National Integration in Tropical Africa* (Berkeley: University of California Press, 1964).

7. For two very different discussions of the similarity in values and orientations of the nationalist leaders of the 1960s, see Edward Shils, "The Intellectuals in the Political Development of the New States," *World Politics,* XII (1960), pp. 329–68, and Frantz Fanon, *The Wretched of the Earth* (New York: Grove Press, 1965).

8. This period is described in detail by Pratt, op. cit., chaps. 5 and 6. It is difficult to pinpoint the period when Tanzania began to reassess the policies it pursued at independence. While it is our contention that the reassessment did not get fully underway until late 1965, Pratt argues that some changes, such as the decision to reduce Tanzania's reliance on former colonial civil servants, began as early as 1962.

9. For a discussion of this period, see Cherry Gertzel, *The Politics of Independent Kenya* (Evanston: Northwestern University Press, 1970), chap. 2, and Colin Leys, *Underdevelopment in Kenya: The Political Economy of Neo-Colonialism* (London: Heinemann, 1974).

10. At the time of Kenya's independence in 1963 there were approximately 60,000 European residents in the country. In contrast, the number of Europeans in Tanzania never rose above 30,000 and reached its peak in the mid-1950s.

11. For details of Nyerere's growing awareness that Tanzania's expectations would not be met, see Pratt, op. cit., chap. 6, and John Okumu's discussion in Chapter 10 of this volume. Pratt describes Nyerere's reaction to Britain's failure to provide sufficient assistance to Tanzania as one of bitter disappointment.

12. Julius K. Nyerere, "The Tanzanian Economy," an address to the Tanzanian National Assembly, June 13, 1966 as reported in Julius K. Nyerere, *Freedom and Socialism* (New York: Oxford University Press, 1968), pp. 165–71.

13. For a discussion that attempts to explain changes in Tanzanian policy almost solely in terms of Nyerere's leadership, see Pratt, op. cit.

14. In his biography of Julius Nyerere, William Edgett Smith quotes Nyerere's own assessment of his days at Edinburgh as follows: "At Edinburgh, my degree was in history and economics. My strongest subject was philosophy. I read a great deal. I had plenty of time to think. My ideas of politics were formed completely. It was my own evolution, but it was complete." Whether or not this "evolution" included his commitment to socialism Nyerere does not say, but the definitiveness of his statement suggests that it does. See William Edgett Smith, *We Must Run While They Walk: Nyerere of Tanzania* (New York: Random House, 1971), p. 59.

15. Julius K. Nyerere, "Ujamaa: The Basis of African Socialism" in *Freedom and Unity* (New York: Oxford University Press, 1967), pp. 162–71. For an elaboration of these ideas see Nyerere's introduction to Julius K. Nyerere, *Freedom and Socialism* (New York: Oxford University Press, 1968).

16. The five published speeches are Nyerere's "Inaugural Address" as the first president of Tanzania (December 10, 1962), "The Second Scramble," an address to the World Assembly of Youth (February 4, 1963), and an address opening the new campus of the University of Dar es Salaam (August 21, 1964) all of which appear in Nyerere, *Freedom and Unity,* op. cit., and "Leaders Must Not be Masters" (February 1966) and "Principle and Development" (June 1966) which appear in Nyerere, *Freedom and Socialism,* op. cit.

17. For a discussion of this position see, Julius K. Nyerere, "The Varied Paths to Socialism" in *Freedom and Socialism,* op. cit., pp. 301–10.

18. For details, see Julius K. Nyerere, "Education and Self-Reliance" and "Socialism and Rural Development" in *Freedom and Socialism,* op. cit., pp. 267–90 and 337–66.

19. Ali A. Mazrui, "Tanziphilia," *Transition* no. 31 (July, 1967); 20–26.

20. Nyerere's proposed solutions to Tanzania's problems, particularly his decisions to pursue socialism by curtailing the consumptive habits of the country's educated elite while emphasizing the development of the rural sector (especially the production of food), closely followed the prescriptions of the popular French socialist and agronomist, René Dumont. Dumont's main argument, as set forth in his widely read book, *False Start in Africa* (New York: Praeger, 1966) was that African states would neither develop nor achieve socialism until they committed their limited human and material resources to the establishment of a sound agricultural sector based on small-scale technologies appropriate to the existing skills of the peasantry. By emphasizing the development of the rural sector, Nyerere was the first African leader to commit his nation to what might be termed "the agrarian path to socialism" and as such became the subject of intense interest.

21. Tanzania's policies generated considerable excitement both within the country and without among those supportive of what Nyerere and his colleagues were trying to achieve. As time passed, however, Nyerere's policies also generated substantial criticism from both the "right" and the "left" of those sympathetic to Tanzania's aspirations, as well as criticism from those who were not. In addition to the discussions carried out by those responsible for the making of public policy, much of the excitement, disappointment, and debate of Tanzania's policies has been an exercise carried out by intellectuals and outside observers who, though students of development, have had no direct stake in the outcome of these policies. It is well to remember that all the contributors to this volume fall within this category, and that they and their colleagues have been a burden which the country by virtue of its unique willingness to embark on a different course to development has had to bear.

22. In 1974, Tanzania's constitution was amended to formalize the supremacy of the party over all other institutions. In 1977 TANU was merged with the Afro-Shirazi Party of Zanzibar to form a single party for the entire country, Chama Cha Mapinduzi (CCM) which in Swahili means the Revolutionary Party.

23. For an incisive discussion of this position as it pertains to Tanzania see Goran Hyden, *Peasants and Underdevelopment: The Tanzanian Experiment and Beyond* (Berkeley: University of California Press, forthcoming). As suggested by Hyden in his introduction: "Our efforts to change modern society are not only artificial but also illusory. What we label 'alternatives' are not really much more than variations of a theme. This is true even of such major shifts as the creation of a socialist society."

24. One need only ponder the internal logic of the term itself to recognize the fact that "development" is by definition an ethical phenomenon. The central idea of *every* concept of development is the notion of a change from some condition existing at T_1 to some "better," and more desirable condition, existing at T_2.

25. Imagine, for example, the application of Walt W. Rostow's theory of the stages of economic growth to the People's Republic of China. See Walt W. Rostow, *The Stages of Economic Growth* (London: Cambridge, 1961).

26. For example, the structural-functional approach to the process of political change as set forth during the 1960s by the members of the Committee on Comparative Politics of the Social Science Research Council.

27. For one notable example of an attempt to speak to the concerns of policy makers, see Warren Ilchman and Norman Uphoff, *The Political Economy of Change* (Berkeley: University of California Press, 1969).

28. For example, in his critical review of Kenyan development policies since independence, Colin Leys repeatedly suggests that Kenya's problems are a result of her attempting to develop within a capitalist framework, and that these problems would not exist had Kenya pursued a course of socialist construction. No data, however, is presented for countries, such as Tanzania, which have attempted to follow a socialist course. See Colin Leys, *Underdevelopment in Kenya, op. cit.*

29. A 1977 study of 24 major parastatals by the Tanzanian treasury concluded that their accumulated loss totaled more than $22 million, or 91 percent of their total share capital. Source: *Weekly Review* (Nairobi), October 31, 1977, p. 7. Nyerere has also called attention to the poor performance of the parastatal sector. See Julius K. Nyerere, *The Arusha Declaration: Ten Years After* (Dar es Salaam: Government Printer, 1977), pp. 33–34.

30. Nyerere, *The Arusha Declaration: Ten Years After, op. cit.*, p. 34. Between 1967 and 1974 industrial output per worker in Tanzania as measured in current prices declined by 14 percent. In real terms, the decline was even greater.

31. Ibid., p. 20.

32. Ibid., p. 19.

33. Ibid., pp. 41–2.

34. Nyerere, "Ujamaa: The Basis of African Socialism," op. cit., pp. 162–63.

35. Nyerere, *The Arusha Declaration: Ten Years After, op. cit.*, pp. 32–37.

36. Consider, for example, the following remarks by Amir Jamal, the Minister of Finance, in a lecture at the University of Dar es Salaam, November 19, 1974. "Any discussion of Tanzania's current economic problems must be in the context of the Arusha Declaration. It is a waste of time to engage in comparisons between Tanzania and other developing states (read Kenya) who have embarked on different strategies of development. . . . Even in normal times the best we can expect is a 5 per cent growth in GNP at constant prices. . . ."

37. For the most thorough discussion of the inequalities of income distribution in Kenya see International Labour Office, *Employment, Incomes and Equality: A Strategy for Increasing Productive Employment in Kenya* (Geneva: International Labour Office, 1972), chap. 5.

38. International Labour Office, *Employment, Incomes and Equality, op. cit.*, Table 25, p. 74. For a critique of the significance of the ILO's findings, see Arthur Hazelwood, "Kenya: Income Distribution and Poverty—An Unfashionable View," *Journal of Modern African Studies* 16, no. 1 (March 1978), pp. 81–95.

39. Official sanction of such ventures is discussed at length in the Ndegwa Report of 1971 that presented the findings of a commission of inquiry into the structure and renumeration of the public service. The report, which was subsequently adopted by the Kenyan National Assembly, saw no reason why civil servants should not engage in private business ventures so long as such involvement did not interfere with their official duties. As stated in the report: ". . . there ought in theory to be no objection to the ownership of property or involvement in business by members of the public services to a point where their wealth is augmented perhaps substantially by such activities." See D.N. Ndegwa, *Report of the Commission of Inquiry* (Public Service Structure and Renumeration Commission), (Nairobi: Government Printer, 1971), p. 14 (paragraph 32).

40. Data indicating the minimal impact of the income tax are presented in the International Labour Office (ILO) report, *Employment, Incomes and Equality*, op. cit., p. 75.

41. One indication of the emergence of an indigenous bourgeoisie in Kenya is the increasing criticism of multinational corporations by Kenyan businessmen who regard MNCs as a threat to the growth of Kenyan capitalism (as distinct from the growth of capitalism in Kenya). See, for example, the views expressed by the Minister of Commerce Eliud Mwanunga in the *Weekly Review* (Nairobi), October 31, 1978.

42. International Association of Agricultural Economists, *World Atlas of Agriculture*, vol. 4 (Novara: Instituto Geografico De Agostini, 1976), pp. 254, 676. The Kenyan government prefers to speak in terms of "good" rather than "arable" land, or land on which there is intermittent rainfall to permit the cultivation of crops at least on the subsistence level. Even under this definition the government estimates that there is now only .88 hectares of land per person, and that this amount is expected to fall to .36 hectares by the year 2000. See *Kenya Economic Survey 1977* (Nairobi: Government Printer, 1977), p. 40.

43. The ILO estimated that as far back as 1969, 300,000 households out of a total of 1.7 million households were landless. See *Employment, Incomes and Equality*, op. cit., p. 33.

44. A major factor contributing to absenteeism has been the time spent on political demonstrations, political education, militia parades, etc. In the course of the debate in the Tanzanian National Assembly on the 1977 budget, Cleopa Msuya, the Minister of Finance, reported that a survey of ten major enterprises in Dar es Salaam found that 820,000 man hours had been lost in 1976 alone on various forms of political acitvity. See "Back to Back," op. cit., p. S-16.

45. Although land cannot be sold in Tanzania, improvements on the land such as coffee bushes, buildings, and so on, can.

46. Nyerere, *The Arusha Declaration: Ten Years After*, op. cit., p. 20.

47. David K. Leonard, "Bureaucracy, Class and Inequality in Kenya and Tanzania," an unpublished paper prepared for delivery at a conference on inequality in Africa held under the auspices of the Social Science Research Council, Mount Kisco, New York (August 1976), pp. 20–21, Table 1, columns 1, 2, and 4.

48. *Employment, Incomes and Equality*, op. cit., Table 28, pp. 78–79.

49. The TANU Guidelines (Mwongozo) as reprinted in the *African Review*, 1, 4 (April 1972), p. 6.

50. For details, especially for 1974 when both Tanzania and Kenya were faced with a sharp rise in expenditures for the import of oil, see Goran Hyden, "Ujamaa, Villagization and Rural Development in Tanzania," *O.D.I. Review* 1, (Sussex, 1975), p. 67. Hyden notes, however, that Tanzania's expenditures for food exceeded those for oil during this period.

51. For perhaps the best articulation of this position see S.M. Lipset's essay, "The Economic Preconditions for Democracy" in S. M. Lipset, *Political Man* (Garden City, New York: Anchor Books, 1960).

52. Though a more equitable distribution of personal income would no doubt enhance the popularity of the regime in the short term, equality alone will not solve, but only mitigate

Kenya's basic problem of too many people on too little land. In the final analysis, Kenya has no choice but to continue to pursue a development strategy which emphasizes growth. At the same time, Kenya must become more successful than it has been at reducing the rate at which its population expands.

PART II

Institutional Alternatives for Political Change

2

PARTY AND PARTY-STATE RELATIONS

John J. Okumu

THIS CHAPTER IS CONCERNED with two questions: First, to what extent are the ruling political parties of Kenya and Tanzania effective instruments for the making of public policy? And second, what are the particular uses to which each ruling party has been put in its respective country? In addressing our analysis to these questions, we shall also compare the distinctive modes of the political process in general, and party development in the two countries.

There are important historical differences between Kenya and Tanzania but their colonial legacy is relatively similar. The Tanganyika African National Union (TANU) was founded in July 1954, seven years before Tanzania became independent in 1961. The Kenya African National Union (KANU) was formed in 1960, only three years before Kenya became independent in December 1963. At the time of independence, both parties were weak in structure and incipient in ideological formation because they were basically anticolonial movements whose main strength lay in their capacity to mobilize the population around slogans and issues that had broad public appeal. Their god was political power, not economic reasoning. It is therefore not surprising that like most nationalist movements in Africa, they became ineffective instruments for development in the era immediately after independence, since their original raison d'etre, independence, was no longer an issue.[1] The objective conditions that created this mode of development are discussed in Chapter 5.

It is important to observe that colonies were managed in a manner similar to that of an administrative state in which decision-making powers are centralized in the state bureaucracy while organized politics, if allowed to exist, is kept to the barest minimum. The colonial state bureaucracy was the instrument used by the colonizing power to reorganize the precolonial modes of production and to maintain law and order. It was therefore logical for African nationalism to challenge both the colonizing power and the colonial state bureaucracy as instruments of exploitation. The colonial state attempted to meet this challenge and to legitimate the state bureauracy by an increase in promotion of educated Africans to senior positions in the civil service, but this effort failed to stem the tide of the African nationalist struggle for independence. Fearing to make a decision that would antagonize the nationalist movements, the colonial state behaved cautiously; on the one hand, expressing feelings of uncertainty and assuming a rather low profile, while on the other hand ensuring the continuity and resiliency of the administration. As a former colonial governor once put it:

> In the latter stages of political advance, pressure by nationalist forces tends to be strong and here, if the government is rigid, there may be an explosion, or if the government is weak, progress may be too rapid in the wrong direction. In fact, where local political forces or movements are powerful, smooth progress depends on imagination as well as firmness on the part of governments, not only on strength but on flexibility.[2]

This process of cooptation continued into the postindependence era and the state bureaucracies of both Kenya and Tanzania retained their leading role in decision-making processes with only marginal influence from either KANU or TANU.

THE COLONIAL CONCEPTION OF POLITICAL PARTIES AND PARLIAMENTARY GOVERNMENT

At independence, Kenya and Tanzania inherited the "Westminster model" of parliamentary government. Under this model, political parties are regarded as electoral organizations whose functions are limited to stimulating popular interest and participation in politics, selecting and campaigning for parliamentary candidates, reflecting the interests and opinions of diverse groups in the society, and providing organized support for the government in power, as well as organizing opposition to it. In this sense, the party as a whole, with the exception of its parliamentary group, is not expected to be at the center of the stage in the policy-making process.

The sovereignty of Parliament, moreover, remains a cardinal concept of the Westminster model. Parliament has supreme power, as well as direct and executive control over legislation; it exercises indirect control over the activities and actions of the cabinet and the state bureaucracy. Legislatively, there are no constitutional restrictions over its authority—the courts are expected to enforce without question all laws it passes. In addition, all other law-making bodies in the system, such as local authorities, exercise only those powers authorized by Parliament. Parliament is also supposed to have control over the state bureaucracy; ministers are responsible to Parliament for their individual decisions as well as all the actions and activities of their departments. Thus while government policy may be made in the cabinet, cabinet ministers must answer to Parliament for all their decisions and can be forced to resign if their decisions fail to obtain parliamentary approval. And because Parliament is the institution that expresses the sovereignty of the people, it is often maintained that it is the center of power and a major source of decisions.[3]

In actual practice, however, Parliament as a source of major decisions suffers from some obvious shortcomings. First, in relation to the state bureaucracy, Parliament is dependent on the bureaucracy for the specialized information and expert advice it requires as raw material in the decision-making process. This applies to the back bench more than the front because ministers enjoy the support of the whole administrative apparatus and are usually thoroughly briefed for every public statement they make and every parliamentary question they answer. Left to its own resources, the back bench, whether in England, Kenya, or Tanzania, suffers from limited access to government departments. And because the state bureaucracy does tend to monopolize important information and is composed of men who are skilled in research and drafting, they have ample freedom not to reveal to the back bench more information than they think is absolutely necessary. This is important in creating a closer working relationship between the cabinet and the state bureaucracy as important arms of the executive.

Second, parliamentary power over decisions is also limited because cabinet ministers, as important agents of the government, are given more powers and opportunities than ordinary members are given to do what they think is good for the general welfare of the country. For this reason, the British parliamentary practice usually encourages criticism of the cabinet by the back bench but discourages the latter from obstructing legislation.[4] Perhaps this is why it is so crucial to maintain party loyalty and discipline within the parliamentary group. Together, these elements, among others, put a limit on the extent to which Parliament can be seen as a major policy-making body. Despite these limitations, the Westminster model does work within the British political culture, in which the parliamentary group is closer to the locus of power and decision making than are the extraparliamentary organs of the party such as the National Executive Committee (NEC).

The Westminster model also provides for the supremacy of Parliament and government initiative in the policy-making process. Under this arrangement political parties are only indirectly involved in public policy making through their election platforms. The power over decisions lies with the prime minister, the cabinet, and the state bureaucracy.

In both Kenya and Tanzania the Westminster model gave the executive branch effective power to initiate and to be the locus of public policy decisions. Each had a National Assembly that was legally regarded as the supreme law-making body. The National Assembly as a whole, however, did not participate in all stages of the policy process. It was a section of it, the cabinet, belonging to the executive branch, that was closely associated with policy, although the assembly was legally responsible for giving legislative effect to decisions.

In this context, political parties in both countries were expected to take back seats in the policy-making process, because the main party organs such as the NECs were regarded as extraparliamentary units. The NECs and other decision-making organs of KANU and TANU could therefore only participate effectively in the policy-making process if they were consulted by their leaders, the two heads of state, who were also the presidents of the two parties. In Tanzania, the NEC of TANU, including President Julius Nyerere, met regularly (once every three months) in the postindependence era. However, in Kenya the NEC of KANU rarely held any meetings. Instead, President Jomo Kenyatta established monthly consultative sessions with the KANU parliamentary group to discuss general issues of development. These consultations were also used to mediate between the government (cabinet) and the back bench whenever a crisis arose over a controversial government bill that backbenchers threatened to defeat. Early in the postindependence era one begins to see that President Nyerere was more fundamentally integrated with TANU, its existence, role, and future, than was President Kenyatta with KANU. Despite these contrasting styles it is important to note that before 1965, when Tanzania established a one-party system, the loci of public policy decisions in both countries remained in the executive institutions. Political parties performed functions not directly concerned with policy making yet qualitative differences were apparent in the way the two parties related to the state.

PARTY-STATE RELATIONS IN TANZANIA, 1961 TO 1965

TANU's relations with the state were closer and more fundamental. The NEC and the National Assembly observed a gentlemen's agreement that policy would be discussed by each at different levels of its formation. The NEC discussed major policy issues in broad outlines while the National Assembly dealt with the questions of how, when, and in what order of priority agreed-upon policies should be implemented.[5] This was in conformity with inherited British parliamentary practices, according to which the National Assembly was seen as an institution of high status with important decision-making powers and control functions. And, in the public eye, the National Assembly maintained a special position derived from the nationalist period, when the Legislative Council was the center of controversy and obtained more publicity and significance than it deserved.

This historical legacy caused members of Parliament to regard themselves as a group apart from and superior to TANU as far as their decision-making role was concerned. As Pius Msekwa has argued, even the prime minister, in the 1962 debate over the republican constitution, contended that the National Assembly was the decision-making body empowered to discuss the proposed constitution. He regarded the National Assembly as "the voice of the Nation and fount of authority, which must remain sovereign."[6] Through it, the people's "supreme authority" in decision making was exercised.

It is important to note, however, that the decision to make Tanzania a republic was first discussed and agreed upon by the NEC before the government proposal was brought before the National Assembly. The prime minister's cautious strategy when introducing the motion suggests that the party's decision in this issue was by no means regarded by TANU's leaders as binding, and if rejected by the National Assembly, it would have been shelved.* The weak position of TANU was also notable for the fact that the principles on which the new republican constitution was based were submitted for debate before the National Assembly,† and that the principle of parliamentary sovereignty was underlined.[7] But from the origin of the issue, it is possible to assert that the NEC and a section of TANU leadership had already recognized the necessity, sooner or later, of asserting the party's position in relation to other decision-making institutions.

The fact that TANU did not press the issue can in part be explained in terms of the issue itself. In the early 1960s it had become accepted practice, in the decolonization process, for an independent former British colony to become a republic within the Commonwealth one year after independence. A republican constitution was therefore expected and would not have been resisted by any of the decision-making organs. In

---

*While Msekwa may be correct in his assessment of the National Assembly's mood on this occasion, I find it difficult to agree with this assessment because there is hardly any evidence to suggest that the NEC of TANU had, at any time, lost an important issue.

†This was quite proper under the Westminster model, which prevailed at the time, for it is possible that attempts to do otherwise would have angered the governor-general and created a charged atmosphere.

fact, becoming a republic was a major demonstration that political independence was finally achieved, because it severed political links with the
British Crown, exercised through the governor-general. Kenya took the
same step by becoming a republic in 1964.

The most significant decision made within the party forums during
this period was the NEC decision in January 1963 regarding the desirability
of changing Tanzania into a democratic one-party state. President Nyerere
was authorized to set up a commission to consider the issue and make
appropriate recommendations as to the form and procedures of the party.
The government was required to give full effect to the concept of a one-
party democracy. Msekwa has rightly argued that this decision was substantially one of the most crucial prior to 1965.[8] For the first time, the
National Assembly was not asked whether or not the decision was right.
That had been decided upon. The National Assembly's main task was to
give the commission's report its legislative approval. There were other
decisions made by the NEC during this period between 1961 and 1965 that
have been discussed elsewhere and will not be reexamined here.[9] The
pertinent point, however, is that, with the declaration of Tanzania as a
republic, TANU began to assert its role in major national policy decisions
and in imposing its will and presence on other national institutions, thanks
to the frequency with which its decision-making organs met to discuss
important issues of national development.

The important party organs referred to above are the National Conference (referred to as the Annual Conference before 1965), the NEC, and the
Central Committee. The National Conference is the supreme organ of
TANU and is responsible for formulating general policy and enforcing it.
It has wide constitutional powers, and can revoke any decisions made by
any other organ of the party or any of its officers. However, because the
intervals between its meetings are long, its effectiveness is reduced. The
day-to-day administration of party affairs is the responsibility of the Central Committee, which meets frequently, while the locus of power is the
NEC. The NEC is formally answerable to the National Conference, but this
does not reduce its effectiveness because its meetings are more frequent—
at least once every three months—and it makes and exercises other functions that cannot await the approval of the National Conference. In this
strategic position, the NEC is capable of overseeing the day-to-day implementation of party decisions by the government. While the National Conference is legally supreme, the NEC is the effective operational organ of
the party. In sum, the most remarkable aspect of the pre-1965 era in
Tanzania was the emergence of a unified and assertive party leadership
that established the preeminence of TANU, particularly the NEC, in the
policy-making process.

PARTY-STATE RELATIONS IN KENYA, 1963 TO 1965

In Kenya the period before 1965 was uneventful insofar as party-state relations were concerned. Kenya became independent under a quasi-federal constitution that attempted to reduce the effective power of the central government by strengthening the regions. However, KANU, the majority party led by Kenyatta, was determined to develop Kenya as a unitary state. As the ruling party, KANU had major operational advantages over its opposition, the Kenya African Democratic Union (KADU); its most important advantage was control over the machinery of the state bureaucracy. In contrast to TANU, however, KANU did not have a unified leadership and KANU's structure was confederated. The decentralized structure of KANU (and also of KADU) was the result of the colonial government's ban against the formation of national political parties between 1956 and 1960; the ban limited the establishment of parties to districtwide organizations, and when lifted, led to the formation of national parties that were loose coalitions of the existing district-based groups. The only issue that united the KANU leadership was the desirability to reestablish a unitary state with a strong executive branch, and an effective parliamentary system—the Westminster model.* Kenya had a unitary government throughout the colonial period, but a quasi-federal or *Majimbo* constitution had been forced upon KANU as a condition for independence in 1963 by the colonial government and KADU, which had been formed to protect the interests of Kenya's smallest tribes.†

Throughout 1964, the KANU government under Prime Minister Kenyatta devoted all its energies to the destruction of the KADU opposition and the Majimbo constitution. A three-pronged strategy was used. First, the state bureaucracy, the only national institution with effective links to the grass roots, was manipulated by the KANU government to prevent the effective development of the regional administrative agencies provided for by the constitution. In this exercise, KANU's control of central government institutions also gave it effective control over regional administration. At the regional level, the KANU government used the civil secretaries (provincial commissioners) to maintain more direct channels of communication between the central government and the regions than those speci-

---

*The KANU election manifesto (1963) indicated that the party was also determined to develop Kenya as a mixed economy.

†The Majimbo constitution was the result of the Lancaster House conference held in June 1963. Under the Majimbo constitution, Kenya gained its independence in December, establishing a bicameral legislature and a series of regional legislative and administrative bodies designed to protect KADU's scattered bases of support.

fied by the constitution. Second, the KANU government refused to implement the financial provisions of the constitution, which required the central government to decentralize financial control among the regions by June 1964, when the regions were to take over full financial responsibility. Finally, the KANU government also refused to transfer certain social services to the regions.[10]

The first year of independence, 1963–64, was therefore a crucial year for KANU and was marked by its decision to refuse to implement the full provisions of the Majimbo constitution. This is, perhaps, the most important decision ever taken by KANU, as a party, on matters of national importance. On December 12, 1964, Kenya became a republic with a president, an act that also marked the functional demise of KANU as a decision-making body in the political system. In contrast to TANU, which became more assertive in decision making after Tanzania became a republic in 1962, KANU suffered a form of benign neglect as Kenya's executive began slowly but effectively to strengthen the executive branch of the government as the fount and locus of public policy decisions. Why was this so?

First, unlike Nyerere, Kenyatta was really not a party man. He had never been personally involved in the actual formation of a political party, although he assumed the presidency of the Kenya African Union (KAU) in 1947 when he returned from London, and of KANU in 1961 when he came out of detention. As noted above, KANU was formed in 1960 out of preexisting and autonomous district political associations that controlled grass-roots politics. The conversion of these district political associations into district branches of KANU was the best way of satisfying entrenched district leaders; Kenyatta, as president of KANU, was deprived of effective access to the grass roots via the party medium. This situation was further aggravated by the fact that factions within KANU were district, and therefore, tribally based.[11]

These factors made it inevitable for Kenyatta to also become a district political boss in the Kiambu area, and in Kikuyuland as a whole, following his release from detention in 1961. This interpretation is verified by the numerous meetings held within and outside KANU circles in 1961 and 1962, to decide which of the Kikuyu members of Parliament would vacate his constituency seat in Kikuyuland to enable Kenyatta to enter the Legislative Council. Eventually a minor legislator, Kariuki Njiiri, agreed to give up his seat. Further, the reports of KANU meetings regarding the selection of the party's representatives to the 1962 Constitutional Conference in London indicate that Kenyatta did not wish to be involved in the debate as to whether Paul Ngei, a former political detainee and a prominent Kamba leader, should be included in the delegation. Thus, between his release from detention in 1961 and the gaining of independence in December 1963, Kenyatta found it difficult to ride over the waves of the long-standing intraparty factionalism, and unify the disparate elements of the KANU coalition. To attempt to solve the problem would have brought him into serious personal conflicts with the other district political bosses at a high cost to his popularity and political prestige.

This situation seems to have led President Kenyatta to decide to remain above the day-to-day conflicts of party politics by assuming the role of *Mzee,* the "father of the nation." Such a role has permitted the president to bypass the party apparatus by establishing indirect political control of the grass roots via a series of informal patron-client hierarchies of which he is the head. It was also inevitable that the president would, sooner or later, establish and govern through a strong state administration that stood outside party control. Thus, once he became president in December 1964, Kenyatta slowly began to neglect and finally discontinue the monthly consultations with the KANU parliamentary group, which had been his practice during the preceding year. Consultations between cabinet ministers and backbenchers, also established during the same year, became infrequent. Ministers finally stopped giving attention to backbenchers,[12] because the locus of power and decision making had shifted almost entirely to the president.

A strong executive was created through a series of constitutional amendments that made the president virtually independent of both party and parliamentary controls. Special reference can be made to the Sixth and Tenth Amendments, as we shall see below. The result was that by 1965 significant differences had emerged in Kenya and Tanzania between KANU and TANU, and the relationships between each party and the executive, legislative, and administrative institutions in the respective countries. Both countries had made radical departures from the Westminster model, but they had taken opposite paths. While KANU became cut off from the decision-making process, TANU asserted its role. TANU's intellectual thrust and vision began to grow vigorously while KANU's declined. And whereas TANU's structural development began to occur at the grass roots with the introduction of a cell system in 1965, no similar development occurred in KANU.*

---

*KANU did create the new position of provincial vice-president in 1966. The purpose of this move, however, was not to give the party new life, but to rid it of its radical element, which subsequently resigned to form a new opposition party, the Kenya People's Union. As a result, the position of provincial vice president fell rapidly into disuse, and was abolished in 1977.

PARTY DEVELOPMENT IN TANZANIA SINCE 1965

For Tanzania, 1965 was the turning point in party-state relations over policy questions. From then on, TANU began to flex its muscles positively. The report of the Presidential Commission on the Establishment of a One-Party State not only gave TANU, and the NEC in particular, a high constitutional status, but also increased its powers, scope, and involvement in governmental affairs. "If anything, the NEC has become a more important organ than it was before 1965: its scope and powers have increased, and it has begun to function in governmental capacities."[13] What was the essence of this new role?

First, the commission recommended that the NEC be concerned with laying down broad lines of policy. Second, it recommended that because of the high status of the NEC, it should have the power to "summon witnesses and call for papers, which is conferred by Chapter 359 of the Laws of the National Assembly and the Sessional Committees of the Assembly."[14] Third, the commission recommended that those members of the NEC "who are not also members of the National Assembly should be paid the same salary and allowances as are paid to Members of Parliament."[15] Subsequently, the TANU constitution was made an integral part of the state constitution. With this done, TANU became a major "constitutional category" whose role and involvement in any aspect of governmental activity could no longer be taken lightly. As Msekwa has asserted, "By making TANU a Constitutional category, the 1965 Constitution of the United Republic of Tanzania set a historical precedent, particularly in terms of legal theory."[16] The significance of this statement is that TANU's new role was not theoretical but real and effective. By paying NEC members the same salary as members of Parliament, a problem of status differentials between the party and the National Assembly was eliminated. Also, the power to call for papers and to summon witnesses gave the party access to a major area of the legislative process, which was bound to increase its power as the final authority in selecting candidates for election to the National Assembly. This act changed the power relationship between the two institutions and was the beginning of effective implementation of party discipline over its members. This was demonstrated in 1968 when the NEC expelled from the party seven parliamentarians who immediately lost their seats.[17] With these changes, the attorney general and the head of the civil service became ex-officio members of the NEC and made expert and confidential advice available for the first time.

Although these changes took place without overt resistance by either Parliament or the state bureaucracy, the issue of party supremacy, which was the essence of its new role, exploded in Parliament in 1968 when the group of seven MPs cited above wanted to find out which body was really supreme, the party (NEC) or the National Assembly. This renegade section of Parliament wanted to reassert the legislature's supremacy over the party in keeping with the Westminster model. It is this issue that led to their dismissal.[18] The expulsions were based on the principle that the members involved were disloyal, and uncommitted to TANU's principles and program. Later in 1968, the NEC further decided that in the future, all major policy papers such as the Second Five-Year Plan and all annual plans would be submitted to it for discussion and approval before being sent to Parliament to be enacted into law.[19]

This has become a normal working procedure between TANU and the state, and underlines the critical role of the party in decision making. The power to discuss and approve development proposals was extended to the District and Regional Executive Committees of TANU when the government was decentralized in 1972.[20] This gave the party a greater supervisory role over regional administration. It also marked a major step toward the completion of a process of structural reforms deemed necessary to fully effect party superiority. The final step toward party superiority was taken in 1975 when the national constitution was amended to make TANU and later, the *Chama Cha Mapinduzi* (the Revolutionary Party, which grew out of the merger in 1977 of TANU and the Afro-Shirazi Party of Zanzibar), the supreme authority in the land. Thus, legally, structurally, and to a great extent substantively, the party has become the most important locus for policy decisions. That TANU is supreme in the Tanzanian political system is no longer a concept; it is a reality. This can be seen in some of the major policy decisions since 1965 as briefly outlined below.

Major decisions made by the NEC in the post-1965 period were numerous and spread over a wide spectrum of government activity. It is not our task here to restate them all, but to mention only a few of the most salient. The first major decision made by the NEC after the establishment of the one-party state constitution in 1965 called for the promulgation in 1967 of the Arusha Declaration and TANU's Policy for Socialism and Self-Reliance. The objective conditions that brought about this decision are fully outlined by Ake in Chapter 5. The second major decision involved the submission of the Second Five-Year Plan for Social and Economic Progress to the NEC for thorough consideration and approval in keeping with an earlier decision of the NEC. The third, and perhaps most daring decision, in terms of sheer size and cost, was the one made in 1972 to decentralize the machinery of government in order to facilitate rural development and stimulate effective democratic popular participation in the planning process. Then came the decision in 1973 to move the capital to Dodoma. These are decisions of a scale that requires political will and commitment, extensive manpower and economic resources, and elaborate institutions to facilitate their implementation. While recognizing the weight of the tasks that lay ahead, President Nyerere was nevertheless able to state his faith in the party's future and ability when he addressed the nation in 1974:

> ... under One-Party Constitution, TANU is supreme. It is able to give directions to Government about the general policy which must be adopted for national development, and it has power to give instructions about priorities of action in any aspect of our national life.
>
> Further, TANU can call the Cabinet, any Minister, or any Government official, to account for their activities and any failure in the execution of their duty. That is at national level. The same is true at local level.
>
> In the localities, the Branch, District, or Regional TANU Committees are the people's representatives. It is their task to guide and supervise the actions of all government officials in their area, and to ensure that our policies are implemented in such a way that they bring maximum benefit to the people as a whole. Further, it is through TANU that the people in our villages and towns can take part in local and national planning for future development. . . .[21]

Implicit in this discussion is the contention that TANU has succeeded in establishing a sufficient capability to play a central role in the making of public policy. To what extent is this judgment valid?

A party's capability to adequately perform tasks such as those TANU has set for itself depends on its ability to command sufficient political and economic resources. The party must be able to get the best and most basic information on which to make decisions. It must also have the capacity to become effectively involved in the actual implementation of its decisions when the need arises. This in turn requires a capacity to recruit and retain personnel who are competent and knowledgeable about their duties, are of high integrity, and are ideologically committed to the party's program. The leadership of the party must also be popular, and maintain the support of the general public. These factors, together with a financially liquid status, considerably enhance the party's capacity to fulfill its objectives. Without these resources, party policies and programs will fall far short of their intended targets.

While it is correct to assert that TANU has experienced tremendous growth in legal and decision-making ability, it is equally important to note that acquisition of legal right has not always gone hand in hand with the corresponding capacity to exercise it. For example, the 1965 constitution gave the party the power to summon witnesses and call for policy papers, but TANU did not exercise this privilege until 1973, when the Central Committee was forced by public pressure (complaints) to summon the managers of Tanganyika Packers (a slaughterhouse), the Dar es Salaam Development Corporation (responsible for food distribution), and the National Agricultural and Food Corporation, to explain why there was an acute shortage of meat in many parts of the country. Likewise, the minister responsible for water supply was called in to explain reasons for a water shortage in Dar es Salaam, while the managers of the National Development Corporation and the National Textile Corporation were questioned on shortages of textile goods in the market.[22]

The reason for not exercising this legal prerogative is perhaps the fact that the party organs may not have understood the circumstances under which this power could be exercised; or that it was considered sufficiently taken care of by the question period in the National Assembly. The first argument is not plausible because the right to summon witnesses and call for papers came about as a result of a conscious desire among the party leadership to put the party into the front line of the policy-making process. The second is possible because the National Assembly, which had become an instrument for enactment and implementation of the party's policies, had always played this role with a good measure of success.

But the party's overall capability continued to grow especially after 1965. While it was unable to attract competent and trained manpower before 1965, the situation improved after that because the government took over full responsibility for payment of all TANU salaries. After this change the party was able to attract a better team of able young men to its service. A system was devised to second senior and experienced civil servants to the party headquarters to enable the NEC to receive better information and well-prepared position papers and drafts. To complete the process, the entire civil service machinery was put at the disposal of the NEC to facilitate the making and the implementation of decisions. Finally, the party organization itself was streamlined by introducing a new election system, enabling the party to ensure that more competent people are elected to party offices at all levels.[23]

Although the government has been subordinated to party control, many civil servants are still unpersuaded by the logic behind the move to strengthen the party, and continue to consider their status as superior to that of most party functionaries. Their claim is based on grounds of better education and longer service, which have, of course, made professionals out of many of them. While this covert and latent conflict is noticeable in the capital city, Dar es Salaam, which has a high concentration of Tanzania's intelligentsia, it is even more apparent, and often overt, in the regions and districts where many party leaders are less educated than most civil servants posted to these areas. The party's leverage at the district level, and in the rural areas in general, remains low. This is not surprising since many of the constitutional changes we have discussed are of recent origin and require time to evolve and mature. The TANU leadership's awareness of this problem is demonstrated by the elaborate leadership-training programs based at Kivukoni College and at other sister zonal colleges. Despite these and other shortcomings—particularly the constraints on public participation in the party's decision-making organs (discussed at length by Frank Holmquist in Chapter 6)—TANU's, and later the Chama Cha Mapinduzi's, evolution has been one of the most spectacular and interesting experiences in postcolonial Africa.

PARTY ORGANIZATION IN KENYA SINCE 1965

Kenya's experience in party-state relations over the same period was, unlike Tanzania's, characterized by tremendous growth in the power and independence of the executive. As mentioned earlier, the process of executive growth was brought about by a series of constitutional amendments between 1966 and 1968. The Sixth Amendment, Act 17 of 1966, published in April of that year stipulated that the fundamental rights of movement, association, and expression would not be contravened if, under the provisions of the Preservation of Public Security Act or detention act, the president exercised his special powers including detention without trial.

The Tenth Amendment, Act 45 of 1968, altered the method of presidential election by stating that in the future, the president would be directly elected by the national electorate at the time of a general election; that all candidates for a general election must be nominated by a political party; that at the time of a general election every political party taking part in the election would be required to nominate a presidential candidate; that at the polls, the ballot paper would pair the presidential candidate and the parliamentary candidate belonging to the same party. This act also altered the provisions for succession by providing that in the event that the office of the president becomes vacant other than at the time of the dissolution of Parliament, an election for president should be held within 90 days. In the interim period, the vice-president would assume the functions of the office but would neither make any decision concerning matters related to the Preservation of Public Security Act, nor appoint or dismiss ministers without cabinet's approval. This amendment also eliminated the requirement that Parliament every eight months should reaffirm its support for an order bringing into force Part III of the Preservation of Public Security Act, which provides for detention without trial. The Tenth Amendment also changed the composition of the National Assembly by replacing the 12 specially elected members, who were elected by the parliamentarians, with 12 nominated members appointed by the president.[24]

These amendments have produced a tremendous cumulative effect that has reduced the power and effectiveness of KANU as a policy-making institution. The net result has been the emergence of government by an oligarchy of cabinet ministers and top state bureaucrats that has become increasingly independent and the occasionally defiant of both Parliament and the party. To cite an example of this pattern, in a parliamentary debate over the proposed Land Control Bill (1967) the then assistant minister for agriculture made the following statement to a backbencher who had proposed an amendment to the bill:

> ... Mr. Deputy Speaker, Sir, the question of this amendment cannot be accepted by us on the Government side. . . . This was clearly stated at the [parliamentary group] meeting by the Minister himself, that it was a Government decision. . . . Therefore, this amendment contradicts the wishes and decisions of the Government. . . .[25]

A more recent example of this pattern occurred in 1974 when Parliament passed the National Assembly and Presidential Elections (Amendments) Bill. The bill was first submitted to the National Assembly in March by a group of backbenchers led by John Seroney, a long-term critic of the government. Though the government had initially frustrated this effort by requiring Seroney and his colleagues to pay for the printing of the bill's text by the Government Printer, it offered no serious objection to the measure during the debate in the House. Following the bill's passage, however, President Kenyatta refused to sign it into law. But what was most troubling to the bill's sponsors were the events that occurred after the presidential veto. In May, the vice-president, Daniel arap Moi, introduced the government's own National Assembly and Presidential Elections (Amendments) Bill, which for all practical purposes was a carbon copy of the original. At the close of the debate, Seroney made the following observation, which no doubt expressed the view of many of his colleagues as well:

> There is a need in this House for a spirit of give-and-take. I find that there is a tendency of some—not all—persons in the Front Benches to be intolerant of any efforts made by Back-benchers. Our Standing Orders do provide quite clearly that Ministers as well as Back-benchers may introduce public bills. . . . We have had only two bills from Back-benchers, and both of them were public. I hope that if the Ministers expect us to support their bills, in the spirit of give-and-take, they should not expect us to keep on supporting their bills, and, perhaps, amend them reluctantly, when they do not do the same.[26]

Further, the Tenth Amendment has been used to detain, without trial, members of Parliament who criticize proposed government policy or action. This has been done even where it is clear from the debate that the motive behind the criticism was either to improve the quality and substance of legislation, or to question irregularities in the handling of government business by certain senior officials.* MPs have naturally been inhibited by such severe disciplinary measures—measures which need not have been employed had the government chosen to discipline its critics within the framework of the KANU constitution, the conventional method for dealing with recalcitrant backbenchers. These actions, coupled with the fact that party organs are rarely activated, have reduced both the party's and Parliament's ability to question government policy, have subordinated the National Assembly to the executive, and resulted in the periodic estrangement between segments of the front and back bench.

It was argued earlier that KANU's role in the making of public policy declined through a process of benign neglect on the part of President Kenyatta, and many of the ministers in his government. Why did this neglect occur? First, because KANU grew out of autonomous district parties with established leaderships that revolved around individual personalities, it failed to overcome this historical peculiarity and developed as a loosely knit confederation with strong district branches, and a weak central executive organ. The executive organ, the National Executive Committee, never succeeded in asserting its personality and program over subordinate organs because the established district bosses jealously guarded their local bases of power, and manipulated the party branches to gain high offices at the national level (for example, cabinet ministers). This tendency facilitated President Kenyatta's move to establish a personal political machine outside the party and thus enabled him to gain access to regional and district bosses and other leaders on an individual basis rather than within an organizational framework. This arrangement makes it easier for him to control and influence them. The weapon of patronage controlled by the executive has become a key instrument in sustaining this pattern of influence—a series of hierarchical networks of patron-client relationships reaching from the president down to the grass roots via cabinet ministers, members of Parliament, and lesser officials such as district and town councilors, and chiefs. In this game, regional and district political bosses, in exchange for patronage, must demonstrate to the president that their tribesmen support him (the president), his government, and its policies. This is what is known in Kenya as creating support for the system by "bringing in the ethnic base." Because this system works, the

---

*For example, in May 1977 George Anyona, an MP, was detained for questioning on the handling of tenders for the supply of rolling stock for the Kenya Railways. He was arrested apparently before he revealed the nature and extent of the irregularities involved. Earlier cases included the arrest and detention of John Seroney, the deputy speaker, and Martin Shikuku, the former assistant minister for home affairs, in 1976.

party has little function in the interim between elections. Its major draw-back is that it encourages both parochialism and factionalism.

A second factor that contributed to the neglect of the party was that its functions were conceived mainly as a machinery to facilitate the election of candidates to the National Assembly; to stimulate popular interest and participation in campaigns, to select candidates for parliamentary office, and to campaign on their behalf. This is supported by the fact that party activity regularly undergoes a resurgence—during the year of general or local government elections—that is characterized by the printing of new membership cards, recruitment of new members, exhortations on the achievements of the KANU government since independence, and so on. Between elections, however, the party goes into a deep slumber, and literally dies. For example, between 1966 and 1969 the party often did not have any funds in its treasury, and was unable to pay rent when threatened with eviction from party headquarters. Its telephones were cut because it could not pay bills. And just before the 1969 general elections, the party had no information regarding the number of paid-up members, which was estimated at the time to be under 3,000. It is because of this cyclical pattern of party activity juxtaposed against the power of the executive and civil service that Kenya is frequently referred to as a "no-party state."

The third, and perhaps the most salient, factor in the syndrome of neglect is that the vital organs of the party have rarely been activated or given any chance to evolve as they should through regular meetings. KANU's Annual Delegates Conference, which is similar in constitutional status to TANU's National Conference, held its first meeting in 1962, almost a year before independence. It did not meet again until March 1966. The NEC, the equivalent of TANU's NEC, met so infrequently that its overall impact on the party's organization and activity ceased to carry any weight. The same was true for the Governing Council.*

An attempt to arrest this decline occurred in February 1966 when Mboya, then secretary general of KANU, announced that a Special Delegates Conference would be held in March at Limuru to reorganize and revitalize the party. The meeting became known as the Limuru Delegates Conference, and discussed two important points. First, it sought to find a way of integrating former leaders of KADU into KANU. KADU, the opposition party between 1963 and 1964, had dissolved itself in late 1964 "in the interest of national unity." Second, the absorption of KADU by

---

*It should, however, be noted that the late Tom Mboya, the former secretary general of KANU, was very devoted to the party. On several occasions he convened seminars for party leaders to discuss the party's role in the development of Kenya. He often stated that KANU would, in the future, become a more vigorous party, once certain obstacles were removed.

KANU could not be effected without the reorganization of the latter. Reorganization was also seen as a method for silencing the radical element in KANU, whose relative strength would be diluted and neutralized by the absorption of the former KADU members. The reorganizational process resulted in constitutional changes that created nine new provincial vice-presidents. All these positions were won by the moderate wing of the party, led by Kenyatta and Mboya. The radicals later left KANU in May 1966 to form a new opposition party, the Kenya People's Union (KPU).

To what extent was KANU revitalized by reorganization? My contention is that the party was weakened, and its members demoralized. First, the provincial vice-presidents, whose tasks were to facilitate recruitment of new members, and to involve the party in rural development projects, have done virtually nothing to promote the party's image (though several have been quite successful at building their own personal political machines). Second, elections for branch leadership in the districts have not been held since 1965 because rival political machines, operated by competing political figures in most districts, make the administration of such elections difficult.

There is also always the possibility that radicals might reenter Kenyan politics by gaining office through party branch or local government elections. Thus in 1968, local government elections were to be contested between KANU and the KPU. A few weeks after the candidates of both parties submitted their nomination papers, the provincial administration was instructed to declare all KPU candidates disqualified on the ground that their nomination forms were not properly filled in. As a result, all KANU candidates were returned unopposed. This, and similar affairs, however, demonstrate the extent to which KANU has been unsure of its own strength and popularity, and requires government intervention to ensure its survival.

In October 1969 the KPU was declared illegal, with the result that the parliamentary elections held in December were contested only by candidates who were members of KANU. In 1970 a small section of KANU's national leaders decided that a revitalization of the party should be attempted to bring new leadership into the organization. A new party constitution was drawn up and approved. The new constitution provided for the election of new national officers following completion of elections at the branch level. Such branch elections, however, have never been held, nor has there been an opportunity for new national officers to be elected. In 1976 another attempt was made to change the party's constitution to enable certain individuals to be elected to high positions in the party's executive organ. A meeting of all branch leaders was convened at State House in Nakuru to go into this matter, and eventually a new constitution was produced that provided for the election of new national officers. However, the election that was scheduled to take place near Nairobi at a party convention in March 1977 was suddenly canceled two days before the final balloting, after many delegates had already arrived at the convention site. Once again, an attempt to revitalize the party organization and leadership was halted before it could reach fruition.

CONCLUSION

As illustrated by the events described in this chapter, the direction of party development, and the nature of party-state relations, in Kenya and in Tanzania are very different, and reflect the different types of political economy each country is trying to pursue. The different paths taken by KANU in Kenya and by TANU in Tanzania also reflect the different sets of objective conditions existing in the two countries, especially during the waning days of the colonial era when the organizational expression of African nationalism took a variety of forms. In Tanzania, the leaders of the nationalist movement were permitted by the colonial government to establish a nationwide organization at a relatively early stage in 1954. Their efforts were also facilitated by the existence of a common African language for political discourse, Swahili, and by the distribution of the country's population across a large number of small ethnic groups, no one of which was capable of dominating the others. Conditions in Kenya were just the reverse. The colonial government's ban on nationwide political parties prior to 1960 forced parties to confine their activities to a single administrative district. The process of party development was therefore highly decentralized and resulted in the formation of a series of autonomous political machines whose defined purpose was usually limited to the promotion and defense of the interests of a single ethnic group. When combined with the concentration of Kenya's population into a relatively small number of large tribes, it is hardly surprising that this sequence of party development made it all but impossible to establish a single, cohesive, nationwide political organization free from the strains of competing sectional interests. It is also not surprising that given these contrasts, TANU became an asset to President Nyerere—an asset he eagerly and creatively attempted to exploit—while KANU was perceived as a potential liability by its leader, Kenyatta, who subsequently consigned it to a minor role in the Kenyan political system.

The net result after a decade and a half of independence is that in terms of their respective capacities to make public policy, and ensure effective implementation of those policies made, TANU has developed a capability that is unique in the African experience, while KANU has not. Only in countries that have gained their independence through armed struggle, as in the territories of Portuguese-speaking Africa, have political parties developed a capacity for decision making equal to TANU's. TANU is thus the exception rather than the rule. And though TANU may consequently serve as a model for parties elsewhere on the continent, KANU's lack of development cannot be ignored, for it is more representative of the condition of political parties in most African states. On balance, however, we would submit that development is better than decay,[27] and in this regard the two parties occupy opposite poles on that continuum.

NOTES

1. See, for instance, Tom Mboya, *Freedom and After* (London: Andre Deutsch, 1963), or Kwame Nkrumah, *I Speak of Freedom* (New York: Praeger, 1961).

2. See Sir Andrew Cohen, *British Policy in Changing Africa* (London, 1959), p. 37.

3. Information used in this paragraph is available in one form or another in standard texts on British government, of which the following are a good selection: J. A. G. Griffith and H. Street, *A Casebook of Adminstrative Law* (London: Sir Isaac Pitman and Sons, 1974), pp. 22–23; A. H. Birch, *The British System of Government* (London: George Allen & Unwin, 1967), pp. 213, 219; Lord Morrison, *Government and Parliament* (London: Oxford University Press, 1964).

4. See P. Msekwa, "Party Supremacy" (M. A. thesis, University of Dar es Salaam, 1974), p. 8.

5. Ibid., pp. 9–11.

6. Ibid., p. 15; see also *Hansard Parliamentary Debates,* June 28, 1962, col. 1085.

7. Ibid., p. 14.

8. Ibid., p. 16.

9. See William Tordoff, *Government and Politics in Tanzania* (Nairobi: East African Publishing House, 1967), chap. 3, especially p. 80.

10. See Cherry Gertzel, *The Politics of Independent Kenya* (London: Heinemann, 1970), chap. 2, especially pp. 23–42.

11. See John J. Okumu, "Charisma and Politics in Kenya," *East Africa Journal,* February 1968, pp. 9–16; George Bennett and Carl G. Rosberg, *The Kenyatta Election* (London: Oxford University Press, 1961); Henry Bienen, *Kenya: The Politics of Participation and Control* (Princeton: Princeton University Press, 1974), chap. 3.

12. Gertzel, op. cit., p. 150.

13. Henry Bienen, *Tanzania: Party Transformation and Economic Development* (Princeton: Princeton University Press, 1967), p. 198.

14. *Report of the Presidential Commission on the Establishment of a Democratic One-Party State* (Dar es Salaam: Government Printer, 1968), p. 17, para. 42, quoted in Msekwa, op. cit., p. 27.

15. Msekwa, op. cit., p. 38.

16. Ibid.

17. Ibid., p. 39.

18. *Hansard Parliamentary Debates,* July 22, 1968; also Msekwa, op. cit., p.33.

19. Msekwa, op. cit., pp. 39–40.

20. Julius Nyerere, *Decentralization* (Dar es Salaam: Government Printer, 1972), p. 11; see also Msekwa, op. cit., p. 40.

21. *Daily News* (Dar es Salaam), February 23, 1974.

22. Msekwa, op. cit., p. 44.

23. Ibid., p. 47.

24. For a review of the amendments to the Kenyan constitution between 1964 and 1969, see Gertzel, op. cit., pp. 174–76.

25. See Kenya, *Official Report,* National Assembly, 1st Parliament, 5th sess., 1967, vol. 12 pt. 2, col. 8213, quoted in Gertzel, op. cit., p. 151.

26. See Kenya, *Official Report,* National Assembly, 2d Parliament, 5th sess., 1974, vol. 34, col. 137.

27. For a discussion of the desirability of a highly developed and institutionalized party organization in developing political systems, see Samuel P. Huntington, *Political Order in Changing Societies* (New Haven: Yale University Press, 1968), chap. 7.

3

LEGISLATORS, ELECTIONS, AND POLITICAL LINKAGE

Joel D. Barkan

OF THE MANY FEATURES of the political economies of Kenya and Tanzania that have been shaped by the colonial experience, few have been so consciously molded to conform to the practice of the former colonial overlord, and then so consciously modified, as the legislative and electoral process. To properly assess the current significance of the related forms of political behavior that make up this process, one must therefore search beyond the purpose for which these activities were initiated during the waning days of colonial rule.

During the years immediately before independence, the British colonial government attempted to repeat in Kenya and Tanzania what it had already attempted in other third-world countries to which it had granted independence, beginning with India in 1947; namely, the transfer of British parliamentary and electoral institutions to non-Western soil. Institutional transfer was viewed as the sine qua non of the process by which the power to govern would be transferred from a government of colonial administrators to a government of indigenous political leaders. As such, self-government was explicitly defined in terms of parliamentary government, specifically, the Westminster model, and not merely by the substitution of black faces for white ones in the administrative agencies that comprised the colonial state.

Having defined self-government, and indeed political development, in terms of the transfer of British parliamentary and electoral institutions to African soil, the colonial government proceeded to phase in the operation of such institutions by rapidly expanding the membership of the Legisla-

I wish to acknowledge the support of the Comparative Legislative Research Center at the University of Iowa for facilitating the field research in Kenya reported in this chapter.

tive Council, and altering the method of selecting its members until a majority of the council was directly elected on the basis of one man, one vote.

This scenario was played out in Kenya in the course of four elections held between 1957 and 1963,[1] and in Tanzania via three elections between 1958 and 1960.[2] In each country, the results were roughly the same, and were typical of the outcomes of elections held in other African countries during this period: (1) the emergence of a single political party as the dominant force in the national legislature, and in the political system as a whole; (2) the transfer of the power to govern, and the granting of independence to an African government formed by the leaders of the dominant political party; (3) the emergence of a structure of political representation that was particularly responsive to local interests and issues, rather than to issues of national concern.

The net effect of these developments, as most students of African politics are well aware, was not the transplantation of Western parliamentary democracy to Africa, but something quite different. Because these political systems were controlled by a single group of political leaders, the process of competition, mutual criticism, and bargaining between government and opposition parties that characterize political life in the West was never established. For the same reason, the legislature never became an important arena for the deliberation and making of public policy. Nor did the electoral process provide voters with a choice of policy alternatives, or a choice between competing governing elites.

While the institutional transfer envisaged by the British never materialized, the legislature and the electoral process continue to exist in both Kenya and Tanzania more than a decade and a half after independence. In contrast to the situation in more than half the countries of sub-Saharan Africa, where these nascent institutions have been shoved aside by military juntas or civilian-run approximations of the colonial administrative state, the legislature and the electoral process have survived, and, in some instances, even thrived. The purpose of this discussion is therefore to examine the significance of this institutional survival, the forms it has taken, and why it has occurred.

THE LEGISLATIVE PROCESS AS POLITICAL LINKAGE

In both Kenya and Tanzania, the strength and longevity of legislative and electoral institutions is a function of the extent to which each links citizens residing on the periphery of these political systems to the center. Because they are not instruments for the making of public policy, the significance of the National Assembly in the two countries lies not in the collective activities of their members, such as the deliberation and passing of bills that transpire within the legislative chamber, but rather in the individual behavior of each member outside.* As such, the legislative institution of importance is not the legislature but the legislator, and it is with his role that we shall be concerned.

To be viable and independent, all political systems must develop mechanisms for linking the central agencies of the state to the population it purports to rule. The political systems of Kenya and Tanzania are no exception to this requirement. Without well-developed linkages—which we define as valved and stable networks for communication and the exchange of resources—between government and the members of a society, public policy cannot be formulated to respond to the needs of the population. Nor can the population be expected to comply with such policies as the state seeks to carry out if its members do not understand the rationale behind these policies, and the benefits they might bring. As in many other third-world societies, however, the linkages that exist between the center and the periphery in Kenya and Tanzania are not spatially extensive, or intensive, in terms of the volume of communication and resources they transmit. Most political linkages in Kenya and Tanzania parallel those of the economy, and are therefore most developed between urban areas and those rural areas that are centers for the production of cash crops for export, or for other export-oriented activities such as tourism and mining. More important, most existing linkages are those of the state administration, many of which were established during the colonial period, and which function for the purpose of facilitating the center's penetration and control of the periphery, rather than to connect the periphery to the center. Regardless of the many services they might provide to the local people, the

---

*Parliamentary practice in both Kenya and Tanzania consists almost exclusively of the deliberation and passage of government-proposed legislation and the questioning of members of the government by backbenchers about the administration of government policy. No private members' bills have been passed by either house for almost a decade, and attempts by MPs to amend government legislation rarely succeed. Despite these basic similarities, some significant differences exist between the parliamentary practices in the two countries. Backbenchers in Kenya are far more active and independent than their counterparts in Tanzania and are occasionally able to push the government to the point that it modifies its own legislative proposals. Efforts by Kenyan backbenchers to use the question period as a mechanism for legislative oversight are more extensive than similar efforts in Tanzania—in part because the Kenyan National Assembly is often in session for several months each year compared to the Tanzanian Parliament, which rarely meets for more than 40 days. Commissions of inquiry are also periodically established by Kenyan backbenchers to delve into government policy, and the annual debates of estimated expenditures by government departments are lively affairs. Press coverage of parliamentary debates in Kenya is also far more extensive than in Tanzania, with the result that prominent backbenchers, as well as ministers, become better known to the general public than do their counterparts in Tanzania.

bureaucrats of the provincial and regional administrations in Kenya and Tanzania who maintain these administrative linkages, and who are responsible for implementing government policy, are by definition and practice, agents of the center. In addition to being charged with carrying out policies determined by the center, these linkers are recruited and evaluated by the center. They are not, except via informal mechanisms, responsible to the local people they are assigned to serve.

In contrast, legislators are elected representatives of local communities, and as such are expected by the people they represent to be agents of the periphery at the center. This is particularly true in agrarian societies where the main lines of political cleavage are of a sectional and territorial nature, and where the level of organized political activity by interest groups and/or social classes that cut across the boundaries of sectional interests is relatively low. In these societies, legislators have the potential for playing a unique role in the political process, because they are frequently the only actors in a position to create and maintain linkages from the periphery to the center. While they may never be an important factor in the actual making of public policy, the process by which the state allocates its resources, they often have the opportunity to affect the pattern by which resources allocated to a given problem are distributed across society at the local level. Legislators are consequently perceived by their constituents not only as their representatives at the center, but as agents capable of extracting resources from the center for the local community.[3]

Data reported elsewhere by this writer, and by others, strongly suggest that most legislators in Kenya and Tanzania share this conception of the legislator's role.[4] For them, the essence of the legislative process is found not in legislating as a member of the National Assembly, but in lobbying on their constituents' behalf vis-a-vis government ministers, senior bureaucrats in charge of ministries that run programs in the rural areas (that is, public works, health, education, agriculture), and the senior members of the provincial and regional administrations responsible for the area in which their constituencies are located. Election to the National Assembly is therefore significant to the extent that it confers on MPs the right to engage in such lobbying, and other entrepreneurial activities through which they provide or obtain resources and services for their constituents. Most important among these activities are efforts to organize and support small-scale self-help development projects in the local community. These efforts at constituency service are what consume the bulk of most legislators' time, and constitute the substance of the linkages they may create between the periphery and the center. They are also the activities on which an MP is judged at election time.

The extent to which legislators in Kenya and Tanzania actually realize this linkage role varies greatly both within and, especially, between the two polities, and is a function of at least five conditions: (1) the inclination and capacity of individual legislators to engage in the type of entrepreneurial activities required to make them successful linkers of the periphery to the center; (2) the amount of access legislators have to the resources of the center for distribution to the periphery, and/or the existence of alternative resources on which legislators can draw; (3) the role of the national political party, the extent and nature of its organization, and the ideological goals to which it is committed; (4) the posture of the civil service toward legislators; and (5) the nature of the electoral process. In the next section we shall consider the first four of these conditions, while the fifth shall be examined in the section which follows.

The Propensity of Legislators to be Linkers

The legislative process as we have broadly defined it is a highly individual and fundamentally entrepreneurial exercise that places a premium on the ability of MPs to deal effectively with their constituents, and with those who distribute state resources. The success of legislators at creating linkages consequently depends on their willingness to go out and organize the members of their constituencies into a significant political base whose support is valued by the center, and to mediate the reciprocal demands voiced by their constituents on the one hand, and by the center on the other. Given the skills and the personality required, it is not surprising that some MPs are more inclined to undertake these tasks than others, and are more adept at it. Not all MPs are extroverts and/or entrepreneurs, and in both Kenya and Tanzania, it is possible to distinguish between those legislators who have grasped the significance of the linkage aspects of the legislative process, and those who are content to confine their efforts to such business as is brought before the National Assembly by government leaders.

A number of observations may be made in respect to the propensity of legislators to define themselves as "externals" or "internals."[5] First, there are still some MPs in the National Assembly of both countries who persist in defining their roles primarily in terms of the deliberation and passage of laws. This is, of course, the conventional Western view of the legislator's role, and one to which the members of the National Assembly in both countries were particularly prone in the periods immediately before and after independence. In the early days of self-rule when the notion of institutional transfer remained a salient legacy of the colonial era, debates in the National Assembly were often lively affairs and given substantial coverage in the press. MPs who had been trained to think of the legislative process in these terms naturally concentrated on the activities which were consistent with this view, by regularly attending parliamentary sessions and participating in the debates which ensued. Such behavior continued throughout the First Parliament in both countries (1960–65 in Tanzania; 1963–69 in Kenya) despite the fact that by late 1964, both were one-party states. Instead of the government and the governing party being challenged by a loyal opposition in the Westminster tradition, backbenchers of the Kenya African National Union (KANU) and of the Tanganyika African National Union (TANU) confronted party leaders on the front bench. This was especially true in Kenya, where the cohesion and discipline of the ruling parliamentary party has never matched that of its counterpart to the south.

Many MPs became so absorbed in parliamentary combat that they failed to grasp the necessity of building a political base in their local communities and linking these communities to the center. From the perspective of the residents of these communities, such MPs went off to the capital after their election and were never seen or heard from again. A great many paid dearly for this omission when they sought reelection. Thus in Kenya in 1969 in the first nationwide elections following independence, 54 percent of the incumbents who sought reelection were defeated.* Similar results occurred in Tanzania, where 58 percent of the MPs who stood for reelection were defeated in 1965 while another 20 incumbents did not even attempt to run.

Backbenchers were particularly vulnerable to the seductions of parliamentary debate. Many viewed active participation in the affairs of the National Assembly as the means for maintaining their visibility with their constituents and for attracting the attention of government leaders whose support they required to obtain resources for their local communities. In contrast, frontbenchers, as ministers or assistant ministers of executive departments, had greater access to state resources. They could thus maintain their local bases of power, and at the same time devote most of their time to the running of their ministries, the parliamentary process, and other business of the center, in a way backbenchers could not.

The lesson of the Tanzanian elections of 1965, and of the Kenyan elections of 1969, was that MPs needed to devote far more effort to solving

---

*Parliamentary elections were also held in parts of Kenya in 1966 and were known as the Little General Election. These elections were held in 29 constituencies represented by MPs who had resigned from KANU to become members of the opposition Kenya People's Union. These MPs were forced to stand for reelection by the government on the ground that they had been originally elected to the National Assembly as members of KANU. Sixty-six percent of the incumbents who stood for reelection were defeated. In contrast to the elections of 1969 and 1974, which have been strictly one-party contests, the Little General Election was a series of hard-fought two-party contests in which the Kenyan government became heavily involved.

the problems of their local communities if they hoped to remain in office. For incumbents, these elections, and others which followed, have basically been referenda on the performance of individual MPs in obtaining resources for their local community. Considerations of MPs' performance as legislators within the National Assembly have had minimal impact. Since the beginning of the Second Parliament in each country (1965–70 in Tanzania; 1969–74 in Kenya), an increasing proportion of MPs have consequently shifted their attention from legislating to constituency service, and other linkage activities.

Access to Resources

The capacity of MPs to play a linkage role is also a function of several conditions beyond an awareness of the need to do so, and the will. Far more crucial, in recent years, has been the availability of resources. Given the limited amount of government resources that are not earmarked for recurrent budget expenditure or tied to major development schemes (as in the case of projects assisted by foreign donors), there is often a shortfall between the amount of resources constituents expect their MPs to obtain for the local community, and what is actually available. To the extent, however, that constituency service consists of organizing and securing government support for small-scale development projects such as the building of schools, health clinics, feeder roads, and wells, the capital required to launch such efforts (as distinct from the funds required to maintain them), is not particularly great, nor beyond the reach of most MPs. Though little hard data are available on the cost of these projects, it would appear that the majority, which are frequently organized on the basis of community self-help, cost no more than $5,000 to $10,000, and many cost less. While projects costing two to three times this amount are not unusual in Kenya, few if any exceed $100,000.[6] The challenge for MPs attempting to organize and link such projects to the center is not, therefore, the existence of resources, but access to them.

Access is a function of the rules of the game pertaining to such activities and of the MP's standing with those senior decision makers, usually ministers, who are in a position to release available funds to claimants. In respect to the former, it matters much whether the national leadership and official ideology encourage and permit MPs to organize community development projects and seek government aid to bring them to fruition. Given the divergent value systems of Kenya and Tanzania, it is hardly surprising that the two countries take markedly different approaches toward legislators engaging in linkage activities of the entrepreneurial nature described above. Put simply, Kenya encourages such activities on the part of its MPs, provided they conform to certain rules of the system, while Tanzania does not. During the presidency of Jomo Kenyatta, efforts by Kenyan MPs to organize the members of their constituencies for the purpose of self-help received official and well-publicized blessings, provided individual legislators did not pyramid the creation of such projects into an independent base of political support from which they might threaten the regime. This practice will most likely continue under Kenyatta's successor, Daniel arap Moi. The challenge to the MP is thus to create a political base that is large enough for the regime to value and coopt, but not so large for the regime to fear.*

Since the mid-1960s, and particularly since the elections of 1969, Kenya has evolved an increasingly specific and semicodified set of procedures by which legislators initiate projects and then obtain a variety of matching grants from the government to sustain them. As such, positive sanctions are accorded to the explicitly entrepreneurial roles MPs play on the periphery. Considerable latitude is given to individuals operating on the periphery, on the assumption that their success will produce both benefits for the rural population and support for the regime—all at a relatively low cost to the center. This laissez faire conception of what constitutes proper activity by legislators is highly consistent with Kenya's greater concern for economic growth as compared to her concern for equality. For while MPs who organize their communities for self-help foster development and link their constituencies to the center, they inevitably buttress their political and socioeconomic status in the process. In Chapter 6, Frank Holmquist argues that self-help and inequality in the rural areas often go hand in hand. The same might be said for linkage and inequality as well.

Under the Kenyan system, MPs make direct claims on the ministers and assistant ministers in charge of the ministries most relevant to the projects and other problems with which they are concerned. The result is that ministers use a portion of their budgets as patronage, and end up playing a role vis-a-vis individual MPs that is similar to the role which the MPs themselves play vis-a-vis their constituents. Where implemented, especially if done on a regular basis, such exchanges of resources for political support establish viable linkages, or linkage chains, between center and periphery of a clientelist nature. By establishing such linkages, MPs both connect their constituency to the center of the political system and

---

*An example of one MP who broke this unwritten rule was the late J. M. Kariuki, who assisted Harambee projects around the country. By providing assistance to both the projects and to the MPs for the constituencies in which they were located, Kariuki developed a large following and something of an independent political base at the national level. Popular, flamboyant, and critical of the government, he was assassinated in March 1975.

further their careers. Moreover, they do so without entering the legislature or engaging in conventional collective legislative activities with fellow MPs.

The linkage chains through which members of the Kenya National Assembly connect their constituencies to the center usually consist of a hierarchy of patron-client linkages as summarized in Figure 3.1. In most cases, these linkage chains embrace four tiers of patron-client relationships. At the apex of the system is the president of the republic who, as the chief patron, coordinates and balances the claims of competing lineages. As head of the government, the president awards government ministries (and the resources of patronage they command) to senior politicians of longstanding reputation who wield power beyond their own parliamentary districts. Ministries have usually been awarded to regional leaders who have demonstrated their ability to "bring in their ethnic base," or region in support of the government. These regional leaders are simultaneously clients of the president and patrons of aspiring younger politicians, including backbenchers in the National Assembly and potential backbenchers. The latter are in turn clients of ministers and patrons of local notables in their constituencies. These notables, some of whom might hold elective office themselves as members of town councils, are in turn patrons of small segments of the general public.

This four-tiered system was established and orchestrated with particular effectiveness between 1969 and 1978 by Kenya's first president, and acknowledged "father of the nation," "Mzee" Jomo Kenyatta. His successors in the presidency will no doubt attempt to do the same, and, in part, will assume office on the basis of whether they are perceived by the most powerful of their potential clients (that is, ministers and regional leaders) as being capable of fulfilling the role of chief patron.

Although this four-tiered system has become a model for center/ periphery relations in Kenya, it does not embrace all members of the National Assembly, nor does it exist on a uniform basis across the country. In some areas, it scarcely exists at all. Because these chains consist of a series of informal, personal relationships, they often break down or fail to develop between one or more of the four levels. Some chains consist of less than four tiers, as where a minister appeals directly to the local notables in his own constituency rather than via an MP, or when a backbencher bypasses the local notables to make direct contact with the people at the grass roots.

Another significant variation occurs with the linkage chains involving the roughly 35 members of the Kenya National Assembly who are assistant ministers. Comprising almost a quarter of the legislature, this group consists mainly of young, energetic MPs who have provided much in the way of constituency service and who, as a result, have been elected by

FIGURE 3.1: Levels of Patron-Client Linkage Structure in Kenya

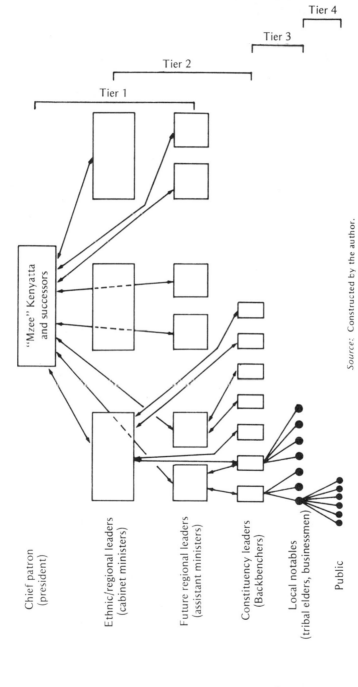

Source: Constructed by the author.

substantial majorities or easily reelected to a second term. Most assistant ministers occupy a somewhat ambiguous position in the system because they are frequently not clients of ministers, nor particularly close to the president. As effective organizers of their constituencies, they are simultaneously regarded as potential regional (that is, ethnic) leaders and a possible source of opposition to the center. Their appointments as assistant ministers by the president may thus be viewed as both a promotion acknowledging their performance to date and an attempt to coopt them to his clientelist system to thwart any tendency to challenge his rule. Whatever the specific reason, assistant ministers enjoy access to government resources superior to that of ordinary MPs. This position enables them to maintain the linkages they have established between their constituencies and the center, and, as we shall see below, enhances their prospects for reelection.

In addition to working within a nationwide system of clientelist linkages, Kenyan MPs seek resources by approaching prominent civil servants both at the center, where they seek to establish working relationships with permanent secretaries, assistant secretaries, and the like, and on the periphery by working with provincial and district commissioners, the district heads of central ministries' field staffs, and provincial and district development councils and planning bodies, where they exist. As might be expected, legislators who are successful in obtaining administrative backing at the district level stand a better chance of getting what they want when they lobby at the center.

Finally, like political entrepreneurs the world over, Kenyan legislators are not unaware of the principle that "money is the mother's milk of politics," and, as a class, they invariably seek to accumulate sufficient personal resources to finance, or at least provide seed money for, the projects in which they are involved. Consistent with the entrepreneurial roles they are expected to play, Kenyan MPs are provided with a variety of opportunities for private accumulation that are formally banned to their counterparts in Tanzania. Kenyan legislators are thus permitted to engage freely in private business ventures. They face no restrictions on the amount of income earned over and above their official emoluments, or on the sources from which it is obtained. Nor are they required to make any public disclosures of their financial interests. MPs are often favored over their fellow citizens when applying for bank loans, while the standards for repayment by MPs that are applied by the banks are likely to be less burdensome. Many Kenyan MPs also sit on government regulatory boards, for which they derive a secondary salary from the state.

In contrast to the laissez faire system of patronage that affords Kenyan MPs access to both state and private resources, the rules of the game within which Tanzanian legislators function are highly restrictive, and the opportunities for obtaining resources are few. Most restrictive are the role expectations for MPs held by the national leadership, which regards entrepreneurial activity by MPs as incompatible with Tanzania's socialist ethic. Whereas in Kenya, MPs are permitted to be active lobbyists for the periphery in exchange for generating regime support, in Tanzania they are expected to confine their activities in their home communities to being agents of the center—primarily by explaining government policies to those residing at the grass roots. Conversely, MPs' activities at the center are largely limited to their formal duties as members of the National Assembly, and here too, the scope for representing the interests of the periphery, particularly concerns specific to a single constituency, is limited. MPs may, and do deliberate legislation proposed by the government, but once a decision is made—invariably in support of the proposal—they are expected to publicly support the decision whatever their personal conviction.[7] With few exceptions, legislation proposed by the leadership is thus debated and ratified.* Such bargaining as does occur over policy takes place behind closed doors in the meetings of the National Executive Committee (NEC) of the party—a body to which only a small number of elected, as distinct from appointed, MPs belong.

Several reasons exist for the limited role Tanzanian leaders assign to members of the National Assembly. First, both members of the National Assembly and the institution itself are perceived as a distraction—if not a threat—to the hegemony of the ruling party. As discussed by John Okumu in Chapter 2, the supremacy of TANU over the National Assembly, particularly the supremacy of the NEC as the source of all major policy decisions, has been asserted by the leadership for more than a decade. Second, and perhaps more significant, is that the leadership understands the inherently individual and entrepreneurial nature of legislative behavior in the context of an agrarian peasant society.

As noted above, any MP wishing to be reelected must devote considerable effort to constituency service and organize the residents of his community into an independent political base. Although such activities are highly appropriate in a political economy based on patron-client capitalism, they are counterproductive in a system committed to achieving equality and collective decision making coupled with party control. Thus while TANU, and subsequently the Revolutionary Party, or *Chama Cha Mapinduzi* (CCM), have provided both the organizational framework and the resources for many of the same patron-client relationships that exist outside a party structure in Kenya, the opportunities for Tanzanian legislators

---

*In 1973, the Tanzanian government proposed a sharp increase in both the progressivity and overall level of the national income tax. The proposal was initially voted down by the National Assembly, at which point Parliament was suspended, and MPs were told to go home and think about their decision. Later that year Parliament was reconvened and the bill was quickly passed.

to become a part of these clientelist networks and to play a linkage role similar to that of their Kenyan colleagues is systematically denied.

MPs are neither encouraged nor allowed to play an independent role in the initiation of self-help development projects in their constituencies, nor can they lobby at the center on their constituents' behalf. Rather, they must tie such efforts into a national system of planning controlled by the party and the center. Since the decentralization and reorganization of the regional administration in 1972, all locally initiated efforts at rural development are first considered by a Ward Development Committee, the lowest agency concerned with projects of this type. Projects approved by Ward Development Committees are subsequently reviewed by development committees at the divisional, district, and regional levels, and ultimately at the national level by *Maendeleo* (the Ministry of Rural Development), the president, and the National Executive Committee of the party. The only role accorded to MPs in this screening process is as members of the development committees at the district and regional levels. This role, however, is at best a marginal one. With more than 40 members, the committees are chaired respectively by the regional and district chairmen of the party. The vice-chairmen are the regional and area commissioners, the most senior civil servants in the rural administrations; the secretaries are the regional and district development directors, the civil servants charged with overseeing all development efforts in the rural areas. The geographic jurisdiction of the Regional and District Development Committees also encompasses several parliamentary constituencies, with the result that MPs must focus their attention beyond the areas they have been elected to represent. These committees consider recommendations from the Divisional and Ward Development Committees, which are dominated entirely by party officials, and on which MPs do not sit, and are in turn responsible to Maendeleo. Though they obviously attempt to articulate the needs of the people they represent, MPs can do little more. Nor do they have the opportunity to significantly modify the national plan for rural development when it is ultimately brought before the National Assembly. While it is possible to conceive of the Regional and District Development Committees as subnational legislatures, the subordination of MPs to party personnel and civil servants is such that the impact of the individual MP is difficult to discern. What is clear, however, is that this system limits the formal opportunities for Tanzanian MPs to create and establish linkages from the periphery to the center by cutting off any privileged access they might have to the resources of the center. Confronted by a massive planning apparatus between the periphery and the center, MPs are for all practical purposes short-circuited out of the linkage process.

Nor is this the only frustration facing Tanzanian MPs. In a system which denies individual access to public resources, access to private resources naturally takes on a greater significance. Here too, however, Tanzanian legislators are at a disadvantage compared to their Kenyan counterparts. Whereas the latter are permitted to engage in an almost unlimited array of business ventures, Tanzanian legislators are subject to a stringent leadership code that prevents them from accumulating sufficient private resources to establish and maintain a personal political machine in their constituencies. MPs are expressly forbidden from receiving rents from their personal property, owning stock in private corporations, and receiving supplemental salaries from the state. The Kenyan practice of appointing loyal MPs to government regulatory agencies and parastatals is avoided.

Tanzanian MPs thus face a dilemma from which there is little prospect for escape. On the one hand, they are subject to the same mass pressures and expectations as their Kenyan counterparts insofar as their constituents elect them to engage in various forms of constituency service and to obtain resources for the local community. On the other, legislators in Tanzania must conform to the expectations and sanctions of the center, which conceives of the MP as something of an errand boy and which has structured the game in such a way as to actively discourage MPs from operating in an independent manner on their constituents' behalf.

Legislators and Parties

A third variable in the linkage equation is the role of the ruling political party in the political system, the nature of its organization, and the ideological goals to which it is committed. Having noted that the individual and entrepreneurial activities MPs must pursue to be effective linkers are more compatible with Kenya's capitalist orientation than with Tanzania's socialist values, we shall confine our attention here to the significance of party role and organization.

As discussed at length by Okumu in the preceding chapter, KANU and TANU evolved in opposite directions, particularly after 1965. Whereas the former suffered from a policy of benign neglect, to the point that it ceased to function as a national organization except to certify candidates at the times of parliamentary and local elections, TANU (and subsequently CCM), evolved into both the supreme policy-making authority in Tanzania, and an organization with increasing capacity to enforce the implementation of its policies down to the grass roots. In contrast to Kenya, where few branches of KANU function at the district level, and where party organs at the location level and below can rarely be found, TANU's presence, especially in the countryside, is pervasive. Party branches hold meetings and function regularly down to the ward level. Party chairmen at the regional and district levels are the most powerful public officials in the rural areas, where they oversee the activities of civil servants in the regional administration. Development committees are likewise under party control. Whereas in Kenya the party has all but ceased to exist, in Tanzania it constitutes an independent set of linkages between the center and the periphery that rivals that of the civil service and that severely retards the development of separate linkage networks by MPs.

Once the viability of TANU's national organization—particularly its potential as an instrument of control—became apparent by the late 1960s, the advantages of the party over MPs as a linkage system also became obvious. Like the linkage networks created by MPs, the party's organization facilitates communication upward from the grass roots. Unlike MP networks, it is also an instrument of the center. Given its formal structure and rules, the linkages between party personnel at various levels are also much less fragile than those created by MPs. Whereas the clientelist chains entered into by MPs, such as those in Kenya, are highly informal and personal networks from which subordinates can and do withdraw when a better patron comes along, individuals within the party structure cannot undertake such shifts with such swiftness or ease. Last, and most obvious, a system of party linkages between the center and the periphery facilitates political control over the rural administration in a way that informal clientelist structures cannot. This advantage has been particularly salient among the leadership of a country attempting to achieve socialist transformation but unsure about the ideological commitment of the civil service assigned to do the job.

The net result is that in Kenya, MPs are usually the leading political figures in their constituencies and are unencumbered by any party organization beyond their control. In contrast, Tanzanian legislators must work within an elaborate and highly centralized party structure in which they have minimal influence and where party organization does not parallel the constituencies they have been elected to represent. Although the lower levels of TANU have often been dominated by local community bosses[8] and permeated with patron-client relationships similar to those found outside the party in Kenya, their existence within the party framework in Tanzania has meant that Tanzanian legislators have not been able to develop personal machines independent of party control.

The Civil Service

The fourth condition affecting the prospects for legislators to develop linkages from the periphery to the center is the posture of the civil service toward legislators. Where the civil service—whether via central government ministries, the rural administration, or parastatal agencies—seeks to monopolize all efforts at developing the rural areas, the opportunities for legislators engaging in activities of constituency service and development are obviously limited. This has been the historical pattern in most African states, including Kenya and Tanzania, and dates back to the colonial period, when the civil service was usually the sole authority charged with and capable of promoting rural development. Given the absence of private institutions, state agencies have always been preeminent in this area. Only in recent years have legislators and party organizations begun to challenge their supremacy. Because of its presumed expertise and the relatively higher education of its personnel, the civil service has often been reluctant to share authority for rural development with those playing political roles. Legislators are invariably perceived by civil servants as being opportunistic, unsophisticated, and disruptive—especially as viewed by recent college graduates, who man most of the key posts in the rural administration.[9]

Given these attitudes, it is not surprising that in most African states, legislators have not been brought into the local planning and distribution process by civil servants in control of the rural administration. This is particularly true in countries where the linkage role of MPs has yet to be fully appreciated and/or where the rural administration is under close scrutiny by party cadres. In Kenya, particularly since the election of 1969, during which time Kenyan MPs were encouraged by President Kenyatta to become involved in Harambee efforts, civil servants have become more tolerant of the entrepreneurial activities of legislators in the rural areas. This increased level of tolerance appears to be the result of a new awareness on the part of both civil servants and legislators that they play different linkage roles that can be mutually supportive of each other. Because of their high education and elite status, and because they are normally posted to areas other than those from which they come, civil servants are invariably perceived as strangers by the members of the communities in which they serve. As a result, many civil servants have come to realize that they must establish a working relationship with the local notables in their areas of service if they are to be effective in obtaining the cooperation of the local population. In this context, legislators are increasingly perceived by civil servants as potential assets. Conversely, legislators have been quick to cooperate with civil servants posted to the rural areas, particularly provincial and district commissioners, because these officials can provide them with many of the resources they need to succeed in efforts at rendering constituency service.

Civil servant tolerance for MPs, however, and the prospects for partnership are more limited and have developed more slowly in Tanzania, where the national party is the supreme policy-making authority, and where the party has already preempted and restricted MPs' linkage activities on other fronts. The existence of party organs down to the grass roots provides civil servants with an alternative and more reliable set of partners to MPs for obtaining local compliance with the policies at the center. From the perspective of the civil servant, local party leaders have a decided advantage over MPs as prospective partners. Although they can facilitate civil servants' dealings with members of the local community, MPs are fundamentally agents of the periphery. In contrast, party leaders are local notables who are to some degree committed—indeed chosen—to be spokesmen for the center on the periphery. While MPs are elected to make demands on the center, the role of local party officials is to mediate between center and periphery interests. As a result, the formal mechanisms for establishing partnerships between civil servants and MPs are almost nonexistent in Tanzania compared to the mechanisms for merging the civil service with the party, for example, the hierarchy of rural development committees.

SUMMARY

Upon considering four of the five major factors that determine the capacity of legislators to build linkages from the periphery to the center, it is clear that Kenya and Tanzania have pursued very different approaches to these aspects of center-periphery relations. During the first five years after independence, the pattern of legislative behavior in both countries was similar and consisted mainly of activities within the legislature. Fundamental differences emerged, however, as pressures intensified for the parliamentarians in both countries to spend more time on service and development activities home in their constituencies, and more time lobbying with cabinet ministers and senior civil servants at the center.

In Kenya, the individual and entrepreneurial nature of the legislative process was recognized early on and has been regarded as consistent with the country's capitalist philosophy. It was also regarded as an asset in the absence of a well-organized national party to complement the provincial administration as the main link between the center and the rural areas. Legislators in Kenya are consequently encouraged by the country's leadership to organize their own local political base in the countryside and plug into the national patronage system. Though the distribution of rewards resulting from this system is rarely equitable, such distribution as does occur generates support for the regime among local elites and the population as a whole. The system is also likely to be particularly responsive to those who make the loudest demands, and as such, provides a useful mechanism for defusing sources of popular discontent.

Tanzania's leadership has also recognized the inherent entrepreneurial nature of legislative behavior but has drawn the opposite conclusions from Kenya when assessing its worth. The unique historical and sociological conditions which gave rise to a unified party in Tanzania permitted the development of a viable system of center-periphery linkages within the party that was not possible in Kenya. Once it became apparent that those center-periphery linkages established by the party were superior to those that might be established by MPs, the scope of activities permitted MPs was increasingly restricted and many activities were brought under party control. Thus, while the linkage role of Kenyan legislators has expanded in recent years, that of Tanzanian legislators has been steadily reduced. Stripped of most of their linkage role, Tanzanian MPs have been increasingly relegated to a role of ratifying government-proposed legislation in the National Assembly, and have been cut off from their political base. Were it not for the regular holding of parliamentary elections, to which we now turn, it is problematic whether this species of political animal would continue to exist.

LEGISLATORS AND THE ELECTORAL PROCESS

Although Kenyan legislators have been encouraged to develop linkages from the periphery to the center while Tanzanian legislators have not, both groups of MPs face similar constraints and hold similar expectations when it comes to getting elected or reelected to Parliament. In one-party systems like Tanzania's , and in no-party systems like Kenya's, the primary purpose of the electoral process is not to provide voters with a choice of policy alternatives or of governing elites. Rather, it is to recruit new individuals into the present ruling elite, promote other individuals in that elite, and to renew the legitimacy of this elite and its mode of governance in the minds of the electorate. The extent to which these objectives are actually fulfilled in Kenya and Tanzania, however, is quite different in each country.

It was noted at the beginning of this chapter that the holding of regularly scheduled parliamentary elections in Kenya and Tanzania sets them apart from most other African countries.* Parliamentary elections have been held in Kenya in 1966 (for only 29 seats), 1969, and 1974, and are expected again in 1979; in Tanzania they were held in 1965, 1970, and

---

*Only Botswana and Zambia have also held elections at regularly scheduled intervals since independence. Other countries such as Senegal and Sierra Leone have also maintained the electoral process albeit on an irregular basis.

1975. Despite the ideological and especially the structural differences between the Kenyan and Tanzanian systems, the character and outcome of the electoral process in the two countries are remarkably alike. Elections in both countries are basically a series of local contests to select representatives of the periphery to lobby at the center. These elections are dominated by discussions of local rather than national issues; questions of ideology rarely arise. They are marked by intense intraparty competition between rival personalities seeking to enlarge or maintain their personal political base in the countryside. In contests involving incumbents, they are invariably referenda on the incumbent's past performance in constituency service.

Tanzania was the first of the two countries to come to grips with the purpose and form of parliamentary elections in the context of a one-party state, following the adoption of a new constitution in July 1965, which designated TANU as the only legal party. To open recruitment to a wide spectrum of the public and give voters a meaningful choice, while maintaining central control, a sequence of procedures was devised beginning with the filing of nomination papers by any member of TANU who could obtain the signatures of 25 supporters. Between 800 and 1,300 individuals have filed nomination papers in each of the parliamentary elections since 1965. Those filing nomination papers are subsequently screened and ranked by secret ballot by the TANU Annual District Delegates Conference in the district where they propose to stand. The rankings of the delegates conference are then forwarded to the NEC, which selects two candidates to contest the election in each constituency. In 1975, the NEC selected 185 candidates to stand in 96 constituencies, including five who were unopposed.

These procedures have been followed with minor modifications for each parliamentary election since 1965. Although screening by party bodies has become more intensive with each successive election, only about 10 percent of the selections of candidates ranked first or second by the Annual District Delegates Conferences have been overturned by the NEC. NEC vetoes have usually occurred in cases of well-known figures who are regarded as troublemakers by the regime or by party officials at the regional level. Moreover, where candidates are nominated to stand unopposed, or where only two candidates are nominated, the NEC must accept the district recommendations. Party input is thus greatest at the district level, where, however, the party organization is dominated by local notables, and where it is consequently as much an organ of the periphery as it is a mechanism for central control.

Nomination of candidates in Kenya is both less formal and complex than in Tanzania, and less subject to party control. For the elections of 1974, any adult over 25 years of age who was literate in English, was a member of KANU for six months, and was prepared to pay a £50 deposit was eligible to run;* 629 individuals ultimately did so in 158 constituencies after being certified by the KANU National Executive Committee as being "loyal to the party."

The KANU National Executive Committee may reject candidates but rarely does so.† No systematic screening of candidates' qualifications for office is conducted as in Tanzania. Nor is a limit placed on the number of candidates who can contest each seat. The result is that in 1974, an average of 3.98 candidates ran in each constituency, and 49 percent of the MPs were elected by a minority of the vote.[10]

Despite these differences in procedure, the electoral process in the two countries tends to produce similar results in terms of who is elected and why. As discussed extensively in the literature,[11] elections in both Kenya and Tanzania have repeatedly been contests dominated by local issues in which voters assess the past and anticipated performance of individual candidates in providing services for their communities. The data confirming this pattern are overwhelming and consist of interviews with and observations of parliamentary candidates in both countries over several elections, as well as surveys of voter opinion.[12] The latter are particularly revealing in that they reflect a fundamental aspect of politics in peasant societies that is often neglected by social scientists and government leaders alike; namely, that the members of these societies, despite their humble backgrounds, are capable of articulating what they regard as their self-interest, and capable of systematically evaluating the performance of public officials in terms of whether it serves their self-interest.

Surveys of voter opinion conducted by this writer and Okumu in Kenya in 1974 and by Jon Moris in Tanzania in 1970 indicate four key points. First, most voters have a clear set of role expectations as to what constitutes the proper duties of a member of the National Assembly.[13] Second, most voters define the role of the legislator primarily in terms of constituency service, particularly the initiation of small-scale development projects in the constituency, and the representation of local interests at the center.[14] Third, most voters, indeed a much higher proportion than in

---

*Kenyan and Tanzanian pounds were equal to $2.80 through 1975, after which it devaluated to $2.30.

†As in Tanzania, the National Executive Committee of the party intervenes in the nomination process to weed out those perceived as troublemakers. Thus in 1974, Oginga Odinga, the former vice-president and head of the opposition Kenya People's Union, had his nomination papers declared invalid when he tried to stand for election in his old constituency in Nyanza. The stated reason for invalidating Odinga's papers was that former members of KPU were required to be members of KANU for three years instead of six months, and that Odinga had failed to meet this requirement. No one knew of such a three-year rule, however, until after Odinga filed, least of all Odinga himself.

industrialized societies, know who their MP is and what he has and has not done to further the interests of the local community.[15] And fourth, the outcomes of parliamentary elections, especially the incumbent's proportion of the vote, and the number of candidates who seek to challenge him for his office, are directly and indirectly a function of voter assessments of candidate performance on those aspects of the legislator's role they value the most.[16]

The significance of these findings is that they suggest that members of peasant societies are probably very different from what conventional wisdom contends them to be. Although they reside on the periphery of the national political system and take a decidedly local perspective of what constitutes the public good, most peasants are not passive political actors ignorant of the national political community within which they live.[17] Nor, as it is often asserted, do they base their political behavior mainly on ascriptive or so-called traditional considerations. Thus, while ethnic background of parliamentary candidates is a very salient factor in the minds of many voters, it is rarely the deciding factor in the way individuals vote. Because possession of the right ethnic credentials is often a prerequisite for being a serious candidate, most serious candidates meet this test. Candidates are thus distinguished from one another on the basis of performance criteria. As such, the electoral process becomes a highly rational exercise. Indeed, compared to parliamentary elections in industrialized countries, where party identification is often the greatest single determinant in the voting decision, voting behavior in Kenya and Tanzania is a model of rational choice.

Given the common considerations of Kenyan and Tanzanian voters, it is not surprising that they elect the same type of people to be their representatives in the National Assembly. A review of the social backgrounds of victorious candidates in both countries indicates that they are invariably much better educated, earn higher incomes, and are much less likely to be farmers, as compared with the average citizen.[18] They also tend to be of higher educational and socioeconomic status than their rivals whom they defeated at the polls.[19] Those elected to office are usually local notables of some renown, men who have been active in civic affairs for many years. Candidates with such credentials are perceived as having the best prospects of advancing the interests of the local community, especially at the center, where access to top decision makers is the name of the game. When seeking to extract resources from the center, sending a typical member of the community to do the job will not do.

The extent to which the electoral system consistently favors those who are already in positions of prominence is readily seen when one compares the rates of electoral success achieved by ministers, assistant ministers, backbenchers, and challengers in the Kenyan elections of 1969 and 1974, and in the Tanzanian elections of 1965, 1970, and 1975. The figures presented in Table 3.1 for Kenya and in Table 3.2 for Tanzania show that, in each election, the higher the office held by the candidate, the greater his prospects for being elected. Though less than half of the incumbents standing for reelection are returned to the National Assembly, there is a marked difference between the prospects of ministers, who have a considerable access to resources for distribution to their constituencies, and the prospects of backbenchers, whose access is limited. Likewise, the prospects of election for backbenchers are roughly twice that for challengers in Kenya, and in recent years more than six times that for challengers in Tanzania. The result is that in both countries the composition of the National Assembly is increasingly a stratification involving two groups: At the top is an emergent oligarchy whose members are regularly returned to office, and which is supported, especially in Kenya, by a group of assistant (junior) ministers and backbenchers who are their clients and who manage to get themselves returned to office, albeit at a lower rate. At the bottom are those backbenchers, roughly two-thirds of the total, who are in office only one term.

It is at the bottom where significant differences emerge between the two countries. Although the rate of reelection among Tanzanian backbenchers is roughly the same as among their Kenyan counterparts, the proportion of backbenchers who did not seek reelection in Tanzania is significantly higher. Since the proportion of elected MPs who are members of the back bench in the Tanzanian National Assembly is also higher than in Kenya, the overall rate of turnover among elected members is higher as

TABLE 3.1:   Winners and Losers in Kenya by Type of Candidate

Year	Challengers	Backbenchers	Assistant Ministers	Ministers	All Incumbents
1974					
Winners	15%	35%	64%	79%	49%
Losers	85	65	36	21	51
N	(496)	(78)	(36)	(19)	(133)
1969					
Winners	20%	37%	63%	74%	46%
Losers	80	63	37	26	54
N	(468)	(86)	(38)	(19)	(143)

Note: Data presented for the 1974 elections are for 140 electoral districts out of a total of 158; data for 1969 are for all 158 districts.

Sources: Daily Nation and *East African Standard* (Nairobi), October 19, 1974; *Daily Nation*, December 8, 1969; and Goran Hyden and Colin Leys, "Elections and Politics in Single-Party Systems," *British Journal of Political Science* 2, no. 4 (October 1972): 396–99.

TABLE 3.2:   Winners and Losers in Tanzania by Type of Candidate

Year	Challengers	Backbenchers	Junior Ministers	Ministers	All Incumbents
1975					
Winners	5%	34%	n.a.	80%	43%
Losers	95	66	n.a.	20	57
N	(968)	(67)	n.a.	(15)	(82)
1970					
Winners	7%	44%	50%	80%	49%
Losers	93	56	50	20	51
N	(1,204)	(62)	(2)	(10)	(74)
1965					
Winners	11%	18%	31%	87%	42%
Losers	89	82	69	13	58
N	(761)	(22)	(13)	(15)	(50)

Note: For 1975, data for junior ministers were combined with those for ministers, and are therefore unavailable as a separate category; data presented are for 96 electoral districts. Data for 1970 are for 120 districts; for 1965, 107 districts.

Sources: Daily News (Dar es Salaam), November 6, 1975, as quoted by Denis Martin, "The 1975 Tanzanian Elections," in Elections Without Choice, ed. Richard Rose, Guy Hermet, and Alain Rouquie (London: Macmillan, 1978); Election Study Committee, eds., Socialism and Participation: Tanzania's 1970 National Elections (Dar es Salaam: Tanzania Publishing House, 1974) pp. 368, 379–447; Lionel Cliffe, ed., One Party Democracy: The 1965 Tanzania General Elections (Nairobi: East African Publishing House, 1967), p. 303, apps. 1B and 1C.

well. These differences, presented in Table 3.3, are undoubtedly a function of the more limited access Tanzanian MPs have to the resources of the center, and of the greater restrictions on their engaging in entrepreneurial efforts at the grass roots. It is also important to note that the proportion of MPs in the Tanzanian National Assembly who are directly elected is substantially lower than the proportion in Kenya. Whereas 93 percent of the membership of Kenya's Parliament is composed of elected MPs, the proportion in Tanzania is now about half. Only 96 members of Tanzania's legislature are currently elected to their seats. The remainder, including 25 regional commissioners, 20 regional party chairmen from the mainland, ten nominated members, and up to 52 members from Zanzibar, are all appointed by the president. These appointments clearly dilute the influence of elected MPs and are intended for this purpose.

The combination of these differences, plus the low prospects for challengers in Tanzania, suggests that although the patterns of voting behavior in the two countries are the same and generate similar results in terms of who is elected and who is not, the ultimate impact of these electoral outcomes on the National Assembly, and on the political system in general,

TABLE 3.3: Turnover and Composition of the Kenyan and Tanzanian National Assemblies, 1965–75

	Kenya		Tanzania		
Turnover/Composition	1969	1974	1965	1970	1975
Backbenchers as a percentage of all elected MPs	64	65	91	88	84
Percentage of backbenchers from previous Parliament who did not seek reelection	15	24	49	33	36
Turnover among elected MPs (percentage of elected MPs serving first term in National Assembly)	58	59	80	70	64
Elected MPs as a percentage of all MPs	93	93	58	61*	48*
Number of seats in National Assembly	(170)	(170)	(185)	(198)*	(198)*

*Estimated on the assumption that the practice of limiting the number of nominated MPs from Zanzibar to 32 was continued after 1970. The number of nominated MPs in the Tanzanian National Assembly can be as high as 62 under the provisions of the National Assembly Elections Acts of 1965, 1970, and 1975, but in practice the number has been approximately 32. The number of seats held by elected MPs was 107 after the elections of 1965, 120 after the elections of 1970, and 96 after the 1975 elections. Since 1964, the number of seats held by elected MPs in the Kenyan National Assembly has stood at 158. Twelve members are nominated by the president.

Source: Compiled by the author.

is quite different. In view of their limited numbers, high turnover, and limited resources with which to construct a political base in the countryside, backbenchers in Tanzania, indeed, elected MPs as a group, are clearly marginal actors compared to their Kenyan counterparts. In Kenya, backbenchers have some prospects of becoming clients of the ruling oligarchy composed of ministers and assistant ministers. In Tanzania, their prospects are virtually nil. Restricted in efforts to become successful entrepreneurs in the countryside, they have little to offer ministers who might be inclined to be their patrons but who are themselves dependent on the president and the party for their posts. The result is that the cleavage between backbenchers and frontbenchers in Kenya is far less pronounced than in Tanzania. In Kenya the National Assembly is permeated by a series of competing clientelist hierarchies in which backbenchers play a subordinate, albeit significant, role. In contrast, the Tanzanian National Assembly is divided between elected backbenchers who are largely frozen out of the political process, and ministers and appointed members who have established a political base within the party.

In Kenya, where KANU has withered from disuse, the electoral process has become an important and increasingly institutionalized mechanism for elite recruitment. In the absence of a well-defined and extensive party organization, the electoral process both allocates and defines the hierarchy of roles that links the periphery to the center. MPs who are reelected to the National Assembly and who are known to have developed an extensive political base in the countryside are tabbed for promotion from the back bench to positions as assistant ministers.* Leaders of longer standing who have developed regional followings become eligible for positions in the cabinet.

Such is not the situation in Tanzania. Because of the alternative linkage networks established by the party, and because of the control the party has established over the access to resources, the electoral process in Tanzania does not recruit leaders so much as it limits the prospects of potential leaders for achieving positions of authority. Those who are persistent enough to surmount the electoral barrier, moreover, find themselves dominated at the center by those who have been recruited through the party ranks.† Not only are their roles as linkers curtailed, but their roles as parliamentarians in the conventional sense are curtailed as well.

IMPACT AND SIGNIFICANCE

In assessing the role of the legislative and the electoral process in Kenya and Tanzania, we have argued that the former is an inherently entrepreneurial exercise for the purpose of linking the periphery to the center, while the latter reinforces and rewards this exercise. That these forms of political behavior should be encouraged in Kenya, and frustrated in Tanzania, is to be expected. Indeed, it would be odd if it were otherwise. The problem for Tanzania, however, is more complex than one of merely

---

*The reader should note that more than 30 members of the Kenyan National Assembly are assistant ministers compared to less than a half-dozen in Tanzania. These positions exist almost solely for the purpose of maintaining an orderly process of recruitment and cooptation into the ruling oligarchy.

†In assessing the electoral process in Tanzania, the reader should keep in mind than we have dealt with the electoral process solely in terms of its significance for the behavior of MPs and for its impact on the National Assembly. The reader should not forget that although those who have been appointed to the National Assembly have been appointed because of their positions in the party, many of these people were elected to their party posts. Space does not permit an analysis of the series of indirect elections through which party leaders rose through the party ranks, but there is no doubt that this dimension of the electoral process in Tanzania is of considerable significance so far as recruitment is concerned. Except at the ward level, however, it is not a process in which members of the general public directly elect their representatives or play a decisive role.

being confronted by a process that is inherently more compatible with a capitalist model of development than with its own.

What is at issue is that Tanzania basically wants to have its cake and eat it too. On the one hand, the country's leadership is committed to the establishment of a democratic polity where the members of society and their representatives play a decisive role in the making of public policy. On the other, it is equally committed to achieving democracy within a socialist framework, a task which requires a transformation in the way most of the country's institutions work. Because socialist construction does not occur automatically, the legislative and electoral process poses a perpetual dilemma: whether the outcome should be the election of representatives of local interests, in which case those with entrepreneurial skills are the ones most likely to be catapulted into office, or the election of leaders committed to advancing the party's program of socialism and self-reliance.

As now structured, the electoral process in Tanzania, as in Kenya, produces more representatives than leaders. Party intervention in the nomination of candidates reduces this tendency somewhat. But, so long as the Annual District Delegates Conference remains the critical stage of party review, and voters continue to evaluate candidates in terms of their potential for constituency service rather than in terms of their commitment to socialist construction, there will be little change in the type of representatives elected to the National Assembly. Short of the NEC making all nominations, and imposing them on the local constituencies, the dilemma now posed for the leadership is unlikely to be resolved.

It is for this reason that Tanzania has adopted what is basically a series of post hoc solutions to the problem of how to develop patterns of legislative behavior that are compatible with the goals of socialist construction, and at the same time elect a Parliament chosen directly by the people. As discussed above, these solutions require MPs to be deprived of the resources they need to carry out linkage activities in the districts and be shorn of much of their influence within the National Assembly. Such solutions, however, limit the capacity of MPs to do the job their constituents elected them to do and are unlikely to generate public support for the legislative and electoral process over the long term.

Given our discussion, the answer to the question raised at the outset of this essay—why and how the legislative and electoral process has survived in East Africa—should now be clear with respect to Kenya. What is not clear, however, is why the legislative and electoral process has survived in Tanzania as well. Two hypotheses offer possible, but by no means definitive, explanations. First, in a country where power and political recruitment are monopolized by a well-organized ruling party, the electoral and legislative process still plays a symbolic role simply by continuing to exist. So long as the Tanzanian National Assembly is regarded as the sole institution for the making of laws (as distinct from the making of policy), it will continue to perform this ritual task and representatives will be elected to become members in this body. In other words, so long as legislative and electoral activities do not alienate the public—and there are few signs that they do—the fact that they perform no more than symbolic functions does not mean that they will go out of business. Indeed, such symbolic purposes as they do fulfill may be of greater significance than our lack of hard data on this question leads us to suppose.

A second, and related, explanation lies in the short- and long-term effects of the electoral and legislative process in countries where it has developed into a significant and substantive feature of political life. Thus in Kenya, where an increasing number of MPs establish linkages from the periphery to the center, and where parliamentary elections are an important mechanism for elite recruitment, some costs may eventually need to be paid as a result of the very success these activities have achieved. Assuming a continuation of the present patterns of peasant voting behavior, each successive parliamentary election will raise the proportion of legislators who possess the skills and the will to be effective linkers. This will eventually result in a higher overall level of vertical integration between the center and the periphery. But the greater the number of linkers and linkages, and the better their quality, the greater will be the total volume of demands made on the center.[20] Once this occurs, the competition for resources between representatives of different constituencies will intensify and politics may evolve into a zero-sum game in which stability cannot long be maintained. In attempting to assess the long-term impact of the legislative and electoral process, one must not forget that we are concerned with the impact of these phenomena in plural societies that are extremely poor and where sectional (and in many cases ethnic) cleavages run deep. The increased level of vertical integration achieved via the legislative and electoral process may thus be the precursor of horizontal disintegration.

In the economic realm, the more effective legislators are in initiating development in their constituencies through small-scale autonomous efforts at the grass roots, the less likely economic change can be effectively coordinated across the entire society. Legislator-initiated development that is the substance of the linkage process is also likely to result in unbalanced development. Those areas which are able to help themselves and qualify for assistance from the center will prosper at the expense of those which cannot. The existence side by side of extensive linkages between the center and those areas of the periphery which are relatively well off, and the minimal linkages between the center and those areas of the periphery which are poor, will ultimately compound the problem of regional inequality and place greater strain on the national political economy.

In sum, the short-term gains accrued by the legislative and electoral process in Kenya may eventually be overtaken by the long-term costs they produce. Conversely, the short-term difficulties of maintaining legislative and electoral activities in Tanzania in the absence of their serving any critical function in the political order may eventually lead to a more restrained and manageable form of legislative politics that can be maintained.

NOTES

1. For discussions of these elections and of this period of Kenyan politics, see George Bennett and Carl G. Rosberg, *The Kenyatta Election: Kenya 1960-61* (London: Oxford University Press, 1961), and Carl G. Rosberg and John Nottingham, *The Myth of Mau Mau: Nationalism in Kenya* (New York: Praeger, 1966).

2. For discussions of these elections and of this period in Tanzanian politics, see Henry Bienen, *Tanzania: Party Transformation and Economic Development* (Princeton: Princeton University Press, 1967), chap. 2.

3. See Joel D. Barkan, "Bringing Home the Pork: Legislator Behavior, Rural Development and Political Change in East Africa," in *Legislatures and Development,* ed. Joel Smith and Lloyd Musolf (Durham: Duke University Press, 1978); Jon R. Moris, "The Voters' View of the Elections," in *Socialism and Participation: Tanzania's 1970 National Elections,* ed. Election Study Committee (Dar es Salaam: Tanzania Publishing House, 1974), pp. 348–49; Kenneth Prewitt and Goran Hyden, "Voters Look at the Elections," and Lionel Cliffe, "Factors and Issues," in *One Party Democracy: The 1965 Tanzania General Elections,* ed. Lionel Cliffe (Nairobi: East African Publishing House, 1967), pp. 283, 301.

4. Barkan, "Bringing Home the Pork," op. cit., and Raymond F. Hopkins, *Political Roles in a New State: Tanzania's First Decade* (New Haven: Yale University Press, 1971), pp. 195–98.

5. For an extended discussion of the different ways that legislators classified as "internals" and "externals" spend their time, see Joel D. Barkan, Chong Lim Kim, Malcolm Jewell, and Ilter Turan, *Legislators and Political Development in Kenya, Korea and Turkey* (Durham, N.C.: Duke University Press, forthcoming), chap. 5.

6. The major exceptions are several regional "Harambee Institutes of Technology," which have been initiated in recent years by groups of MPs and ministers from the area. Most prominent among these are the Kiambu Institute of Technology, a Harambee project of extraordinary scale in Central Province that is presently seeking financial support from foreign foundations, and RIAT, the Ramogi Institute of Advanced Technology, a similar institute in Nyanza to serve Luo interests, but which has experienced considerable difficulty as a result of bickering among Luo leaders. For further details see E. M. Godfrey and G. C. M. Mutiso, "The Political Economy of Self-Help: Kenya's 'Harambee' Institutes of Technology," *Canadian Journal of African Studies* 8, no. 1 (1974): 109–33.

7. Raymond F. Hopkins, "Constituency Ties and Deviant Expectations Among Tanzanian Legislators," *Comparative Political Studies* 4, no. 3 (October 1971): 326.

8. See Bienen, op. cit., chap. 10, for a description of this tendency in the mid-1960s. Findings presented by several third-year honors students in theses for the Department of Political Science at the Universtiy of Dar es Salaam in 1975 indicate that the pattern described by Bienen remains very much entrenched.

9. Joel D. Barkan, *An African Dilemma: University Students, Development, and Politics in Ghana, Tanzania and Uganda* (New York and Nairobi: Oxford University Press, 1975), p. 165.

10. The number of candidates permitted to stand in each constituency in Tanzania was specifically limited to two in order to insure that each member would be elected by majority. For details of the discussion of this problem by Tanzanian leaders, see Belle Harris, "The Electoral System," in *One Party Democracy: The 1965 Tanzania General Elections,* ed. Lionel Cliffe (Nairobi: East African Publishing House, 1967), p. 22.

11. Joel D. Barkan and John J. Okumu, " 'Semi-Competitive' Elections, Clientelism, and Political Recruitment in Kenya," in Richard Rose, Guy Hermet, and Alain Rocquire, eds., *Elections Without Choice* (London: Macmillan, 1978); *Socialism and Participation,* op. cit.; Goran Hyden and Colin Leys, "Elections in Single-Party Systems: The Case of Kenya and Tanzania," *The British Journal of Political Science* 2, no. 4 (October 1972): 389–420; and *One Party Democracy,* op. cit.

12. For extensive reports of survey findings, see Barkan, "Bringing Home the Pork," op. cit.; Barkan and Okumu, " 'Semi-Competitive' Elections, Clientelism, and Political Recruitment in Kenya," op. cit.; Moris, "The Voters' View of the Elections," op. cit., pp. 312–64; and Kenneth Prewett and Goran Hyden, "Voters Look at the Elections," op. cit., pp. 273–98.

13. Barkan, "Bringing Home the Pork," op. cit., and Moris, "The Voters' View of the Elections," op. cit., pp. 348–51.

14. Barkan, "Bringing Home the Pork," op. cit.

15. Barkan and Okumu, op. cit.

16. Ibid. See also Joel D. Barkan, "Comment: Further Reassessment of the 'Conventional Wisdom': Political Knowledge and Voting Behavior in Kenya," *American Political Science Review* 70, no. 2 (June 1976): 452–55.

17. For more on this important point, see Fred M. Hayward, "A Reassessment of Conventional Wisdom About the Informed Public: National Political Information in Ghana," *American Political Science Review* 70, no. 2 (June 1976): 433–51; Barkan, "Further Reassessment of the 'Conventional Wisdom'," op. cit., and especially James C. Scott, *The Moral Economy of the Peasant* (New Haven: Yale University Press, 1976) chaps. 1 and 2.

18. Hyden and Leys, op. cit., pp. 410–11; and Cliffe, "The Candidates," in *One Party Democracy,* op. cit., pp. 261–66.

19. Hyden and Leys, op. cit.; Cliffe, op. cit.

20. James C. Scott has referred to this process as "inflationary democracy." See Scott, "Patron-Client Politics and Political Change in Southeast Asia," *American Political Science Review* 66, no. 1, (March 1972): 111–12.

4

ADMINISTRATION AND PUBLIC POLICY

Goran Hyden

HOW SIGNIFICANT IS THE ROLE of government administration or bureaucracy in public policy making in Kenya and Tanzania? How similar or different are the patterns of policy making in the two countries? These are the principal questions to which this chapter addresses itself. The discussion is pursued in the light of two major arguments that have dominated our conceptions of bureaucracy in developing countries. The first is that the bureaucracy in these countries enjoys a high degree of institutional autonomy and hence dominates the policy-making process. The second is that bureaucrats constitute a dominant social class and thus have more influence over policy making than any other group. Without rejecting the value of a class or an institutional analysis, the argument pursued below is that public policy making in the two countries can be best understood only if the range of variables considered is allowed to extend beyond what has been used in the two approaches mentioned above. More specifically, by using a contextual approach, we want to demonstrate that in Kenya and Tanzania institutional autonomy is hardly the most important characteristic of the government bureaucracy. In a similar fashion we argue that social class position alone does not help us understand the extent to which bureaucrats exercise influence over public policies in these countries.

THE AUTONOMY OF THE BUREAUCRACY

A common argument in the literature on developing countries is that the bureaucracy in these societies enjoys a significant institutional autonomy and thus dominates the policy-making process. This position is contrasted with the argument that, in bureaucracies in Western and

Communist countries, there exists a sovereign political body that contains bureaucratic influences. One of the first to put forward this argument was Fred Riggs, who in his book on administration in developing (or "prismatic," as he preferred to call them) societies states:

> A phenomenon of utmost significance in transitional societies is the lack of balance between political policy-making institutions and bureaucratic policy-implementing institutions. The relative weakness of political organs means that the political function tends to be appropriated, in considerable measure, by bureaucrats. Intra-bureaucratic struggles become a primary form of politics.[1]

A number of scholars have accepted, wholly or in part, the point that imbalanced political development results from the preponderance of the executive over all other branches of government in developing countries. Ferrel Heady,[2] S. N. Eisenstadt,[3] and Lucian Pye[4] follow a similar line of argument. Pye concluded, with reference to Vietnam (before the Communist takeover) and Pakistan that "power and authority are concentrated in the realm of administrative officialdom."[5] Writing on Africa, David Abernethy states that the bureaucracy plays a crucial role in economic development by influencing the level of available financial resources, the development strategies that are drawn up, and the manner in which plans become concrete programs and projects. He adds that in the absence of strong private-sector forces to stimulate and control development, the bureaucracy may well be the only instrument a country's leaders have to attain ambitious economic objectives.[6] Bereket Selassie follows a similar line of argument when he writes that due to its monopoly of administrative and technical skills the bureaucracy becomes very difficult to control. It is simply too strong for other institutions to challenge.[7]

Y. Dror disagrees with this view of the policy-making process in developing countries, which he instead characterizes in the following manner: "In its internal composition and in its modes of operation, the political executive in developing countries tends to follow the pattern of court politics: much power is concentrated in one leader, for whose favour various cliques engage in struggle with each other."[8] Under these circumstances government bureaucracy cannot supply very many rational components, and the cumulative result is that in most developing countries, according to Dror, the senior civil service, as an institution, contributes much less to public policy making than in developed countries. It reinforces the weaknesses in the behavior patterns of the politicians instead of compensating for them. A similar view is held by R. S. Milne, who questions whether the bureaucracy in developing countries possesses the behavioral traits that make a planned approach to development possible.[9]

African civil servants, reflecting on their own position, render support to the view that their voice is not so influential, after all. Writing from a long personal experience in Ghana, A. L. Adu notes that it is not surprising that in most African countries the civil service no longer has the initiative in the formulation of operational policies.[10] Although the programming of general policies should be the responsibility of the civil service, it is, in Adu's view, the usual situation nowadays to see ministers working out their own detailed programs, supervising the execution of these programs, and carrying out functions which should properly be discharged by civil servants. The conclusion to be drawn from Adu's account is that the official division of functions between politicians and civil servants is not strictly followed in African governments. Other senior civil servants in Africa share this view. Because traditions and conventions are not yet fully established, "ministerial control" is often interpreted as "absolute discretion." To survive in such situations civil servants tend to tailor their views to suit their political masters.[11] Through patronage and spoils the politicians dominate the policy-making process. The implication is that there has been a qualitative change in the relations between politicians and civil servants after independence. While the political heads, before independence, upheld a strict division of functions and a relationship based on the observance of impersonal rules, their postindependence successors have created a diffuse atmosphere in which personal discretion is much more important. The work of the civil servants is less routinized and is subject to frequent, sometimes major, interventions by the political heads.

The Social Power of Bureaucrats

While the argument about the relative autonomy of bureaucracy is based on institutional analysis, there are those who have examined the position of the bureaucrats in the context of the social structure prevailing in postindependence African countries. The civil servants have latent interests in common with other groups in society, and they may facilitate, or take direct political action to promote, these interests. Michael Lofchie notes that the segmented nature of the institutional bureaucracy makes it very difficult for civil servants to seize state power.[12] A. Zolberg, while agreeing with Lofchie, shows, by citing the examples of Benin (Dahomey) and Upper Volta, that the civil servants can create conditions, through protracted strikes, for example, that provide opportunities for their class allies in the army to take over state power.[13] Thus, in order to understand the role that civil servants may play in the policy-making process, it is necessary to go beyond a purely institutional analysis. Here Zolberg echoes a point which is fundamental to Ruth First's explanation of military takeovers in Africa and which points in the direction of a Marxist class analysis.[14]

Writing about the problems facing the more militant regimes in Africa, Marxist scholars have maintained that one of the principal hurdles to radical transformation in these societies has been the class interests of government bureaucrats. Being in a socially privileged position, they have had sufficient power to defend their interests. K. Fitch and M. Oppenheimer show how Kwame Nkrumah failed to reduce the class privileges of the civil servants and the army officers and eventually fell victim of his own inability to tackle this issue.[15] Claude Meillasoux argues, with reference to Mali, that as a result of Modibo Keita's socialist policies, bureaucrats came in fact to occupy an even stronger position than before.[16] They developed the characteristics of a social class: control of the economic infrastructure and use of it as a means of exploitation, control of the means of repression, and resort to various other devices to maintain dominance. Issa G. Shivji entertains a similar argument.[17] By socializing the means of production, the "bureaucratic" bourgeoisie, including politicians, civil servants, and parastatal managers, becomes the dominant force in society. Its members control the manner by which the surplus produced in society is distributed. Politicians, rather than having an antagonistic relationship with the civil servants and managers, share with them a common class interest. That is what, according to Shivji, holds back a radical transformation of the Tanzanian society.

Taken together, the literature reviewed above offers many interesting insights into the policy-making process in the developing countries. Considered separately, however, it is clear that each author tends to reduce his analysis to one limited set of variables. Some focus exclusively on the manifest role of bureaucrats in policy making and on institutional relations. Their critics, in turn, reduce policy making to a question of patronage politics or defense of hidden class interests. In whatever direction the analysis is twisted, it does inevitably simplify the policy-making realities. Certain interesting features are left out. This becomes clear if attention is paid to how policies are made in Tanzania and Kenya.

POLICY MAKING IN TANZANIA: "WE MUST RUN WHILE OTHERS WALK"

Tanzania is a country which tries to make great strides forward under conditions which are very difficult. It is one of the poorest countries in Africa. Its productive forces are still developed only to a limited extent. Agriculture dominates, and most production is by small-holder peasants, many of whom are only marginally integrated into a cash economy. Secondly, while colonization of the territory was a brutal process and led to resistance by the local population, the transition to political independence was peaceful. Furthermore, the social structure is still fluid and class stratification is only emerging. In these circumstances a revolutionary consciousness is not developing in a spontaneous manner. It has to be induced from above by a political leadership that is willing and anxious to overthrow remnants of the past. In order to prove its commitment to radical transformation of the society, Tanzania's political leadership has developed a mode of policy making that in many respects contradicts the conventional assumptions associated with models of policy making. I have elsewhere labeled this the "we-must-run-while-others-walk" mode.[18]

It has four main features. The first is the strong urge to do everything and do it at once. The ambition is to maximize as many social values as possible through policies which serve to mobilize new resources for the achievement of these very values. This is manifested in the way various programs and policies are presented as "frontal attacks" (for example, the *ujamaa* program), "operations" (the movement of people into villages), and "matters of life and death" (efforts to raise agricultural production). Because the social values pursued rarely are operationalized in advance, the aspiration to maximize is pursued with an implicit acceptance of the fact that one may have to settle for a less ambitious target than the one officially pronounced. Thus, the approach resembles that of the fisherman who, when throwing his net into the water, is aware that while he pulls it back some of the catch may escape.

The second feature of Tanzanian policy making is that policy makers often decide on matters without first having obtained full and detailed knowledge of the possible consequences of their decisions. They start "running" and take the consequences as they occur. In this respect, they come close to the approach that Alfred Hirschman has called the "motivation-outruns-understanding" style of policy making.[19] Full understanding of what can or cannot be achieved with existing resources is not regarded as a precondition for making a policy. Instead, the political decision is made first, often under dramatized circumstances, in order to produce a sense of rapid advance. In this approach ends always justify means: the ultimate objective is considered above any cost considerations. The decision which led to the Arusha Declaration in 1967 is the best case in point. One could expect that the nationalization of the major means of production would create severe disturbances in the production and service sectors, given the shortage of qualified local manpower. Yet the decision was made, and although costs were incurred, the benefits later proved to be considerable: The people of Tanzania achieved a closer control of their own economy; local managers got an opportunity to take responsibility for public corporations and thereby gain valuable experience.

The third feature of Tanzanian policy making is the unwillingness of policy makers to use the past as a source of guidance for the future. Being associated with colonial rule, from which the leadership seeks a break, the past is to them, by and large, irrelevant. Dror has identified this inclination as a main feature of policy making in most developing countries.[20] Tanzanian policy makers, therefore, like their colleagues in many other developing countries, do not always tread on familiar grounds but make moves into the unknown—the assumption being that the right policies are not necessarily those chosen from the realm of what is considered feasible in economically rational terms. The solution to a problem is not always found where there is light; it may well be hidden in the dark. Thus, the task of policy makers becomes, in Hirschman's terms, that of "zeroing in" on a new policy that would otherwise be ruled out by conventional criteria of rational calculation. In the field of cooperative development, for instance, the government has experienced serious management problems. Cooperative societies have often been more of a burden than an asset to their members. A wealth of experience gained during the colonial years has been available to the policy makers, but they have preferred to find their own solutions. We have seen the ujamaa villages being established as an alternative solution to the problems in the cooperatives. More recently this has been followed up by compulsory villagization. The emphasis has always been on solutions which are believed to have an indigenous touch, that is, which come closer to the available local know-how than the policies introduced by the British before independence.

The fourth feature of the prevailing mode of policy making in Tanzania is that employees in the public sector are compelled to work in a context where public expectations constantly exceed what can actually be attained by the incumbent officers. This makes many of the latter develop a sense of anxiety. The assumption behind this approach is that this anxiety or insecurity is beneficial as it makes the officers clamor for more security through improved performance. In this respect, the Tanzanian approach differs from the finding of Peter Blau that initiative occurs only with job security.[21] It is more in line with the view of A. Gunder Frank, who has argued that "overdefined" roles, that is, where role expectations cannot actually be satisfied by incumbents, often produce positive results.[22]

The Rationale of the Tanzanian Approach

We have already argued that the mode of policy-making in Tanzania has developed out of the need to achieve radical transformation under conditions, which in themselves, are not very revolutionary. It appears the Tanzanians argue that by appealing to goals or targets that are beyond any realistic achievement, they can achieve more than if they relied on conventional models of policy analysis and policy making. They can mobilize hidden resources which would not be put to use if they depended only on econometric cost-benefit analyses.

Another reason why the conventional conceptions of policy making have been discarded in Tanzania is that the country does not really have its development problems at arm's length. These problems are so pressing for the decision makers that they rarely have the time to plan the next move. Under such circumstances it is not only natural, but often also justified, if policy makers abandon their disposition of routinization. Instead of extolling the values of efficiency and calculative rationality or evaluating measurable results, they resort to the use of intuitive rationality or extrarational factors in policy making. Ideological spontaneity is encouraged and a certain amount of youthful risk taking permitted. President Nyerere's assertion that development depends on people rather than on things, and his notion that people learn while doing, are both manifestations of this orientation. In this respect there exists a similarity between Tanzania and Maoist China.

Hirschman, basing his approach primarily on experience in Latin America, has defended a mode of policy making similar to that in Tanzania. In his view, it is called for because of the uneasy combination of the pressing nature and the low degree of understanding of problems that often characterizes policy making in developing countries.[23] To try out widely different policies, that is, to make moves into the unknown, may be useful when understanding is limited. Similarly, when feedback information on policy outcome is limited or poor, mistakes may have to be of large proportions to make policy makers find time and resources for effective corrective action. This approach, however, which stresses the commitment to achieving goals or ends rather than finding the optimal means to achieve ends, cannot be wholly separated from the need for finding optimal solutions. As the Tanzanian case demonstrates, if the jumps are too many and too often, and if policy makers fail to learn how to find adequate means to achieve their new objectives, costs become significant. The dilemma of the policy maker in these circumstances is to know exactly which of his moves into the unknown is worth giving adequate resources to complete.

In this kind of situation the prevalence of overdefined roles may also have its positive effects. The gap between ends and means of roles surrounded by excessive expectations may generate enterprise and initiative, so sorely needed in countries anxious to enjoy rapid social and economic progress. It gives the incumbents a substantial range of discretion and permits innovation and adaptation. Gunder Frank's conclusion, not very different from that of Hirschman, is that as long as there is only a single desired direction of change, and it is known and accepted by the policy makers, reliance on excessive role expectations is appropriate.[24] The discretion enjoyed under such circumstances may help to combat the dangers of routinization and facilitate the initiation of new policy moves.

Implications for Government Administration

The mode of policy making that has developed in Tanzania after independence does imply a lot of changes for those who occupy central roles in the government administration. For many civil servants it has been difficult to adjust to this new way of policy making. If its potential benefits have not been realized, it is in large part due to the fact that government officials have been slow in accepting its implications. For the ordinary bureaucrats who prefer to march at a steady pace in well-organized columns, it is too youthful and energetic. Many civil servants feel that they have been thrown out of gear.

One of the things which they are uncomfortable about is the fact that they have been overwhelmed by new policies and programs in which the conflicts between ends and means have not been resolved in advance. Their opportunity to influence the formulation of a given policy has been very limited, and they have consequently been forced to resolve conflicts between ends and means, that is, to sort out feasible alternatives of implementation, only after the decision to go ahead with a certain policy or program has been made. In some cases, like the decision to introduce universal primary education (UPE) by 1977, the civil servants have really responded positively and constructively. They have worked out feasible ways of implementation which do not hamper the execution of other already existing programs in the government. In other cases, however, the civil servants have really been thrown out of gear. A good example is the 1975 Operation Maduka. The then prime minister, Rashidi Kawawa, directed that all private retail shops should as soon as possible be replaced by cooperative ventures. The political heads in Tanzania's 20 regions reacted very differently. Some decided to order the closure of private shops as a matter of urgency. Others suggested a phasing-out plan. Still others waited to see what was going to happen. In this, like so many other cases, the bureaucrats have not been able to act in a concerted manner—characteristic of a group of people concerned with defending their class interest. The sudden and bold policy initiatives that have been so typical of Tanzania since independence have forced the civil servants into a defensive posture. Because the politicians, and notably the president himself, have seized the initiatives, the discretion of the bureaucrats as a social class has been very limited.

This does not mean, however, that the civil servants lack influence. If it is accepted that policy making does not consist of one big decision alone, but rather is a series of decisions at different levels, it can be argued that the Tanzanian civil servants do have some influence on the shaping of policy programs. Once the principal decision has been made by the party, the minister, or the regional commissioner, the ball is thrown into the court of the civil servants. As executing agents, they have to interpret the policy and devise a feasible implementation strategy. In so doing, they are invariably forced to modify the original policy objectives as resources rarely permit the attainment of the ambitious targets set by the politicians. It should be remembered, however, that through the system of party supremacy, written into the constitution since 1975, the civil servants are kept on their toes. Any modification that they introduce must be justified. The political decisions are generally regarded as being beyond criticism, and therefore the blame for any shortcoming always tends to fall on the executing agencies.

In order to make this system work, it has been necessary to centralize the control over the bureaucracy. The system of local government was abolished in 1972. This means that local patrons have lost much of their influence over the lower levels of government administration. It also means that the mediating influence that such people have often had on policies affecting their respective home areas has declined. The masses, particularly in the rural areas, cannot rely on the protection of a local patron in the same way they could prior to 1972. Since then, and particularly after they were moved into villages in 1974, the rural masses have come to stand eye to eye with the government authorities in a manner not known before. There have also been increasing pressures on government officials to penetrate village life. The practice now is for civil servants at the district level to be allocated villages in which they regularly work and for which they are personally responsible. Since these officials are not local patrons, but officers whose career depends on how well they attain targets set by the central authorities, it is expected that they will ensure a more effective implementation of government policies. Another measure that has reinforced the central control over the bureaucracy is the increase in number of senior officials appointed by the president or the prime minister. All senior positions in the regions and the districts, as well as in parastatal bodies, are nowadays political appointments.

The outcome of all this is, that while the civil servants today have a stronger leverage over the population at large, they can hardly be said to represent an institution enjoying a great amount of autonomy; nor do they work in a setting resembling the Weberian ideal-type bureaucracy. They do not enjoy the security of tenure; nor can they be sure that their expert views are being seriously considered in the formulation of policies. The civil servants regularly find themselves being whipped by politicians who accuse them of inefficiency, among other things. This has understandably demoralized many civil servants, particularly since politicians have resorted to the "we-must-run-while-others-walk" mode of policy making, even when there has been no reason for it. This excessive use of the policy-making mode, referred to as "platform policy making," has been condemned by the president. Whether demoralized or just inclined to play it safe, bureaucrats in Tanzania are aware that showing commitment to the policies as pronounced by their political leaders is more important than offering a rational critique of these policies based on some kind of cost-benefit analysis. Thus, even in those cases where the search for optimal solutions has been necessary to support bold policy moves into the unknown, civil servants have often refrained from substantive criticisms. The notion that "we are all engaged in a huge task of transforming our society," which requires solidarity, is a much more powerful behavioral guide than the idea that the civil servants stand outside the political mainstream and only offer technical advice based on rational ends-means calculations.

In those places where it works, there is a genuine team spirit developing, and the policy-making process probably has a greater chance for success than if the politicians and civil servants were to stick to roles very strictly defined, as in Western democracies. However, in places where it does not work, it is clear that the Tanzanian system has its costs. If a genuine sense of trust is nonexistent, the tendency among civil servants is to tailor their feedback reports so as to please their political bosses. This becomes particularly harmful in a system where policies often emerge without a proper assessment of feasibility or of costs and benefits. In such a system, full understanding can only be obtained in the process of implementing policies. Therefore, reliable information about policy outcome is a sine qua non for the successful operation of the Tanzanian mode of policy making.

With the assistance of McKinsey consultants from the United States, who were invited to design the decentralization system, the government of Tanzania has tried to institutionalize plan-implementation procedures, including a reporting system. The effects of these attempts, however, have been limited. Reports have not always been written, and when written, they are usually submitted late. Senior officers have been unable, and sometimes unwilling, to make use of the data supplied from below. Many junior staff members have consequently sensed a lack of appreciation by their superiors. This has significantly reduced the potential value inherent in a system of overdefined roles.

The administrative and managerial innovations proposed by the McKinsey consultants were all based on the assumption that what Tanzania needs is a stable and well-defined system of government. Indeed, much of what they proposed was absolutely contrary to the mode by which policies are made in Tanzania under the principle of party supremacy. That their proposals were so readily accepted must be explained by the fact that they passed through a committee of senior civil servants. The latter were responsible for accepting the proposals, and they found no objection to a system of management that would potentially enhance their security and influence.

Many of the principal features of the system introduced by the McKinsey consultants have subsequently been ignored. The civil servants have not been allowed to enjoy a higher degree of security in their positions; nor has their influence on policies increased. They do have some influence, and they certainly have more influence than many other groups in the society, but in comparison with the political leadership they have much less. The bureaucratic bourgeoisie, when forced to run, has been constantly falling—and not without costs to the country's development. The questions is, How many times can the political leadership allow its civil servants to fall without losing its own credibility?

POLICY MAKING IN KENYA: "WE MUST PULL WHILE OTHERS PAUSE"

As in Tanzania, much of postindependence politics in Kenya has centered on the issue of bureaucratic influences on policy making. We have seen how a deep and genuine urge to deal radically with the problems of underdevelopment in Tanzania has generated a mode of policy making which to a large extent has thrown the bureaucracy out of gear. In Kenya, political aspirations have been more pragmatic. Politics has been more competitive and like a tug of war. People have formed groups based on tribal and similar ties, and have attempted to preempt opportunities for other such groups. The well-known call for *harambee* has been seriously applied within the context of relatively small groups and organizations, but has, at the same time, generated a lot of instability in the political system and uncertainty in the policy-making process. The mode by which policies are often made in Kenya can best be called the "we-must-pull-while-others-pause" exercise.

In order to contain the disintegrating tendencies inherent in such a system, the government of Kenya has tried to retain the well-established central administration inherited from the colonial authorities. Some observers of the Kenyan political scene have described the country as an example of imbalance in the growth of political institutions. Cherry Gertzel,[25] John R. Nellis,[26] and John J. Okumu[27] have maintained that the government bureaucracy is more mature, and thus more powerful, than other political institutions. Their argument is based on two major assumptions: that the administration inherited from the British has retained its dominance after independence; and that administration overshadows politics because the ruling party is weak. While this argument may have been valid in the first years after independence, some important qualitative changes that have taken place in Kenya in recent years have considerably reduced its validity. The notion of the Kenyan bureaucracy as being very powerful and above factional politics must be questioned.

The colonial administration in Kenya, as elsewhere in Africa, was a classical bureaucracy—it loyally performed the functions of maintaining the status quo and safeguarding the privileges and interests of its masters. However, the presence of a significant number of European settlers added a complication because they constituted a rival group of masters to the British government in London. The political history of preindependence Kenya centers on this problem; colonial administrators often experienced a conflict of loyalty between the interests of the government in London and those of the white settlers in Kenya.[28] It is important to note here, however, that this rivalry was confined to that sector of the population which shared, with the administrators, a concern to control the African majority. It did not undermine the powers of the bureaucracy over the majority of the population. It remained an important means of control, as was dramatically illustrated during the Mau Mau uprising.[29]

Against this background, it is not surprising that many Africans, on the eve of independence, argued in favor of reducing the central government's powers. This orientation was manifested in the Majimbo constitution, the first to serve independent Kenya. However, given the instability of the political alliances formed immediately before independence, the first KANU government was unwilling to practice the principles of the constitution.[30] Instead it tried to recreate a strong center, an intention that was confirmed in the 1964 republican constitution, the one that Kenya still officially follows. Thus, the attempts to introduce any significant structural changes in the government organization were blocked. This fact is used as evidence that the civil service in Kenya has remained very powerful in the policy-making process. We doubt, however, whether the fact that structures did not change is enough proof that the civil service in Kenya operates in a fashion similar to its colonial predecessor—exercising, as a cohesive institution, wide powers over the rest of society.

Although the withdrawal of Europeans in the civil service in Kenya was not quite as extensive and rapid as in many other African countries, it was significant enough to pave the way for a predominantly indigenous civil service. The Africanization process meant that a totally new group of people, with aspirations very different from their European predecessors and under different pressures from the domestic society, were put in charge of the bureaucratic institutions. While the British often deliberately stayed away from contacts with the local population, the Kenyan civil servants could not afford to ignore their roots in the local social structure. The former were a group of socially well-established officers who did not have to worry about their position in society. The latter, on the other hand, had to prove to themselves, to their relatives, and to their local peers that they could make it. This led to a scramble for prestige and power in which extraorganizational ties, notably tribal connections, were important.

In the first five years after independence, Africanization was pursued primarily in the public sector. It was possible to become a civil servant in the senior ranks within a short period of time. It offered both high salary and high status. African ambitions, therefore, were to get good and secure jobs. Those who were able to take greatest advantage of this situation fell into two categories: civil servants, previously confined to the middle levels of the colonial administration, who, by upgrading, were allowed to succeed their European or Asian bosses; and new graduates from universities in East Africa and overseas. With reference to the latter, Okumu has written that "they were originally attracted to the civil service not out of missionary zeal but because of the security offered by life appointment with its regular salary and perquisites."[31] The bureaucracy, then, was not so much considered an instrument for the pursuit of public policy as it was an avenue of promoting private ambitions and interests. In Tanzania, where these tendencies were also present, they have been deliberately curbed since the Arusha Declaration. In Kenya, on the other hand, they have been officially condoned. The Ndegwa Commission in 1971 recommended that civil servants be allowed to have private businesses along with their public duties, provided that these interests are publicly declared.[32] The Keyna government has subsequently approved a system of rules similar to those recommended by the commission.

As a result of this policy, many civil servants in senior positions have gradually become as interested in their own businesses as in the public offices they occupy. Some have resigned from the civil service in order to pursue their businesses more effectively. The majority, however, have remained in office. For them it has not been easy to maintain a distinct line between private and public interests, and there is little doubt in the minds of most Kenyans that many civil servants have taken advantage of their position when it comes to granting licenses and allocating other benefits. The private sector has taken on an increasing importance for Kenya's emerging bourgeoisie as the number of job opportunities in the public sector, particularly at the middle and higher levels, has declined.

The effort to preempt opportunities for others, which is such a key feature of Kenyan policy making, is no longer directed only toward securing jobs for the boys, but more toward extracting services and benefits from various public institutions. This, as we shall see below, has had definite implications for the political system in general, and government administration in particular.

The Rationale of the Kenyan Approach

Colonial penetration in Kenya was both deeper and more extensive than it ever was in Tanzania. The majority of the population have been more drastically affected by colonialism. This does not mean that they are necessarily less traditional than in Tanzania. In fact, it appears that Kenyans often resort to quasi-traditional forms of organization in order to defend and promote their interests. The competitive nature of the economic system that was introduced during the colonial time—and which, by and large, has been further developed in the same direction after independence—has, by destroying essential features of the traditional social organization, caused insecurity and suspicion. In order to cope with this situation, people have developed and maintained social bonds primarily with those who can be most trusted, that is, members of the same clan or neighborhood, and at the national level, members of the same tribe or subtribe. Thus, in the midst of a rapidly increasing social stratification in the country, tribal and other such associations and groups are rich and poor together. The former become the patrons of the latter. The political system is as strongly divided vertically as it is horizontally.

The colonial authorities managed to govern this system by remaining immune to the pressures for patronage. By staying aloof and reducing the amount of resources controlled by the local African leaders, they could effectively practice a system of divide and rule. After independence, when the British had withdrawn, no group could lay claim to total control of the central government; although attempts have been made to monopolize political control, no group has yet succeeded. The political system in Kenya has been characterized by intense, sometimes bitter, political factionalism. Only President Kenyatta has been able to stand above this factionalism. He has taken the position of the British, and in addition to resolving struggles between political groups, he has effectively managed to rule by playing one group against the other. This has been manifest in the succession struggle, that is, the quest for control of the government when President Kenyatta dies. Although Kenyans in general believe that the Kiambu Kikuyus have benefited most from Kenyatta, he has not allowed any one politician to appear as his natural crown prince.

Thus, Kenyans continue to live in uncertainty and insecurity, and it is not a coincidence that the question "What is going to happen when Kenyatta is gone?" occupies such a prominent position in their minds.

While it is true that Kenya has provided an attractive investment climate for international capital, it is also true that managers of many multinational companies are either very cautious or even reluctant to invest money in the country. They view the tug-of-war-like mode of policy making as a threat to stability and therefore to their capital. Reports of political detentions and assassinations serve to confirm their fears. So do financial deals that officially, or unofficially, are said to have been concluded through the use of bribes.

While many foreigners find it difficult to accept and adjust to the Kenyan way of making policies, the local people are extensively involved in it. They know that it is necessary to pull, and pull at the right time. Frank Holmquist has shown how this works in the context of local politics.[33] People in the villages, sublocations, or locations come together to do self-help work and use their own contributions as a leverage to bargain for government funds. Thus, the competitive nature of policy making encourages a certain type of resource mobilization that would not otherwise take place. To be sure, the government is not always able to respond positively to these local contributions and offer a supplementary support. Yet this system forces the government leaders to be more responsive than they would otherwise be. Most politicians know that their position is, in large part, dependent on their ability to respond, with supplementary resources, to those initiatives that have been taken by local groups or associations. Thus, in their own way, Kenyan officials also serve in overdefined roles.

Implications for Government Administration

The question of tribalism and tribal patronage has been the foremost issue in Kenyan politics since independence. The nature of this phenomenon, however, has changed over the years. In the first years of independence, when the private sector was still virtually closed to Africans and there was still opportunity for rapid promotion in the public service, the main manifestation of tribal patronage was the acquisition of jobs through tribal contacts. In the competitive atmosphere that prevailed, it was necessary to rely on the support of influential fellow tribesmen inside the public service. This practice did not necessarily mean that incompetent people were recruited to higher and middle-level positions in the civil service. Most candidates were adequately qualified, but in this situation the support of an influential tribesman often became crucial. Although we do not know exactly how widespread this phenomenon was, there is little doubt that, given the competitive atmosphere and the lack of trust in the institutions established by the British, it did flourish. The former chairman of the Public Service Commission has testified that his institution often found itself competing with tribal and other such informal cliques anxious to promote the interests of their members.[34]

This form of tribal favoritism was particularly prominent in the years when the public sector offered the most attractive career opportunities. As these opportunities have gradually disappeared, the nepotism and tribal favoritism in job allocation and promotion within the civil service have lost some of their significance. This does not mean they have completely disappeared. Civil servants, like politicians, are often asked to assist relatives and fellow tribesmen to acquire jobs in the government. Remaining opportunities for applying that kind of favoritism, however, are nowadays confined to the lower levels; it may still be possible to help somebody get a clerical post or one requiring no skills at all. But even at that level, chances for practicing tribal favoritism are getting more and more limited.

It is clear that tribalism, when practiced in this context, is wholly informal. Only a small number of people are normally involved, and they form a clique that exercises influence beyond what the formal rules and regulations prescribe. This may be called the invisible form of tribalism. While extremely difficult to prove, everybody knows that it is there.

This informal practice has also been used in other decision-making contexts in the Kenyan government. During the last years of the 1960s, MPs became increasingly worried about corruption in the allocation of farms and businesses taken over from departing noncitizens. A Parliamentary Select Committee was set up in 1971 to probe into corruption, nepotism and tribalism, and more specifically, how some people have "acquired five or six businesses in a limited time."[35] This could be taken as evidence of a public concern with illegal practices in the public and private sectors. To some extent this may be so, but the debate preceding the establishment of the committee suggested that the primary reason for its creation was a genuine worry that members of a few select tribes in the country were able to acquire advantages and privileges at the cost of others.[36]

In recent years, as Kenya's emerging bourgeoisie has increasingly looked to the private sector as their primary sphere of activity, the work of tribal groups has become more formalized, organized, and thereby open. This is what makes some people believe that tribalism has gone from bad to worse in the country. What has happened is that the old tribal associations among the Luo, Luhya, and Kamba people have become increasingly involved in public affairs. New associations of a similar nature, sometimes encompassing people from only one division or location, have also been formed. In all these associations civil servants are often called upon to play an important role. They are, at least unofficially, expected to serve and promote the interests of their members inside as well as outside government service. For the associations it is crucial to have representatives in key public positions.

The most interesting and, by now, the most powerful of these associations is the Gikuyu Embu and Meru Association (GEMA), which was formed in the early 1970s with a view to promote the interests of members of these tribes more effectively. The growing Kikuyu domination of public affairs in Kenya, for which GEMA to a large extent is responsible, manifests itself both inside and outside the public sector. One study of the ethnic composition of leading government positions in Kenya reveals that the Kikuyu strengthened their control over the public service between 1969 and 1972.[37] The increase of Kikuyus has been manifest in senior positions both in the civil and military services. The appointment of Kikuyus to these senior positions is at least in part related to the slow but steady rise of a national bourgeoisie in Kenya, dominated by members of this particular tribe. The Kenyan bourgeoisie has always struggled in the shadow of the more powerful representatives of the international bourgeoisie present in the country. The prevailing notion in the early 1970s was that the Kenyan bourgeoisie was merely a *comprador* ally of international capitalism.[38] It is only more recently that the achievements of the Kenyan bourgeoisie have been subject to reevaluation. Nicola Swainson, for instance, has shown that the number and size of local Kenyan enterprises have increased and that local capital has moved more and more into production, something which has been achieved through successful lobbying to restrict foreign capital in these sectors.[39] In this competition with foreign capitalists a separate organization known as the GEMA Holding Corporation, established in 1973, has been most prominent. It serves as an investment agency, as well as a bank, for indigenous, notably Kikuyu, capital. Managed by some of the most experienced Kikuyu capitalists, this corporation in 1975 took over one of the largest brick and tile manufacturing plants in Kenya, formerly owned by an American multinational company. It has other industrial investments underway, and the GEMA faction of the emerging Kenyan bourgeoisie is now commanding the move of local capital into industry.

Most capitalists in Kenya are not as strong as the GEMA group. They will therefore have to continue their reliance on cooperation with foreign capital or on support from the state. The latter is preferred, and the pressures on the government to assist the local capitalists to launch production have increased in recent years, as both the number of budding capitalists has increased and the capital on the private market becomes more difficult to come by. Connections with politicians as well as civil servants in senior positions have become important, and the latter have found it more and more difficult to stay out of the pull-while-others-pause exercise. The attempt by the local capitalists to use the state for their own development tends to intensify tribal rivalry; thus, in order to succeed, the various factions have to dig their positions much deeper. In this situation, one can hardly describe Kenyan civil servants as faceless bureaucrats lacking a set of priorities of their own and pursuing their work mechanically, according to a given set of rules. By being officially or unofficially allied with tribal and other similar associations, they are frequently called upon to assist in extracting public resources for the benefit of these associations.

CONCLUSIONS

Many of the political efforts in both Tanzania and Kenya have been directed toward removing the decision-making powers of the civil service as an institution. In Tanzania, this has happened because of its desire to move rapidly in a socialist direction. The political leadership has not trusted the ability of the civil service to "run" on its own; instead, it has tried to force it to run by elevating the ruling party to the position of supreme policy-making organ in the country. Many civil servants have found themselves demoted or even dismissed; they have lost much of the political protection they enjoyed in earlier years. In these circumstances it has no longer been rational for the civil servants to behave as their institution formally requires. Civil servants have therefore abdicated their conventional function and sought affiliation and solidarity with the ruling party. The notion of the civil service as a counterbalancing force to the political organization has lost much of its validity. It is not very easy to see how the government bureaucrats can pursue their interests as a class. They do exercise more influence than workers and peasants do, but that is true of all countries. What is more interesting is that by being forced to run while others walk, the constraints imposed on them are so great that much of their effective power is gone.

The constraints operating on the Kenyan civil servants are of a different nature: There the civil service is increasingly being asked to serve the interests of local capitalism. In the competition with international capitalism and in the rivalry among the local factions of Kenya's emerging bourgeoisie, the civil servants are repeatedly being forced to declare their interests. Their identity as public servants is gradually undermined. They become absorbed by local factions that try to preempt the powers of other such factions. The bureaucrats are internally divided and lack the independence that would make them the power elite. Because of these divisions, and because knowledge and other essential resources needed for development are increasingly available among Kenyans outside the public service, the position of the bureaucracy has weakened over the years. Both as an institution and as a class, the bureaucracy is fragmented; it is not a dominant class, nor is it at present a cohesive institution serving the bourgeoisie without favor and fear.

The notion that the bureaucracy constitutes the major scene of policy making, as implied by Riggs and others with reference to developing countries, does not hold true in the cases of Kenya and Tanzania. Much the same can be said of the view that the bureaucrats in the two countries constitute a dominant class because of their position in the contemporary social structure. That the civil servants have some influence on policy making is not refuted, but they are not more influential in Kenya and Tanzania than they are anywhere else. If anything, they are less influential, for the reason that the civil service, as David K. Leonard has emphasized,[40] is only a power unto itself under two conditions: it enjoys sufficient external support to feel protected; and it possesses a monopoly of knowledge and expertise. These conditions do not prevail in Kenya and Tanzania.

This chapter has served to raise doubts about, rather than to verify, existing conceptions of bureaucracy in developing countries. If anything, it has shown the need for these conceptions to be further researched. Our discussion has also shown how both Tanzania and Kenya have developed their own modes of policy making, which in major respects differ from the conventional decision-making models developed in Western countries. Some of the effects of these modes, both positive and negative, will be discussed in subsequent chapters, where a number of substantive policy issues are more carefully examined.

NOTES

1. Fred Riggs, "Bureaucrats and Political Development: A Paradoxical View," in *Bureaucracy and Political Development,* ed. J. LaPalombara (Princeton, N.J.: Princeton University Press, 1963), p. 120.

2. Ferrel Heady, *Public Administration: A Comparative Perspective* (Englewood Cliffs, N.J.: Prentice-Hall, 1966).

3. S. N. Eisenstadt, "Political Development," in *Social Change,* ed. A. and E. Etzioni (New York: Basic Books, 1964) pp. 310–23.

4. Lucian Pye, "The Political Context of National Development," in *Development Administration: Concepts and Problems,* ed. I. Swerdlow (Syracuse, N.Y.: Syracuse University Press, 1963) pp. 25–44; see also Lucian Pye, *Aspects of Political Development* (Boston: Little, Brown, 1966).

5. Pye, "The Political Context," op. cit., p. 25.

6. David Abernethy, "Bureaucracy and Economic Development in Africa," *African Review* 1, no. 1 (1971): 101.

7. Bereket H. Selassie, *The Executive in African Governments* (London: Heinemann, 1974), p. 215.

8. Y. Dror, *Public Policy-Making Re-Examined* (Scranton, Pa.: Chandler Publishing Co., 1968), p. 113.

9. R. S. Milne, "Mechanistic and Organic Models of Public Administration in Developing Countries," *Administrative Science Quarterly* 15 (1970): 57–67; see also his "Decision-Making in Developing Countries," *Journal of Comparative Administration* 3, no. 3 (1972).

10. A. L. Adu, *The Civil Service in Commonwealth Africa* (London: Allen & Unwin, 1969), p. 240.

11. See, for instance, "The Changing Role of the African Administrator," Part 1, in *A Decade of Public Administration in Africa,* ed. G. Hyden and A. H. Rweyemamu (Nairobi: East African Literature Bureau, 1975).

12. Michael Lofchie, "Political Science, Bureaucracy and Development" (Paper presented at the University of East Africa Social Science Conference, Makerere University College, December 1966).

13. A. Zolberg, "The Military Decade in Africa," *World Politics* 25 (1973): 313.

14. Ruth First, *Power in Africa* (London: Penguin, 1971).

15. K. Fitch and M. Oppenheimer, *Ghana: End of Illusion* (New York: Monthly Review Press, 1966).

16. Claude Meillasoux, "A Class Analysis of the Bureaucratic Process in Mali," *Journal of Development Studies* 6, no. 2 (January 1970): 97–110.

17. Issa G. Shivji, *Class Struggles in Tanzania* (Dar es Salaam: Tanzania Publishing House, 1975).

18. G. Hyden, " 'We must run while others walk': Policy-making for Socialist Development in the Tanzania-type of Politics," *Economic Research Bureau Paper 75.1* (Dar es Salaam: University of Dar es Salaam, 1975).

19. Alfred O. Hirschman, *Journeys Towards Progress* (Garden City, New York: Doubleday, 1975).

20. Dror, op. cit.

21. Peter Blau, *The Dynamics of Bureaucracy* (Chicago: University of Chicago Press, 1975).

22. A. Gunder Frank, "Administrative Role Definition and Social Change," *Human Organization* 22, no. 4 (1964): 238–42.

23. Hirschman, op. cit.

24. Gunder Frank, op. cit.

25. Cherry Gertzel, *Politics of Independent Kenya* (Nairobi: East African Publishing House, 1970), pp. 166–73; see also her article, "The Provincial Administration in Kenya," *Journal of Commonwealth Political Studies* 4, no. 3 (1966): 201–15.

26. John R. Nellis, "Is the Kenyan Bureaucracy Developmental? Considerations in Development Administration" (Paper read at the Conference on Comparative Administration, Arusha, September 25–28, 1971).

27. John J. Okumu, "The Political Setting," in *Development Administration: The Kenyan Experience,* ed. G. Hyden, R. H. Jackson, and J. J. Okumu (Nairobi: Oxford University Press, 1970), pp. 25–42.

28. For an account of the early colonial period in Kenya, see M.P.K. Sorrenson, *Origins of European Settlement in Kenya* (Nairobi: Oxford University Press, 1968). The situation in subsequent years is described, for example, in *So Rough a Wind: The Kenya Memoirs of Sir Michael Blundell* (London: Weidenfeld & Nicolson, 1964); see also A. E. Brett, *Colonialism and Underdevelopment in East Africa: The Politics of Economic Change 1919–39* (London: Heinemann, 1973).

29. Carl G. Rosberg, Jr. and John Nottingham, *The Myth of Mau Mau* (New York: Praeger, 1966).

30. Gertzel, *Politics of Independent Kenya*, op. cit., pp. 32–72.

31. Okumu, op. cit., p. 38.

32. Public Service Structure and Remuneration Commission, *Report of the Commission of Inquiry* (Nairobi: Government Printer, 1971).

33. Frank Holmquist, "Implementing Rural Development Projects," in *Development Administration: The Kenyan Experience,* op. cit., pp. 201–29.

34. William M. Wamalwa, "The Role of the Public Service Commission in New African States," in *A Decade of Public Administration in Africa*, op. cit.

35. *Daily Nation* and *East African Standard* (Nairobi), September 18 and October 2, 1971.

36. Ibid.; see also editorial in *Sunday Nation* (Nairobi), October 24, 1971.

37. John R. Nellis, "The Ethnic Composition of Leading Kenyan Government Positions," *Research Report No. 24* (Uppsala: Scandinavian Institute of African Studies, 1974).

38. Colin Leys, *Underdevelopment in Kenya: The Political Economy of Neo-Colonialism* (London: Heinemann, 1975).

39. Nicola Swainson, "The Rise of a National Bourgeoisie in Kenya," mimeographed (Dar es Salaam: University of Dar es Salaam, 1977).

40. David K. Leonard, "Bureaucracy, Class and Inequality in Kenya and Tanzania" (Paper presented at the Conference on Inequality in Africa of the Social Science Research Council, Mt. Kisco, N.Y., October 6–9, 1976).

PART III

Contrasting Strategies for Development and Underdevelopment

5

IDEOLOGY AND OBJECTIVE CONDITIONS

Claude Ake

TO UNDERSTAND IDEOLOGY and its role in social change, it is necessary to pay close attention to the objective conditions that produce it. This point is elementary but important. Unfortunately, it is often forgotten. For instance, it is sometimes assumed that development is a matter of adopting the correct ideology. Implicit in this assumption is the further assumption that ideologies determine political behavior and public policy. While these assumptions are not entirely false, they are highly misleading. Ideologies are not original but derivative. It is essentially objective conditions that produce ideologies and determine when, where, and to what extent particular ideologies hold sway. Once they are generated, ideologies become an integral part of objective conditions and, as such, help to shape consciousness as well as the very objective conditions which generated them.

The fact that ideology and objective conditions act on and react to one another does not mean that they have equal status. Objective conditions clearly constitute the more fundamental of the two phenomena. For it is objective conditions that must first define not only what we can do, but also what we can think. To be sure, there is a sense in which consciousness or thinking precedes action, that is, precedes our manipulation of the objective conditions. However, this does not contradict the primacy of objective conditions, for people necessarily think about their circumstances; thinking is necessarily problem oriented, arising from the contradictions of a person's objective conditions.

Comparison of Kenya and Tanzania provides a useful insight into the nature of ideology and its relation to objective conditions and public policy. It is popularly assumed that Kenya and Tanzania are two radically different countries, particularly in their ideological orientations. It is also assumed that they are pursuing correspondingly different policies in order to realize their aspirations. As a matter of fact, Kenya and Tanzania are not so different. The gross exaggeration of the differences between them arises from the tendency to make ideology too autonomous, to dissociate it from existential conditions, and even make it the determinant of these conditions. If objective conditions are taken as the point of departure, it is readily seen that there cannot be such drastic ideological and policy differences between Kenya and Tanzania. Be that as it may, I am not interested in minimizing the differences between the two countries; still less do I want to decide a priori, whether they are great or small, fundamental or incidental. Even if it could be done, such an exercise would not be very useful or interesting. What I want to do here is try to define and account for the differences between Kenya and Tanzania, and to indicate their significance. This will necessarily amount to clarifying the nature of ideology and its relation to objective conditions, on the one hand, and to public policy on the other.

To begin with, the objective conditions of the two countries are similar in many fundamental ways, because of their colonial experience and its associated syndrome of underdevelopment and dependence. These conditions produced, in both countries, a virtually identical ideology—the nationalist ideology that guided the struggle for independence. Let us briefly consider the colonial situation and its relation to the nationalist ideology it produced. The salient features of the colonial situation were as follows:

1. The presence of an occupying power.

2. Monopoly of economic and political power by the occupying power.

3. An occupation ideology that represented the colonized as less than human, that legitimized their brutalization, subordination, and exclusion from economic power and political participation.

4. Existence in the colonial economic structure of contradictions that produced an indigenous petty bourgeoisie.

5. Inherent contradictions of the colonial system that severely checked the upward mobility of this petty bourgeoisie and frustrated the very aspirations that the colonial system had imparted to this emerging class.

6. The existence of a colonized population alienated and frustrated by the discrimination and oppression of the occupying power, and ready to be socialized into radical politics.

7. Systematic inculcation by the colonizing power of a sense of inferiority.

8. Pillage of the resources of the colony.

The stark contradictions of the colonial situation generated an anticolonial movement. In both Kenya and Tanzania, as well as most of Africa, the character of this movement was essentially the same. First, the leadership of the movement came from the most acculturated, indigenous people, who bestraddled the two worlds of colonizer and colonized and became, so to speak, the incarnation of colonial contradictions. Second, the major power resources of this leadership were the colonized people. But these people were only an effective resource insofar as they were politicized and mobilized; so the thrust of the movement was in the direction of mobilizing as many people as possible and, hence, in phrasing issues for the broadest appeal. Third, the colonial situation was such that the argument between the colonizers and the nationalist movement resolved itself into the assertion of one exclusive claim to rule against another; neither side could accept the legitimacy of the other's claim to power without nullifying the premise of its own claim.* Fourth, and most importantly, the anticolonial movements in most of colonial Africa, including Kenya and Tanzania, evolved rather similar ideologies, with the following characteristics:

1. Emphasis on political as opposed to economic factors. This obviously reflects the available power resources of the nationalist leadership.
2. Rehabilitation of the pride of the colonized—a necessary negation of the colonizer's policy of representing their victims as less than human in order to legitimize their inhumanity toward them.
3. Emphasis on discrediting the colonial system by exploiting the grievances against it. Since these grievances arose from the very logic of a system that negated self-determination, freedom, and equality, the anticolonial movement necessarily affirmed these values.
4. Virtual silence on the character of postcolonial society. Thus the ideals of self-determination, freedom, and equality found no concrete articulation. Perhaps the major determinant of this ideological trend was the peculiar character of colonial politics, which resolved into two exclusive claims to rule, and rendered irrelevant any debate on how to rule.

This was the type of ideology with which Kenya and Tanzania came to independence; and one could hardly expect radically different public policy in these countries in the years immediately following independence.

---

*In the final analysis the excuse for colonization was that the colonized were less than human. This assumption was incompatible with granting their claim to rule. That is one side of the coin. The other side is that the colonized could not accept the sharing of power without giving legitimacy to the colonizer's denigration of their humanity.

The point is that one is not simply deducing public policy from ideology, but rather anticipating a similarity of policies from a similarity of ideologies, because the similarity of ideologies reflects a similarity in objective conditions.

However, to posit the similarity of public policies in the immediate postindependence era does not take us very far. We need to specify and appreciate the substance of this similarity; in order to do this, we have to go back briefly to the objective conditions. In dealing with the objective conditions of the preindependence era, I did not place any emphasis on the socioeconomic character of the leadership of the anticolonial movement. But this is precisely what needs emphasis in order to reveal the substance of the policy similarities in question. Fortunately, there is no difficulty in specifying the socioeconomic character of this leadership: It was a petty bourgeoisie—kulaks, teachers, lawyers, engineers, journalists. This nascent class was created by colonial education, and by the limited economic opportunities the colonial system offered. It was at the top of the newly created stratification system of the indigenous population, and hence considered itself as heir to the colonial system. The characteristics of the ideology with which the war against colonialism was waged reflected a consciousness that was more inclined to inherit control of a socioeconomic system than to revolutionize it (there were a few notable exceptions, namely in Mozambique, Angola, and Guinea-Bissau). This partly explains the emphasis on politics as opposed to economics, the abstract discussion of equality and freedom, the emphasis on unity against a common enemy, the reluctance to spell out their image of the future—typical characteristics of petty bourgeois radicalism.[1]

The policies associated with this consciousness in the early years of independence included:

1. a notion of progress as Westernization
2. a notion of development as economic growth
3. a tendency to see the obstacle to development in terms of fundamental institutional weaknesses, especially the shortage of highly trained personnel
4. accommodation with neocolonialism
5. containment of the revolutionary pressures released by the mobilization of the masses into politics, and with expectations of material betterment and greater political participation.

The postindependence policies of Tanzania and Kenya ran along these lines; given Kenya's popular image as the classic neocolony, it is perhaps unnecessary to show this here. For those who are interested in documentation, I refer them to the Development Plan (called the Red Plan) presented in the Kenya Parliament on June 10, 1964. Since this plan was prepared very hastily after Kenya achieved independence on December 12, 1963, it was necessary to revise it even during the plan period (1964–70). A new version, called the Green Plan, was produced in 1966. Both documents fully corroborate the assertion made here regarding Kenya's policy trends.

OBJECTIVE CONDITIONS IN TANZANIA

In the case of Tanzania, corroboration is to be found in the first Five-Year Development Plan, which was launched on July 1, 1964. This was the first phase of what was expected to be a 15-year perspective plan covering the period up to 1980. To illustrate briefly, the plan's major goals to be achieved by 1980 were as follows: (1) the doubling of per capita income, (2) self-sufficiency in manpower except for the most highly skilled occupations, and (3) the improvement of life expectancy from 35 years in 1964 to 50 years by 1980. These goals clearly indicate a conservative consciousness primarily interested in amelioration of the existing order rather than its revolutionary transformation. The plan also provides ample evidence of the Tanzanian leadership's willingness to collaborate in the maintenance of Tanzania's neocolonial dependence. For instance, of the government's development expenditure of $285.7 million, $222.7 million, or 78 percent, was expected from external sources.

Since the years immediately following independence, the differences between Tanzania and Kenya have grown. To be specific, Tanzania's ideology has become more radical, very insistent on its commitment to building a socialist society. The major change in it occurred in 1967, with the proclamation of the Arusha Declaration.[2] But it has since been repeatedly reaffirmed, and even reinforced, for instance, in the TANU guidelines (1971),[3] *The Rational Choice* (1973),[4] *The Arusha Declaration Ten Years After* (1977),[5] and the *CCM Constitution* (1977).[6] Public policies—notably, villagization, decentralization, and the parastatal system—are increasingly defended in terms of their contribution to the realization of a socialist Tanzania. In the case of Kenya, there has been no change on this scale in ideology or public policy.

Why has this change occurred in Tanzania? The immediate cause of the change was the enormous difficulties the Tanzanian leadership encountered in the first two years of independence. Of the $222.7 million expected as the total contribution to development expenditure from external sources, only $33 million had actually been obtained during the first half of the plan period. This was a very serious setback considering the fact that the plan had originally anticipated (as noted above) that 78 percent of all development expenditure would come from external sources. Availability of resources for implementing the development plan was greatly reduced by the fluctuations of the international commodity market. It was most unfortunate that Tanzania's two leading export crops, sisal and cotton, were also the most adversely affected. "The average sisal price for all grades fell from an average (f.o.b.) £105 per ton in 1964 to one of £68 per ton in 1967, a decline of 35 percent. In 1966 prices started to fall in February and there was a drop of Sh. 80 [$11] per ton by the end of April. Further weaknesses developed during September . . ."[7] Cotton prices suffered much the same fate—the price index for cotton stood at 83 in 1966, only 3 points higher than that for sisal. During the plan period, production was hampered by drought. The drought which occurred in 1965 was not quite as serious as the one in 1961, but it led to a substantial decline in the production of sisal groundnuts, maize, rice, seed beans, and pulses. In addition to all this, total employment fell by 5.4 percent in 1965 and 4 percent in 1966, while the cost of living increased by 10 percent in 1965 and 5 percent in 1966. For the period 1965–66, the earnings of employees in the public and the private sector increased by about 13.5 percent on the average, so that for this group there was a marginal increase in real income; but the group represented a small proportion of the population. The Development Plan had projected an increase of 6.7 percent in GDP, but for the period 1964–66, the increase was only 5 percent. There were also manpower problems. At the beginning of the plan period, 154 top-level positions were scheduled to be filled by overseas recruitments to help carry out the objectives of the Development Plan. However, only 75 of these recruitments were made, and then these were offset by 75 new vacancies.[8]

It was in the face of these difficulties that the Arusha Declaration was promulgated and that TANU embarked on the pursuit of socialism and self-reliance. As far as self-reliance is concerned it is quite easy to see that Tanzania was making a virtue of necessity; remember that Tanzania had expected foreigners to provide as much as 78 percent (Sh. 795 million) of its development budget, but during the first half of the plan period external sources contributed only Sh. 236 million. To avoid disaster, Tanzania had to mobilize more capital internally. Indeed, for the period 1965–1966, local funds eventually accounted for just over 62 percent of development revenue. It was the same situation with the top-level personnel needed for implementing the plan. As we have seen, Tanzania did not succeed in obtaining the manpower it had expected to recruit from abroad, and was finally pushed into self-reliance by its rather moderate attempt to assert its political independence. For instance, during the period of the first plan, Tanzania lost Sh. 50 million in aid from West Germany and the United Kingdom, because it broke diplomatic relations with the United Kingdom and received a trade delegation from the German Democratic Republic.

Tanzania suffered further punitive economic sanctions from the United Kingdom by rejecting the demand that it pay pensions to British civil servants who had worked for the colonial regime.[9]

What about socialism? To begin with, it should be noted that what is at issue is not the scientific socialism of Marxism-Leninism, but a Fabian or evolutionary socialism or, at best, a Gotha Program of socialism. The Arusha Declaration makes this clear enough: revolution is rejected for evolution; class struggle is repudiated; there is no conception of the dictatorship of the proletariat. The move to this mild socialism was one of defensive radicalism,[10] undertaken to mobilize mass support and legitimize a regime under the threat of economic collapse. The proclamation of socialism created a new sense of purpose. The rhetoric against inequality and exploitation was bound to appeal to peasants and workers who had scarcely any property to lose, but everything to gain, by the more equitable distribution of wealth—never mind that there was scarcely any surplus to redistribute. There was the additional advantage that, insofar as the new radicalism made the masses more favorably disposed toward their leaders, it was easier for the leadership to get more effort from the masses. And the better effort would facilitate development, which would, in turn, reinforce the legitimacy of the government. Finally, there is every indication that the new socialist ideology was calculated to nourish the spirit and faith in the face of a diminishing ability to nourish the flesh. This might explain the drama which surrounded this launching of socialism—the marches, the endless public meetings, the emotional speeches.

Usually when a ruling class is confronted with the crisis of economic stagnation, it tends to do one of two things—move toward the left, or try to deal with frustration, and its associated revolutionary pressures, by repression. Why then did Tanzania move to the left, instead of moving to the right or simply becoming more repressive? It was more advantageous to move to the left. Some of the advantages, such as winning the loyalty of the masses and getting more effort from them, have already been mentioned. No less important was the fact that, in material terms, the ruling class of Tanzania had nothing to lose, but everything to gain, by such a move. To appreciate this point, one must first note that the ruling class of Tanzania had a particularly weak material base—a fact related to the character of colonialism in Tanzania. The British made even less effort at development in Tanzania than in Kenya, because (unlike Kenya) Tanzania was not chosen as a settler colony. Because of the lack of development in Tanzania, there was less surplus to share; the petty bourgeoisie was smaller and weaker economically than in Kenya. Since Tanzania was not a settler colony, the colonizing power made a rather more perfunctory effort to create a bourgeoisie to perpetuate neocolonial relations after independence. Thus the petty bourgeoisie that inherited the power in Tanzania,

was more petty than bourgeois. The move to the left was not really problematic, precisely because the petty bourgeoisie was numerically small and
not so well-off. Indeed, the move to the left gave this petty bourgeoisie an
excellent opportunity to consolidate its political power as well as
strengthen its material base; an immediate effect of the move was an
enormous expansion of state control. This expansion immensely increased
the economic resources under the control of the government.

OBJECTIVE CONDITIONS IN KENYA

These circumstances did not prevail in Kenya. Kenya was able to
achieve the targeted average annual increase in GDP for the period of her
first Development Plan, 1964–65. There was an increase in the average per
capita product of over 3 percent.[11] Agricultural expansion barely fell short
of the plan target mainly because of coffee berry disease, which reduced
coffee production in 1967 and 1968. However, small holders' gross farm
income grew at an average of about 10 percent. Despite the fact that the
level of investment fell below expectation, Kenya could be said to have
been prospering. The target rate of increase in production for the economy
was achieved, the planned increase of per capita real consumption was
achieved, employment opportunities increased considerably,[12] average
wages increased by 30 percent over the plan period, and as already indicated, the average income of small farmers also increased substantially.
It is no wonder that the Kenyan government chose to enhance its legitimacy by appealing to its success in realizing the "fruits of Uhuru."

The process of class formation advanced more rapidly in Kenya than
in Tanzania. It was a stronger economy, and somewhat more developed
because it was a settler colony. Since the economic stake of the colonizers
was much higher in Kenya, they made a greater effort to protect it against
the threat of African nationalism. They tried to create a Kenyan bourgeoisie whose interests would be tied to those of international capitalism. The
major policy of bourgeoisification was the land settlement scheme, the
transfer of the European farms to Africans. Indeed, up to 1968, about
2,306,600 acres had been transferred to Africans. The land transfer scheme
was a rather brilliant stroke of colonial policy. In effect, farmland was
being bought from European farmers and sold to Africans. But the settlers
got good, and sometimes, inflated prices for land they had taken illegally
in the first place, and had developed by crassly exploiting African labor
and by taking advantage of extension services supported by the African
taxpayers. The money for buying the land was provided by the United
Kingdom and other Western sources. The Africans who got the land were
grateful for a real opportunity to become prosperous; they were getting

rather easy loans to buy out well-established farmers. In the meantime, the loans and grants the Kenya government got from abroad for this transaction ensured neocolonial dependence. The Africans who took over the European farms had a vested interest in this dependence. The same type of policy was pursued in the industrial sector. There was much emphasis placed on taking Africans into partnership; several funds were established for Africans to buy shares in foreign-owned businesses and to establish new enterprises.[13] By the early years of independence, the development of the process of class formation was such that the African petty bourgeoisie would have had much to lose if policies similar to those of the Arusha Declaration had been adopted.

IDENTIFYING DIFFERENCES

The differences between Tanzania and Kenya are clear and interesting. They have given us some appreciation of the relation between ideology and material conditions. However, there is a danger of treating such differences as fossilized determinations. It is necessary to proceed dialectically, if only because we are dealing with a dynamic world. States of being are merely phases of transition; differences and identities are constantly mediated and transformed; consciousness and material conditions interact and modify each other—as a process of change, the world can be comprehended only by the dialectic method.

The very differences between Tanzania and Kenya that we have discussed have in a sense generated their own dialectical negation. The advancement of the process of class formation has revealed, and to some extent, radicalized the contradictions in production relations in Kenya. Kenya's relatively rapid economic expansion, largely financed by foreign investment in the industrial-service sector, and the source of increasing inequality in the distribution of real income, demonstrated the problem of growth without development. Finally, Kenya's apparent acquiescence in neocolonial dependence now looms large, as a contradiction, for a ruling class which came to power on the wave of a struggle against imperialism. These factors have put Kenya under powerful pressure to resort to defensive radicalism.

In Tanzania, on the other hand, defensive radicalism is generating powerful reactionary pressures. Critics at home and abroad have represented Tanzania's economic failures as the effects of its leftism, its ideological "constipation," and lack of realism. Most importantly, defensive radicalism has institutionalized state capitalism, has made the ruling class more secure politically and economically, and inevitably conservative. Those who became socialists because they had nothing to lose must now curb socialism because it has given them a lot to lose. However paradoxical it may seem, one may say that the differences in the objective conditions of Kenya and Tanzania are moving them toward similar paths of development.

And now, add the current similarities. It is all too easy to forget how much postcolonial societies in Africa, such as Kenya and Tanzania, have in common. The dissimilarities impress us because they are more interesting and, in a sense, more conspicuous, because of the almost monotonous similarity of these societies. It would be inappropriate here to undertake a comprehensive analysis of the objective conditions that constitute these similarities. However, it is necessary to mention the following conditions, which are particularly consequential for the structure of politics and policy making: the division of society into exploiters and exploited; the desperate poverty among the peasants and workers; the high degree of political consciousness created by the nationalist movement; the very slow pace of economic development, especially in the rural areas; and the dependence on international capitalism.

These conditions are the very core of the syndrome of underdevelopment. They are the background of much that is happening in postcolonial Africa. Their influence is so decisive that one must be very wary about positing fundamental differences in the patterns of political and economic development of African countries, including Kenya and Tanzania. The public policies of these two countries are largely variations on the same theme. For instance, the ruling classes in Kenya and Tanzania are equally concerned with consolidating their power, and are doing it in rather similar ways: nonparticipation and, in some cases, depoliticization of the masses and peasants, and within the party system, and the extension of public ownership of the means of production.

The dynamics of the syndrome of underdevelopment generate strong revolutionary pressures. For instance, the slow pace of economic development means persistence of scarcity, which translates into frustrations easily mobilized against the system. Neocolonial dependence undermines the legitimacy of a ruling class which came to power in a struggle against colonialism. Attempts to further development invariably reveal the necessity of destroying the present production relations.

In the face of these revolutionary pressures, the rulers of Africa have resorted to coercion and defensive radicalism.[14] Here again, Kenya and Tanzania are no exceptions. So it is not really accurate to conclude that Tanzania moved to the left after independence, while Kenya did not. In fact, Kenya and many other African countries have moved to the left, although in an even more superficial way than has Tanzania. To illustrate, Kenya is increasingly emphatic on the fact that its policy is based on African socialism. To be sure, it is a toothless type of socialism, which masks the capitalist policies of the Kenyan bourgeoisie.[15] But one must not miss the significance of the fact that Kenya finds it necessary to criticize capitalism and advocate a version of socialism. Kenyan policy statements are increasingly paying attention to the value of equality, and freedom from exploitation. More importantly, they are even beginning to spell out both equality and freedom from exploitation in economic terms, as more equitable distribution of the surplus.[16] Once more, commitment to equality and the ending of exploitation is more apparent than real; nevertheless it is still significant that this particular pose is being adopted. In Kenya, as in most of Africa, public control of the economy is being extended, and is being defended in terms of socialist values and as part of a heroic effort against imperialism.

In the light of these considerations, I am inclined to posit that the ideological differences between Kenya and Tanzania are essentially differences in degree rather than in kind—certainly not analogous to the difference between capitalism and socialism. The ideologies of both countries reflect their very similar objective conditions. Tanzania is interesting not so much because it is profoundly different, but because it is an image of the future (that is, of course, extrapolating from the current state of social forces; but these forces are in process too, subject to change, and do not rigidly determine the future). What makes Tanzania different is that certain tendencies (especially defensive radicalism) that are inherent in the objective conditions of postcolonial Africa have already become manifest in Tanzania while they are still only latent in most other places such as Kenya.

NOTES

1. A convenient way of testing my characterization of the nationalist ideology would be to examine the selections in Gideon-Cyrus M. Mutiso and S. W. Rohio, *Readings in African Political Thought* (London: Heinemann, 1975).

2. Tanzania, *The Arusha Declaration and TANU's Policy on Socialism and Self-Reliance* (Dar es Salaam: Government Printer, 1967).

3. Tanganyika African National Union, *TANU Guidelines on Guarding, Consolidating and Advancing the Revolution of Tanzania and of Africa* (Dar es Salaam: Government Printer, 1971).

4. Julius K. Nyerere, *The Rational Choice,* Address delivered at the Sudanese Socialist Union Headquarters, Khartoum, Jan. 2, 1973 (Dar es Salaam: Government Printer, 1972).

5. Julius K. Nyerere, *The Arusha Declaration Ten Years After* (Dar es Salaam: Government Printer, 1977).

6. Chama Cha Mapinduzi, *CCM Constitution* (Dar es Salaam: Government Printer, 1977).

7. Ministry of Economic Affairs and Development Planning, *Mid-Term Appraisal of the Achievements Under the Five-Year Plan July 1964-June 1969* (Dar es Salaam: Government Printer, 1967) p. 24.

8. Ministry of Economic Affairs and Development Planning, *First Year Progress Report on the Implementation of the Five-Year Development Plan* (Dar es Salaam: Government Printer, n.d.).

9. M. D. Mkumbwa, "The Tanzanian Economy Ten Years After Independence," in *Rasilimali* (Dar es Salaam: Tanzania Investment Bank, n.d.), p. 9.

10. For a discussion of the concept of defensive radicalism, see my study, "The Congruence of Ideologies and Political Economies," in *The Political Economy of Contemporary Africa*, ed. Peter Gutkind and Immanuel Wallerstein (Beverly Hills: Sage Publications, 1976), pp. 198–211.

11. Government of Kenya, *Development Plan 1970–74* (Nairobi: Government Printer, n.d.) p. 29.

12. Ibid, pp. 68–69.

13. For insight into the process of bourgeoisification in Kenya see Colin Leys, *Underdevelopment in Kenya: The Political Economy of Neo-Colonialism 1964–71* (Berkeley and Los Angeles: University of California Press, 1974); International Labour Office, *Employment, Incomes and Equality: A Strategy for Increasing Productive Employment in Kenya* (Geneva: International Labour Office, 1972).

14. For a fuller picture of the forces pushing the postcolonial societies of Africa toward defensive radicalism, see my study, "The Congruence of Ideologies and Political Economies," op. cit.

15. See Government of Kenya, *Kenya Government Sessional Paper No. 10 of 1965: African Socialism and Its Applications to Planning in Kenya* (Nairobi: Government Printer, 1965).

16. For example: Government of Kenya, *Development Plan 1970–1974* (Nairobi: Government Printer, n.d.); *Development Plan 1974–1978* (Nairobi: Government Printer, 1974).

6

CLASS STRUCTURE, PEASANT PARTICIPATION, AND RURAL SELF-HELP

Frank Holmquist

THE CONTRASTING DEVELOPMENT PATHS of Kenya and Tanzania are a natural invitation for comparison. Occasional ritual mention of African socialism notwithstanding, Kenya can be characterized as a classic example of African peripheral capitalist development aided by a long-repressed petty bourgeoisie and peasantry, and built upon the foundations of international capital.[1] Tanzania has not cut all ties to international capital but it has diminished all forms of domestic capitalist activity; and it has officially opted for a self-reliant participatory brand of socialism, which, according to President Julius Nyerere, has yet to be realized but is possible via an evolutionary strategy. In Tanzania, the participatory theme is so prominent that at times development is virtually defined in terms of mass participation. According to President Nyerere: "Development brings freedom, provided it is development of people. But people cannot be developed; they can only develop themselves."[2] The 1971 guidelines of the Tanganyika African National Union (TANU) make the point more boldly:

> Any action that gives them (the people) more control of their own affairs is an action for development, even if it does not offer them better health or more bread. Any action that reduces their say in determining their own affairs or running their own lives is not development and retards them even if the action brings them a little better health and a little more bread.[3]

There would appear to be very different prospects for significant peasant participation in the political system in Kenya and Tanzania, given

---

This paper was originally presented at the 18th Annual Meeting of the African Studies Association, in San Francisco, October 29–November 1, 1975.

their radically different development philosophies and strategies. But if we glance at the postindependence development history of both countries, we cannot help being struck by the extraordinary and continuing peasant-based *harambee* (self-help) movement in Kenya and its comparative absence in Tanzania despite vigorous activity just after independence.[4] I will try to explain this paradox and, in the process, illustrate the crucial political role of the rural petty bourgeoisie and the peculiar halfway brand of self-help that is characteristic of Kenya's harambee. Self-help processes are here defined as those requiring at least a minimum of community organization, involvement, and initiative, and a community contribution of finance and labor, or both, to any project. I will also confine my attention to larger projects involving the building of schools, health facilities, community centers, roads, and bridges.

A basic theoretical assumption is that any discussion of the phenomenon of mass participation must acknowledge the context of class relations in the society at large as well as the nature of existing political structures. This perspective alerts us to the fact that various degrees and kinds of peasant participation may perform very different functions within different class structures. Participation may be a means by which ruling classes coopt dissent, provide an illusion of progress, and deflect attention from all important policies and mechanisms of appropriating peasant surplus.[5] But, on the other hand, broad-based participation may be a vehicle of peasant power throughout the political system and a means by which peasant advances are consolidated and protected. At the very least, this paper will show how an awareness of class relations provides a tool for explaining why peasant participation happens or fails to happen, and why, if it does occur, it takes on a particular character depending on the class and political structures at large.

The key general questions to be answered in this chapter are, why does peasant participation of a certain variety occur in some countries and not in others, and why does such participation in any one country vary over time? In particular, we will try to explain why both Kenya and Tanzania experienced high rates of self-help development of a halfway variety just after independence, and why Kenya's rate has continued at a rather high level up to the present time, while Tanzania's has declined rather precipitously and shows no signs of reviving, contrary to official expectations.

EXPLANATIONS OF PEASANT SELF-HELP

Various explanations have been offered for the self-help phenomenon in Kenya. The government, despite its qualms about certain aspects of self-help, would probably credit itself with having the rational foresight to announce such a policy. But this explanation wrongly assumes a high degree of government leverage, through ideas, on a process based on peasant initiative. It also begs the question of why, since the explanation naïvely assumes that abstract rationality determines policy choice among a pool of alternatives, regardless of the political interests of people making the policy. G. C. M. Mutiso claims that a center-periphery (paralleling an urban-rural) division within Kenya broadly reflects different cultures, and self-help is a defensive strategy of the periphery to squeeze what it can out of a seemingly opulent and arrogant center.[6] Edgar Winans, on the other hand, offers more of an economic and cultural explanation at a macrolevel when he argues that, within Kenya, higher rates of self-help correlate with relatively prosperous areas having good communications and a relatively homogeneous language and culture.[7] Another key interpretation along related lines is that of Philip Mbithi and Rasmus Rasmusson, who zero in on the self-help movement at the group and project level. They see local social organization as the building blocks of the entire movement, because through these groupings, individuals derive reference points, obtain ego reinforcement, and articulate their identity and experience within the context of a high degree of social control. In the process "individuals gain a consistent socially reinforced definition of their situation and hence develop strong in-group/out-group relationships under different contexts."[8] Mbithi and Rasmusson criticize variants of the center-periphery approach for their assumption of a critical awareness on the part of the peasantry of what is going on at the policy-making and budgeting center. They argue, furthermore, that such approaches fail to adequately deal with factors motivating individuals to make extraordinary sacrifices and extensive commitments of time and money to self-help activity.

The above approaches (dangerously abbreviated here) do not exhaust the field of possible explanations, nor are they mutually exclusive. A full explanation would have to integrate aspects of them all, and that remains to be done. My own attempts to explain Kenya's self-help have emphasized the timing of the movement, which correlated with basic changes of political structure and leader-follower relationships in the society at large.[9] In short, there appears to have been a trigger pulled at the time of independence that gave rise to intense community organizing and community competition in both Kenya and Tanganyika, which were often, though certainly not always, oriented to extracting resources from governmental or various private agencies. The timing of all this appears crucial because community cultures and solidarity mechanisms were a constant—they existed before independence. Thus the cultural explanation begs the question, why self-help at that time? The same question is begged by theories emphasizing a crucial threshold of economic development that must be crossed before self-help takes off. Community culture, social organization, and local economies did not radically change at independence—but ruling structures beyond the community did. It would appear then that changes at points removed from the village set off the very real dynamics of self-help in the villages described so well by Mbithi, Martin Hill, Geoff Lamb, Edmond Keller, and others.[10]

But while changing political structures may be the immediate cause, I no longer think they provide a satisfactory explanation of the phenomenon, if only because political structures ultimately reflect, though often imperfectly, class relations and the fortunes of competitive segments of each class. It will be argued here that the real prime mover of self-help in both Kenya and Tanzania at independence, and in Kenya to the present day, was a segment of a particular class—namely, the rural petty bourgeoisie. The thesis is that the character and rates of self-help in Kenya and Tanzania ultimately depended upon the balance of power in rural areas between two segments of the petty bourgeoisie: a rural segment (wealthy peasants, African trading and commercial elements, and local immobile civil servants); and a bureaucratic segment (transferable civil servants at the national level, and, in Tanzania, salaried party officials) that was transferable throughout the country and was largely recruited on the basis of educational attainment.* For reasons to be explained below, the locally based rural wing of this class generally needed self-help to preserve and advance their political and economic positions, while the bureaucratic segment did not need it and tended to see it as a nuisance and occasionally as a threat.

The reader should be reminded that the focus here is on the question of how social amenities are developed—that is, the presence or absence of peasant participation, here defined in terms of self-help—not on how many social amenities exist. The issue of quantity is of course very important, but it also involves a comparison of available resources, the density of existing facilities per capita, and their quality, which will not be attempted here. For example, Tanzanian peasants may, for a variety of reasons, find a greater percentage of public resources channeled toward their amenities than might their Kenyan neighbors. But the evidence suggests that the process by which this occurs is not very participatory and clearly not in accord with Tanzania's official notion of a thoroughgoing participatory process; nor is Kenya's process really thoroughgoing, as will be explained below.

---

*Needless to say, there is not always a clear distinction between the rural petty bourgeoisie and its bureaucratic counterpart in rural politics, let alone in the self-help process. Many bureaucrats play by the bureaucratic rules and roles outside their home areas, but readily abandon them when struggling for leadership and power at home.

AN OVERVIEW OF CLASS AND POLITICAL STRUCTURE UP TO INDEPENDENCE

Colonial rule was bureaucratic rule. Colonial regimes created cadres of clerks and functionaries to act as liaisons with, and controllers of, the peasantry in order to either reorient peasant growing patterns to satisfy metropolitan raw-materials requirements and meet the need for adminis- trative revenue, or structure peasant subsistence capabilities so as to induce peasants to offer their labor cheaply to other growers or extractive indus- try. The linchpins of the ruling structure were, of course, the chiefs who dominated most channels to higher authority. Once initial resistance to colonial rule was quelled, the system was reasonably secure for colonial designs until the indigenous petty bourgeois leadership grew too large to be readily coopted. Rural agitation for political independence in the 1950s in both countries usually meant agitation against the colonial bureaucracy and especially local chiefs. Despite occasional spontaneous protests, crucial protest leadership was largely drawn from the rural petty bourgeoisie, who, unlike the chiefs, were not effectively incorporated into authority structures despite their economic credentials.[11] We should remember, however, that some chiefs made peace with the protest before indepen- dence.

The rural petty bourgeoisie's bid for local power was generally backed by the peasantry. On top of a general desire to boot out the foreigners, there was specific opposition to land policy, Asian commercial elements, and a host of agricultural improvement policies, from destocking to tie ridging, which were often imposed without popular consultation, or in spite of actual opposition. The peasant majority also had no fondness for chiefs when these popularly unaccountable local rulers were virtually fro- zen in power by colonial authority, thus leaving considerable leeway for abuses of power involving everything from virtual requisitioning of women as brides, to a host of corrupt practices benefiting the practitioner and his kin.[12] The overt peasant demand was that, at the very least, authorities be rotated, but more significantly it was a demand to increase the number of authorities so that every community and interest would have one of its own people in a position of effective power.

Thus pluralist ideology was, not surprisingly, formed and popularized by the rural petty bourgeoisie, who wished to advance and consolidate themselves in the political realm. And, as we might expect, the local ideology during the nationalist phase did not question the biases of the social structure. The peasants and the rural petty bourgeoisie could find a consensus on the need to simply "open up the system" and allow those with potential influence to have actual influence in key decision-making bodies.

In both countries, independence catapulted a small segment of the petty bourgeoisie into control of state structures at the very top. This was perhaps the most important consequence of independence. But equally important, for an understanding of rural politics and development, is the fact that independence marked not only the triumph of the majority of the rural petty bourgeoisie over a minority local segment under government employ (especially chiefs), but also a partial triumph of the majority over central government bureaucracy in general.[13] Thus, at the time of independence the central government bureaucracy was at its weakest point in decades in the countryside, because it was forced to cede political ground to a powerful alliance of the peasantry and the rural petty bourgeoisie. The bureaucracy was also in the throes of Africanization, which lent a momentary note of uncertainty to its action.

Thus, one irony of nationalist agitation was that, while it forced the Africanization of state structures and the creation of political parties, it also unleashed forces that partially undermined these structures due to the fragmented, locally focused nature of political organization and to the ad hoc nature of peasant mobilization, which left a rather autonomous rural petty bourgeoisie firmly in leadership positions. A host of research and writing has, somewhat belatedly, acknowledged this fact for all of Africa, and Henry Bienen outlined it very clearly with regard to Tanzania.[14] While Bienen's focus was on the party, TANU, it is evident that all state structures had limited fiat in rural areas. In both countries, it was evident that large numbers of the rural petty bourgeoisie manned the interstices between the peasants and the state structures that were formerly dominated by chiefs and other bureaucratic personnel. They were now the patrons and brokers of rural politics, whom the bureaucracy and the party would have to deal with in most relations with the peasant majority.[15]

There were, however, important differences of class structure and political organization between Kenya and Tanganyika that would only come to light as time passed. The rural petty bourgeoisie was more firmly entrenched politically in Kenya, where local government structures had a longer and sounder tradition, and where the pattern of the use of ethnic notables as ambassadors to the center was almost inevitable, given the late development of party organization and Kenya's peculiar passage to independence. TANU had a somewhat more coherent center and a well-developed organizational structure, despite the manifest weaknesses described by Bienen. Furthermore, its leadership was a slightly more urbane sort that was not as closely tied to rural ethnic constituencies. Indeed, except for the West Lake and Kilimanjaro regions, the entire development of the rural petty bourgeoisie in Tanzania was limited due to the very poverty of the country itself. Also, the Swahili cultural homogeneity that overlaid innumerable ethnic units, none of which was large enough to dominate the others, tended to diminish the influence of rural and ethnically based petty bourgeois politicians at the center.

POSTINDEPENDENCE RURAL DEVELOPMENT STRATEGIES

At independence neither ruling group assuming power had a clear idea of what rural development policy would look like; but it is not accidental that both countries announced a strategy of self-help as core policy. The policy accurately reflected the structure of power in the countryside. In lieu of strong party organization based on a peasant majority, the policy simply acknowledged that it was the rather independent rural petty bourgeoisie that had the most effective contact with, and influence upon, the peasantry.[16] This stratum was best suited to capitalize on peasant expectations and mobilize the peasants to do something for themselves in lieu of powerful and resource-rich bureaucracies. One could argue that the policy of rural self-help was a policy by default, in the sense that party and bureaucratic structures lacked a clear vision of a rural future. I would argue, however, that self-help policy and the prominence of the rural petty bourgeoisie were almost inevitable, given the structure of power in the immediate postindependence situation.

Both governments also saw self-help as development "on the cheap," despite relatively unforeseen long-term costly implications of project maintenance. In the fiscal year 1962–63, the then Tanganyikan government directly allocated less than .3 percent of all government expenditure to self-help, the cornerstone of its rural policy at that time.[17] In 1967, the Kenyan government allocation amounted to only 6 percent of the total expenditure on self-help.[18] Both regimes announced similar policies amounting to "government helps those who help themselves." The ball was in the peasant court and some remarkable things happened.

Community Strategy in Self-Help

Social-amenity development is the most popular form of development. To most peasants development means, above all, schools, health facilities, roads, and community centers, rather than fertilizers, crop rotations, and hybrid seed. And, because the former are public rather than private family-farm projects, community organization is required.

The government carrot of possible aid for locally initiated projects set up criteria of merit eligibility for those funds. Neighboring communities became intensely aware that they were competing with each other for the very scarce aid needed to complete a school or a dispensary, or to obtain government agreement to maintain the facility. Thus communities engaged in a preemptive development strategy—that is, they tried to preempt the field of contestants for scarce government assistance by building early and, if possible, high-quality projects.

Communities also knew that politics determined who got what, and they usually tried to mobilize rural petty bourgeois notables for the task of extracting outside aid and providing an organizational core for the whole effort. This usually required notables to pursue intense lobbying with local government or private organizations that had money to spend, or it involved the more or less subtle task of influencing bureaucrats who controlled the major purse strings to give aid to or maintain a facility. Communities searched for patrons and offered themselves as clients.[19] This political dynamic afforded most communities the added hope that they could attract government attention through the efforts of their petty bourgeois patrons.

Rural Petty Bourgeois Strategy in Self-Help

Why did the rural petty bourgeoisie respond positively to all this community action? The answer can be found in the fact that members of the rural petty bourgeoisie were in competition with each other for scarce political roles—roles which could be used to enhance one's economic standing as well as general social and political prestige. The sifting and winnowing process in leadership selection was inevitably complex, but after independence in both Kenya and Tanzania, elections were used more than ever before to distinguish the ins from the outs in Parliament, parties, and district and local councils. The triumph of the rural petty bourgeoisie at independence also saw the rise of the electoral process to regulate combat among them, and the structure of leadership accountability changed in the process; competitive elections are a resource for the citizenry, enabling them to at least hold leaders partially accountable.[20] With the peasantry demanding social amenities and having some leverage over their leaders, the latter had to help communities extract funds from governmental and private sources in order to prove their worth to the population. One might even say that rural petty bourgeois leadership needed self-help activity, since the bureaucracy resolved most of the functions of programmatic policy making for itself. Besides job finding, assistance for self-help projects was about the only arena within which the rural petty bourgeoisie could play a demonstrably useful public role.

It should also be pointed out that self-help development did not threaten the status of the rural petty bourgeoisie as a class, although competition among them affected the political fortunes of individuals. Self-help took the community social structure as a given and even strengthened the political clout a person had—the more likely that that person was to garner assistance for projects, the more popular the person would be. Thus, there was a perverse incentive to create, rather than diminish, inequality. Potential leaders who were economically representative of the peasant majority were useless and not likely to lead for long, unless they were well connected to high-level patrons.

Further, the rural petty bourgeoisie had a very personal and permanent interest in local amenity development; they used the crudest local roads, sent their children to local schools, and their families used the local dispensary. They had a far more immediate and long-term interest in local amenity development than their centrally recruited and transferable class counterparts in the bureaucracy.[21]

What Kind of Self-Help Was It?

The result of the alliance in self-help between the peasantry and the rural petty bourgeoisie was more social-amenity projects than either regime expected or even wanted.[22] Perhaps the most important lesson of the remarkable self-help efforts in Kenya up to now, and in Tanzania shortly after independence, was that the peasantry could accomplish rather staggering feats of development if the political environment provided minimally favorable conditions. While this observation begs innumerable questions of process, I will try to show how the interests of the bureaucracy did not generally correspond with those of the peasantry in self-help activity. In particular, it will be argued that the bureaucracy in both Kenya and Tanzania has tried to muzzle, if not curtail, self-help because the entire self-help process threatens the bureaucracy's managerial functions, its ideology, and ultimately, its means of survival through the control of surplus peasant production.

Before describing the bureaucratic reaction to self-help in both countries, it is useful to compare the nature of Kenya's and Tanzania's self-help to a very different case—that of China.[23] The African cases might be termed a halfway approach and the latter, full-blown self-help. The halfway variety refers to a situation in which the bureaucracy keeps a rather tight rein on many aspects of the policy-making and maintenance functions related to social amenities. With regard to education, for example, the hiring and compensation of teachers, the recruitment of students, and the determination of curriculum, in Kenya and Tanzania, goes on at a level far removed from the locality. In China, on the other hand, it appears that the process is more decentralized, and more education policy is open to local debate and hence is better geared to local needs than is education in East Africa. It also appears that Chinese localities have considerable control over all important purse strings, in education and across a variety of policy areas including health facilities, where local producing units nominate, hire, and fire local paramedical and more highly trained personnel. In Kenya and Tanzania, with the recent exception of a few new paramedical workers in the latter, health policy and personnel supervision is thoroughly controlled by ministry officials.[24] Similarly, scattered accounts of irrigation and water development in China contrast rather markedly with similar descriptions for Kenya and Tanzania, where the process (except for occasionally requisitioned local labor) is largely controlled by outside bureaucratic personnel and is often dependent on expensive imported equipment.[25]

Despite the fact that, at the time of independence, self-help construction was allowed and even encouraged in both countries, the bureaucracy clearly did not undertake a systematic and intensive effort to turn more of the policy-making and maintenance functions of amenities over to peasant-controlled institutions. The bureaucratically determined rules of the game said that scarce personnel, experts, and often sophisticated equipment were necessary before certain amenities would be allowed to function.[26] The peasants knew this and calculated a strategy of doing just enough to get more facilities. With a few notable exceptions (that is, the *harambee* secondary schools), peasants usually had no intention of doing more than build the facility.[27] After that they were willing to be dependent upon bureaucratic management. Only a broad-based educational effort, and perhaps a permanent organizational framework of communal production to generate surplus wealth, could alter this congruence between bureaucratic rules and peasant intentions in the halfway mode of self-help.

Of course, the halfway style of self-help was also convenient for the rural petty bourgeoisie. While the process went far enough to need their assistance as intermediaries between the peasantry and the bureaucracy, it usually did not go so far as to develop permanent, democratic, and multipurpose organizations that could organize amenities largely on their own. Thus the halfway character of self-help in Kenya and Tanzania has been dictated by the interests of the petty bourgeoisie as both bureaucrats and local notables. A more full-blown variety of self-help would be an index of a radically different fate for the entire class.

THE BUREAUCRATIC REACTION TO SELF-HELP

After a year or two the bureaucracy in both countries (including party bureaucrats in Tanzania) became alarmed by the proliferation of self-help projects. From the bureaucratic point of view, development was now out of control. The problem was suddenly one of trying to partially demobilize the peasantry because they were doing too much rather than too little. The bureaucratic counterattack was couched in terms of the rationale and structures of planning. By channeling local development projects into planning structures, peasant initiative could be gradually eroded while bureaucratic power could be augmented and its control over local development reasserted.

The bureaucratic rationale for planning and control went something like this: Self-help was thought to be inefficient and wasteful, leading to poor grades of construction; community competition often led to a duplication of services and chaos in the construction process. Self-help, it was argued, also encouraged political attempts to influence bureaucratic allocations, which only disrupted budgeting processes and operating procedures. Self-help was also said to be frustrating the peasantry when outside assistance failed to materialize or when the government refused to take over a project and meet recurrent costs. Such situations brought a feeling of disillusionment with the regime when it was seen that local effort met with little or no matching response from government and that dispensaries, for example, remained without medicine or personnel. A general bureaucratic complaint was that self-help was not directly productive; large sums of money diverted to social amenities yielded, at best, long-term increases in productivity. The implication was that, instead of investment in health, for example, a more immediate payoff to the economy would come from putting that money in fertilizer. In equity-conscious Tanzania another argument suggested that self-help exacerbated already unequal development between regions, because well-endowed areas were better able to help themselves by exerting their initiative and coaxing government funds for project maintenance.

It is not hard to detect the self-interest of the bureaucracy's rationale. It implies that more bureaucratic control is the solution, when in fact, existing bureaucratic controls helped create the typical problems of the halfway style of self-help. As long as the bureaucracy did not allow or actively educate the peasantry to take more responsibility, in whatever institutional form, for road, health, and educational policy, and to manage projects largely by themselves, it was only rational for each community to initiate projects and overdevelop its area in hopes of gaining government support. Self-help waste and duplication resulted partially from the fact that communities rightly saw themselves in intense competition with each other for access to extremely scarce and expensive government resources. Peasant frustration over a lack of government response, and consequent political dangers to the regime, could have been partially alleviated if the bureaucracy worked more actively to remove themselves from some of their maintenance roles. Presumably, bureaucrats did not want to suffer the loss of their current dominant role in the process, nor could most think beyond the ideology of modernization, which legitimizes their role as providers of development. Political intrusions into bureaucratic operations were also an inevitable product of the tensions between the bureaucracy's financial and general control of the social-amenity development process, and a rural elected leadership trying to provide some evidence of their value to constituents. The bureaucratic complaint that self-help was not immediately productive was correct—immediately productive investment was sacrificed for social-amenity infrastructure. But production, especially of taxable export crops, keeps the bureaucracy in salaries, and one must beware of the self-interest involved. It should also be remembered that the pace of social-amenity development is a product of class relations. There is a peasant priority interest in social amenities. Needless to say, for the isolated peasantry, health facilities can literally be a matter of life and death. It is no accident that, on taking power, mass-based revolutionary regimes, as witnessed by China and Cuba in particular, immediately embark upon major programs of social-amenity development. The argument in Tanzania, that regional equity requires strict bureaucratic allocation of resources, obviously sacrifices the immediate primary goal of participation for an important but secondary one of regional equity. The problem involves finding an appropriate balance between two partially contradictory goals.

In order to implement its planning strategy, Tanganyika in 1962 set up Village Development Committees (VDCs) throughout the country; the VDCs could aggregate isolated party units and consult with the bureaucracy before starting projects. Communities were required to fill out forms asking for the permission of district and regional authorities to undertake projects requesting government funds.[28] Although national priorities deserve top consideration, the immediate effect of this move was to put communities in the role of supplicant, and village committees tended to become receptacles of instructions from above. As a consequence, according to James Finucane's study of the Mwanza Region, attendance at VDC and other self-help meetings declined, and self-help tapered off as members saw few returns for attendance.[29] In 1969, VDCs were amalgamated into a smaller number of Ward Development Committees (covering roughly three times the area of VDCs), a move that further withdrew the committees from the peasantry. The bureaucratic rationale for this change was that VDCs were inefficient as planning units and had a low caliber of personnel.[30] Tanzania has since put an increasing emphasis on planning structures, as indicated by the 1972 decentralization proposals discussed below.

Similarly, Kenya elaborated a procedure by which projects had to be registered with the Department of Community Development in order to be eligible for aid. Despite a hierarchy of community development committees (manned by officials and nonofficials) designed, as in Tanzania, to give some order to the whole process, little order, let alone planning, occurred.[31]

Comparing the fate of early self-help in Kenya and in Tanzania, it is evident that Tanzania's bureaucrats have been far more successful at muzzling local initiative than their counterparts in Kenya. While it is true that bureaucratic power has rebounded in Kenya since the years immediately following independence, and while it is likely that the bureaucracy and especially the chiefs have played a greater controlling role in the past few years, it is also evident that the relatively independent power of Kenya's rural petty bourgeoisie has not capitulated to the bureaucracy, as it has been virtually forced to do in Tanzania.[32] The result is that halfway self-help continues in Kenya while it is comparatively rare in Tanzania. Aside from the fact that Tanzania's rural petty bourgeoisie was less fully developed from that element in Kenya, an adequate explanation of this trend requires a more detailed look at the evolution of the two segments of the petty bourgeoisie in both countries.

PETTY BOURGEOIS CONFLICT IN KENYA

The power of the bureaucratic segment of the petty bourgeoisie revived after 1964 in Kenya, but it never overwhelmed the rural petty bourgeoisie and it has not snuffed out the self-help process. The rural petty bourgeoisie did, however, lose ground when roughly 80 percent of district council budgets were lost to central government ministries as education, health, and local road maintenance responsibilities were transferred.[33] This move took considerable immediate patronage out of the hands of a number of local politicians; but the patronage style of self-help still existed, with the power of effective patronage concentrated in the hands of members of Parliament at a higher level. Patron-client networks continue to pyramid in such a way as to indirectly link villages to high-level politicians. And, of course, all this occurs outside the confines of the Kenya African National Union (KANU) party structure, which continues to wither away as time passes.

The style of leader, encouraged by President Kenyatta, is the ethnically and lineage-based constituency representative, whose role is to act primarily as ambassador from a constituency (as long as dissidence from the regime occurs within acceptable bounds), and only secondarily as representative of government to the people. With each successive national election in Kenya, the key local issue has increasingly become one of determining which candidate has done more for self-help—who has best served as self-help catalyst and organizer, and who has extracted the most governmental aid for the most projects? Despite the increasingly coercive nature of the regime, the avenue to national stature for most politicians (except for a small group recruited by Kenyatta) still requires a reasonably popular local base.[34]

Although its local political influence is being challenged by the bureaucracy, the rural petty bourgeoisie remains a key prop of the regime; the bureaucracy has encroached upon but not overwhelmed them. As a result, latitude for self-help leadership continues to exist, while national policy is directed toward maintaining and strengthening rural petty bourgeois interests: in commerce, through Africanization and loan policies; in local notable-led cooperatives, through rather limited government intervention compared to Tanzania; and in agriculture, as agricultural extension service is skewed in the direction of bourgeois interests, and as they buy more land following national registration of titles.[35]

PETTY BOURGEOIS CONFLICT IN TANZANIA

As one would expect under a regime striving for democratic socialism, the rural petty bourgeoisie in Tanzania has not held its own. But rather than giving clear indications of emerging peasant power, considerable evidence suggests that socialist direction in Tanzania has primarily meant the expansion of both bureaucratic power and numbers in rural areas. In the process the rural petty bourgeoisie has been increasingly shunted aside or coopted into government or party bureaucracy. This has resulted in the partial loss of the rural petty bourgeoisie's free-wheeling independence as they are subject to the hierarchical principle and are, furthermore, required (by the Leadership Code of the Arusha Declaration) to divest themselves of petty capitalist operations, which makes them even more dependent on their salaries and their bureaucratic role (although some conceal business operations through use of family and friends). The rise of the bureaucratic principle can be seen in virtually all rural institutions.

Cooperatives

Agricultural cooperatives for the marketing of cash crops such as coffee were key avenues for rural petty bourgeois leadership, but despite the wholesale proliferation of cooperatives in recent years, the power of their elected managing committees has been increasingly undermined as staff hiring, policy formulation, and general oversight functions have been transferred to government personnel.[36] In the process, the local petty bourgeoisie has lost much of its patronage powers and, hence, political clout.

District Councils

Primary-education, health, water, and local road functions were, as in Kenya, taken out of district council hands in 1969. But unlike Kenya, councils were eventually abolished in 1973 and were turned into hopefully productive institutions in the form of development corporations. In the process a key institution of rural petty bourgeois power was simply eliminated.

Members of Parliament

MPs, by all accounts, have become less significant as constituency representatives.[37] Every effort has been made to define their role as party and government representatives, and patronage pleas are actively discouraged. They have a far more difficult time obtaining national publicity than their Kenyan counterparts, and collectively their power as the key national deliberative body has declined in favor of the indirectly elected and nominated TANU National Executive Committee.[38] The 1975 decision to amalgamate constituencies, allowing only one MP per district, will probably further diminish their power.

The Rural Development Fund

Begun in 1967, the Rural Development Fund (RDF) was designed to give spot funds to local, and often self-help, projects of all kinds. The allocating committees were, however, dominated by bureaucrats, and in 1969 the first Presidential Circular required that the money be spent on directly productive projects in *ujamaa* (collectivized) villages.[39] More popular social-amenity projects were not destined for aid.

Ujamaa (Villagization) Policy

Ujamaa (villagization) policy has an obvious antiwealthy, peasant bias in theory although in a few cases, wealthier peasants have been able to divert it to their own ends or sabotage it altogether.[40] The most notable fact of ujamaa, however, is that it has not become a peasant-based movement. Virtually all studies suggest that the peasants are not convinced that the ujamaa policy is good for them and, as a result, the majority of communal plots currently account for a very small portion of total production and income, although the percentage varies from place to place, with a preponderance of plots in the poorest areas.[41] The early, post-1968 government strategy of spontaneous implementation had little effect. The second strategy, that of exchanging social amenities for token ujamaa, recognized the popularity of social amenities but failed to stimulate serious peasant interest in communal production and proved very costly to the government.

The third, post-1973 strategy found the initiative still with the bureaucracy, but in lieu of sufficient carrots of aid, force was used and villages were created, while little effort was made to change the mode of production. (In the aftermath of the villagization campaigns of 1974 the emphasis in several areas has been on private cultivation in a block-farming context rather than on communal production.) Because the peasants are still to be convinced, there has not been a noticeable trend toward more self-reliance and declining dependence on the bureaucracy.[42]

The Party

Bienen outlined the rather decentralized nature of TANU, in which local branches led by the rural petty bourgeoisie often went their own way, regardless of the intentions of the party at the center. The *kumi-kumi* (party cell) system was set up in 1964 but has received little systematic attention since then. The cells serve primarily as dispute-settling institutions and tend to do little party work as such.[43] With the Leadership Code in 1967 and the requirement that party leaders divest themselves of capitalist activity, there may have been some turnover of party leadership. But new or old leadership could do little for development when it had no direct leverage on policy or funds at branch, district, or regional levels.[44] Local elected personnel could only attend various development committees, which were usually dominated by bureaucrats. Thus the party has grown more coherent over the years, but coherence has been obtained at the cost of increasing bureaucratization and declining mass participation.

There is a fundamental distinction between appointed and elected TANU officials, and it is the former that hold key positions in the party at all levels. Soon after independence, party and government structures were merged in the persons of regional and area commissioners. As time passed, virtually all elected roles in rural Tanzania have been eliminated or weakened. There are no elected bodies directly controlling significant purse strings in development. The elected TANU group in rural areas appears to act more as a publicity arm of the regime rather than as a powerful independent force.

Decentralization

Administrative decentralization, announced in 1972, was intended to expand peasant participation, increase bureaucratic efficiency, and facilitate planning.[45] Most observers agree that what was actually administrative deconcentration (as opposed to decentralization of power outside the bureaucracy), has not increased peasant participation—a conclusion that can be reached simply by examining the formal structure and the extent of elected representation.[46] A recent study of selected development projects by a team from the University of Dar es Salaam (as part of a larger project) suggests that "there is good reason to suspect that decentralization has in fact increased the power of local civil servants at the expense of both TANU and elected officials."[47]

Since a larger percentage of the development budget (eventually 40 percent but as of 1975, only 14 percent) will be spent by the regions, under the direction of TANU regional executive secretaries (formerly called regional commissioners), administrative deconcentration is likely to raise the morale and efficiency among bureaucratic field personnel, speed up project implementation, and perhaps even stimulate peasant production.[48] But the elaborate, if not elephantine, planning structure will probably yield virtually unusable local "shopping lists" rather than integrated participatory planning.[49] It is interesting to note that in one region, according to a former regional development director (that is, the top regional executive officer), the announcement of decentralization and the spending of more money by regional authorities brought forth considerable self-help activity in his region. Health facilities, especially, seemed to blossom all over and often without the bureaucracy knowing in advance. The popular initiative was, however, diluted by party and government bureaucracy as these institutions continued to force all government assistance through planning channels, and soon the initiative died out. If the bureaucracy intends to develop amenities according to its own criteria and largely with its own funds, there can be little or no incentive for any peasant initiative. The University of Dar es Salaam study of development projects found that decentralization did not have a positive effect on self-help.

> The proportion of self-help projects with good popular performance appears in our sample to have declined with decentralization. In 1971–72, 64% of the self-help projects were judged to have good participation, whereas in 1974–75 the percentage was only 29.[50]

While the rural petty bourgeoisie, as noted above, often received special benefits from halfway self-help in proportion to their power in the process, Tanzania's bureaucrats may have become a more prominent beneficiary of rural project development in proportion to the expansion of their power under decentralization. According to the University of Dar es Salaam study, the "main change in beneficiaries as a result of decentralization has been [among] the civil servants, whose welfare was enhanced by 13% of the 1971–72 projects studied but by 37% of the 1974–75 ones."[51]

It is evident that the relatively independent power of the Tanzanian rural petty bourgeoisie has been progressively defused by cooptation into party or government hierarchies, or by the removal or emasculation of institutions formerly dominated by them. Despite their momentary strength just after independence, they were not a crucial prop of the regime and, hence, could be gradually eliminated from even local positions of strength. (But they could not be rooted out of village leadership positions, as numerous reports from ujamaa villages indicate; this could only be accomplished by an aroused peasantry.) While their removal is an appropriate consequence of a socialist direction, their demise was not in favor of the peasant majority, but rather, of the bureaucratic wing of the same petty bourgeois class. As a result, the peculiar halfway brand of self-help under rural petty bourgeois tutelage tended to decline, if not die out, in proportion to the decline of the protectors, while a more thoroughgoing self-help characteristic of some peasant-based revolutionary regimes failed to emerge in its place.*

James Finucane's monograph provides a detailed look at Tanzania's rural politics, administration, and the question of peasant participation. His profoundly pessimistic conclusions should not go unnoticed:

> My findings considered with other studies indicate quite clearly that participation of the general citizenry in the decision making of the national political system had not notably increased nor changed in nature since the last decade of colonial rule, the ideological and rhetorical images arising from a fairly intense amount of intraelite participation in discussions about what to do with the general citizenry notwithstanding.... With the tendency on the part of the national leadership to consider as national some of those resources which formerly were regarded as local (e.g., those of the co-operatives and of the district councils), and to rely almost exclusively upon indirect methods of skimming the economic surpluses out of the rural areas (sales taxes rather than local rates and produce cesses), the participation of the rural population in making decisions about those activities which affect them directly and which link them with the national policy has lessened. This lessened politics of diversity was not replaced by an increase in the politics of mass enthusiasm.[52]

CONCLUSION

We should be aware of the broader political economies of Kenya and Tanzania in order to put this story of comparative self-help in perspective. The general significance of self-help for peasant welfare pales in light of the mechanisms of appropriation and use of peasant surplus, which condi-

---

*Joel Samoff indicates, in a personal communication, that in 1974 in Kilimanjaro, where the rural petty bourgeoisie is strongest, he and Rachel Samoff found that "local people still do build schools and clinics usually encouraged by churches ... even where local officials announce that staffing and equipment will not be available from government funds."

tion the overall development directions of the two states and cannot be adequately discussed here. Self-help is not the main political or development event. It is a kind of sideshow, but it is significant for what it reveals about the overall structure of power in the two states—the contrasting interests of self-help of the bureaucratic and the independent rural petty bourgeoisie; and the extraordinary desire of the peasantry to improve their immediate social-amenity circumstances, and the lengths to which they will sacrifice for it if a few minimally favorable conditions apply.

Our study of the evolution of self-help in the two states emphasizes the often ignored fact that self-help and social-amenity development is about power—whether it will happen, who will initiate it, and who will control it. It would appear that explanations of self-help relying on community-group dynamics, the level of overall community economic development and social infrastructure, center-local tensions, or changes of political structure, are all necessary for a general explanation of the phenomenon, but what they fail to make explicit is the fact that not all class and political structures even allow self-help, and some will allow and encourage only a halfway variety. The Kenyan and Tanzanian cases indicate that, while the petty bourgeoisie dominated the rural power structures and took over the reins of state at independence, there was a basic, though generally unfocused, struggle between a rather independent petty bourgeois rural segment and a bureaucratic segment. They were struggling over which would provide a core social base of support for the regime as a whole, and which would dominate the countryside. Ultimately, one may view the struggle as a contest determining which segment would appropriate more of the peasant and worker surplus.

It is important to remember that halfway self-help blossomed in both countries just after independence, when the bureaucracy was at its weakest point in relation to the rural petty bourgeoisie and the peasantry as a whole. As both party and state bureaucratic power reemerged in Tanzania, especially after the clear socialist direction announced in 1967, self-help activity fell off, only to be used by the party and government in a very different form when free labor was needed. This experience should once again give pause to those who believe that a large and modern bureaucracy is necessarily an instrument for peasant welfare. It may well be the very opposite—a structure for surplus appropriation that takes more than it gives, while tending to preclude peasant participation, local organization, mass skill development, and the use of local resources and technology.

The rural petty bourgeoisie in Kenya has facilitated a considerable amount of the halfway style of self-help activity, because it is in their interest to do so; just as it is in the interest of the bureaucracy to dampen local initiative and control it. But the Kenyan rural petty bourgeoisie will only encourage rural self-help when they can dominate it through their role as the intermediary between peasants and government. We presume that if their dominance began to erode, and self-help organization took on a more permanent character, with a new and more representative leadership that refused to deal through rural patrons, or that actively opposed them, the rural petty bourgeoisie would unite with their class allies—the bureaucracy—to curtail it.[53]

The gap between rhetoric and the reality of peasant participation in Tanzania vividly suggests that the class structure has not fundamentally altered as bureaucratic institutions have grown stronger. Among its several major accomplishments, Tanzania has made remarkable strides toward a more egalitarian distribution of income and wealth as big and small capitalists have been challenged, and many displaced. But these facts should not obscure the evidence that worker power is honored far more in form than in fact, and that there are not even the scant beginnings of a democratic, peasant worker-based party organization.[54] The closing off of effective mass participation for the sake of the dubious rationality of pervasive bureaucratic planning delays the process of grappling with the vital issues of democracy at all levels and the necessary institutional context of participatory socialism. Of course none of this is news to many Tanzanian leaders, least of all President Nyerere. It only serves as a reminder that there is no shortcut to participatory socialism through a bureaucracy of party or government. And with regard to this discussion in particular, rural peasant participation is not advanced by the replacement of rural petty bourgeois leadership by a bureaucratic segment of the same class.

NOTES

1. See Colin Leys, *Underdevelopment in Kenya* (Berkeley: University of California Press, 1974); and Roger Van Zwanenberg, "Neocolonialism and the Origin of the National Bourgeoisie in Kenya Between 1940 and 1973," *Journal of East African Research and Development* 4, no. 2 (1974).

2. Julius Nyerere, "Freedom and Development," in *Freedom and Development* (New York: Oxford University Press, 1973), p. 60. Nyerere also argues that there can be no socialism without democracy.

3. "T.A.N.U. Guidelines on Guarding, Consolidating and Advancing the Revolution of Tanzania, and of Africa," *The African Review* 1, no. 4 (April 1972):6.

4. I emphasize the comparative absence of self-help in Tanzania compared to Kenya. I am fully aware that genuine self-help goes on in Tanzania, but all evidence, faulty though it is, suggests that Tanzania's incidence of self-help falls short of Kenya's and it has markedly declined over time. For Kenya, see the annual statistical summaries in the Ministry of Economic Planning and Development, Statistics Division, "The Output of Self-Help Schemes, 1967: A Statistical Analysis," mimeographed (Nairobi: Ministry of Cooperatives and Social Services, Community Development Division, August, 1968), and Philip Mbithi and Rasmus Rasmusson, "The Structure of Grass-roots Harambee within the Context of

National Planning," mimeographed (Nairobi: University of Nairobi, Department of Sociology, December 1974). No summary of statistics is available for Tanzania but the current paucity of local initiative in self-help is noted in Bismarck Mwansasu, "Giving Power to the People," *The Standard,* (Dar es Salaam), April 3, 1972, and in James Finucane, *Rural Development and Bureaucracy in Tanzania: The Case of Mwanza Region* (Uppsala: Scandinavian Institute of African Studies, 1974). One must be careful to distinguish local involvement and initiative from government-induced, or required participation. There is a good deal of the latter in Tanzania as evidenced by case studies of rural water supplies and health center construction. See Gerhard Tschannerl, "Rural Water Supplies: Is 'Politics' or 'Technique' in Command?" (Paper no. 52 presented at the Annual Social Science Conference of the East African Universities, Dar es Salaam, December 18–20, 1973), and William Mayer, "Implementation and Control Under Decentralization: Tanzania's Rural Health Centre Programme" (M.A. thesis, University of Dar es Salaam, Department of Political Science, 1974).

5. In the context of a peasant society where most heads of households own their own land, struggles over the appropriation of peasant surplus by other classes may take many forms not requiring the actual loss of land—the major means of production. See Leys, op. cit., p. 192. He says these ways may include: "appropriation at the level of exchange, through adverse rural-urban terms of trade and through monopoly elements in the process of collection, processing and selling peasant-produced commodities for foreign markets; regressive taxes of various kinds, legal and illegal, which in effect transferred surplus from the poorer to the richer families; the similarly regressive burden of the co-operatives' and marketing boards' administrative costs, which supported a substantial part of the salariat by means, in effect, of flat-rate charges on every unit of output from both the capitalist and the peasant sectors of agricultural production; by the strong bias in the provision of services in favour of the richer peasant households as well as of the salariat and small and large-scale owners of capital in the towns; and so on."

6. The summary of studies cited here reproduces the summary in Mbithi and Rasmusson, op. cit., of two papers by G. C. M. Mutiso, which I have not had a chance to view myself: "Mbai Sya Eitu: A Low Status Group in Centre-Periphery Relations," mimeographed, 1973, and "Towards Metapolicies on Improving on Rural Welfare," Nairobi, mimeographed. See also E. M. Godrey and G. C. M. Mutiso, "The Political Economy of Self-Help: Kenya's 'Harambee' Institutes of Technology," *Canadian Journal of African Studies* 4, no. 1 (1974): 109–33, and Frank Holmquist, "Implementing Rural Development Projects," in *Development Administration: The Kenyan Experience,* ed. Goran Hyden, Robert Jackson, and John J. Okumu (Nairobi: Oxford University Press, 1970).

7. Edgar Winans, "Local Initiative and Government Response: Development Politics in Kenya" (Paper presented at the annual meetings of the African Studies Association, Philadelphia, November 8–11, 1972).

8. Mbithi and Rasmusson, op. cit., p. 41.

9. Frank Holmquist, "Toward a Political Theory of Rural Self-Help Development in Africa," *Rural Africana,* no. 18 (Fall 1972):60–79.

10. Philip Mbithi, "Harambee Self-Help: The Kenyan Approach," *The African Review* 2, no. 1 (June 1972):147–66; Martin Hill, "Self-Help in Education and Development: A Social Anthropological Study in Kitui, Kenya," Staff Paper (Nairobi: University of Nairobi, Bureau of Educational Research, 1974): Geoff Lamb, *Peasant Politics: Conflict and Development in Muranga* (Sussex, England: Julian Friedman Publishing, 1974); and Edmond J. Keller, "Harambee: Educational Policy, Inequality and the Political Economy of Rural Community Self-Help in Kenya," Staff Paper (Nairobi: University of Nairobi, Bureau of Educational Research, 1975).

11. John Lonsdale, "Some Origins of Nationalism in East Africa," *The Journal of African History* 9, no. 1 (1968):119–46; Lionel Cliffe, "Nationalism and Reaction to Enforced Agricul-

tural Change in Tanganyika during the Colonial Period," in *Socialism in Tanzania,* vol. 1; ed. Lionel Cliffe and John Saul (Nairobi: East African Publishing House, 1972).

12. This was evident in my own research in Kisii District, Kenya. The coercive powers of chiefs in Kenya's central and eastern provinces are outlined in detail in Robert Tignor, "Colonial Chiefs in Chiefless Societies," *Journal of Modern African Studies* 9, no. 3 (1973): 339–59.

13. I have noted this in Kisii District, and Cherry Gertzel shows how it was briefly institutionalized in the independence arrangement. See her study, "The Provincial Administration in Kenya," *Journal of Commonwealth Political Studies* 4, no. 3 (November 1966). Michaela Von Freyhold observes the same, in regard to Tanga, Tanzania, in "Government Staff and Ujamaa Villages (The Tanga Experience)," mimeographed (Dar es Salaam:University of Dar es Salaam, Department of Economics, n.d.).

14. Henry Bienen, *Tanzania: Party Transformation and Economic Development,* rev. ed. (Princeton: Princeton University Press, 1970).

15. This pattern describes a central tendency: It did not happen everywhere. It was more likely in wealthier peasant growing areas than in poorer ones with limited internal stratification, education, and wealth. The pattern is rarely omitted in political observations on rural Kenya, but less common in descriptions of poorer Tanzania, although Bienen, op. cit., provides general support for the idea. For other evidence of postindependence clientelism in Tanzania, see Tschannerl, op. cit.; Astrid Nypan and Mariken Vaa, "Leadership, Organizational Structure and Development—Two Meru Villages" (paper presented at the Seminar on Changes in Tanzanian Rural Society and Their Relevance for Development Planning, Leiden, December 7–11, 1970), especially pp. 43, 54; Paul Collins, "The Working of Tanzania's Rural Development Fund: A Problem in Decentralization," *East African Journal of Rural Development* 5, nos. 1 and 2 (1972), especially p. 156; and H.U.E. Thoden Van Velzen, "Staff, Kulaks, and Peasants," in *Socialism in Tanzania,* vol. 2, ed. Lionel Cliffe and John Saul (Nairobi: East African Publishing House, 1972), p. 168.

16. By 1963 there was no community development staff in 23 districts in the then Tanganyika, according to Joseph Nye, "Tanganyika's Self-Help," *Transition* 3, no. 11 (November 1963): p. 38. President Nyerere resigned as prime minister to devote his time to building the postindependence party. Self-help was also intended to facilitate party building, but, according to William Tordoff, it had little positive effect in this direction. See his study *Government and Politics in Tanzania* (Nairobi: East African Publishing House, 1967), p. 160.

17. Nye, op. cit., p. 37.

18. Ministry of Economic Planning and Development, op. cit.

19. There has been a spate of literature on the clientelism phenomenon. The articles I have found most useful are James Scott, "Patron-Client Politics: Political Change in South-East Asia," *The American Political Science Review* 66, no. 1 (March 1972), and Richard Sandbrook, "Patrons, Clients, and Factions: New Dimensions of Conflict Analysis in Africa," *Canadian Journal of Political Science* 5, no. 1 (March 1972):104–19. On clientelism in Kenya see Joel D. Barkan, "Bringing Home the Pork: Legislator Behavior, Rural Development and Political Change in East Africa," in *Legislators and Development,* ed. Lloyd Musolf and Joel Smith (Durham: Duke University Press, 1978), and Joel D. Barkan and John J. Okumu, "Semi-Competitive Elections, Clientelism, and Political Recruitment in a No-Party State: The Kenyan Experience," in *Elections Without Choice,* ed. Guy Hermet et al. (London: Macmillan, 1978).

20. Scott, op. cit., pp. 109–13, Barkan and Okumu, op. cit.

21. K. J. Davey cites examples from Tanzania and Uganda that illustrate this difference of interest in local amenity development and the consistent tendency of district councilors to overspend council budgets. See his excellent study, "Local Bureaucrats and Politicians in East Africa," *Journal of Administration Overseas* 10, no. 4 (October, 1971):276–77.

22. On the Tanzanian reaction see Nye, op. cit.; Clyde Ingle, *From Village to State in Tanzania* (Ithaca: Cornell University Press, 1972), p. 62; and Tordoff, op. cit. The negative Kenyan bureaucratic reaction was clearly evident in Kisii during 1967–69. In some quarters there was an attitude of near panic: "Over the previous three years, construction of self-help projects had alarmingly increased and there were charges that they were getting out of control. Things had to be put right quickly, therefore, or there would be wastage of effort on the part of self-help groups." Kenya, *Department of Community Development and Social Services Annual Report 1967* (Nairobi: Government Printer, 1971), p. 2.

23. I do not wish to set up a rigid polarity, nor imply that China has not gone through many political and administrative changes. The existing literature, however, provides a rather striking contrast. See John Gardner and Wilt Idema, "China's Educational Revolution," and Marianne Bastid, "Levels of Economic Decision-Making," in *Authority, Participation, and Cultural Change in China*, ed. Stuart R. Schram (London: Cambridge University Press, 1973); E. L. Wheelwright and Bruce McFarlane, *The Chinese Road to Socialism* (New York: Monthly Review Press, 1970); Joshua Horn, *Away with All Pests* (New York: Monthly Review Press, 1966); Science for the People, *China Walks on Two Legs* (New York: Avon Books, 1974); Byung-Joon Ahn, "The Political Economy of the People's Commune in China: Changes and Continuities," *Journal of Asian Studies* 34, no. 3 (May 1975):631–58; Victor Sidel, *Serving the People* (New York: Beacon, 1974); and Wilfred Burchett with Rewi Alley, *China: The Quality of Life* (Baltimore: Penguin, 1976).

24. See H. K. Colebatch, "Government Services at the District Level in Kenya: Roads, Schools and Health Services," IDS Discussion Paper no. 38, (Brighton, England: University of Sussex, Institute of Development Studies, May 1974), and a somewhat dated article by M. Segall, "The Politics of Health," in *Tanzanian Studies*, no. 1 (Dar es Salaam: Tanzania Publishing House, 1972).

25. Tschannerl, op. cit.

26. Ibid. Davey, op. cit., also notes the bureaucratic tendency to maximize project quality at the expense of quantity.

27. Godfrey and Mutiso, op. cit., p. 120.

28. Violaine Junod, "Some Problems in the Coordination of Local Development in Tanzania" (Paper presented at the Workshop on Penetration, Nairobi, September 29–October 1, 1967).

29. Finucane, op. cit., pp. 89–90.

30. Davey, op. cit., p. 279.

31. This was my experience in Kisii District. See also Cherry Gertzel, "The Provincial Administration and Development in Kenya, 1965–68" (Paper presented at the annual Universities of East Africa Social Science Conference, Dar es Salaam, December, 1970). Robert Chambers has written extensively on the failures of rural planning in both countries. See his study, "Planning for Rural Areas in East Africa; Experience and Prescriptions," in *Rural Administration in Kenya*, Management and Administration Series: no. 2, ed. David K. Leonard (Nairobi: East African Literature Bureau, 1973), and his book, *Managing Rural Development: Ideas and Experience from East Africa* (Uppsala: Scandinavian Institute of African Studies, 1974). Also, on Tanzania see P. R. Lawrence et al., "Regional Planning in Tanzania: Some Institutional Problems," *Eastern Africa Journal of Rural Development* 7, nos. 1 and 2 (1974).

32. Godfrey and Mutiso, op. cit., and Barkan, op. cit., indicate a more active role for Kenyan chiefs and the bureaucracy in bigger projects. These observations further justify our placing the local immobile civil servants, such as chiefs, in a category apart from their more mobile and transferable bureaucratic counterparts.

33. Colebatch, op. cit.

34. On the 1969 elections see Goran Hyden and Colin Leys, "Elections and Politics in Single Party Systems: The Case of Kenya and Tanzania," *British Journal of Political Science* 2, no. 4 (October 1972). For the elections of 1974 see Barkan and Okumu, op. cit.

35. Looking at Kenya, David Leonard argues that because "the Kenyan system is dominated by a class which has a strong base outside the public sector, its bureaucrats are much more subject to external demands than are their Tanzanian counterparts." The strongest external voice comes from the Kenyan bourgeoisie, but "petty bourgeois demands generally receive a sympathetic response from the administration, especially when they are made on junior civil servants who belong to the same class." See David K. Leonard, "Bureaucracy, Class and Inequality in Kenya and Tanzania" (Paper presented at the Social Science Research Council Conference on Inequality in Africa, Mt. Kisco, N.Y., October 1976, p. 30). See also Goran Hyden, *Efficiency Versus Distribution in East African Cooperatives: A Study in Organization Conflicts* (Nairobi: East African Literature Bureau, 1973), and Joseph Ascroft et al., "Does Extension Create Poverty?" *East Africa Journal* 9, no. 3 (1972).

36. See Hyden, op. cit. For a wealth of material on cooperatives and rural policy in general, see Rural Development Research Committee, ed., *Rural Cooperation in Tanzania* (Dar es Salaam: Tanzania Publishing House, 1975). In the aftermath of the villagization campaign of 1974 the role and probably the number of primary cooperative societies have been expanded while higher-level cooperative unions have been abolished.

37. Helge Kjekhus, "Parliament in a One-Party State: The Bunge of Tanzania, 1965–70," *Journal of Modern African Studies* 12, no. 1 (March 1974):19–43. For a local level view see Finucane, op. cit., chapter 5. According to a voter survey prior to the 1970 elections, most respondents wanted the MP to support local wishes rather than the government's in any dispute. See Jon R. Moris, "The Voter's View of the Elections," in *Socialism and Participation: Tanzania's 1970 National Elections,* ed. Election Study Committee (Dar es Salaam: Tanzania Publishing House, 1974).

38. Pius Msekwa, "Toward Party Supremacy: The Changing Pattern of Relationships Between the National Assembly and the National Executive Committee of TANU Before and After 1965" (M.A. thesis, University of Dar es Salaam, Department of Political Science, 1974).

39. Collins, op. cit.

40. For evidence of this see John Sender, "Some Preliminary Notes on the Political Economy of Rural Development in Tanzania, Based on a Case Study on the West Usambaras" (Paper presented at an Economic Research Bureau Seminar, University of Dar es Salaam, November 16, 1973).

41. The largely unpublished literature on ujamaa is now considerable. For a good, if dated, summary view with bibliography see P. L. Raikes, "Ujamaa and Rural Socialism," *Review of African Political Economy* 1, no. 3 (May 1975):33–52. See also Jonathan Barker, "Socialism and the Rural Sector in Tanzania" (Paper presented at the 72d Annual Meeting of the American Political Science Association, Chicago, 1976). On the basis of data collected in four regions in early 1975, Dean McHenry suggests that only 40 percent of ujamaa villages practice communal production, and that within them, communal production provides only a small fraction of total peasant income. See his study, "Rural Policy Divergence: Communal Farming in Ujamaa Villages" (Paper presented at the annual East African Universities Social Science Conference, Nairobi, December 1975), and his study, "Peasant Participation in Communal Farming: The Tanzanian Experience," (Paper presented at the annual meetings of the African Studies Association, Boston, November 1976).

42. Goran Hyden, "Ujamaa, Villagization and Rural Development in Tanzania," *ODI Review* (Sussex, England), no. 1 (April 1975):53–72. Hyden appropriately warns against expecting instant success in ujamaa or in other aspects of Tanzania's transition to socialism. He cites a village that has made rather tortured moves in a positive direction, although it should be noted that progress was often in spite of government or in opposition to it, rather than because of it.

43. Joel Samoff, "Cell Leaders in Tanzania," *Taamuli* 4, no. 1 (Dar es Salaam, December 1973). On the fragmented and weak nature of local TANU branches see Joel Samoff, "The

Bureaucracy and the Bourgeoisie: Decentralization and Class Struggle in Tanzania" (Paper presented at the annual meetings of the African Studies Association, Boston, November 1976).

44. The generally poor participatory state of the party in rural Tanzania is vividly portrayed in Finucane, op. cit., and in five B.A. theses written in 1974 for the Department of Political Science, University of Dar es Salaam, by Udi Kabuka, H. J. Mosha, Mathias Misanga, C. R. S. Muzo, and C. T. Nuduru. See also the B.A. thesis by Rwekaza S. Mukandala (1976).

45. Julius Nyerere, *Decentralization* (Dar es Salaam: Government Printer, 1972).

46. R. Baguma, "Decentralization as a Strategy for Rural Transformation in Tanzania: Causes and Prospects" (Paper presented at the annual Social Science Conference of the East African Universities, December 1973). See similar comments in Finucane, op. cit., and in Paul Collins, "Decentralization and Local Administration for Development in Tanzania," *Africa Today* 21, no. 3 (Summer 1974):15–25.

47. David Leonard with Goran Hyden, Justin Maeda, and Samuel Mushi, "An Analysis of a Pre-Test Sample of Development Projects Implemented Under Tanzania's Decentralized Administrative Structure," Working Paper no. 75, University Research Project on Government Decentralization and the Management of Rural Development in Tanzania (Dar es Salaam: University of Dar es Salaam, 1975), p. 8.

48. Ibid., p. 13.

49. For comments on experience in the West Lake region see Jannik Boesen, "Tanzania: From Ujamaa to Villagization," IDR paper A. 76.7 (Copenhagen: Institute for Development Research, 1976).

50. Leonard et al., op. cit., pp. 23–24.

51. Ibid, pp. 17–18. The authors take care to point out that this result is not statistically significant.

52. Finucane, op. cit., p. 173.

53. The everyday tendency for staff and kulak to ally in the village is discussed in Van Velzen, op. cit. A second-hand story from Kuria, Kenya, in 1970 tells of two priests organizing peasants to collect funds to set up maize-grinding mills in competition with other private, often near-monopoly, operations whose proprietors were political allies of the local MP. As the peasant organization became a success economically, it grew into a rather militant group in opposition to the MP and his mill-operating cohorts. The MP did everything he could to get the organization banned and declared subversive. An apparently similar case from Tanzania involved the disbanding in 1969 of the Ruvuma Development Association of very successful ujamaa villages by the TANU National Executive Committee (contrary to Nyerere's vote), following long-term complaints by bureaucrats, TANU officials, and local politicians that it was "too independent" (read too much of an independent political threat). See Ralph Ibbot, "The Disbanding of the Ruvuma Development Association, Tanzania," unpublished typescript (London, November 1969).

54. Of course, the issue of worker power and a peasant-based party is never even broached in Kenya. Issa Shivji, op. cit., summarizes the condition of Tanzania's halting worker-power movement. On the rationale and design for a cadre party in Tanzania, see the excellent study by William Luttrell, "Villagization, Cooperative Production and Rural Cadres: Strategies and Tactics in Tanzanian Socialist Rural Development, mimeographed (Dar es Salaam: Institute of Finance Management, n.d.).

7

RURAL DEVELOPMENT POLICY AND EQUALITY

S. E. Migot-Adholla

RURAL DEVELOPMENT: AN OVERVIEW

ALTHOUGH IT IS GENERALLY TRUE that the majority of the poor in third-world countries reside in the rural areas, it is also generally true that commercial farmers and rural entrepreneurs are among the wealthiest groups in these societies. The constellation of factors contributing to inequality and underdevelopment in third-world countries is obviously broad and complex, but the approaches to solving these problems usually fall within one of two categories. On the one hand are the approaches followed by most third-world governments, and supported by the major agencies that dispense international aid. These approaches tend to treat each case of rural development as being unique, and to develop a separate program for each.[1] Such programs are usually limited in scope, and have narrow and specific goals. Most of them concentrate on increasing the agricultural productivity of individual farmers and involve the diffusion of better agronomic technology, extension of credit, and community self-help projects.

Programs of this type have generally had only marginal and very limited success in terms of improving the overall condition of the rural poor, as the dismal growth rates in third-world agricultural production attest.[2] The failure of these programs to achieve any appreciable results may be attributed to the fact that, almost invariably, they take the structural and institutional status quo for granted, thus allowing those strategic positions to divert resources to their own interests. In addition, such programs have singularly suffered from what has been termed "cafeteria programming," the selection of projects which have potential for the greatest visibility, and which have the possibility of quick success in order to enhance bureaucratic images of efficiency. The interplay of these factors tends to link bureaucratic interests with those of the wealthier groups of farmers, thus reinforcing the structural status quo.[3] But perhaps more significant, such programs have often been so heavily capitalized that once external aid is stopped, local inertia soon sets in because of the lack of local resources to maintain the projects.

The second approach to the problems of rural development is the centralized approach, which is generally identified with extensive central planning, collectivization, and cooperative farming experiments in socialist countries. This approach adopts a frontal attack on rural poverty and inequality through the transformation of rural social structures and institutions and the redistribution of land resources. In addition to attempting to increase agricultural production, this approach aims at enhancing the direct participation of the rural population in the economic and political processes of development. Its advantages are to be found in its ability to marshal resources more effectively and to fit programs in the total national picture more realistically. Centralized planning, however, often creates bottlenecks at the top, and entails the use of qualified expertise in the determination and implementation of projects. Directives from the center also tend to be so broad and far-reaching that they have sometimes led to the stifling of local enthusiasm as the scope of local initiative has narrowed and eventually disappeared. This in turn has led to a feeling of alienation among local farmers, and characterizes what has been disparagingly termed "command farming." As a result of this political and psychological problem, which is related to the question of incentives, the centralized approach to rural development usually fails to achieve per capita productivity rates similar to those obtaining in capitalist agriculture. But productivity per capita is only one of the measures of development, and probably not a very useful one so long as it does not directly relate to income distribution of real life.

The two approaches outlined here have been posed in their extreme to emphasize the contrast. Although underlining different ideological positions, these approaches are rarely so divergent in practice, especially in the developing countries, many of whose economies are planned and managed from the center. Indeed, many rural development programs combine elements of both approaches in varying proportions depending on the ideological orientation of the groups in control of political power. Nevertheless, within Africa, Kenya and Tanzania perhaps best exemplify these two approaches to rural development, for each leans heavily toward one approach over the other. These two countries share a number of common features, the most important of which is that the bulk of their populations, more than 90 percent, live in rural areas and derive their livelihood from agriculture. They are both poor, having per capita GNPs equivalent to $220 and $170, respectively, and both have been classified by the United Nations as being among the poorest countries, which some observers now refer to as the fourth world and which others have termed the "extreme periphery." The two countries both claim to subscribe to some variant of socialism. In the case of Kenya, African socialism is essentially a rhetorical justification of policies which are basically capitalist. Kenya consequently attempts to raise rural incomes through the profit incentive and individual enterprise. Questions of equity and income distribution are given little thought, in the hope that this would eventually be solved when general levels of wealth have increased. Tanzania, on the other hand, espouses an ideology of *ujamaa,* or socialism and self-reliance, which is to be achieved through cooperative work and living in collectivized villages throughout rural Tanzania. Although neither of the two countries has made any claims to support any variant of scientific socialism, that is, Marxist-Leninism, Tanzania has made the most concentrated attempts at structural transformation and the eradication of sources of extreme inequality.

Policies developed in Kenya and Tanzania have both been praised as potentially successful and condemned as disastrous failures by their respective supporters and critics, observers who often base their judgments on criteria other than those accepted in the two countries. This study broadly examines the efficacy of the two countries' policies in structural transformation and in the eradication of extreme poverty among the rural population.

RURAL DEVELOPMENT POLICY IN KENYA, 1953–77

Although it is generally recognized that political independence in Kenya came about partly as a result of the Mau Mau revolt, the far-reaching and persistent nature of the policies formulated in response to the issues that had sparked the revolt has not been given prominence. An understanding of the political and economic reforms of the Mau Mau period, however, is crucial for understanding the political economy and rural development policies of Kenya today. For reasons that shall be discussed later, present government policies for rural development are in large part a continuation and an elaboration of policies established by the colonial government during the closing days of imperial rule.

The Mau Mau revolt had arisen out of the conflict over the land alienated early in the twentieth century for the exclusive occupation of Europeans. More generally, however, the revolt had its causes in the social discrimination, economic exploitation, and political subjugation of the

African people by a racially distinct colonial-settler minority.[4] While more acute in the rural areas, these problems did not spare Africans in the emergent urban centers of the country. In many African agricultural areas, the land was exhausted from overcropping and was being eroded as a result of overstocking. On the other hand, fertile land of high potential was often fragmented into handkerchief-sized plots as a result of traditional tenure and succession systems that guaranteed each son a share of the land. In the White Highlands, many European-owned farms were also only marginally productive, though for different reasons. A lack of capital and a scarcity of labor often resulted in land lying idle or not being farmed to capacity. In the urban areas, wages were low, and target labor led to rapid turnover of personnel, and low levels of skill formation. Capital for expansion was also scarce.

Typical of the government at that time, major policy formulation had to be justified by a commission of experts, and the Mau Mau era witnessed a barrage of reports focusing on various aspects of the political economy: the Troup report (1954), the Carpenter report (1954), the Swynnerton Plan (1954), and the Royal East Africa Commission report (1955).[5] The Troup report, addressed to problems of farming in the White Highlands, was overtaken by events. One of its major recommendations, for instance, was to increase European immigration and settlement. It is rather reminiscent of recent campaigns for white immigration in Rhodesia and South Africa at a time when racial conflict over questions of resource allocation and political participation has intensified.

The Carpenter report was primarily concerned with urban wages, although there was a section on rural wages. It argued for the stabilization of urban labor through increased wages and proposed the determination of wages through collective bargaining.[6] The third report, which came to be known as the Swynnerton Plan, dealt with problems of agriculture in the African areas and embodied a series of proposals designed as counter-revolutionary to the Mau Mau.[7] In the long run the plan aimed at revolutionizing African agriculture through the introduction of individual tenure and the cultivation of profitable export crops hitherto prohibited to Africans. The plan envisaged and encouraged the creation of landed and landless classes in the African reserves. Arguing for the eventual concentration of land resources in the hands of the most efficient producers, it anticipated an exodus of surplus labor from the land and their absorption into industry. Lastly, the Royal East Africa Commission report of 1955, with the broadest terms of reference, endorsed the need to promote commercial agriculture and private enterprise among Africans. One of its most important recommendations was the abolition of racial distinctions in land holding, and can thus be seen as the first official negation of the white settlers' hope for economic and political domination.

Both the Swynnerton and the royal commission reports had perhaps the greatest impact on Kenya's political economy, many aspects of which persist today. The reports based their assumptions for the expected agrarian revolution in Kenya on the experience of seventeenth-century Britain, and suggested standard textbook methods for its implementation. But the recommendations did not take serious account of the international alignment of economic forces that would prevent the realization of a commensurate industrial revolution to give full effect to the agrarian revolution. In the absence of an industrial revolution, the effect of the introduction of individual tenure and commercialization of land would be to aggravate landlessness and polarize rural classes: rich farmers as opposed to the landless and poor peasants. This process, however, has not been unidimensional as residual customary ties and obligations have tended to mute the process of polarization. Thus the land-tenure reforms initiated during this period set off two opposite trends—concentration of land resources in fewer hands, and increased fragmentation especially among the poorer peasants.

Apart from the land-tenure reform comprising consolidation and registration in the name of individual title holders, the Swynnerton Plan is memorable for allowing Africans to cultivate profitable export crops, hitherto an exclusive monopoly of white settlers. Ecologically, such crops as coffee, tea, pyrethrum, and later, dairy produce were restricted to high-rainfall, fertile land in the highland areas adjacent to the white-settler farming region. The expansion in small-farm production of these crops by Africans benefited from many years of research that had been conducted for settler farmers in the highlands to develop high-growing crop varieties, agronomic practices, and methods of disease and pest control. But the African highland areas, in addition to being the areas where land pressure had been acute, were the areas of intense Mau Mau activity and experienced the greatest expansion of administrative staff and infrastructure, primarily to control guerrilla activity, which was effectively contained during the first four years of the rebellion (1952–56). It was thus possible to take advantage of the expanded administration and the emergency regulations to force the quick completion of the land-reform process in these areas.

Following the individualization of land tenure via the registration of individual titles, it was possible for farmers to obtain credit for agricultural development, and the agricultural extension service was expanded in these areas, partly to guarantee that loans obtained were correctly used. Prices paid to farmers were also manipulated to provide further incentives for the production of export crops. But there was also concern among white settlers that the crops grown by Africans, unless closely supervised during cultivation and strictly graded, would lower the quality of Kenyan produce, and adversely affect Kenya's markets overseas. Very stringent grading measures were consequently instituted, and persist today, a fact which explains the relatively high quality of Kenya's small-holder farm produce.

In purely productive terms, the combined effects of land-tenure reform, agricultural credit, expanded extension service, and the benefits of research conducted for settler farms started what can be justifiably seen as a green revolution in the limited sense that it led to higher yields and better quality.[8]

These developments, however, were initially confined to areas of high-potential land on the fringes of the then White Highlands. In the rest of the country, inhabited by the majority of the African population, the land was marginal, and while conservation and soil improvement measures were recommended and, in a few cases, supported by government programs, no profitable export crops were adopted. Consequently, agriculture in these areas continued to stagnate despite the later extension of the land-tenure reform campaign to the whole country.

To the extent that the orientation of agricultural extension institutions, credit agencies, and the pricing policies discriminated against food crops grown by Africans, it can be argued that the policies embodied in the Swynnerton Plan may, in effect, have contributed to the underdevelopment of marginal agricultural areas. With respect to nutritive value, Judith Heyer has illustrated that the switch to the better-priced maize in some of these areas led to the abandonment of the more nutritious and drought-resistant sorghums and millets.[9] There can also be little doubt about the ecologically limited nature of the benefits of reform programs instituted under the Swynnerton Plan. One significant long-term effect was to dramatize regional income inequality. And in a situation where ecological and administrative regions also coincided with ethnic and linguistic boundaries, such inequalities immediately took on political dimensions, fueling ethnic animosities and undermining the evolution of a sense of nationhood. Within the high-potential areas these policies sharpened disparities in land and income distribution, setting into motion even more acute demands by the landless for redistribution of the extensive white-settler farms among Africans. Politicization of the land question became particularly explosive in the years immediately preceding independence, and was compounded by the release of 60,000 Mau Mau detainees, many of whom had no land, and by the coincident insurgency of the underground Land Freedom Army and Kiama Kia Mingi. The demand for land also increased as a result of rising productivity and profitability of small-holder farming under the Swynnerton Plan, and as a result of rising unemployment in the urban areas.[10]

White settlers and government bureaucrats alike feared a wave of land seizures following independence. To preempt such land grabs and stem possible revolt against the new government, portions of the former White Highlands were added onto the African reserves beginning in 1961 and subdivided for occupation by the landless and unemployed and by progressive African farmers. This program, called the Million Acre Settlement Scheme, initially aimed to settle some 6,000 peasant families, but by 1971 the number of families settled through the scheme was roughly 34,000.[11] Although popularized as a measure to Africanize the former White Highlands, it is important to note that the scheme affected only a small fraction of the land previously preserved for European occupation, and was basically only an extension of the existing African reserves.* But the settler instruments of privilege were retained in the settlement areas: marketing procedures, pricing systems, farming organizations, credit institutions, all of which favored the products of large-scale farms. Like the Swynnerton Plan, the Million Acre Scheme was intended in the short run as a counterinsurgency measure aimed at containing rural unrest on the eve of independence. That it left from three-quarters to four-fifths of the former White Highland areas intact affirms the desire of the outgoing colonial regime to Africanize the White Highlands without affecting the patterns of resource distribution in any fundamental way.

Nor did this policy change after independence. By 1968 the subdivision of large farms was effectively abandoned. Since then, the purchase of whole farms by individual Africans or groups (companies or cooperatives) has been encouraged by the availability of loans for such purchases from government credit institutions, as in the case of the Million Acre Scheme. The repeated justification given by the government for keeping large farms intact has been a presumed level of greater efficiency accorded to large units over small ones. But as demonstrated convincingly by Colin Leys in his analysis of government figures comparing large- and small-holder production, large farms have often been the least productive agricultural units in Kenya. Moreover, it has been the owners of large farms who have been the ones most likely to default on the repayment of their loans.[12]

The extent to which the policies of the Kenyan government have not dealt effectively with the problem of inequality in the distribution and ownership of land can be seen in Tables 7.1 and 7.2. As indicated in Table 7.1, which presents the changes in the distribution of ownership of large farms between 1954 and 1971, little progress was made toward reducing the overall level of inequality during this critical period that embraced the containment of the Mau Mau, the formal end to colonial rule, and the

---

*Although other groups had lost the greatest proportion of their land during the earlier alienation process, the resettlement scheme in formerly alienated land appears to have favored the Kikuyu disproportionately, a fact which has heightened ethnic tension, particularly over land.

TABLE 7.1: Changes in the Size of Large Farms: 1954–71

Number of Hectares	1954		1963		1971	
	Number of Farms	Percent of Farms	Number of Farms	Percent of Farms	Number of Farms	Percent of Farms
49 and under	467	14	578	17	741	23
50–399	1,162	37	1,288	38	1,253	40
400 and above	1,535	49	1,502	45	1,182	37
Total	3,164	100	3,368	100	3,175	100

Source: Roger Van Zwanenberg, "Neocolonialism and the Origin of the National Bourgeoisie in Kenya between 1940 and 1973," *Journal of Eastern Africa Research and Development* 4 (1974): 174.

TABLE 7.2: Size Distribution of Large Farms, 1970

Size of Farm (hectares)	Number of Farms	Percentage of All Farms	Estimated Total Area (thousand hectares)	Percentage of All Farm Land
0–50	741	23.3	15	0.6
50–99	304	9.6	23	0.8
100–299	685	21.6	134	5.0
300–499	471	14.9	186	6.9
500–999	498	15.7	373	13.9
1,000–1,999	243	7.6	364	13.5
2,000–3,999	107	3.4	321	11.9
4,000–19,999	111	3.5	1,273	47.3
20,000 and over	15	0.5		
All sizes	3,175	100.0	2,690	100.0

Source: International Labour Office, Employment Incomes and Equality (Geneva: International Labour Office, 1972) p. 36.

consolidation of an independent African government. While the proportion of large farms that contained more than 400 hectares declined from 49 to 37 percent, the proportion of land concentrated in a few large holdings remained very high, as shown by Table 7.2.

So far, an attempt has been made to show that the present rural development policy in Kenya is a direct continuation of the policy originating from the need to diffuse insurgency during the Mau Mau revolt and in the period immediately preceding independence by extending the privileges and institutional benefits of settler agriculture to some Africans. But the policy, while recognizing the evolution of polarized classes in the long run, has supported the better-placed, more enterprising, and often wealthier individuals, especially those in the more fertile highland areas engaged in commercial farming. In these areas there has been an impressive increase in the value of small-farm production, averaging nearly 10 percent per year since independence. But the effect of this on income distribution, given the pattern of resource distribution, has not been encouraging. Indeed, it is estimated that landlessness and the extent of rural poverty have become more acute. In 1972 the International Labour Office (ILO) estimated that in 1969 roughly 30,000 peasant households in Kenya, or 17 percent of all households, had no land, while the average amount of arable land available to each member of the rural population was only 0.8 hectares. In view of Kenya's high rate of population growth (2.9 to 3.1 percent per annum), and the fact that only 11 percent of Kenya's land area is composed of arable land, these figures are no doubt grossly out of date.[13]

Although land-tenure reform, particularly the registration of individual titles, has now covered nearly all agricultural areas, farmers in marginal and low-potential lands have had hardly any visible benefits. In some cases the relative poverty of these areas has been compounded as a result of the adoption of Harambee self-help projects as the method for mobilizing resources for rural infrastructure. Embracing the popular biblical dictum "To those that have, more will be given," the Kenya government has generally supported individuals and communities able to demonstrate their own resourcefulness. This policy guideline was stated clearly soon after independence in 1965 by the government in its famous sessional paper on the application of African socialism to Kenya. It continues to be the basis of policy today:

> To make the economy as a whole grow as fast as possible, development money should be invested where it will yield the largest increase in new output. This approach will clearly favor the development of areas having abundant natural resources, good land and rainfall, transport and power facilities, and people receptive to and active in development.[14]

As discussed by Joel Barkan and Frank Holmquist in Chapters 3 and 6, respectively, the local people, abetted by local political leaders or other members of the local elite, use Harambee self-help projects as a device to extract more government resources for the local community. By encouraging Harambee projects, the government thus undermines its own official long-term plans to spread development across the country on a more efficient and equitable basis. As Holmquist observes, "The strategy of self-help groups is to purposely go beyond the plan, because they probably would not receive aid without preemptive local effort. . . . Rather than helping to shift the burden of development from government, self-help activity may serve to generate even more demand upon government from below."[15] As such, a policy of rural development that emphasizes rapid economic growth, and that seeks to stimulate growth through an expansion of export agriculture on the one hand, and through Harambee projects on the other, is also a policy that exacerbates the degree of inequality between regions. Communities with relatively fewer local resources are likely to have their underdevelopment compounded, while those with more resources will grow and prosper as these inequalities become cumulative.

This strategy for rural development also has some important implications for the distribution of income within regions, of which some have already been noted. As observations of one particular type of Harambee project show, "Although conspicuous donations are being extracted from the elite, most local contributors are in lower income groups, particularly small farmers."[16] Thus it can be argued that Kenya's self-help program constitutes a form of regressive taxation. This, however, is not to overlook the tremendous resources that have been generated to support locally identified projects, even if some of these have only been partially completed, abandoned, or found unusable after completion.

In summary, one can point to the success of Kenyan rural development policy in increasing agricultural productivity and, therefore, rural incomes in some areas. Since independence, the commercial agricultural sector, which is now almost completely in African hands, has annually made steady, and occasionally spectacular, real gains of between 2 and 10 percent in the value of total production.[17] Kenyan agriculture is one of the most productive on the African continent. Despite the continued emphasis on the production of export crops, Kenya is virtually self-sufficient in foodstuffs, a condition which is in sharp contrast to that found in many other independent African states. Prices of foodstuffs to consumers in Kenya are also much lower compared to prices in neighboring countries, for example, Tanzania, Uganda, and Zambia. The significance of this important aspect of the Kenyan developmental experience has been aptly summed up by Roger Van Zwanenberg: "While it is probably true that large numbers, probably the majority of the people, have benefitted by independence, so many people have benefitted materially that the expectation of opportunity is widespread, even among some of the poorest peoples."[18]

Kenya's policy of growth and the Africanization of land ownership, however, has not led to a more equitable distribution of rural incomes; indeed, as we have argued, the result has been just the opposite. Nor has the government attempted to deal boldly with this issue, as underscored by its repeated refusal to impose a land tax on large land holdings, or a ceiling on the extent of such holdings.* In respect to rural policy, Kenya is thus a classic example of the trickle-down model of development, which assumes that the critical question is not whether inequality exists, or even whether the extent of inequality is becoming more pronounced, but whether everyone's share of the national pie, large or small, continues to expand.

As suggested by James C. Scott in his important study of peasant agriculture in Burma and Vietnam, there is much historical evidence to support the official Kenyan view, provided the minimum material security

---

*The most vociferous demands for such limitations on the size of land holdings come from members of the Kenyan National Assembly. These demands are usually made by backbenchers critical of the government. Perhaps the most outspoken proponent of such limitations was the late J. M. Kariuki.

of the peasant can be guaranteed.[19] If this is the proper term of reference, however, the question remains as to whether present government policy in Kenya, despite its past success, can continue to guarantee the minimum material security of all farmers in the years ahead. The answer to this question is suggested, but by no means clear.

On the one hand, skeptical observers, including those of the ILO, note that the gap between rich and poor is increasing in Kenya, while the number of landless peasants, and the number of rural residents who are underemployed (and consequently the number of migrants to the urban areas who are likewise underemployed, or unemployed) are also rising.[20] Kenya's high rate of population growth, combined with its limited amount of high-quality land, also suggest that in the long run (25 to 50 years) the critical issue may not be the question of land inequality, but rather, whether—even in a situation of full equality or of semiequality—there is sufficient arable land to support the country's population.

On the other hand, less pessimistic observers point to the current boom in Kenyan agriculture as a result of the expansion of small-holder production of tea, and record coffee production and world coffee prices. As for the long-term situation when the sharp rises in the production and prices of export crops level off, it is hoped that the expanding industrial sector—despite its emphasis on capital-intensive technology—will take up the slack. It must also be noted that beginning in the mid-1970s, perhaps in response to the sobering findings of the ILO study, the Kenyan government started to expand settlement opportunities for landless peasants in northeastern Kenya along the Tana River. In contrast to earlier settlement schemes, these new settlements involve the opening up of new areas of cultivation rather than the takeover of existing farms, and, as such, contribute to the overall expansion of the agricultural sector. These settlements, which are largely populated by migrants from Central Province, are also a source of less ethnic friction than were earlier efforts at creating new settlements in some areas of the Rift Valley. They are also important for maintaining the sometimes tenuous security of Kenya's frontier with Somalia.

While the Kenyan government has begun to accelerate the expansion of these and other settlement schemes to respond to the unceasing demand for land, it is doubtful whether such efforts will effectively deflect demands for the equalization of land holdings and/or guarantee a livelihood for that sector of the rural population which is presently being squeezed below the line of subsistence. The size and rate of expansion of these settlements relative to the demand is still small, while the cost of such programs is high. Thus, while Kenya's policy of rural development has not dealt directly with the problem of land inequality, it is apparent that indirect solutions to this sensitive issue are beginning to be sought.

RURAL DEVELOPMENT POLICY IN TANZANIA, 1961–77

Independence in Tanzania did not come through any struggle similar to that in Kenya, nor was the issue of land distribution and inequality a major source of conflict. Although Tanzania had been a site for European settlement since before World War I, the settler community was less than one-third the size of its Kenyan counterpart, and was largely confined to two areas—the Southern Highlands, and the region between Arusha and Moshi—which were roughly 500 miles apart. Tanzania's resources of arable land relative to its population are also considerably greater than that of its northern neighbor.[21] Soon after independence, however, the new leadership in Tanzania offered socialism as an option for development, although at the time it was deliberately defined as an abstract set of values without reference to social forms necessary for its realization. Indeed, the implementation of any socialist policy did not take place until six years later when the ruling party adopted the Arusha Declaration, which argued that socialist organization and self-reliance provided the surest alternative for development. To the extent that this policy proposed a break from the previous forms of economic and social organization, it may be said that Tanzania opted for fairly significant structural transformation and change in the patterns of resource allocation. But this position was arrived at after much debate and examination of the factors impinging on Tanzania's overall prospects for development.

The first development plan, launched in 1964, proposed a series of village settlements to act as demonstration centers in a program that was envisaged to eventually lead to the transformation of the Tanzanian rural economy. This program, which had been proposed by the World Bank and designed by Israeli experts,[22] consisted of 23 settlement schemes and cost more than £2 million. It was later abandoned when it was found to be expensive beyond the means of the country. The villages were overcapitalized, providing housing, farm machinery, seeds, and even food to the initial settlers. Administrative overheads were equally large, although the level of productivity was not impressive.[23] Typical of development thinking at the time, 80 percent of Tanzania's development budget was expected to be financed from foreign sources. But five years after independence such a partnership with the rich countries had not materialized. The promise of industrialization proved illusory, and the price of sisal, which had supported the country's foreign exchange earnings, had fallen by more than 50 percent. As discussed by John Okumu in Chapter 10, Tanzania's support for the liberation struggle in the neighboring Portuguese colony of Mozambique, and the breaking of diplomatic relations with Britain over the Rhodesia issue, further isolated Tanzania and compounded her economic problems.

Thus, Tanzania, perhaps more than any other African country at the time, learned the emptiness of the prevailing doctrine of partnership in development. By 1966, the lesson led to the abandonment of the expensive World Bank transformation approach to rural development, and to the adoption of an improvement approach, which stresses marginal increments with resources being directed to progressive farmers or specific program areas. More significantly, the lesson led to the promulgation a year later of the Arusha Declaration, in which President Nyerere articulated Tanzania's shift to a strategy of socialism and self-reliance. The major goals of theDeclaration are well known and need not be repeated here. Clarification of these policies as they pertained to rural development came in two policy pamphlets issued by the Tanganyika African National Union (TANU) later that year—*Socialism* and *Rural Development and Education for Self-Reliance.*[24] The general argument of the two documents provided for political education for party officials and activists, inculcation of socialist values, and a spirit of self-sacrifice among future elites in the upper reaches of the education pyramid, specifically through a national service program and a radical reorientation of primary-school education so that it would be relevant to rural life. But more significantly, provision was made for the gradual transformation of rural life from scattered family plots toward cooperative forms of living and working—the *ujamaa* villages, which have become the most popularized but perhaps also the most controversial aspect of Tanzanian rural development policy.[25]

There is no doubt that Tanzania's policies are farsighted and idealistic, but their implementation has not always been encouraging. As outlined in 1967, the policy of ujamaa was to be democratically implemented through voluntary participation of the rural masses and largely by their own resources. This position was further underlined in the *TANU Party Guidelines* of 1971, which emphasized the principle of local initiative and self-management and which argued that it was "not correct for leaders and experts to usurp the people's rights to decide on an issue just because they have the expertise."[26] But the initial statements about ujamaa obviously derived from the experience of the earlier village settlement program, whose failure was not to be repeated. The new villages were to be organized collectively and run by peasants themselves, without large-scale capital inputs from outside. A prototype of such self-reliant villages was already in existence in the guise of the Ruvuma Development Association, comprising villages that had been started by enterprising members of the TANU Youth League without government initiative. Following this example, the ujamaa villages were intended to be politically implemented, through education and mass mobilization of peasants. An important part of this depended on demonstrating to the peasants the benefits of cooperative organization and communal living, which in turn assumed that those who were to do the explaining would themselves have a clear grasp of the principles of socialism and the specific technical and social conditions in each part of the country.

As the policy paper on ujamaa itself recognized, there were two kinds of inequality in rural Tanzania that paralleled those already discussed in Kenya: There were regional inequalities in which the overall level of development and farm income was much higher in the areas which produced export crops, for example, Kilimanjaro and West Lake, than those which did not. Within these areas, as indeed in other areas, small groups of individuals had also gained disproportionate wealth, and often, political power as well via control of the local party organization, cooperative unions, and other local institutions. Thus regional inequality and rural class formation were two tendencies that ujamaa policy was designed to rectify. The strategy adopted was to focus on the poor rural areas, especially those in the southern regions of the country, thus making a frontal attack on rural poverty. In fact, this was the specific rationale for the first government-coordinated campaign in the early 1970s to resettle in villages those peasants from the poorest regions, which produced no export crops.[27]

Given this strategy, it is also important that a disproportionately large number of the civil servants in Tanzania come from the regions of export crop production where resistance to ujamaa was strongest. This coincidence is largely explained by the legacy of colonial policy, which concentrated educational facilities in the areas of high potential, and by the greater ability of the residents of these areas to pay for education in their communities. In the context of ujamaa implementation, this has been a particularly significant factor because the government has had to rely on civil servants, as a result of an absence of party cadres in sufficient numbers to do the job. There were also few local political leaders who were themselves clear about the aims of ujamaa. Finally, as noted by Philip Raikes, some political leaders have adopted a bureaucratic and authoritarian style of leadership.[28] Thus it emerged that although ujamaa was to be implemented voluntarily by peasants, it was also a government policy, and, as such, the responsibility of civil servants, who measured success not so much in terms of transforming social relations within the villages as they did in terms of the number of villages established and the proportion of the population resettled in the new units. By training, inclination, and ongoing practice, administrators were accustomed to working through more receptive progressive farmers. Imbued with liberal doses of elitism, the administrators saw themselves as the bearers of modernity to a traditional peasantry.

In such circumstances, the democratic self-management of peasants often proved incomprehensible, if not antagonistic, to the bureaucratic patterns of thought. As a result, the goals of ujamaa were redefined; emphasis shifted from the cooperative and democratic aspects of management to a program of villagization—a longstanding policy dating from colonial times when the purpose was population control and provision of services.* Indeed, given the multitude of varying ecological and socioeconomic situations, different types of villages emerged after varying degrees of planning. The process of voluntary decision making by peasants through political education was replaced by one of bargaining over production targets and material inputs and involving differing degrees of coercion.[29] Raikes has identified several major categories of ujamaa villages, depending on the mode of their formation.[30] Naturally, such categories are not intended to be discrete or exclusive in any sense. They serve the limited purpose of giving clarity to the major trends of ujamaa development.

The first, and probably the earliest category of villages, dating back to 1968, are the self-initiated villages, which were started by peasants without prompting from the government officials, and which exemplify genuine attempts at self-reliant cooperative production. The second category of villages have been called "signposted" ujamaa villages—these were created overnight by declaration where a village already existed. Many traditional villages have turned ujamaa in this fashion, partly out of the need by officials to demonstrate the growth of ujamaa in their areas of jurisdiction. Some of the villages in the original village settlement scheme of the early 1960s are also to be included here. For this kind of village, it has been necessary subsequently to promote some form of communal production where none existed before signposting. The third most common type of ujamaa village, however, is that for which the Tanzanian government has provided various material inducements in the form of social services, subsidies, or grants of equipment and sometimes food. The majority of the villages created in the early 1970s in the poor regions and in the special campaign areas have been formed this way. This was a rational choice from the outset of the ujamaa program, insofar as it was justified by economies of scale against scattered and nucleated settlement. But such incentives also raise problems, some of which are discussed below.

The fourth, and most recent category of villages, are those founded through coercion. The use of coercion was clearly very minimal until after 1971, and particularly after the drought and food shortages beginning in 1972 and continuing into 1974. The government's resorting to coercion to

---

*In terms of population control the concentration of villages in the southern regions can be partly explained by the need for self-defense capabilities against the Portuguese attacks. In these regions, Mtwara and Ruvuma especially, self-defense and ujamaa were organized at the same time.

implement ujamaa was largely the result of what it regarded as the slow pace of villagization, despite the provision, at great cost,[31] of various social services and amenities to induce peasants to resettle on their own. Estimates of the number of people living in ujamaa villages vary widely, in large part because different observers employ different definitions of what constitutes a genuine ujamaa village, and what does not. However, by early 1973, it was generally acknowledged that the proportion of the population residing in ujamaa villages was somewhere in the neighborhood of 15 percent.[32]

In November 1973 TANU decided that all peasants in the country should be enrolled in villages within three years, through compulsory measures if necessary. Many civil servants interpreted this to mean that it would be even better if accomplished in one year. The result was a major dislocation of part of the rural population, which alienated many peasants, and greatly exacerbated the already serious problem of food shortages caused by the drought. Overzealous efforts by civil servants occurred during the course of several regional operations in which large numbers of people were summarily rounded up, at short notice, together with their belongings and trucked off to the site of their new village several miles away. In some cases, these moves were accompanied by the destruction of existing homes to insure that those moved would not return. Nonetheless, the regional operations did succeed in accelerating the pace of villagization, and by the end of 1974 some observers estimated that the proportion of the population residing in villages could be as high as 65 percent.[33]

It also appears that in the course of the drive to enroll the entire population in ujamaa, emphasis shifted in 1974 from formation of villages as socialist institutions to formation of villages as purely economic institutions.[34] Thus the term ujamaa has been replaced by "development villages," although it is assumed that the latter would in time evolve into socialist organizations. One result is that kulak ujamaa villages have emerged in some areas, particularly areas of high population density (and, hence, of surplus labor), and areas of cash-crop production. In some instances, "groups of wealthy farmers have formed 'ujamaa villages' which are closer in nature to joint stock companies, by dint of which they have been able to get hold of land previously used for other people or other purposes."[35] Only a minority of villages fall into this category, but the potential for such abuse cannot be ignored.

It is thus clear that the variety of situations and the differing dynamics of the local political economies have necessitated implementation of ujamaa in different ways. For the majority of villages, however, it is fair to say that material inducement and a certain amount of bureaucratic coercion have been employed, especially in recent years. This has resulted in several criticisms of the implementation of ujamaa, including those from the extreme left and the right, which point to bureaucratic coercion and the stifling of local initiative in decision making. To members of the extreme left, that is, Marxists, ujamaa suffers from a failure to come to grips with the existing class structure in the rural areas. The solution, therefore, lies in a campaign based exclusively on class considerations, which would eradicate rich peasants, local notables, and bureaucrats. The right, on the other hand, sees ujamaa as a form of welfare for the poor that merely drains resources from the most productive elements in the country. For its part, the Tanzanian government falls somewhere in between these two viewpoints, having committed itself to the eradication of absolute rural poverty and extreme regional (though not necessarily class) inequality as the first item on the development agenda. In the long run, the goal is to promote communal production in the entire country, including the export-crop areas currently least affected by the villagization process.

The frontal approach to villagization has also been compared to the forced collectivization in Russia in the 1930s, but the comparison may be farfetched. For in Russia, force was the only method used, if not the predominant one, while in Tanzania, we have seen that material inducement, at least until 1973, was the predominant method. But there is also a stark difference of aims, as suggested by Raikes:

> In Russia, forced collectivization had a clear purpose in squeezing more surplus out of the peasantry for the transformation of the economy in a massive industrialization effort. . . . In Tanzania there is as yet no plan for the overall transformation of the economy, and many of the *ujamaa* villages are entirely integrated into the previous dependency pattern through the production of export crops. Still more seriously, the *ujamaa* policy, far from generating or squeezing more surplus out of the peasants, appears to be a major drain on surplus, and likely to become more so.[36]

Raikes's point is underscored by the huge expenditures made by the Tanzanian government to finance villagization. Whereas in 1967 the government spent $6.3 million on agricultural development, in 1975 and 1976 the figure was $56 million in each year.[37]

This brings us to what is by far the most serious and valid criticism of Tanzania's ujamaa policy, at least in the short run; namely, that so far it has not led to any significant increases in agricultural productivity comparable to those found among small holders in Kenya but, on the contrary, has led to its decline. Only fragmentary data are available, but the broad outlines of the picture are clear. Between 1967 and 1973, the average annual rise in total output was only 2.7 percent at constant prices—the same as the estimated annual rate of population growth—and between

1970 and 1974 the marketed production of major cereal crops declined in each year except in 1972.[38]

Part of this decline in production, especially prior to 1974, can be attributed to the serious drought conditions that affected much of the northern part of the country. The sharpest decline, however, occurred in 1974 and was mainly a result of the dislocations caused by the accelerated process of villagization during that year. Many of the regional operations were carried out with little thought given to their impact on production, particularly the production of food. In some cases, peasants were forced to abandon fields which had already been planted, and they had to replant in the vicinity of their new villages after the season for doing so had passed. In others, peasants attempted to maintain their old plots by traveling back and forth between their fields and their new places of residence, an effort which expended much energy and time. In still other cases, those moved into new villages refused to farm at all.*

So serious was the decline in food production in 1974 and early 1975 that Tanzania was forced to import massive amounts of maize, wheat, and other cereals to feed its population. Thus, during the 1973/74 fiscal year, the National Milling Corporation (NMC), which was responsible for all grain purchases, both foreign and domestic, obtained 70 percent of its maize and 48 percent of its wheat from foreign sources, whereas it imported 41 percent of its maize and none of its wheat the year before. During the 1974/75 fiscal year, the full impact of the rural dislocations was felt when the NMC had to obtain over 90 percent of its maize and almost 80 percent of its wheat from foreign sources.[39]

By 1975, these imports had pushed Tanzania to the brink of financial disaster. The country's foreign-exchange reserves, which had been carefully built up over the preceding decade, and which had stood at a record high as late as February 1973, were exhausted, and Tanzania was forced to seek and accept emergency loans and grain shipments from the World Bank, the United States, Great Britain, Canada, and Sweden.[40] As indicated in Chapter 10 by Table 10.1, Tanzania's trade imports rose from $489 million in 1973 to $813 million in 1974 and to $843 million in 1975.

---

*Resistance was particularly strong in the area around Iringa, where, ironically, the local Hehe population had provided the most resistance to earlier efforts at villagization by both the Germans and the British during the colonial era. Though never formally acknowledged by the government, it was widely rumored that two government extension workers were shot during the course of the villagization operation in the Iringa area in 1974. The area was also the scene of the assassination in 1971 of Wilbert Klerru, the administrator in charge of villagization for the region. Klerru's confessed murderer was a rich peasant who said he had been frustrated by the administrator's strong-handed and overly bureaucratic methods of implementing ujamaa by declaration. It should be noted, however, that resistance of this type has been largely confined to areas of fairly large-scale kulak and cash-crop agriculture.

While part of these increases can be attributed to the rapid rise in the cost of petroleum imports, and to the inflationary spiral that affected the Western industrial economies during this period, the greatest proportion of the increase in imports, particularly from the United States and Canada, was attributable to food.[41]

Despite these figures, and despite their own claim that upward of 70 percent of the population were resettled between 1973 and the end of 1976, President Nyerere and the other government leaders have regarded the ujamaa policy as a success, and have refused to acknowledge (at least publicly) that the food shortages of 1974 and 1975 were a result of the villagization campaigns. On the other hand, the president and the government do acknowledge that Tanzania's most pressing problem is that of declining production, both in the agricultural and manufacturing sectors, and that production (especially in agriculture) must be raised if socialism is to be achieved.[42] As a result, Tanzania, since 1976, seems to have embarked on a policy of rural consolidation now that villagization has, for the most part, been accomplished. Production, rather than collectivist production, has been decreed the goal of the immediate future, and sanctioned as being consistent with the country's basic goal of socialist development. Prices to farmers, moreover, particularly for foodstuffs, have been raised to provide a stimulus to this end.[43]

It must also be recognized that, since 1976, domestic production of foodstuffs has started to rise, while imports have declined sharply. These figures suggest that it would be both unfair and hasty to judge the villagization program on the basis of its first few years of operation alone. Rural inequality cannot be eliminated without radical departures from the status quo, and since such departures are, by definition and necessity, of a revolutionary nature, it is not surprising that there have been serious dislocations in the short run. Moreover, one must not forget that whereas small-holder cash-crop agriculture in Kenya can boast almost 20 years' experience, and government assistance, the majority of ujamaa villages are only three years old.

Given that development is ultimately an ethical rather than a quantitative value, we may pose the question about what improvements ujamaa has brought to the rural poor in Tanzania in these terms. Here there can be no ambiguity about the success of the policy, largely experimental as the program still is, and however varied its impact in different areas and individual villages. The ujamaa policy has indeed brought about significant changes in Tanzania's political economy, and has the proven potential for bringing about a fundamental structural transformation of the rural sector of Tanzanian society in the long run.

As our discussion has shown, Tanzania's transition toward socialism in the rural areas has been neither uniform nor smooth, and the goal of a self-reliant, self-managed, and collectively organized peasantry is far from being achieved. Nevertheless, it would be premature to reach a final judgment on the policy solely on the basis of its implementation to date. Indeed, it would be facile to assume that there would be no mistakes in undertaking such a monumental task as accomplishing the relocation of nearly 13 million people in villages in the course of only nine years.

CONCLUSION

In this brief outline of Kenya's and Tanzania's rural development policies we have tried to illustrate how the former has retained the institutions of privilege under the colonial-settler society and accelerated the class development that was initiated as a deliberate counter-revolutionary measure during the Mau Mau insurgency. That there have been some economic successes as a result of this strategy cannot be doubted, even if the political assumptions on which it is based may prove unrealistic in the long term. But the economic success of Kenya's green revolution needs also to be placed within a wider context, taking into account Kenya's privileged position within the East African common market area. As noted above, the presence of white-settler agriculture was undoubtedly beneficial to agricultural research, the results of which after 1954 were made available to the small-scale farmers. However, the incentive for the small-scale farmers to increase their production must also be explained in terms of the buoyancy of the Kenyan market, and particularly the rapid expansion of processing industries in the period following World War II.

In Tanzania, on the other hand, there were no restrictions on cash-crop production; indeed, Africans had been producing profitable cash crops in the high-potential agricultural areas since the 1930s. But Tanzania's economy during British colonial rule was always subordinate to that of Kenya. Indeed, as discussed by Okumu in Chapter 10, Tanzania was a major market for Kenyan goods, and consistently ran a balance-of-trade deficit with its northern neighbor. It can be argued, then, that at independence, Tanzania was starting at a disadvantage relative to Kenya. Its economy was much less diversified; it relied on one crop, sisal, for a large part of its foreign exchange; and it was dependent to some extent on Kenyan goods and, especially, on the East African regional institutions, both public and private, which were controlled from Nairobi.

The adoption of rather austere policies, especially after the dramatic fall in sisal prices in the early 1960s, was in part a response to these rather adverse circumstances as well as others, including Tanzania's general inability to attract sufficient foreign aid and foreign private investment to facilitate its initial plans for development. So too were the policies adopted after the Arusha Declaration of 1967. Thus, whereas Kenya's policy of rural development has been purposely built upon the existing set of social relations, political power, and economic privilege found in the rural areas, Tanzania's has sought to transform the rural sector.

If we look ahead not ten, but 50, years from now, assuming no fundamental change in the basic model of development each country pursues, Kenya's economy will probably not appear qualitatively different from what it is now. There will be perhaps fewer large farm owners, but the basic problem of landlessness will undoubtedly be more acute than it is today. Tanzania, on the other hand, will perhaps not have achieved any spectacular level of development, but at least there will be no rural destitution. Part of this difference will result from the relative availability of arable land in the two countries, rather than from the developmental policies each will have pursued. But if a parallel may be allowed, Kenya will probably look more like present-day Mexico, or perhaps India, and Tanzania perhaps more like North Korea.

To get that far, however, both countries will have to adopt a more pragmatic posture toward the rural sector than that which they have pursued so far. Neither Kenya's unregulated capitalism nor Tanzania's command socialism will achieve what their proponents claim in the rural sector if they continue to evolve strictly within the terms of recent policy. Kenya's tentative attempt to create new land opportunities for the landless, and Tanzania's recognition that increasing production is a requisite for socialist transformation, indicate that the leadership of both countries are respectively aware of the fragility of their efforts and achievements to date. For until most people have some meaningful stake in the social order, that order, regardless of the model of development on which it is based, will not survive.

NOTES

1. An evaluation of this type of program is contained in Vernon W. Ruttan, "Rural Development Programs: A Skeptical Perspective" (Paper presented at the Colloquium on "New Concepts and Technologies in Third World Urbanization," University of California, Los Angeles, May 17–18, 1974). See also Alvin Bertrand, "Definitions and Strategies of Rural Development: A Search for Coherence and Congruity," *Sociologia Ruralis* 12, nos. 3/4 (1972): pp. 233–51.

2. See *United Nations Statistical Yearbook, 1973* (New York: United Nations, 1974), p. 24. Between 1961 and 1972, the so-called decade of development, the overall rate of economic growth in the rural areas of most third-world countries barely increased, while the per capita purchasing power (at constant prices) of most rural residents in most cases declined. Taking 1963 = 100 as the base year, indexes of economic growth for the rural sector by region are as follows:

Region	1961	1972
Africa	96	101
Asia	100	97
Latin America	100	98
Middle East	96	109
World	99	104

3. On class relations in the countryside and implementation of development policies, see Philip L. Raikes, "Differentiation and Progressive Farmer Policies" (Paper presented at the East Africa Agricultural Economics Society Conference, Kampala, June 1972).

4. For an extended discussion of the causes and events leading up to the nationalist insurrection, see Carl G. Rosberg, Jr. and John Nottingham, *The Myth of Mau Mau* (New York: Praeger, 1966).

5. See Troup, *Colony and Protectorate of Kenya, Report of the Inquiry Into the General Economy of Farming in the Highlands* (Nairobi: Government Printer, 1953); F. W. Carpenter, *Report of the Committee on African Wages* (Nairobi: Government Printer, 1954); R. T. M. Swynnerton, *A Plan to Intensify the Development of African Agriculture in Kenya* (Nairobi: Government Printer, 1954); and United Kingdom, "The Royal East Africa Commission of 1952–1955 Report," Cmd. 9475 (London: Her Majesty's Stationery Office, 1955).

6. Measures suggested by the Carpenter committee and subsequent attempts to stabilize urban labor have only partially succeeded, in the absence of adequate security and retirement benefits for the majority of urban workers. In these circumstances the security of membership in an extended family, contingent upon rights over land, has operated against the development of a permanent urban industrial proletariat. A correct description of the bulk of African urban workers sees their families as comprising two households, one in the city and the other in the country. See Gary P. Ferraro, "Urban and Rural Identities in East Africa: A False Dichotomy," *Southern Anthropological Society Proceedings* 8 (1974): 92–105; T. G. McGee, "Peasants in Cities: A Paradox, A Paradox, A Most Ingenious Paradox," *Human Organization* 32, no. 2 (1973): 135–42; and, especially, Thomas S. Weisner, "One Family, Two Households: Rural-Urban Network Model of Urbanism," *Annual Conference Proceedings* (University of East Africa Social Science Council) 8 (1969): 1001–23.

7. See M. P. K. Sorrenson, "Counter Revolution to Mau Mau: Land Consolidation in Kikuyuland, 1952–1960," mimeographed (Kampala: East African Institute of Social Research, June 1963).

8. Evaluations of the small-holder program show that production per acre is much higher for coffee, tea, maize, and dairy products than it is in the larger mixed farms or plantations. More recent statistical analysis also demonstrates that the profit margin is higher for smaller than for larger farms; thus in one area the optimum size of land is between 4 and 7 hectares. But considering that the average size of land holdings in the area is only 0.4 hectares, it becomes obvious that it is the wealthier small-holder farmers with relatively larger holdings who are in a position to maximize profits. See Rodney Wilson, "Land Control in Kenya's Small-holder Farming Areas," *East African Journal of Rural Development* 5, nos. 1/2 (1972): 123–40.

9. Judith Heyer, "The Origins of Regional Inequalities in Smallholder Agriculture in Kenya, 1920–1973," *East African Journal of Rural Development* 8, nos. 1/2 (1975): 171.

10. See Gary Wasserman, "Continuity and Counter-Insurgency: The Role of Land Reform in Decolonizing Kenya, 1962–1970," *Canadian Journal of African Studies* 7, no. 1 (1973): 133–48.

11. The Million Acre Scheme was initially financed by a £7.5 million loan from Britain, the Commonwealth Development Corporation, and the World Bank. It was subsequently

supplemented by other schemes, and ultimately embraced 1.5 million acres. About 500,000 people are estimated to have been settled under these schemes, or roughly 4 percent of the Kenyan population in 1970. For details on the evolution of the Million Acre Scheme, see Colin Leys, *Underdevelopment in Kenya* (Berkeley: University of California Press, 1974), pp. 73–75.

12. Ibid., pp. 92–96.

13. International Labour Office, *Employment Incomes and Equality: A Strategy for Increasing Productive Employment in Kenya* (Geneva: International Labour Office, 1972), pp. 33–34. The ILO's estimate of 0.8 hectares per person was based on the population in 1969, and on an estimate that 11 percent of Kenya's land area is suited for cultivation. According to the International Association of Agricultural Economists, however, the figure is closer to 2.8 percent if one limits the estimate of the amount of arable land to land that is of reasonable quality and has reliable rainfall. With an estimated population of 13.8 million in 1978, this means that the average amount of arable land per person in Kenya is now approximately .12 hectares. See International Association of Agricultural Economists, *World Atlas of Agriculture*, vol. 4 (Novara, Italy: Instituto Geografico De Agostini, 1976), p. 254.

14. See Republic of Kenya, *African Socialism and Its Application to Planning in Kenya*, Sessional Paper no. 10 (Nairobi: Government Printer, 1965), par. 133. For a brief critical evaluation of the economic implications of the paper, see Peter Marris, "Economics Is Not Enough," *East Africa Journal* 3, no. 11 (February 1967): 19–26.

15. Frank Holmquist, "Implementing Rural Development Projects," in *Development Administration: the Kenyan Experience*, ed. Goran Hyden, Robert Jackson, and John Okumu (Nairobi: Oxford University Press, 1970), p. 223.

16. E. M. Godfrey and G. C. M. Mutiso, "The Political Economy of Self-Help: Kenya's 'Harambee' Institutes of Technology," *Canadian Journal of African Studies* 8, no. 1 (1974): 118.

17. See the section on agricultural production in the Kenyan *Economic Survey*, which is published annually by the Government Printer, Nairobi. For a summary of the rates of growth of commercial agriculture in Kenya, see Table 1.2.

18. Roger Van Zwanenberg, "Neocolonialism and the Origin of the National Bourgeoisie in Kenya between 1940 and 1973," *Journal of Eastern African Research and Development* 4 (1974): 172.

19. James C. Scott, *The Moral Economy of the Peasant* (New Haven: Yale University Press, 1976), especially chaps. 1 and 2.

20. International Labour Office, op. cit., chap. 1.

21. Based on the estimates of the International Association of Agricultural Economists, 4.5 percent of Tanzania's land area is considered arable. Based on an estimated population of 15.1 million in 1978, this means that the average amount of arable land per person in Tanzania is now approximately .26 hectares, which is slightly more than double the amount of .12 hectares per person in Kenya. See International Association of Agricultural Economists, *World Atlas of Agriculture*, vol. 4. (Novara: Instituto Geografico De Agostini, 1976), pp. 254, 676.

22. See International Bank for Reconstruction and Development, *The Economic Development of Tanganyika* (Baltimore: Johns Hopkins Press, 1960), and B. Kaplan, *New Settlement and Agricultural Development in Tanganyika* (Jerusalem: State of Israel, 1961).

23. See P. M. Landell-Mills, "On the Economic Appraisal of Agricultural Development Projects; the Tanzanian Village Settlement Schemes," *Agricultural Economic Bulletin for Africa* (United Nations, Economic Commission for Africa), no. 8 (1966).

24. Julius K. Nyerere, *Education for Self-Reliance* (Dar es Salaam: Government Printer, 1967), and *Socialism and Rural Development* (Dar es Salaam: Government Printer, 1967).

25. In proposing the ujamaa policy, President Nyerere argued that the new policy was a modern actualization of the principles of traditional African society, whose foundation consists of respect for each person, the sharing of property, and the obligation to work. I have argued elsewhere that there is no direct relationship between traditional forms of communal

living and modern cooperatives, and that to suggest such a link is to promote a myth, albeit a useful one, intended to justify a program that may not be popular among certain categories of the population; see S. E. Migot-Adholla, "Traditional Society and Cooperatives," in *Cooperatives and Rural Development in East Africa,* ed. Carl G. Widstrand (Uppsala: Scandinavian Institute of African Studies, 1970), pp. 17–38.

26. Tanganyika African National Union, *Mwongozo wa TANU* [TANU party guidelines] (Dar es Salaam: Government Printer, 1971).

27. Calculations show that by 1971, more than 55 percent of the ujamaa villages and 88 percent of the population residing in them were located in only 4 regions out of the 18. See Antony Ellman, "Development of *Ujamaa* Policy in Tanzania," in *Rural Cooperation in Tanzania,* ed. L. Cliffe, P. Lawrence, W. Luttrell, S. E. Migot-Adholla, and J. S. Saul (Dar es Salaam: Tanzania Publishing House, 1975), p. 321, table 2.

28. This and the following paragraphs on problems of implementation of ujamaa policy are a summary of the incisive account by Philip Raikes, "Ujamaa and Rural Socialism," *Review of African Political Economy,* no. 3 (May–October 1975): 33–53.

29. Michaela von Freyhold has labeled this "planning and bargaining," in "Government Staff and Ujamaa Villages in Handeni," mimeographed (Dar es Salaam: Department of Economics, University of Dar es Salaam, 1972), cited in Raikes, op. cit.

30. Raikes, op. cit., p. 44.

31. Hyden estimates that approximately $70 million was spent on ujamaa between 1969 and 1974, an average of $14 million per year. See Goran Hyden, "Ujamaa Villagization and Rural Development in Tanzania," *O. D. I. Review* (Sussex, England), no. 1 (April 1975): 64.

32. Ibid., p. 56.

33. Ibid., p. 67. See also Dean E. McHenry, Jr., "Rural Policy Divergence: Communal Farming in Ujamaa Villages" (Paper presented at the annual conference of the Universities of East Africa Social Science Council, Nairobi, December 15–21, 1975), p. 3.

34. Hyden, op. cit., p. 67.

35. Raikes, op. cit., p. 45.

36. Ibid., p. 47.

37. The figures were those cited by President Nyerere in his own critical review of the performance of Tanzanian agriculture. See Julius K. Nyerere, *The Arusha Declaration: Ten Years After* (Dar es Salaam: Government Printer, 1977), p. 19.

38. "Back to Back: A Survey of Kenya and Tanzania," *The Economist,* March 11, 1978.

39. These figures are estimates given in "Statement of Maize and Wheat Supply and Distribution for the Period 1969/70 to 1974/75," mimeographed (Dar es Salaam; National Milling Corp., 1974).

40. Michael F. Lofchie, "Agrarian Socialism in the Third World: The Tanzanian Case," *Comparative Politics* 8, no. 3 (April 1976): 483.

41. Hyden, citing statistics from the Bank of Tanzania, notes that imports of food exceeded those of petroleum beginning in the first quarter of 1974. The same conclusion can be deduced, albeit only in rough dimensions, from the data in Table 10.1. Thus the reader will note that, while in 1975 imports from the United States and Canada ballooned to 15 percent of Tanzania's total, Tanzania's imports from oil-producing countries dropped to 17 percent. See Hyden, op. cit., p. 67.

42. See Nyerere, *The Arusha Declaration: Ten Years After,* op. cit., pp. 19–22.

43. Ibid., p. 20. The prices paid farmers for such cash crops as coffee and tea, however, so far have not kept pace with the rise in the world price of these products. It is as a stimulus to food production, however, where the need is greatest, to avert a repeat of the shortfalls of 1974–75.

8

URBAN POLICY

Richard E. Stren

By THE SECOND HALF of the 1970s it was becoming increasingly clear all over the third world that the urban population explosion was producing a crisis of monumental proportions. Although most third-world societies outside Latin America are predominantly rural, their larger cities have been growing at historically unprecedented rates,[1] while resources to cope with demands for employment and services have been severely limited. The results of these twin pressures are that many basic services (such as housing, water supplies, and health facilities) have been deteriorating in quality and general accessibility, and that the distribution of scarce benefits has increasingly favored the rich and the powerful.[2] In its influential attempts to improve both the efficiency and distribution of urban services, the World Bank has stressed the importance of comprehensive urban policy and its articulation within a wider development strategy.[3] But most African governments have yet to develop explicit urban policies, much less situate such policies within an overall economic, social, and political strategy for national development. Kenya and Tanzania are unusual in this respect, since their urban policies have been well established for some time, and interrelate closely with their clearly stated development strategies.

In analyzing urban policies in Kenya and Tanzania, and the planning framework within which they have been set since independence, we will attempt in this chapter to suggest how urban processes are reflective of a deeper dimension of political and economic life. The boundaries of this

This chapter is an extensively revised and updated version of an earlier article entitled "Urban Policy and Performance in Kenya and Tanzania," which appeared in the *Journal of Modern African Studies* 13 2, (1975). The author wishes to thank Cambridge University Press for permission to reproduce sections of the original article in this chapter.

dimension are established by the goals of growth and redistribution; Kenya has stressed the first, and Tanzania, the second. But neither emphasis is free of important gaps between general goals and ultimate performance. How these gaps have emerged will be clear from an analysis of urban policy and performance in the two countries. In the discussion which follows, three policy areas are singled out for more intensive examination—land allocation, housing, and urban planning. The material which covers these areas is extensive enough to permit comparison, and the policy areas themselves are particularly important for low-income groups in both countries.

URBAN POLICY AND PERFORMANCE IN KENYA

Policy

In the first few years after independence, Kenya did little to define its urban development policy. The value of private buildings constructed in the main towns—a sensitive indicator of economic growth—fell precipitously from $2.9 million in 1959 to $581,000 in 1963, and did not begin to rise appreciably again until 1967.[4] At the same time the urban population was swelling; from 1948 to 1962, census figures showed an average rate of growth of 6.3 percent per annum.[5] Taking the African population of the two largest towns, Nairobi and Mombasa, the figures were 6.5 percent and 7.1 percent, respectively, compared with 2.8 percent for the whole country. Between the 1962 and 1969 censuses, the number of Africans in Nairobi and in Mombasa grew at a compound annual rate of 11.1 percent and 7.6 percent, respectively.[6] These growth rates, in combination with the decline in private building, put tremendous pressure on the government to deal with housing in a more aggressive manner.

The government initially responded by calling in the experts. Subsequently, a UN report published in May 1965 found that the country was experiencing "a serious housing problem"; moreover, in comparison with accommodations for other people, African housing was of poorer quality and overcrowding was "extreme."[7] Machinery to deal with these shortages fell into two categories: regulatory and developmental. On the regulatory side, in 1967 tribunals were set up in the main towns, with powers to control rents on unfurnished dwellings with a "standard rent" of $112 or less. In theory these tribunals (under a new Rent Control Act) should have been able to regulate all rents in lower- and middle-income housing throughout the country. As a developmental response, the government, following a suggestion from the UN report, established in 1967 a National Housing Corporation (NHC), with powers to directly undertake housing projects throughout Kenya, as well as to make loans to local authorities, who would handle the building and managing of the projects. The NHC was to be a more vigorous descendant of the former Central Housing Board, which needed "to have a new image in playing a role which is in keeping with the spirit of the new, independent Kenya."[8]

The *Development Plan, 1970–1974,* recognizing "an imperative need to accelerate the creation of inexpensive urban housing for the low income groups," stipulated that all government funds given to the NHC would be for houses costing $430 or less. Even at this figure, only 17 percent of urban households could afford more expensive housing. As a gesture to the very lowest income groups, however, the plan also specified that 33 percent of the NHC funds allocated would have to be spent on site-and-service schemes in urban housing; these would provide planned alternatives to the "large and expanding illegal squatter areas near the urban centres." Finally, in addition to planning for the physical growth of Nairobi and Mombasa, it was proposed to take "positive steps . . . to decentralize future urban growth" among seven other towns designated as "major growth centres."[9]

The government's expressed commitment to site-and-service schemes for the lower-income groups was consistent with its eventual support, in principle, of many of the innovative recommendations of the 1972 study by the International Labour Office (ILO), *Employment, Incomes and Equality.* Recommendations of this study that were accepted by the goverment included the abandonment of slum demolition for its own sake, and "vigorous action" to raise incomes and facilitate more employment in the "informal sector."[10] In supporting part of the redistributive program implied by the ILO study, the Kenyan government was backed by a major World Bank study of the country's economic policies.[11] In the new *Development Plan 1974–1978,* policy objectives regarding low-income settlements were, nevertheless, phrased almost as if the ILO study had never existed. Thus, the government pledged itself, inter alia, to "ensure that housing design and construction conform to government standards and that each housing unit constructed in urban areas shall have at least two rooms, plus its own kitchen and toilet"; and, in addition, "to ensure that . . . no additional unauthorized housing settlements are erected . . . [and that] slums are removed when satisfactory alternative housing has been found. . . ."[12]

In general, the new plan document seemed to reinforce the existing urban development strategy in Kenya, with the ILO recommendations playing at best a marginal role in policy objectives and analysis. While the previous plan allocated some K£12.69 million to the NHC,[13] the new plan gave the NHC about twice as much at current prices (K£5.44 million).[14] As in the previous plan, all NHC funds were earmarked for housing units costing no more than K£1,200; this time, however, the proportion to be spent on sites and services was raised to fully 61 percent of the total NHC program.[15] Following a study by Robert Merrill (a sites-and-services expert and former adviser to the World Bank and the Tanzanian goverment) in 1975, the NHC set up a Site and Service Department and published an elaborate set of guidelines for a nationwide program.[16] By 1977 the government was considering an additional program that would involve some 20,000 new site-and-service plots, together with the upgrading of many existing squatter settlements in Nairobi, Mombasa, and Kisumu.

Performance

In the period under review two main biases appear in the implementation of urban policy in Kenya: a disproportionate extension of services and benefits to middle- and upper-income groups, and an emphasis on prestige development in Nairobi.

The construction program of the NHC illustrates the first bias very clearly. As Table 8.1 shows, the corporation spent a total of K£20,155,800 on 12,932 conventional housing units from 1969 to 1975, for an overall average cost per unit of K£1,559. During 1974 and 1975, inflationary pressures produced average unit costs of K£2,000 and K£1,760, respectively. The average cost of an NHC house in 1974 was roughly twice what an average civil servant could afford.[17] Thus, as the third plan period was getting underway, the average cost of public housing completed was already much higher than the maximum cost permitted to the NHC in the plan itself. According to the 1975 *Economic Survey,* problems in Nairobi were severe:

> Nairobi City Council's waiting list for houses indicates a growing shortage of houses in Nairobi, and probably in the country as a whole. The number on the waiting list in Nairobi had risen to a peak of 27,756 by March, 1975. In Nairobi 60 percent of the people on the waiting list earned less than K.Sh. 833 a month compared with a rental of K.Sh. 650 a month for a three-bedroomed flat in Nairobi's most recently completed housing scheme. The sharp rise in building costs is making it progressively more difficult for people on low incomes to be provided with adequate housing.[18]

In addition to its public housing activities carried out through the NHC, the government also builds for its own civil servants.[19] Over the five-year period from 1970 to 1975, the Ministry of Works built 3,675 units of lower-cost "institutional housing" and 599 units of higher-cost "pool housing," for government employees. The average cost of these units had reached $1,310 and $1,900, respectively, by 1975, suggesting that a large

TABLE 8.1: Kenya National Housing Corporation: Units Completed, and Cost, 1969–75

	Site-and-Service Units		Conventional Units		
Year	Number	Cost (K£)	Number	Cost (K£)	Total Cost
1969	48	4,000	1,880	2,644,000	2,648,000
1970	169	39,000	2,171	2,442,000	2,481,000
1971	1,465	313,000	1,737	1,902,000	2,215,000
1972	2,100	271,000	2,498	4,425,000	4,696,000
1973	96	16,000	1,094	2,145,000	2,161,000
1974	0	0	1,441	2,882,000	2,882,000
1975	363	168,500	2,111	3,715,800	3,884,300
Total	4,241	811,500	12,932	20,155,800	20,967,300

Sources: Ministry of Housing data, 1973; Statistical Abstract 1974 (Nairobi: Government Printer, 1974); Kenya, Economic Survey 1976 (Nairobi: Government Printer, 1976); National Housing Corp., Annual Report, 1975 (Nairobi: NHC, 1975).

element of public subsidy was involved in renting these houses to (already relatively affluent) civil servants at a cost they could afford.

Other factors besides cost have further narrowed the group to whom the benefits of public housing schemes accrue. Because market rents in Kenya's towns are considerably greater than the monthly repayment costs to the local authorities who manage public housing schemes once they have been built by the NHC, tenant-purchase houses are seen as an especially lucrative investment by the political and economic elite. The allocation committees of the municipal councils have been the focus of most intense political pressure, with the result that strict adherence to waiting-list and points procedures (as prescribed by the Ministry of Local Government) has often been circumvented. Subletting of public rental housing and tenant-purchase housing is very widely spread in Kenya, although it is, in most cases, formally illegal. A study of a tenant-purchase scheme administered by the Thika Municipal Council found that five-sixths of the houses were not occupied by the original purchasers; houses had been rented out on a room-to-room basis, thus tripling the number of households in the scheme as compared to original estimates, and changing the way the houses were used; and many landlords were collecting total rents which were approximately double the amount of the monthly payments to the municipal council.[20] And for the Pumwani Redevelopment Scheme (Phase 1) in Nairobi, Janet Bujra discovered in 1971 that just over half the landlords who had been allocated the new flats no longer lived in them. These absentee landlords made the biggest profits, since, compared with the charges to the city council of from $32 to $39 per month, they were receiving market rents of from Sh. 350 to Sh. 425 per month. The landlords who had been able to take advantage of this particular scheme were among the wealthiest in Pumwani, in the first place. The same trend was noted in the Pumwani Relief Scheme, where more than half the original tenant-purchasers sublet in order to take advantage of the difference between open-market rents ($39 per month) and repayment charges to the council ($19 per month).[21]

Conventional housing is not the whole story. As we have seen, the two most recent plans have clearly recognized that, because of costs, those in the lowest-income groups—whom the government has explicitly committed itself to help—cannot afford the payments on conventionally built houses or flats. The alternative is site-and-service schemes, according to which public authorities organize the plots and lay in minimal services, while the individual plot allottees are expected to build their own houses. As the figures in Table 8.1 show, the government has been very slow in living up to its public commitments in this field; out of a total of K£ 20,967,300 spent during 1969–75 on all forms of public housing, only K£811,500, or 4 percent—as compared with the targets in the two plans of 33 percent and 61 percent—was spent on sites and services. Although the NHC now seems to recognize its responsibility to improve performance in this area, its general manager feels that political opposition is the key problem. As he puts it:

> Politicians, both at local and national levels, are anxious to see their constituents housed in modern buildings constructed to a reasonably high standard; and in many urban areas there is opposition in principle to the concentration of housing development in Site and Service Schemes. This opposition must be overcome to enable the (Site and Service Scheme) Programme to be satisfactorily completed. So, some means must be sought to reconcile the views between what is politically and socially desirable on the one hand and, on the other, what is economically possible.[22]

The general manager's remarks apply especially well to the large, World Bank-financed site-and-service project in Dandora, in the eastern part of Nairobi. Although planning for the 6,000-plot Dandora scheme was underway as early as 1972, and an agreement was signed with the World Bank for a concessionary loan in 1974, construction work was repeatedly interrupted by Ministry of Health objections to what it considered unacceptably low standards for ventilation and plot coverage in the "core units."[23] Although World Bank and Nairobi City Council pressure ironed out these problems by early 1977, another, smaller project at Kibera had already been halted for similar reasons. In any case, the projected cost per unit in the Dandora scheme was substantially above what low-income families could afford, and inflationary construction costs promised to limit the target population still further.

These biases in the implementation of public housing programs are not compensated for in other directions. The rent-control machinery, for example, is not effective in helping the poor. In some low-income areas there have been physical threats against rent-control officials. And, indeed, legal safeguards under the Rent Control Act are not easily within the reach of most Africans because of complicated procedures and charges.[24] As for approved housing constructed by the private sector, which is much greater in value than that built by the government, the great majority are expensive houses far beyond the reach of both the provisions of the Rent Restriction Act and lower-income groups.

The typical response to this kind of urban policy bias all over the developing world has been that of squatting, in various forms, and Kenya is no exception. In 1971 a comprehensive study estimated that one-third of Nairobi's population was living in "uncontrolled and illegal housing."[25] The largest single area was Mathare Valley, where it was estimated that about 50,000 people were living. In Mombasa, Kenya's second largest town, it is more difficult for the authorities to control residential building, since most residential land is in private-freehold tenure, and constant police action against rate-paying landowners who permit illegal building would undermine the political support of the local authority. In 1969 a detailed study estimated that 31 percent of all residential land was occupied by "unplanned temporary" housing, and that 47 percent of the inhabitants of Mombasa—or, some 116,000 of the total population of 247,073 —lived in such housing.[26]

Urban officials in Kenya have tried to regulate squatting in two main ways: through by-law application and large-scale demolition. Municipal by-laws require that all plans for building within the city boundaries be submitted to the local councils for approval. Although in 1968 a new set of building by-laws containing lower (Grade-2) standards was appended to the main regulations, specifically for designated lower-income areas in the larger towns, most squatter housing, and even site-and-service housing, is beneath the Grade-2 levels, according to various criteria. In any case, fully effective controls through by-laws depend on three factors, which are rarely present at the same time: a vigilant, honest building inspectorate with cooperation from the police and the administration; an adequately staffed town planning agency; and the political will to demolish structures which do not meet established standards.

The demolition of low-income slum or squatter areas has a long history in Kenya, dating back to the early days of Nairobi when the government demolished African villages in order to oblige all Africans to live in a single location for natives. During most of the colonial period, the government systematically razed so-called shantytowns within Nairobi, in many cases not even attempting to provide alternative accommodations for those who lost their homes. Through the emergency period, from 1952 to 1960, these operations were tied to two political objectives: screening possible subversive elements—mainly the Kikuyu, Embu, and Meru—and controlling immigration to the city. When the emergency regulations were lifted in early 1960, the flood of Kikuyu migration from areas surrounding the city swamped the administration. Thousands of Africans began to trade without licenses and to build wherever they could find land. After the new central government consolidated its power during the mid-1960s, there were several large demolition and clean-up campaigns aimed at ridding the city's central area of squatters.

In 1970, the year following National Assembly elections, the City Council of Nairobi, together with the administration and the police, mounted a massive clean-up campaign extending over several months. According to a careful strategy, which covered all the major squatter areas except Mathare Valley and Kibera, city council *askaris* and police would arrive at dawn to surprise the people before they left for work, finishing their demolition in time for lunch. During 1970 this campaign resulted in the demolition of about 10,000 squatter dwellings, leaving some 50,000 people homeless. Although there was public criticism of this campaign, it was supported by the cabinet,[27] and President Kenyatta later told a council delegation he did not want Nairobi to turn into a "shanty-town."[28] Since then, the city council has regularly demolished visible shanties along road reserves, in the central city, and on state and city council land.

As a partial exception to the policy of regular demolition, two large areas of substandard housing have been relatively untouched: Dagoretti and Mathare Valley. Both have, in recent years, been represented by powerful national politicians who have vigorously worked to protect their constituencies. Neither area is likely to be seen by casual European tourists visiting Nairobi.

Although Dagoretti is a semirural area on the outskirts of Nairobi, Mathare Valley is only a few miles from the city center. Mathare was subject to periodic demolition until 1971, when the whole string of villages was improved with roads, streetlighting, and water and sanitary facilities, following an outbreak of cholera elsewhere in Nairobi. Although there are still occasional crackdowns on the women who brew *chang'aa*, the city council has demolished only when called in by administrative officers. Thus, while the population of Mathare grew by an estimated 36.8 percent between 1971 and 1976 (to a total of about 69,000), the number of dwellings increased by only 11.4 percent during the same period.[29] In general, the growth of illegal housing in Nairobi has been contained, if by no means completely controlled. But with few services being extended to existing substandard areas so far, the effect is that more and more overcrowding takes place in increasingly unhealthy conditions.

The second dimension of urban policy bias in Kenya is the disproportionate share taken by Nairobi in physical development. While both the 1970–74 plan and its successor have sought to spread development more evenly among other urban growth centers, no trend in this direction is evident from official statistics. From 1967 through 1975, Nairobi's share of the value of new private construction in the main towns actually rose from 78.3 percent to 81.8 percent although there was some variation from year to year.[30] But from 1970 through 1975, Nairobi's total share for all years stood at 77.8 percent. Moreover, the value of new public building during the 1970–75 period was only 42 percent of the value of private building; most of this public building appears to have taken place in Nairobi.[31]

An important reflection of Nairobi's disproportionate share in national urban development is the slow growth of trade and employment elsewhere. In the case of Kisumu, Kenya's fourth largest town, Africanization of the central business district in the early 1970s caused such a fall in trade that a local reporter for a major newspaper referred to it as "a dying town."[32] Nairobi's share in total reported earnings, as shown in Table 8.2, is considerably larger than its share of the total population in the main towns. Moreover, Nairobi's share of total earnings rose consistently from 1969 to 1973, while the share of almost every other official growth center fell or remained relatively static during this period.

The most significant exception to this pattern of dominance by Nairobi is in the field of tourism. Partly as a result of strong European demand for package tours to the Kenyan coast, and of government promotion of coastal tourism in general, Mombasa and the coast have moved close to Nairobi in terms of available hotel beds. In 1970 Nairobi had 41.4 percent of available beds (per night) in the country, and Mombasa and the coast had only 34.1 percent.[33] But by 1975, after considerable expansion in and around both urban areas, Nairobi's share stood at 40.3 percent, and the share of Mombasa and the coast at 39.0 percent.[34] Since in recent years tourism has earned roughly as much foreign exchange as coffee (with the exception of the period of very high coffee prices), the development of luxury tourism around Nairobi and Mombasa is a major element in the government's overall economic strategy. In both Nairobi and Mombasa, there is a strong feeling among members of the administrative elite that clean cities and a high quality of urban services are necessary in order to maintain the tourist trade. The modernness of Nairobi is also taken as a sign that the country has developed. Thus, when Kenya celebrated her tenth anniversary of independence in December 1973, the capital's imposing skyline (dominated by the K£4 million Kenyatta Conference Centre)

TABLE 8.2: Reported Earnings in Main Towns of Kenya for Selected Years, Compared with Population in 1969

Town	1969 Population	Percent	Reported Earnings, 1969 Total (K£ 1,000)	Percent	Reported Earnings, 1971 Total (K£ 1,000)	Percent	Reported Earnings, 1973 Total (K£ 1,000)	Percent
Nairobi	509,286	57.0	72,504	69.8	88,160	71.5	106,311	72.7
Mombasa	247,073	27.7	18,536	17.9	20,844	16.9	25,858	17.7
Nakuru	47,151	5.3	4,086	3.9	4,555	3.7	4,784	3.3
Kisumu	32,431	3.6	3,515	3.4	3,819	3.1	3,512	2.4
Thika	18,387	2.1	1,318	1.3	1,739	1.4	2,281	1.6
Eldoret	18,196	2.0	2,167	2.1	2,376	1.9	1,231	.8
Nyeri	10,084	1.1	1,236	1.2	1,328	1.1	1,399	.9
Kakamega	6,244	.7	256	.2	260	.2	542	.4
Embu	3,928	.4	201	.2	229	.2	402	.3
Totals	892,700	99.9	103,819	100.0	123,310	100.0	146,320	100.1

Sources: Kenya *Statistical Abstract 1974* (Nairobi: Government Printer, 1974), p. 272; Kenya, *Kenya Population Census, 1969 Volume II* (Nairobi: Ministry of Economic Planning and Development, 1969), p. 2.

was prominently displayed in the press, in newsreels, and on television as a symbol of the country's progress.

URBAN POLICY AND PERFORMANCE IN TANZANIA

Policy

Until the late 1960s, Tanzania, like Kenya and almost all other African countries, had an ad hoc patchwork of policies to deal with her growing urban problems. As elsewhere on the continent, private construction in mainland Tanzania fell sharply at independence. Although the fall in private building was more than offset by government building in the urban areas, the value of all construction never regained its former levels even by the late 1960s.[35] Meanwhile, the African population was growing rapidly. In Dar es Salaam there had been an average rate of increase of 9 percent per annum from 1948 to 1957,[36] but this had shot up to 14 percent between the 1957 and 1967 censuses.[37] High rates of growth, especially for the African (and predominantly low-income) population, were also notable for a number of other, smaller towns.

Until the watershed Arusha Declaration in 1967, Tanzania pursued a building and a land-control strategy to alleviate the pressure for urban housing and community services. The building strategy began with the establishment in 1962 of the National Housing Corporation (NHC), then given a very broad mandate "for the provision of houses and other buildings in Tanganyika by means of financial assistance and otherwise."[38] After taking over 4,389 low-cost houses that had been built by the colonial government and administered by local authorities, the corporation made "a heroic attempt to seriously cope with the housing problem."[39] The first major program, concentrating in Dar es Salaam, on the initiative of President Nyerere, involved clearing some of the old slums on the periphery of the central business district (in Magomeni especially), and replacing them with new, single-story houses that were rented out to the previous owners. The Tanzanian NHC was to operate very differently from its Kenyan counterpart:

> Unlike the National Housing Corporation in Kenya, which is essentially an institution for channelling finance to private-sector contractors, the National Housing Corporation in Tanzania immediately set about building up its own capacity for the implementation of construction projects. And its methods of operation are essentially different from the system prevailing in the private-sector. Projects are planned and designed by the National Housing Corporation staff; materials are standardized, centrally-produced, and delivered on-site by the National Housing Corporation

itself—or by its subsidiary, 'TACONA'. Teams of craftsmen and labour-
ers are then employed directly, on a piece-work basis, and supervised by
the National Housing Corporation's own building inspectors, who have
been trained specifically for this function.[40]

Whereas, as late as 1975, the Kenyan NHC employed only about 170 staff
members, Tanzania's NHC employed several thousand staff and full-time
workers during most of its active period.

During the first plan period, from 1964 to 1969, about 70 percent of
the 5,705 low cost houses built by the Tanzanian NHC came under the Dar
es Salaam slum-clearance scheme.[41] Although what constitues a low-cost
house has never been clearly defined either for or by the NHC, almost all
its efforts have focused on this category of accommodations. During the
five-year period, the corporation received some T£3.47 million from the
government, and was able to raise an additional T£970,000 from the
Federal Republic of Germany, which also provided significant technical
aid. The total from these two sources, however, was only about 25 percent
of the target figure in the plan.

The second major approach to urban development throughout the
1960s was the control and allocation of land by the government. Under a
series of acts beginning in 1963,[42] all freehold land was converted to
government leasehold, and the previous owners were now obliged to pay
rent. Conditions for development were laid down for the use of all urban
land, with the details agreed upon by the Town Planning Division and the
Lands Division. The zoning policy of the colonial government, which
divided residential urban land into low-, medium-, and high-density areas,
was continued, but the emphasis on plot allocation and the provision of
services was shifted from the former European areas to the high-density
(and low-income) African areas.

In the early 1970s the Land Division prepared for public allocation
some 6,000–7,000 plots annually, most of them in high-density urban
areas. The bulk of these were given out with year-to-year rights of occupancy. This would allow the occupant, upon payment of a premium down,
and an annual land rent, to build a temporary structure using traditional
materials. Before any new urban area is laid out for such development, it
is the practice in Tanzania to fully compensate the people living there for
the value of their crops and buildings. Only after the area has been compensated and cleared for surveying, can it be developed. At this point the
funds and responsibility for the services that must be provided—water,
roads, sewerage or septic tanks, community facilities, and so on—are
shared among a number of different government divisions and parastatal
organizations.

Once the Arusha Declaration had proclaimed the primacy of socialist rural development, new emphases began to appear in Tanzania's urban policy. The *Second Five-Year Plan, 1969–1974* announced three new directions. First, moves were to be taken to decentralize certain government functions, and to locate new industries, where possible, away from Dar es Salaam. Eight towns throughout the country were selected for "concentrated urban development" over the plan period.[43] Second, in order to minimize the resources devoted to urban development, and to maximize the spread of benefits to all classes, the NHC was to increase its rate of house construction, and at the same time to limit itself to a cost range of T£300–550 per unit.[44] Medium-cost houses would be financed either privately, or through the Permanent Housing Finance Corporation at commercial rates of interest. Finally, for the bottom end of the urban income scale, the NHC and the Ministry of Lands, Housing and Urban Development (formed in 1968 to unite most of the urban-specialist divisions) were to develop a program for the annual provision of some 5,000 sites-and-services plots. The plan projected that the public sector would provide from 35,000 to 40,000 houses and housing sites over the five-year period.

The next major urban policy initiative came in April 1971 when the government announced that, under the newly passed Acquisition of Buildings Act, it was taking over all rented buildings with a value of T£5,000 and over. An Office of the Registrar of Buildings was created to administer the 2,900 properties acquired, whose estimated value was some T£32.5 million.[45] This move was justified as a logical outcome of the country's commitment to socialism, and compensation was promised; as it happened, most of those who lost their buildings were members of the Asian community. (Because of mistakes, or successful appeals to a tribunal, about 300 of the original total had been returned to their owners by 1973.)

But the problem of wealthy urban landlords was just the tip of the iceberg. The feeling following the Arusha Declaration of 1967 was that government and parastatal officers, who were in most cases paying highly subsidized rents for their state-owned dwellings, should be required to pay in accordance with their incomes. Those with secure housing were clearly among the privileged. People were saying, "It is more difficult to get a room in Dar es Salaam than it is to get a job."[46]

In late 1972, the cabinet decided that all government and parastatal employees occupying public housing would be charged on a sliding scale according to their incomes. Although no exact estimate of the costs of this decision was made at the time, it was felt that the upper-income earners, who would pay more rent under the new system, would in effect be subsidizing the lower-income earners, who would generally be paying less than before.

At the same time the cabinet also decided to reduce the loan ceiling on publicly financed projects from T£3,750 to T£2,000 per house; to improve selectively the services in existing squatter areas (until then officially considered illegal) and to upgrade those houses which met minimal standards; and to review existing by-laws so as to permit the maximum use of traditional and local building materials. In a major institutional change, in January 1973 the Tanzania Housing Bank was established to replace the old Permanent Housing Finance Corporation (PHFC).[47] The Housing Bank could borrow at less than commercial rates from the treasury, and was expected to have a substantial effect on the finance of low-cost housing in urban areas and *ujamaa* (collectivized) villages. By the end of its first year of operation, the Housing Bank was working closely with the newly created Sites and Services Directorate in the Ministry of Lands, Housing and Urban Development. Significant support for the concept of sites and services came from President Nyerere, who cautioned against Tanzanians "thinking in terms of 'international standards' instead of what we can afford and what we can do ourselves."[48] Applying this idea to housing, he said:

> ... although we know that most of our people cannot afford the mortgage or rental costs of the cement house, we persist in promoting its construction. Obviously it is more comfortable, and lasts longer. It is a case of the best being the enemy of the good. [But] for most people the only effective choice is between an improved and an unimproved traditional house—they cannot afford the cement house; ... instead we should concentrate on the development of Site-and-Service projects so that people can build for themselves houses which are appropriate to their income, and which can be gradually improved over time.[49]

Perhaps the most dramatic policy decision during the 1970s was the announcement in November 1973 that the capital would be moved from Dar es Salaam to Dodoma, 300 miles to the west. According to the resolution of the National Executive Committee of the Tanganyikan National African Union (TANU), the transfer would take place gradually over ten years, at an estimated cost of T£185.5 million; after a great deal of debate within the party over the question, only three of the 18 regions had opposed the move. In announcing TANU's decision, the president said "that the transfer of the capital would help stimulate development in the country because of the centrality of the new site."[50] The decision was clearly consistent with the overall scheme of administrative decentralization that the government had begun in earnest more than a year earlier.[51] By 1975, a five-year program was approved by the Capital Development Authority for the development of Dodoma; over this period, about 5,000 civil servants would be transferred from Dar es Salaam to Dodoma, and some 10 percent of national development funds would be spent on the new capital.[52] Although Dodoma's population was only 45,000 in 1975, its projected population for 1985 was 170,000. The physical planning of Dodoma was to be carried out under a *National Capital Master Plan,* published in May 1976. Having taken a close personal interest in the preparation of the *Master Plan,* President Nyerere concluded that it was "consistent with the ideology of Tanzania."[53] Among the elements of the *Master Plan* that the president chose to emphasize in his foreword to it were the use of locally produced, low-cost materials; the building of an efficient public transport service; and the planning of the town around a series of small connecting communities within which cooperative activities would be easily organized.

Performance

The evolution of urban policy in Tanzania since the Arusha Declaration is an expression of the need to achieve consistency with a strong and well-articulated ideological position. This ideology is almost exclusively formulated by President Nyerere. If the urban policy choices deriving from Nyerere's ideological guidelines have appeared rational and even laudable to most outside observers, their implementation has often fallen far short of their intentions. While some critics would point to insufficient ideological training and commitment among leaders and middle-level cadres,[54] more intransigent reasons for the gap in implementation are the severe shortage of human and material resources in Tanzania,[55] combined with external factors over which the government has had little control. Whatever the reasons, the slow pace and the occasionally misdirected bias of implementation have worked the greatest disadvantage on the urban poor.

Both the first and second plans gave the NHC a major role in providing low-cost urban housing. During the first plan period, as we have noted earlier, the NHC was able to obtain only about 25 percent of the funds it had expected from overseas sources, and 70 percent of the low-cost housing it built in Dar es Salaam was part of a slum-clearance scheme that added nothing to the existing housing supply. The Dar es Salaam slum-clearance scheme was, in addition, an economic liability, since the new lessees (and former landlords) were frequently unable to pay their rents to the corporation—thus contributing to the NHC's continuing financial weakness.*

---

*When the traditional Swahili-style houses were demolished and new houses built, the former owners were given leases by the NHC, for which they were required to pay a fixed monthly rent. Since they could charge little more to their tenants for the rooms in the new houses, the owners often found it impossible to pay rent to the NHC.

While the drafters of the second plan stated that "the absolute achievement of the National Housing Corporation had been very consider-able," they acknowledged that the net addition to the housing stock of less than 400 units per year "just touched the fringe of the housing problem."[56] Once slum clearance was halted in the late 1960s, the corporation found it difficult to obtain funds. While the NHC does some work for other parastatals, and had even built for the middle-income market through loans from the PHFC (now the Tanzania Housing Bank), the bulk of its work is in low-cost housing, financed directly by treasury grants. In the 1970s, these grants began to diminish considerably, from a high of T£ 1,070,000 in 1970/71 to a low of T£125,000 in 1973/74. For the fiscal year 1976/77, thanks to a loan from West Germany, the NHC was allocated the sum of T£355,000—all for a major redevelopemnt project in the Buguruni area of Dar es Salaam.[57] But in that year, no funds were channeled directly to the NHC from internal sources in Tanzania. The diminution in avail-ability of funds, particularly from internal sources, reflects a number of factors. First, the treasury has been dissatisfied over the poor financial controls and rent collection activities of the corporation. The problem of controls came to the surface in 1976 when, after an investigation, 111 employees of the corporation were dismissed for financial irregularity, including the general manager. A second problem has been the NHC's failure to keep costs to a minimum. Thus, while the second plan had clearly specified a ceiling of T£550 per house, the average low-cost house put up by the NHC in 1973 cost T£920. By 1977 a low-cost NHC house ran as high as T£4,000![58] A third factor reducing the NHC's internal financial support was the changing developmental emphasis in Tanzania in the 1970s. With development funds becoming scarce in any case, because of world economic conditions and the high price of oil imports, what was available was earmarked mainly for rural development and the ujamaa village program. As a result of all of these factors, the NHC's output fell during the 1970s, reaching an all-time low of 138 low-cost units during 1972–73.

In terms of numbers of plots produced, the surveyed-plot allocation program of the Lands Division was more successful than the NHC pro-gram. In 1971, for example, the division issued 7,305 new certificates of short-term rights to occupancy in urban areas; in 1972 the figure was 6,331. But this was still far from enough to meet the demand for Dar es Salaam alone; the waiting list for high-density plots totaled approximately 15,000 applicants at the end of 1972. In spite of direct presidential pressure to speed up allocation, the procedure remained cumbersome and expensive. A great deal of money had to be paid to compensate squatters and other interests before land could be cleared for surveying, and when surveyed plots were made available, services for the plots (such as roads, water, schools) were rarely ready on schedule. In a 1969 report the barriers created for the poor and uneducated by land development procedures were described as follows:

> The entire administrative process is designed to deal with the individual applicant who is prepared to undertake the development of an urban plot. Not only does this kind of system present problems for accommodating high rates of urban growth, but it is in fact quite inaccessible to the majority of the people. The legal framework and administrative process derive from a context quite foreign to most urban dwellers in Tanzania, particularly those who are relatively new to the urban environment. The aggressive, well educated and better paid urban dweller will be much more capable of getting a plot for himself than low-income rural migrants who lack formal education and the skills relevant to urban living.[59]

A study done by the government in 1972 estimated that under normal conditions it could take 280 days for an applicant to receive a certificate of right of occupancy to land scheduled for development.[60] In view of the annual demand for new urban housing in the country (estimated at 13,750 low-cost units in 1972),[61] it is clear that the combined efforts of the NHC and the plot-allocation program were woefully inadequate.

A greatly expanded site-and-service program seemed the answer to shortfalls in conventional procedures. It will be recalled that the second plan called for 5,000 serviced sites per year. By the end of the plan's third year, however, only 795 sites had been made available—all in a single area of Dar es Salaam. Moreover, the costs of this project put it "beyond the reach of most low income families."[62] The problems of this particular project did not dim the planners' enthusiasm for the site-and-service concept, but they underlined the necessity for careful financial planning. In 1973, following a study of the Ministry of Lands, Housing and Urban Development, done by a management consultant team, an Urban Development Department was set up within the ministry, with its own commissioner. Within the new department, a Sites and Services Directorate was given substantial authority to develop new schemes. In 1973 the directorate submitted a formal loan application to the World Bank for a massive five-year program involving 18,250 plots in Dar es Salaam, Mwanza, and Mbeya. A loan of T£3 million was approved by the World Bank in July 1974 and the program got underway shortly thereafter. The loan provided components for new sites as well as for the upgrading of existing squatter areas. A brief survey of the completed program in 1977 described it as follows:

The basic services consist of earth roads with stormwater drainage, public water kiosks (with 1 kiosk per 50 houses), electricity and street lighting along major roads, community education centres, dispensaries and/or urban health centres, markets, and in some cases, garden centres. Squatter areas were surveyed in blocks to enable the residents to obtain legal Rights of Occupancy and house construction loans were available through Tanzania Housing Bank. The standard of services was deliberately kept low (at approximately Sh. 2,000 per plot compared to the previous average of Sh. 8,000 per plot) so that more plots and houses could be serviced than previously. As implemented, basic services were provided for 9,000 existing squatter houses and 8,500 new sites in Dar es Salaam, Mbeya and Mwanza. The planning period for the programme was 2½ years and the construction period was an additional 2½ years, i.e., 1973–1977 for the total programme.[63]

Work on this scheme was so successful that World Bank officials considered it "their best sites and services programme."[64] In 1977, negotiations were underway for an additional International Development Association (IDA) loan to cover another phase of the program. Supporting the new emphasis on squatter upgrading and site-and-service construction, the Tanzania Housing Bank rapidly expanded its operations. In 1974, it lent a total of just over T£3 million for the construction of 1,811 houses in both urban areas and ujamaa villages; in 1975, it lent over T£6 million for 2,754 houses.[65]

The important shift in emphasis in Tanzanian urban policy toward sites and services and squatter upgrading was partially a result of the growing squatter problem in the main towns. For Dar es Salaam, a comprehensive count carried out for the year 1969 showed 14,720 squatter houses within the statutory planning area (which went somewhat beyond the legal boundaries of the city). Using similar methods, another count was carried out for the year 1972, and this showed 27,981 squatter houses in the same area—an average compound annual increase of 24 percent over three years.[66] On the basis of these figures and some other assumptions, it was estimated that in 1972 about 44 percent of the total population of greater Dar es Salaam lived in squatter areas. This figure must now be higher, since in 1975 approximately 40,000 squatter houses in Dar es Salaam represented some 53 percent of the population, again estimated, of 586,000.[67] For Dodoma, observers noted that once the decision was taken to make it the new capital, squatting in peripheral areas grew rapidly. In 1974, approximately 49 percent of Dodoma's population lived in "unauthorized" housing.[68] Although existing squatters in Tanzania are recognized as having rights to the land they occupy, the growth of squatting in the main towns is a severe planning problem since services must somehow be organized on the basis of irregular settlement patterns. Most squatter areas are poorly serviced as it is, and it will be some time (if ever) before most of them benefit from upgrading programs. A survey carried out in the early 1970s showed that, in comparison to nonsquatters, squatters in Dar es Salaam were generally poorer, had significantly less formal education, and were more heavily engaged in the nonwage sector of the urban economy.[69]

It has already been noted that the Acquisition of Buildings Act, passed in 1971, deprived many Asians of their rental properties. Although the act was not manifestly racist, many thousands of Asian families subsequently left the country. Moreover, most medium-sized private construction firms were wiped out, since they had invested their profits in buildings and were using rents for working capital. While no new housing was created, there was a severe drop in construction capacity.

The new income-based rental policy announced by the government in early 1973 applied only to public employees living in government, parastatal, or NHC housing. Totally unaffected by the measure were almost all lower-income urban workers, and the bulk of middle-income clerks and administrators who had to find their own housing, often in the squatter areas.

Ideally, this rental policy should be evaluated in the light of the government's overall strategy to redistribute income. To the extent that the overall strategy was being applied consistently, government policy in the sphere of public rentals should have had smooth and predictable results. For the 1970s, the data available are limited and somewhat mixed in terms of the trends they show. President Nyerere has stated that by the end of 1976, the highest public-sector salary after direct taxes were deducted was only about nine times the minimum wage after tax; this proportion had been reduced from 20:1 at the time of the Arusha Declaration, and, from about 50:1 at independence.[70] Notwithstanding this general movement in public-sector wages and salaries, the effects of inflation during the period 1969–75 seem to have been felt more by low-wage urban households than high-wage urban households.[71] Chronic shortages of essential consumer goods also operated to the relative disadvantage of rural households and the urban poor. In addition, new urban wage jobs were going disproportionately to the more educated by the early 1970s.[72] Those without, or with little, formal education were thus finding themselves either unemployed or having to find work within the more insecure confines of the urban informal sector. Since it has been shown in independent studies that formal education and level of urban income are very highly correlated in Tanzania,[73] the conclusion seems inescapable that those at the lower end of the urban income (and educational) scale have, at the very least, not improved their position over recent years. Their situation has certainly been worsened by the failure of the government, after 1971, to hold the urban-rural income differential down in order to prevent massive migration of job seekers to the urban areas.[74] Thus, while the rental policy has probably tended to slightly redress inequalities of income among a select group within the public sector, there is evidence that many of those whom the policy did not affect have seen their real incomes deteriorate.

A final important aspect of Tanzanian urban policy that can be evaluated is the strategy of deconcentration outside Dar es Salaam, including the move of the capital to Dodoma. At least during the early years of the second plan, no administrative machinery was set up to influence the siting of new industries in the eight growth towns. The decentralization of administrative functions has been more successful. Significant urban planning, surveying, and land-allocation functions are now undertaken in many regions, and the situation is improving as more qualified staff are posted every year. Since 1973–74, annual budgets have been drawn up by the regions themselves, in cooperation with the prime minister's office. The whole decentralization exercise is given added impetus by the push to Dodoma, although for reasons of finance the pace of building and of transferring staff to the new capital has been much slower than originally anticipated.

KENYA AND TANZANIA: A COMPARISON OF URBAN POLICIES

As the foregoing analysis of urban policy and performance has illustrated, there are not only broad similarities, but also some crucial differences, between these two East African neighbors. While the approaches and problems are shared by many other African countries, the divergencies stem largely from different social and political parameters in the policy process.

The Main Areas of Convergence

In both countries, as we have seen, a disproportionate amount of industrial development has been sited in the capital city, despite official intentions to the contrary. Thus in 1970, Dar es Salaam had 46.0 percent of the total recorded urban employment in Tanzania, up from 44.2 percent in the previous year.[75] In 1971, the comparable figure for Nairobi was 55.0 percent, up from 53.8 percent a year earlier.[76] The statistics thus show that the employment share of the largest cities is growing. But this dominance is clearly linked to population, a factor which is almost impossible to influence by deliberate governmental policy. According to the most recent census returns, Dar es Salaam in 1967 had 45.2 percent of the total urban population in towns over 10,000 in Tanzania, while Nairobi had 54.9

percent of Kenya's urban population. Given the exceptionally high growth rates of these two cities, there is no reason to assume that these proportions are declining.

Both Kenya and Tanzania have officially committed the bulk of public housing funds to low-income groups. But in both countries—though to a much greater extent in Kenya—the efforts of the specialized parastatal organizations in this field have been biased in favor of middle-income groups, in the area of conventional housing. Substantial site-and-service programs failed to materialize until very recently. The two housing corporations are among the most dynamic in Africa, but their failure to provide adequately for low-income groups is consistent with experience elsewhere on the continent. If Kenya has made some important changes in the direction of relaxing municipal by-laws to permit lower-standard development (by the mid-1970s Tanzania had not yet amended its 1956 building code), the overall effect of regulatory action—at least in Nairobi—is to preclude low-income groups from conventional, permanent housing, and to heavily bias the provision of services toward authorized rather than unauthorized areas. In both Kenya and Tanzania, the number of urban squatters has been growing more rapidly than the population in the authorized, planned areas.

The Context of Policy Divergence

Beneath these broad similarities, a close comparison of urban policies shows some extremely important differences. In general, there has been more innovation in Tanzania in terms of the large number of decisions taken in recent years to alter the distribution of benefits to major groups within and between urban and rural areas. These decisions have already been outlined, but the most important include the active development of a national site-and-service program; the de facto recognition of existing squatter settlements, coupled with the intention to gradually improve services to them; a new rental policy in regard to civil servants, related to income; the establishment of the Tanzania Housing Bank; and the decision to move the capital from Dar es Salaam to one of the least-developed regions.

With one exception, policy in Kenya has tended to consolidate earlier decisions on urban patterns, and no new institutions have been created; the policy exception was the enactment of the Local Government Adoptive By-Laws (for Grade-2 buildings) in 1968. What looked like another major exception was the central government's decision to allocate, beginning in 1968, 50 percent of the graduated personal tax (GPT) collections from Nairobi and Mombasa for redistribution to poorer local authorities. But there is no evidence that the treasury actually used the funds for this purpose, and in any case, the remittances were stopped in 1971, GPT being abolished altogether in 1974.

Policy innovation, however, is meaningless in the absence of effective implementation. While Tanzania has pushed very far to draw out the urban policy implications of an ideology that stresses rural socialist development, it has until recently paid less attention to strengthening the bureaucratic machinery necessary to carry out the new policies. It is true that local government in Tanzania has a much shorter history than that in Kenya; but the local authorities have been much weaker as well. For example, urban and district councils employed 28, 971 in Tanzania in 1968, as against 63,100 in Kenya.[77] At the end of 1973, the Dar es Salaam City Council was officially disbanded, its functions being taken over by the regional development director, with three district committees each covering a part of the greater Dar es Salaam area. It is too early to evaluate how this arrangement has worked in practice, but well before this decision was taken, the city council had shown itself to be a relatively ineffective organization.

This weakness of local councils in Tanzania has meant that various central government departments have been responsible for carrying out almost all the recent urban policy decisions. The Dar es Salaam City Council had, for example, only one professional town planner on its staff in 1973. This meant that virtually all the detailed planning for the capital was done in the Ministry of Lands, Housing and Urban Development; but in 1971 its Town Planning Division had only six professionals on the staff, with responsibility for the whole country. By contrast, the Town Planning Department in Kenya had 14 professional staff members in 1971, while the Nairobi City Council had, in addition, at least half that number of town planners. In Kenya, the stability and continuity of governmental machinery tends to be seen as an end in itself; in Tanzania, institutional structures are often changed to achieve consistency with evolving developmental goals.

While it is valid to characterize Tanzania's overriding objectives as "socialist rural development," it is not easy to summarize Kenya's goals of development in such a concise phrase. Alongside a framework of rather extensive controls over, and government participation in, certain sectors of the economy (for example, agriculture and tourism), there is a vigorous private sector bounded only by the injunction that it Africanize its personnel as rapidly as possible. The varying development emphases lead to a different bias in urban policy, despite common problems of performance. In Tanzania, the bulk of governmental activity and development funds for the urban areas are intended to benefit lower-income groups; at the same time, active attempts are made to promote cooperative, socialist activities, and to prevent the gap between urban workers and rural peasants from widening. In Kenya, where we have seen how some programs at least ostensibly aim at lower-income groups, other schemes—notably, the building of municipal markets, loan support for the Africanization of trade, the building of numerous housing estates with public funds, and the lending policies of the commercial banks—tend to benefit mainly those with property or capital.

These differences are also reflected in the strategies of the two countries toward the promotion of international tourism, many of the facilities for which are located in urban areas and use urban-based infrastructure. Kenya has actively encouraged international tourism through the building of high-class hotels, the modernization of its airports, the importation of luxury commodities for the tourist trade, and the insistence on high buildings and public health standards in the towns. Tanzania, on the other hand, has been concerned more with the negative social effects of rich tourists and a luxury tourist establishment in what the government sees as a poor, socialist country struggling for self-reliance.[78] By not aggressively promoting tourism, Tanzania has not been under the same pressure as Kenya to upgrade its facilities or to import costly luxury goods. Although no comparable figures on tourist-generated revenue are available for the two countries, in 1975 Kenya recorded over five times as many hotel beds occupied as Tanzania recorded.

These variations in policy are related to a number of more general independent differences between the two countries. Foremost among these differences are political structures and attitudes, and income distribution. Each of these factors will be discussed in turn.

Political Structures and Attitudes

The single party in Tanzania is a mass organization, from the local leaders in the ten-house cell system, covering all the urban and most of the rural areas, to an ongoing national headquarters and executive structure. Technical decisions are first approved by the economic committee of the cabinet after extensive scrutiny by the civil service, but the National Executive Committee of TANU meets regularly with the president, and most, if not all, important decisions are taken with its sanction. While the party has been concerned about its role in implementing development policies, its importance in establishing general strategy and goals is unquestioned.

In Kenya, the ruling party, the Kenya National African Union (KANU), has played virtually no role in any major recent policy decision. The headquarters of KANU amounts to little more than a few offices; at the district level, the branches play essentially a nomination role at election time. Thus, while the continued vitality of the mass party in Tanzania obliges policy makers to take the needs of the poorest areas and lowest-income groups into consideration, the same kind of institutional pressure does not exist in Kenya.

The degree to which lower-income urban needs are effectively articulated through the political machinery is partly a reflection of the attitudes and interests of the governing elite. The prevailing attitude toward urban development in Tanzania was well expressed in the 1967 Arusha Declaration, first written in draft by Nyerere, and published by the TANU National Executive Committee:

> We must not forget that people who live in towns can possibly become the exploiters of those who live in the rural areas. All our big hospitals are in towns and they benefit only a small section of the people of Tanzania. Yet if we have built them with loans from outside Tanzania, it is the overseas sale of the peasants' produce which provides the foreign exchange for repayment. Those who do not get the benefit of the hospitals thus carry the major responsibility for paying for them. Tarmac roads, too, are mostly found in towns and are of especial value to the motor-car-owners. Yet if we have built those roads with loans, it is again the farmer who produces the goods which will pay for them. What is more, the foreign exchange with which the car was bought also came from the sale of the farmers' produce. Again, electric lights, water pipes, hotels and other aspects of modern development are mostly found in towns. Most of them have been built with loans and most of them do not benefit the farmer directly, although they will be paid for by the foreign exchange earned by the sale of his produce. We should always bear this in mind.[79]

Later in the same document, a "leadership code" was proposed whereby TANU and government officials were prohibited from owning shares or directorships in any private company, receiving more than a single salary, or owning houses for rent.[80] This code has, on the whole, been successfully enforced. In effect, it separates the interests of TANU and government officials from specifically urban-based enterprise, since there is no restriction on a leader's development of his rural farm, so long as he is not "associated with the practices of capitalism or feudalism." This antiurban bias is in turn partially a reflection of the fact that few, if any, of the top political leaders represent towns or areas adjacent to the capital. If TANU's development as an effective nationalist party—out of associations that "were essentially rurally based" and indicated "the resentment of country people against outside interference"[81]—is a valid interpretation for the preindependence period, the government that TANU formed later has been no less rural in its predispositions. And within Dar es Salaam, the strength of the party in lower-income and squatter areas effectively precludes programs which do not have an important redistributive component.

Kenyan political leaders have been less explicit on the rural-urban dichotomy. Besides a formal commitment to rural development in the Second Five-Year Plan, there is Kenyatta's frequent "back to the land" exhortation, with the related implications that urban areas are breeding grounds of immorality and crime. Kenyatta's view that urban areas must be clean and modern, and his opposition to sites and services, are in direct contrast to Nyerere's position that international standards are inappropriate for Tanzania and that sites and services should be supported.

Kenya's unequivocal support for urban development is reflected by a much higher level of budgetary allocation for the Kenyan NHC. At the same time, urban local authorities in Kenya have spent significantly greater amounts per capita on services than have their Tanzanian counterparts.* These differences cannot be explained in terms of dissimilar overall levels of expenditure by the two governments, since in recent years total recurrent and development expenditures in both countries have been roughly equal. Even the slightly greater level of urbanization in Kenya does not account for the magnitude of differences. Of course, considerably more income is generated in Kenya's cities because of the wealth of the Asian and expatriate communities living there, particularly in Nairobi; but this in itself does not explain why the government has spent so much more on public housing and other services that benefit the African community.

A major reason, I would submit, is political. Unlike the Tanzanian example, many influential cabinet ministers (including the president himself) come from areas in the Central Province within commuting distance of the capital. Not only have many of their constituents migrated to Nairobi for work, maintaining their *shambas* (small plots) and continuing to contribute to family upkeep and self-help projects in their home areas; but many politicians and civil servants have become heavily involved in land and business in the capital city. Elite investment in tourism on the coast is also significant. Government support for a fairly high level of urban services, and in particular for tourism and the development of the prestige image of Nairobi, is unlikely to diminish so long as these interests are congruent.

Income Distribution

A second, and complementary dimension that helps to account for the greater ideological thrust toward lower-income benefits in Tanzania is related to class structure. Without entering into a detailed discussion of the attributes of class in urban African society, suffice it to say that any

---

*In 1969, for example, the Nairobi City Council spent $50, on average, for every member of the city population; the Mombasa Municipal Council spent $23; and the Dar es Salaam City Council spent $13.

analysis in depth must start with the known data on income distribution. While it is not easy to achieve exact comparability, some survey data fortunately exist for the principal urban areas in both countries. The data for Kenya are based on a survey of 1,146 households in Nairobi, Mombasa, and Kisumu during 1968–69, and include all main forms of cash and noncash income. The data for Tanzania, on the other hand, are based on a random survey of 2,140 individuals in Dar es Salaam, Tanga, Mwanza, and Arusha in 1971, and do not include noncash income.[82] Admittedly, these data are not perfectly comparable; the figures for Kenya refer to households, and include noncash income, while those for Tanzania refer to all income-earning individuals, and are derived from a survey carried out two years later. The time difference, however, is an advantage here, since the greater income earned by households in the Kenyan sample would be to some extent canceled by natural increases in individual incomes over two years in Tanzania.

For all the problems implicit in such a comparison, there is a striking difference in income distribution. The bulk of the Tanzanian sample (59.2 percent) was earning less than $42 per month, while only 24.2 percent of the Kenyan sample was in this income class. At the other extreme, only 8.5 percent of the Tanzanian urban workers earned $140 per month or more, in contrast with 27.8 percent of the Kenyan households sampled. In spite of the lack of a precise comparison, the differences are so great that two conclusions are inescapable: in Tanzania, proportionally speaking, many more workers received low wages, and far fewer had relatively high salaries. Since these figures were collected, urban income inequalities have almost certainly increased in Kenya.

These differences in income distribution are an important parameter in urban development. On the one hand, the greater proportion of middle- and upper-income earners in Kenya (and again, especially in Nairobi) puts considerable pressure on both the local and central government to provide higher-standard services and facilities.[83] On the other hand, in the Tanzanian environment, any policy which does not at least attempt to benefit lower-income groups will alienate the government from the overwhelming majority of the urban population. Quite apart from elite interests and political structure, some of the differences in urban policy in the two countries are undoubtedly a reflection of contrasting class structures.

CONCLUSIONS

In this chapter I have compared urban policy and performance for the postindependence period ending in 1977. The tendency in Kenya has been to consolidate the policy pattern begun during the later colonial period, although relatively successful performance has only covered up problems of equity. Policy in Tanzania has moved progressively away from the past, but performance has often bogged down because of inadequate resources. These substantially differing approaches are related to broader systemic factors, such as overall socioeconomic goals, political structures, and income distribution. If this is not surprising, in view of what we already know about the differences between the two political systems, there is nevertheless a general point to be drawn from this type of comparison.

It is obviously not sufficient to characterize policies in a particular African state as, say, "progressive" or consolidative, without taking account of the quality of implementation. If a country is poor, and its bureaucratic resources are limited, attempts to put too much pressure on administrators to effect change will, in the end, invite stagnation, and a situation whereby only those with access to the bureaucracy and its agencies will get what they need. Unless performance is improved, this is a danger that always lurks beyond policy innovation in Tanzania. For regimes where policy change has not been radical, and where bureaucratic capacity has been developed to more adequate levels, the problem for policy makers may be how to cope with demands from all sections of urban society, and not merely how to meet targets or to maintain services in a formal sense. In a rapidly urbanizing society where the bulk of the new migrants are in the lower-income groups, Kenya's urban bureaucracy will increasingly have to come to terms with the problem of equity.

NOTES

1. Kingsley Davis, *World Urbanization 1950–1970, Volume II: Analysis of Trends, Relationships, and Development* (Berkeley: Institute of International Studies, 1972), pp. 163–235; and Paul Bairoch, *Urban Unemployment in Developing Countries* (Geneva: International Labour Office, 1973), pp. 7–24.

2. The most succinct overview of these trends is in World Bank, *Urbanization: Sector Working Paper* (Washington, D.C.: World Bank, 1972).

3. See, for example, ibid, pp. 60–61; World Bank, *Housing: Sector Policy Paper* (Washington, D.C.: World Bank, 1975), pp. 26–27; and Orville Grimes, *Housing for Low-Income Urban Families* (Baltimore: Johns Hopkins University Press, for the World Bank, 1976), pp. 92–94.

4. Kenya, *Statistical Abstract, 1968* (Nairobi: Government Printer 1968), p. 91.

5. Kenya, *Kenya Population Census, 1962*, vol. 3, *African Population* (Nairobi: Ministry of Economic Planning and Development, 1966), pp. 23, 82.

6. See International Labour Office, *Employment, Incomes and Equality: A Strategy for Increasing Productive Employment in Kenya* (Geneva: International Labour Office, 1972), p. 49, for the Mombasa figure. The Nairobi estimate has been altered to make allowance for boundary changes.

7. Lawrence Bloomberg and Charles Abrams, *Report of the United Nations Mission to Kenya on Housing* (Nairobi: Government Printer, 1965).

8. Kenya, National Assembly, *Official Report,* vol. 12 (Nairobi: National Assembly, June 8, 1967), col. 773.

9. Kenya, *Development Plan, 1970–74* (Nairobi: Government Printer, 1969).

10. The Kenyan government's formal response to the ILO study is contained in *Sessional Paper on Employment,* no. 10 (Nairobi: Government Printer, 1973).

11. John Burrows, *Kenya: Into the Second Decade* (Baltimore: Johns Hopkins University Press, for the World Bank, 1975).

12. Kenya, *Development Plan, 1974–1978,* part 1 (Nairobi: Government Printer, 1974), p. 473.

13. Kenya, *Development Plan, 1970–1974,* op. cit., p. 516.

14. Kenya, *Development Plan, 1974–1978,* op. cit., p. 475.

15. Ibid, p. 477.

16. National Housing Corp., *Site and Service Schemes, Guidelines for an Administrative Procedure* (Nairobi: NHC, 1976).

17. The average public service wage in 1974 was Sh. 671 per month, as noted in Kenya, *Economic Survey, 1975* (Nairobi: Government Printer, 1975), p. 42.

18. Ibid, p. 145.

19. The figures in this paragraph are taken from Kenya, *Economic Survey, 1976* (Nairobi: Government Printer, 1976), p. 128.

20. Housing Research and Development Unit, *Two Housing Schemes in Thika: User-Reaction Survey* (Nairobi: University of Nairobi, 1972).

21. Bujra, Janet, "Pumwani: The Politics of Property" (Unpublished report on a research project sponsored by the Social Science Research Council, Dar es Salaam, 1973).

22. National Housing Corporation, *Annual Report 1975* (Nairobi: D. L. Patel Press, 1976), pp. i–ii.

23. Personal communication to the author.

24. This interpretation of the operation of the rent-control tribunals is based on an interview with the administrative officer, Rent Restriction Tribunal, Nairobi, on November 22, 1973. A strong denunciation of the tribunal system can be found in Y. P. Ghai and J. P. W. B. McAuslan, *Public Law and Political Change in Kenya* (New York: Oxford University Press, 1970), pp. 289–90.

25. David Etherton, *Mathare Valley: A Case Study of Uncontrolled Housing in Nairobi* (Nairobi: University of Nairobi, Housing Research and Development Unit, 1971), p. 4.

26. Kenya, Town Planning Department, "Housing in Mombasa," mimeographed (Nairobi, 1969), p. 4 and app. A, sec. 13.

27. *East African Standard,* November 21, 1970.

28. *Nairobi City Council Minutes, 1970–1971* (Nairobi: Nairobi City Council, 1971), pp. 2497–98.

29. Kenya, "Low Cost Housing and Squatter Upgrading Study," *Progress Report No. 7* (Nairobi: Government of Kenya and World Bank, 1976), pp. 24, 28.

30. Kenya, *Economic Survey 1976,* op. cit., p. 123.

31. Ibid., pp. 124–25.

32. Leo Odero Omolo, "Kisumu: A Dying Town," *The Sunday Post* (Nairobi), September 23, 1973.

33. Kenya, *Economic Survey 1975,* op. cit., p. 157.

34. Kenya, *Economic Survey 1976,* op. cit., p. 138.

35. Tanzania, *Statistical Abstract, 1970* (Dar es Salaam: Government Printer, 1972), p. 137.

36. J. E. G. Sutton, ed., "Dar es Salaam: City, Port and Region," of *Tanganyika Notes and Records* 71, Special Issue (1970): p. 18.

37. Tanzania, *1967 Population Census,* vol. 2 (Dar es Salaam: Government Printer, 1970), p. 164.

38. Tanzania, *National Housing Corporation Act* (Dar es Salaam: Government Printer, 1962), chap. 481.

39. Manfred A. Bienefeld and H. H. Binhammer, "Tanzania Housing Finance and Housing Policy," in *Urban Challenge in East Africa,* ed. John Hutton (Nairobi: East African Publishing House, 1972), p. 186.

40. Jill Wells, *The Construction Industry in East Africa,* Paper no. 72.2 (Dar es Salaam: University of Dar es Salaam, Economic Research Bureau, May 1972), p. 21.

41. For an evaluation of this scheme, see Gerhard Grohs, "Slum Clearance in Dar es Salaam," in Hutton, ed., op. cit., pp. 157–76.

42. This legislation is discussed in detail in Tanzania, Ministry of Lands, Housing and Urban Development, "Achievement in Ten Years of Independence," mimeographed (Dar es Salaam, 1971), pp. 14–17; and in R. W. James, *Land Tenure and Policy in Tanzania* (Nairobi: East African Literature Bureau, 1971), pp. 93–166.

43. These towns were Tanga, Arusha/Moshi, Mwanza, Mtwara, Mbeya, Morogoro, Dodoma, and Tabora. See Tanzania, *Tanzania Second Five-Year Plan for Economic and Social Development, 1st July 1969–30th June 1974,* vol. 1 (Dar es Salaam: Government Printer, 1969), p. 181.

44. Ibid., p. 191.

45. Ministry of Lands, Housing and Urban Development, op. cit., p. 54.

46. Cited by Marcelino Komba in "Housing Problem in Dar," *The Nationalist* (Dar es Salaam), August 5, 1970.

47. Details of these policy decisions can be found in Tanzania, *Hali ya Uchumi wa Taifa Katika Mwaka, 1972–73* [Economic Survey, 1972–73] (Dar es Salaam: Government Printer, 1973), pp. 85–86.

48. Julius Nyerere, *The Arusha Declaration: Ten Years After* (Dar es Salaam: Government Printer, 1977), p. 25.

49. Ibid, pp. 29–30.

50. *Daily Nation* (Nairobi), October 2, 1973.

51. For details of the reorganization of the central government in accordance with this scheme, see Julius Nyerere, *Decentralization* (Dar es Salaam: Government Printer, 1972).

52. Tanzania, *National Capital Master Plan, Dodoma, Tanzania* (Toronto: Project Planning Associates, 1976), pp. 21, 89–90.

53. Ibid. p. viii.

54. See, for example, Lionel Cliffe and Griffiths Cunningham, "Ideology, Organization and the Settlement Experience in Tanzania," in *Socialism in Tanzania,* vol. 2, ed. Lionel Cliffe and John S. Saul (Nairobi: East African Publishing House, 1973), p. 139.

55. G. K. Helleiner, "Socialism and Economic Development in Tanzania," *Journal of Development Studies* 8 (1972): 183–204.

56. Tanzania, *Second Five-Year Plan,* op, cit., p. 189.

57. Tanzania, *Mpango wa Maendeleo wa Mwaka 1976–77* [Annual Development Plan, 1976–77] (Dar es Salaam: Government Printer, 1976), p. 56.

58. Personal communication to the author.

59. PADCO, *A Proposal for an Urban Development Corporation in Tanzania* (Washington, D.C.: PADCO, 1969), p. 20.

60. Tanzania, Ministry of Lands, Housing and Urban Development, "Report of Committee for Work Improvement," schedule 2, mimeographed (Dar es Salaam, 1972).

61. Tanzania, Minstry of Lands, Housing and Urban Development, *Urban Housing Needs 1972–1976* (Dar es Salaam: Ardhi Planning Unit, 1971).

62. Tanzania, Ministry of Lands, Housing and Urban Development, *Sites and Services Project* (Dar es Salaam: 1973), p. 9.

63. Minstry of Lands, Housing and Urban Development, "The History of the Ardhi Planning Unit 1970–75: The Development of Ardhi's Settlement Policies and Programmes," mimeographed (Dar es Salaam: Ardhi Planning Unit, n.d.), p. 3.

64. Personal communication to the author.

65. Tanzania, *Hali ya Uchumi wa Taifa Katika Mwaka 1975–76* [Economic Survey for the Year 1975–76] (Dar es Salaam: Government Printer, 1976), p. 92.

66. These calculations are discussed in greater detail in Richard Stren, *Urban Inequality and Housing Policy in Tanzania: The Problems of Squatting* (Berkeley: University of California, Institute of International Studies, 1975), pp. 59–62.

67. Ministry of Lands, Housing and Urban Development, 1977.

68. Tanzania, *National Capital Master Plan,* op. cit., Technical Supplement no. 1., p. 38.

69. Stren, op. cit., pp. 77–98.

70. Nyerere, *The Arusha Declaration Ten Years After,* op. cit., p. 16.

71. For evidence on the effects of inflation on different urban income groups, see Bank of Tanzania, *Economic and Operations Reports* (Dar es Salaam: Bank of Tanzania).

72. H. N. Barnum and R. H. Sabot, *Migration, Education and Urban Surplus Labour: The Case of Tanzania* (Paris: OECD Development Centre, 1976), p. 64.

73. See, for example, ibid., and M. Von Freyhold, "The Workers and the Nizers," mimeographed (Dar es Salaam: University of Dar es Salaam, Department of Sociology, 1972).

74. Barnum and Sabot, op. cit., p. 89.

75. Tanzania, *Survey of Employment and Earnings, 1970* (Dar es Salaam: Bureau of Statistics, 1972), p. 37.

76. Kenya, *Statistical Abstract, 1972* (Nairobi: Government Printer, 1972), p. 216.

77. Tanzania, *Statistical Abstract, 1970,* op. cit., p. 174, and Kenya, *Statistical Abstract, 1972,* op. cit., p. 211.

78. For the debate between radicals and conservatives over the value of international tourism to Tanzania see Issa Shivji, ed., *Tourism and Socialist Development* (Dar es Salaam: Tanzania Publishing House, 1973).

79. Julius Nyerere, *Freedom and Socialism* (Dar es Salaam: Oxford University Press, 1968), pp. 242–43.

80. Ibid., p. 249.

81. Lionel Cliffe, "Nationalism and the Reaction to Enforced Agricultural Change in Tanganyika During the Colonial Period" in *Socialism in Tanzania,* vol. 1, ed. Lionel Cliffe and John S. Saul (Nairobi: East African Publishing House, 1972), p. 22.

82. The Kenya survey is taken from International Labour Office, op. cit., p. 346; the Tanzania data were computed by the author from the National Urban Mobility and Employment Survey of Tanzania, carried out by Manfred Bienefeld and Richard Sabot.

83. For an extensive treatment of upper-income biases in the housing program of the Nairobi City Council, see Frederick T. Temple, "Politics, Planning and Housing Policy in Nairobi" (Ph.D. diss., Massachusetts Institute of Technology, 1973).

9

THE EDUCATION SYSTEM AS A RESPONSE TO INEQUALITY

David Court

THIS CHAPTER EXAMINES the attempt* of Kenya and Tanzania to deal with the universal problem of how to reconcile inequalities in the distribution of rewards with a concern for equality.[1] It argues that in both countries the mainspring of educational policy is a desire to alleviate the potentially disruptive consequences of inequality, although for different purposes and by different means. The broad purpose of the study is to compare contrasting educational practice in Kenya and Tanzania from this perspective, as a way of illuminating two distinctive modes of development. More specifically, it attempts to identify some of the contradictions and dilemmas inherent in their particular use of education. Finally, it uses this analysis to make a speculative assessment of how each is faring in the task of building a relatively integrated polity.

While there are important historical differences between Kenya and Tanzania, a major aspect of their colonial legacy is similar: They both inherited institutions and conditions tending toward the intensification and perpetuation of existing economic inequalities, while at the same time, the achievement of independence had released popular expectations of social equality and improved welfare.[2] Their urgent common problem was how to fashion policies for improving general living standards while accommodating and utilizing the popular demand for equality.[3] Given that even if the will had been present, the capacity was insufficient, to apply

*This chapter is an edited version of an article originally published in the *Journal of Modern African Studies* 14, no. 4 (1976). The author wishes to thank Cambridge University Press for permission to reprint the original article.

direct coercion in the task of redistribution, a more gradual process was inevitable, along with measures to secure popular accommodation to the persistence of various forms of inequality. Fifteen years after independence, it is clear that the fundamental difference in the development policies of the two countries lies in the nature of their ideological response to inherited institutional inequality.

At the heart of Tanzanian social policy has been a direct attempt to reduce disparities between individuals and regions by measures aimed at redistributing rewards. This has been part of a larger policy of social transformation emphasizing the goals of socialism, rural development, and greater self-reliance. In Kenya, social ideology is less explicit and less frequently voiced, but it can now be clearly inferred from the trend of events. While there have been some attempts to reduce disparities in regional resources in Kenya, there is much less concern than in Tanzania about individual differences in wealth and status. Indeed, it is clear that such differences are seen as necessary and beneficial. The response to individual inequalities is the propagation of a concept of social justice that aims less at the equalization of wealth and status than at the equalization of opportunities to compete for the most privileged positions.

Although the most visible difference between the two countries is the relatively greater attempt of Tanzania to create conditions of individual equality, both countries are inevitably involved in the task of securing a measure of popular acceptance of inequality. In Kenya, gaining this acceptance centers on positive justification of the functionality of individual differences, whereas in Tanzania the opposite emphasis prevails in the attempt to downplay their importance, and their existence in the face of the larger equalities of a new political culture. In both countries education is centrally involved in the task. The fact that Tanzania and Kenya face a similar task, and start from a similar background, makes the difference in their chosen methods particularly interesting, and comparative analysis notably rewarding.

EDUCATION AND SOCIAL CONTROL

At independence, the immediate practical problems of day-to-day continuance, and the psychological pressure to demonstrate that the country could now be run more efficiently than had been true under the colonialists, combined to ensure that initially the inherited structure was kept intact. The immediate perceived need was that of producing the technologists and administrators to replace departing expatriates. Given this perception, it was likely that the new ruling elite would take over not only existing positions, but also their underpinning normative structure, defining relationships between education, wages, and occupations as well as their associated rewards and life style. Equally inevitable was the consequence that access to these rewards would become the measure of popular aspiration in defiance of economic realities. As a result, the ruling elites were faced with mass demands for economic and social equality that they were ill equipped to meet, but could not ignore.

In this kind of situation the problem of ruling elites is how to maintain social stability in the face of inequalities in the distribution of rewards and status that pose a danger of potential instability. Sociological analysis has drawn attention to three distinctive types of social control by which the range of response to inequality can be characterized: (1) coercive power to force acceptance of situations of inequality; (2) abolition of the conditions and causes of inequality; and (3) efforts to justify the existence of inequality and secure acceptance of it. Each of these has been the subject of extensive theoretical elaboration.[4] Actual social-control measures tend to emphasize one of these while drawing in varying amounts on the other two. While all states rely on a degree of coercion in maintaining the unequal distribution of resources, there are very few—South Africa and Rhodesia are obvious exceptions—that rely on it almost exclusively to secure the subordination of the underprivileged majority by the privileged minority.

Most states attempt to achieve a measure of consensus, and do so by emphasizing one of two contrasting approaches. One approach reflects class theory in affirming that inequalities are both unjust and unnecessary, that they derive from the power of the privileged class, and that they can be abolished. Resultant policy aims at the progressive elimination of inequalities of rewards and status, and at the replacement of a value system reflecting the reward structure and life style of a dominant elite, by a mass culture and consciousness.

The contrasting approach described by functional or stratification theory argues that inequalities arise out of the needs of society for occupational specialization, and are not only inevitable but actually beneficial for all, because they provide the incentive necessary for greater economic efficiency. The essence of derived policy is the attempt to justify inequalities and achieve their acceptance by making the rules governing the distribution of rewards seem legitimate in the eyes of all, including those who benefit least from them. Because the reward structure tends to be a reflection of elite interest, this approach can be viewed as an attempt by the ruling group to persuade subordinate groups to accept its reward structure and value system. To the extent that the elite is successful at this, the potential for conflict arising from inequalities is thereby reduced.

Clearly, this brief summary grossly oversimplifies two major themes of sociological inquiry, but does so in order to indicate the larger context in which the education policies of Kenya and Tanzania can usefully be placed.

Education is one of the most important mechanisms of social control in all societies. In the first place, education is central because of its relationship to social mobility. This provides an opportunity for some people to move from the lower to the upper ranks in society, and so tends to ease some of the incipient tensions associated with inequality. Furthermore, by offering a personal escape route from low status it tends to weaken interest in collective efforts by those who remain. To the extent that upward mobility is a reality for some, and is believed to be possible for all, it serves to disperse some of the incipient antagonisms of the disadvantaged toward the advantaged. In this regard, in countries without universal primary education, the mere expansion of the lower levels of schooling, by broadening the base of subsequent selection, perhaps contributes to the mobility of a few who would not otherwise have benefited; but it certainly increases the semblance of mobility and opportunity that is a safety valve against popular discontent.

Schools in most societies are the main channel of social mobility, and in East Africa they are almost the exclusive one. Because the distribution of educational opportunity at the upper levels is tantamount to distributing future status, acceptance of the validity by which the educational system sanctions and certifies passage from one stage to the next is critical for the process of social control. The effectiveness of these allocative devices depends upon the extent to which they are valid by some objective criteria, and permit upward mobility without obviously discriminating against those of lower status.

The second way in which education may serve as a mechanism of social control is through its ability to socialize its clients. There is now extensive evidence to confirm that one of the main socializing effects of hierarchical and selective school systems having a close connection with the occupational reward structure is to instill in students levels of aspiration and expectation appropriate to their likely future position.[5] Parents and pupils tend to be acutely aware of the academic status of different types of schools and their relative ability to promote the social mobility of their students. Thus the very effect of selection for one type of school rather than another is to trigger a degree of anticipatory adjustment to future roles and rewards in a process which is continued within the differentiating procedures of the classroom. As the educational pyramid in most countries is sharply tapering in shape, the main socializing effect of education is to prepare the majority of students to accept relatively low status and small rewards.

An additional, and much less conclusively documented, socialization effect of schools is their ability to impart a chosen ideology, or consensus values. The argument here is that schools are able to inculcate adherence by students to a set of common values, or a sense of common identity or ethic—be it based on patriotism, socialism, or whatever—that overrides or renders insignificant inequalities based on social and occupational roles. Thus when inequality is confronted it seems acceptable or irrelevant in relation to the higher-order unifying set of values to which all adhere. To the extent that schools are able to promote such a culture, they are able to be mechanisms of social control.

THE IDEOLOGICAL RESPONSE TO INEQUALITY

In Tanzania, official socialist ideology is clear, frequently voiced, and contained in a variety of public documents.[6] It denies the need for rewards and status differences, and has, as its goal, the achievement of widespread equality of material conditions. Inequalities are viewed as neither necessary nor useful, but as ethically unjust and dangerously impractical to social and economic development. Policy, in consequence, has been targeted at the elimination, or at least reduction, of the outstanding disparities in wealth between individuals and regions. It has aimed simultaneously to reduce the privileges of the elite, and to raise the conditions of the masses. Measures aimed at the former have included the reduction of luxury imports, the tightening of personal car loans, and above all, the application of a leadership code that severely curtails supplementary money-making opportunities through rents or other forms of private enterprise.

Tanzania is unique in Africa as a country where the elite has reduced and limited its own rewards and opportunities for personal profit. Measures aimed at raising general living standards include the channeling of investment resources into rural development, and particularly the *ujamaa* village schemes, while the move to decentralize finance and control, and the decision to move the capital city to a more central and rural location, are at least partially inspired by this goal. There can be no doubt that a central aspect of Tanzania's response to the problem of inequality is the attempt to reduce its most striking manifestations:

> [According to Julius Nyerere] . . . the wage differentials in Tanzania are now out of proportion to any conceivable concept of human equality; . . . such differentials in economic levels easily come to be taken for granted as correct; and they lead to social differentiation and attitudes supporting inequality. They encourage the attitude of mind where groups of specialized wage-earners, whose services we need, claim more pay because of the comparative incomes of other specialized groups whose society they aspire to join. It does not seem to happen that anyone compares himself with those at the bottom economic level.

It is essential, therefore, that we in Tanzania, as a society, should recognize that need to take special steps to make our present situation a temporary one, and that we should deliberately fight the intensification of that attitude which would eventually nullify our social need for human dignity and equality. We have to work towards a position where each person realizes that his rights in society—above the basic needs of every human being—must come second to the overriding need of human dignity for all; and we have to establish the kind of social organization which reduces personal temptations above that level to a minimum.[7]

However, while efforts to distribute available resources more equitably are a central tendency, significant inequalities of condition remain, and their persistence intensifies the need for measures to secure acceptance of this situation. Salary differentials among wage earners remain, as do sizable differences in the relative wealth of farmers; and wages in the public sector are tied to levels of educational attainment, although the differences between the highest and the lowest paid, and between the intervening levels, are less in Tanzania than in Kenya. Furthermore, the gap between the rewards of the elite and others cannot be measured solely by nominal salary scales, but needs to take into account such perquisites as access to housing, transport, and foreign exchange. These inevitable continuing distinctions help to explain the social-control element of educational policy in Tanzania—that is, the attempt to develop a mass political consciousness, and to create a political culture exemplified in the life style of the new Tanzanian, who is worker or peasant. The essence of this policy is the attempt to build up and diffuse mass understanding and internalization of those common attributes that together form the basis of Tanzanian citizenship.

The official response to inequality in Kenya is less unequivocally stated than in Tanzania, but is implicit in a variety of policy statements and in the speeches of leaders. The 1974–78 Development Plan summarized future policies toward income distribution as follows:

In order to achieve the social objectives of the Plan, measures will be undertaken to minimize income differentials. Firstly, the better-off members of the community will contribute proportionately more to Government revenue through taxation. All will continue to have the opportunity to contribute also through voluntary *Harambee* [self-help] projects. Secondly, the focus of the last plan on development of rural areas, where incomes are lower than the national average, will continue. Thirdly, Government's provision of education and health services will be accelerated. Finally, the present plan provides opportunities for everyone to participate actively in the economy and in so doing improve his standard of living. Such improvements are bound to be achieved more quickly by some than by others, however. *Equal income for everyone is therefore not the object of this plan. Differences in skill, effort, and initiative need to be recognized and rewarded.* [emphasis added]

Increasingly the message of the elite is a version of the functional theory of stratification implied in the last sentence of the preceding quotation. Variations in individual rewards are seen as necessary forms of incentive. Such inequalities are justifiable because they reflect differences in achievement and in the individual's contribution to society. This being so, the goal of social justice consists less of equalizing rewards than of providing everyone with an equal chance to demonstrate and be rewarded for ability. The unstated rationale for this meritocratic ideal is the notion that people can accept inequalities, and relative personal deprivation, if they believe that they have an equal chance to benefit, and do not choose to question the criteria by which merit and hence mobility are determined.

A comparison of the Ndegwa Commission Report in Kenya and the TANU (Tanganyika African National Union) Guidelines (Mwongozo) in Tanzania provides an instructive contrast in elite ideology.[9] Both are documents produced by the governing elite and dealing with public-sector remuneration. The Ndegwa Report provides a concise ranking of civil-service occupational categories in terms of their perceived importance to society and their required educational qualifications, and proposes corresponding reward levels, with an overall ratio of 36:1 for the highest- as opposed to the lowest-paid workers. These differentials are supported in the text by justifying language.[10] The TANU Guidelines differ starkly from the Ndegwa Report in both content and tone. The emphasis is on reduced elite privileges and salaries. A similar contrast is evident in the types of symbolic and socially respectable behavior that the respective leaders feel they should display. In Kenya, the standard ritual is to lead a local fund-raising effort, and to make a large personal donation to a harambee project. A similar scale of individual contribution by a Tanzanian leader would be grounds for investigation by the anticorruption squad! Instead, the corresponding symbolic gesture is to participate in a communal project of ditch digging or brick making.

The preceding discussion has summarized an approach which seems helpful to understanding some relationships between education and society in East Africa, and has outlined the social-control ideologies of Kenya and Tanzania. It is now possible to investigate the broad proposition that viewing educational development as a means of social control helps to explain aspects of its use in Kenya and Tanzania, and also illuminates the difficulties and inevitable limits of educational policy. The thesis is that, while the official response to the existence of inequality propagates the notion in Tanzania of equalizing economic status, and in Kenya of equalizing competitive opportunity, in both countries actual educational practice implicitly serves to secure acceptance of objective inequalities.

TANZANIA: SOCIAL EQUALITY AND SOCIALIZATION

Two main political emphases in educational policy have followed from Tanzania's desire, on the one hand, to create a more egalitarian society, and on the other, to reconcile people to remaining inequalities. In the first place, there has been a direct attempt to reduce social inequality by broadening the base of educational provision and removing ascriptive barriers to access. Secondly, there has been an increase in the political and socialist content of what is taught as a way of developing common basic attributes of Tanzanian citizenship among students.

Educational Provision

In line with a view of education as, in the first instance, a common right and a social service, there has been an attempt to alter the pattern of distribution of educational resources, such that relatively more resources are directed toward meeting basic mass needs, and less go to producing a small, highly educated class. In practice this has meant a reduction in the proportion of the total education budget going to secondary and tertiary education, and a corresponding increase in the proportion going to primary and adult education.

Adult education has received particularly strong emphasis in Tanzania in the past five years. The afternoon use of primary schools for adult-literacy classes is now widespread, and a number of carefully coordinated campaigns are believed to have effectively reached up to two million people.[11] The proportion of total Ministry of Education expenditure allocated to adult education went up from 4 to 8 percent in the two-year period 1971/72–1973/74. Primary-school fees have been abolished, and the decision to try to implement universal primary education by 1977 means that, in the future, primary education will receive a much greater proportion of government expenditure than the present 50 percent of Ministry of Education allocations.

A corollary of the emphasis upon diffusing a basic educational service for all—indicated by the resources devoted to primary and adult education —has been the deliberate attempt to curtail and control the expansion of secondary and higher education. Since 1967, the government has attempted to relate secondary-school enrollment to tight manpower projections, and to prevent the kind of uncontrolled expansion that has taken place in Kenya. At the same time, where expansion has been authorized, the new facilities have been provided in previously deprived areas of the country in an attempt to reduce the historical imbalance in the distribution of educational facilities.

Accompanying this broadening of the base of educational provision have been various attempts to alter the terms of access to the higher levels of the school system so as to benefit previously less-privileged groups. This has involved the attempt to downgrade examinations and to introduce additional criteria of selection. This did not work well when tried at the primary level, because of the heterogeneity of the system and the scope for patronage and nepotism, but has now been resurrected under the new selection procedures for the University of Dar es Salaam. To be considered for admission here, a prospective student will now be required to have not simply suitable academic qualifications, but also several years' working experience, and a strong recommendation from his employer and TANU branch regarding his "suitability in terms of character, general work performance, and commitment."[12]

Corresponding to the shift in the pattern and terms of access to education have been changes in content, aimed at providing knowledge and skills that will be immediately useful. At the primary level there is an emphasis upon agriculture, and an attempt to integrate subject teaching into the local context. Secondary schools have been classified according to a number of vocational biases—for example, technical, commercial, craft, and agricultural. Perhaps the outstanding example of the attempt to produce relevant knowledge was the health campaign of the Institute of Adult Studies, which aimed to spread knowledge of preventive techniques for combating the six most common diseases in Tanzania.[13]

Socialization

The second distinctive feature of Tanzanian education is its heavy political content. A major objective of the system is to raise the level of collective political consciousness so as to inculcate an understanding of the conditions of Tanzania's underdevelopment, the principles of Tanzanian socialism, a sense of national pride, an appreciation of the dignity of labor; and to foster a spirit of cooperative rather than individualistic behavior and forms of production. It is hoped that, through these means, students can be linked to the rest of the population in a sense of common citizenship that overrides the different and potentially unequal roles they may be called upon to play. There is a heavy reliance on the curriculum and the context of school experience for the achievement of these goals.[14] The subject matter of political education stresses the condition of Tanzania's underdevelopment, and the socialist means to its alleviation, within the wider struggle of the third world and the liberation of the African continent.

It is hoped that these cognitive goals can be achieved through such devices as political education classes, paramilitary training for the people's militia, and the encouragement of an active TANU Youth League in the schools. The inculcation of the socialist values of cooperation and social obligation are to be achieved in the course of regular collective agricultural work, now an integral part of the school curriculum, and by structuring the school organization so as to create an environment which reinforces socialist modes of operation. For those who complete from 4—11 years of formal education—national service provides a period of intensive exposure to manual work, political education, military training, and contact with those who have less formal education.

Complementing direct measures of curriculum change have been efforts designed to foster cultural nationalism. The most important of these has been the intensified use of Swahili as a medium of instruction and as a means of politicization. Thus, teaching in all but a handful of primary schools is done in Swahili, and it is also used in those secondary-school subjects, such as history and political education, which are taught throughout the country by Tanzanians. At the same time the language itself has been developed for the purpose of conveying certain political concepts which are central to the task of socialist education. A further effort in the direction of cultural independence has been a heavy emphasis upon the training of Tanzanian teachers for the purpose of ending dependence upon foreign teachers. The effect of this policy can be gauged by the relatively smaller number of foreign teachers employed in Tanzanian secondary schools than in their Kenyan equivalents. More broadly, there has been a concern, albeit little implemented, to identify educational standards that are exclusively Tanzanian and not a product of the international inheritance.

DILEMMAS OF TANZANIAN EDUCATION

There can be little doubt that educational policy has been concerned about social inequality in Tanzania during the past seven years, and that some progress has been achieved. Following the earlier removal of the most glaring racial and ethnic barriers to educational opportunity, the expansion of primary education and the emphasis on adult education, plus the establishment of government secondary schools in underprovisioned areas, have brought previously ignored groups into communication with the rest of the society. Similarly, it seems clear that the emphasis upon political education has served, at the very least, to imbue students with a stronger sense of national identity and political consciousness than would otherwise have been the case. At the same time there is now a growing awareness in Tanzania of the extent to which educational practce is falling short of aspiration in fostering the movement toward a more egalitarian society. In particular, what little evidence there is suggests that schools are making only modest contributions to the development of the kind of values that are believed to be necessary for the building of socialism.

Contradictions are becoming increasingly visible. For example, the authoritarianism of classroom practice is a standing contradiction of the goal of participatory and cooperative modes of interaction. The emphasis upon downgrading external reward structures is belied by the continued primacy of examinations in motivating students. Even more fundamentally, despite the stress on curtailing the expansion of secondary schools, there has been a mushrooming of private fee-paying schools. These problems are the outgrowth of some of the wider dilemmas that Tanzania faces in the attempt to restructure the relationship between its educational and social systems. The difficulty is the familiar one of creating egalitarian forms of education in advance, in a society where these values are not yet widespread.

A number of continuing characteristics of Tanzanian society have had implications for the effectiveness of the egalitarian objectives of educational policy. The most important of these has been the strength of the continuing relationship between the structures of formal education and those of wage-paying employment, such that educational attainment remains the sole route to material rewards and status. The familiar relationship between education and status is even stronger in Tanzania than it was previously, because one effect of the repression of private enterprise has been to remove the main alternative means to upward mobility. For assessing the effectiveness of Tanzania's educational response to problems of inequality, it is helpful to detail some of the dilemmas the country faces. Educational practice is constantly confronting the task of trying to reconcile contrasting tendencies: between equality and efficiency, between moral and material incentives, between politics and productivity, between elite leadership and mass participation, and between insularity and dependency.

Nation Versus Region

One dilemma centers on the problem of alleviating the historical inequalities of regional and ethnic access to primary and secondary schools that have resulted from the differential patterns of localized demand generated during the colonial period. Rapid achievement of relative parity of access requires sustained discrimination in favor of historically deprived areas, such as Shinyanga and Mara, and against the more advantaged regions, such as Kilimanjaro and West Lake. Yet by virtue of their early comparative advantage, groups from those advantaged regions are strategically entrenched in the structures of society to the point where there is a high political and economic price to their alienation. Tanzania has attempted to alter the unequal pattern of regional access to education by concentrating educational resources on previously deprived areas. At the same time, secondary-school selection has been done on a regional basis, which has the effect—because of variations in the socioeconomic conditions, and the quality and quantity of primary schools—of establishing different standards of entry and hence an indirect quota system. Implicit in the recent addition of nonacademic criteria to selection for university entry is the potential for further engineering the pattern of educational opportunity, but again there are political and practical limits to this kind of manipulation.

The University of Dar es Salaam does not intend to dispense altogether with academic qualifications. The pool of those who, among other desired qualities, possess the new minimum academic requirements is likely to be dominated by those from areas which have depth in their stock of educated youth, that is, the richer, better-endowed regions whose students are already disproportionately represented at the university. Thus one paradoxical effect of the new admission procedures could be to intensify present regional imbalance in the student body.

A similar manifestation of the strength of the constraints on the central manipulation of regional access to education is illustrated by the recent rapid growth of private secondary schools in Tanzania. The demand for these has been concentrated precisely in those areas which have had the best-quality primary and secondary schools, but which are suffering from present government policy. Approximately one-third of the total enrollment at the secondary level is private. This phenomenon—reminiscent of the mushrooming of harambee secondary schools in Kenya during the late 1960s and early 1970s—is indicative of the continued strength of the public demand for academic education; and its political overtones are evident in the fact that the government has chosen to accept and regulate many of these schools, although the effect of such a large private sector is to perpetuate the disproportionate advantages of already advantaged regions and ethnic groups.

Moral Versus Material Incentives

One of the fundamental objectives of Tanzania's social policy is to develop moral, rather than material, incentives as a means of mobilizing the population. The accompanying problem is to decide the speed with which this can and should occur. This is inevitably a long-term educational task, and to abolish financial and individual incentives before moral and collective ones are widely accepted is to risk inducing a widespread apathy. The dilemma results from the fact that schools are expected to lead in the development of the new values. Yet the elimination of a system of external rewards based on examinations and related to subsequent salary differentials—prior to the development of the new values outside education—results in a loss of motivation among students. There is some evidence that one immediate effect of Tanzania's very tentative attempts to reduce the influence of external rewards was to lead some to choose not to go to school, and others to lose interest in continuing with their education.[15]

This vicious circle is proving hard to break. The extent of elite willingness to accept relatively low financial rewards suggests at least partial orientation to nonmaterial rewards, but it is hard to assess the extent of coercion implicit in their response. Certainly there is an element of coercion in the bonding of students and the job direction associated with Tanzania's manpower policies, and particularly the decentralization exercise. Similarly, the frequent official campaigns against laziness and drunkenness, and the instances where uninhibited coercion has been employed in the villagization process, support the view that moral incentives, and the hope of collective as opposed to individual rewards, are not yet providing the motivational force that is sought in Tanzania's social policy.

The Elitist Implications of Manpower Policy

The emphasis upon primary and adult, rather than higher, education is indicative of the primacy of egalitarian objectives in Tanzania, and of the desire to prevent the growth of an excessively large technocratic elite. But other policies, such as the emphasis on manpower planning and the vocationalization of secondary schools, seem to attenuate this commitment. The dilemma arises from the fact that Tanzania requires technical and administrative skills of a high order, which must be developed through formal education, with the almost inevitable consequence that their holders will constitute a technocratic and bureaucratic elite. The self-serving quality of its members depends on the extent to which their schools have imparted a sense of social obligation, to share the skills they have gained at a cost to society, and on the nature of the distinguishing privileges to which they have access by virtue of their training. Although Tanzania's progressive tax structure and strict import licensing have served to reduce the gap between the richest and poorest sections of the population, there are continuing salary differentials tied to educational attainment.

The members of Tanzania's ruling elite are characterized by their educational background, their disproportionate access to the resources of the state, and a life style that distinguishes them from the mass of the population. While the leadership code prevents the excesses of conspicuous consumption and conflict of interest that characterize their counterparts in Kenya, they remain a separate ruling and bureaucratic elite. Yet, paradoxically, it is this group which is expected to spearhead the transformation of Tanzania to a socialist and more egalitarian society. Present policy assumes that the educational system will be able to instill the virtures of self-sacrifice and social duty that will enable the elite to lead in egalitarian change while contributing technical expertise. However, the character of manpower planning seems to preclude such an easy reconciliation of these alternative influences.

Tanzania's manpower planning in the past has tended to assume a continuation of existing patterns of employment, and to concentrate on the replacement of expatriate personnel and on educational efforts to provide the qualifications possessed by those expatriates. Combined with a context where educational attainment remains geared to widely differential monetary rewards, the effect, as John Saul suggests, is predictable: "The logic of the market and the rhetoric of manpower planning thus combine into a heady brew of nascent elitism and the latter is not a particulary encouraging starting point from which to take up an important and creative role in the struggle for egalitarianism."[16]

The mere fact of manpower planning has the monopolistic effect of guaranteeing the more privileged positions to university graduates. If at the same time, the elite who are the beneficiaries of this monopoly are able to actually convince the wider population that—in the words of the current slogan—"we are all workers," the implications of such mystification have a totalitarian tone. The critical question concerning the seriousness of this specter is the social-class origin of those who, in conditions of restricted access to education and private enterprise, do reach the university. The system is too new for more than rudimentary trends to be apparent. In the meantime, it is perhaps pertinent to recall that a policy of restricting the upper echelons of education, combined with a broadening of opportunity for limited early education, served to sustain an exclusive British elite throughout the second half of the nineteenth and the first half of the twentieth century. In Tanzania, from the perspective of those who are most interested in the achievement of a genuinely egalitarian society, the elite are increasingly being viewed as an inevitably exploitative group, fitted into a network of foreign contact: while making minor practical concessions to Tanzania's socialist goals and major rhetorical obeisance, they are seen as the real obstacles to the achievement of that socialist policy.

Politics Versus Productivity

As an outgrowth of the need for simultaneous development of technical skills and a sense of social obligation to use them for the good of society, there is the problem of striking a balance in instruction between political and professional education. Partly to restore a historical imbalance, and partly because the entrenchment of social inequality is viewed as a greater threat to long-term development than present poverty, educational policy is giving great emphasis to developing political and social consciousness among students. Yet to be effective contributors to Tanzanian development after school, students must have skills and competence, as well as the new values of Tanzanian socialism, and thus the rigorous learning and teaching of these skills cannot be dispensed with. The danger of unbalanced emphasis is exemplified, some argue, in some departments at the University of Dar es Salaam, where students have a precise understanding of the nature of Tanzanian underdevelopment and its relationship to world economic and political conditions, but do not have the basic technical skills to solve local practical problems and thereby relieve the very condition of dependency that they deplore. At the secondary level the evidence suggests that neither political nor technical instruction is being done well. K. F. Hirji has painted a chilling picture of the state of political education:

> The contents are dominated by sloganeering and sycophancy, the emphasis being on forms, appearances, declarations rather than scientific understanding of social reality. . . . Thus the atmosphere in which political education is imparted becomes an artificial one in which pretence rather than genuine commitment prevails and where critical thought is unceremoniously banished. Not infrequently it turns into a tug of war between the pupils and the teacher as to who can praise the government most. It is no wonder that neither the pupils nor the teacher care to understand what they say or remember it outside the classroom. Rather than permeating the entire curriculum and organization of the school, political education has been relegated to the level of a compulsory examinable subject a pass in which is essential if one is to proceed to the next stage of education.[17]

It is equally clear that political education is inadequate not simply because it is being sacrificed to the demands of the technical subjects:

> It is common to find teachers frequently skipping classes, not concerned about completing the syllabus, not bothered about correcting homework, etc., let alone any nationalistic or socialistic commitment, even the commitment of a conscientious teacher towards his pupils is becoming a rare phenomenon.[18]

Insularity Versus Dependency

A further dilemma concerns that extent to which Tanzania is able to disengage from inherited educational practices and values derived from outside the country, without destroying general faith in the process of education. While international yardsticks in the form of examinations and concepts of institutional schooling now seem to have questionable relevance to what Tanzania requires of its schools, it is proving difficult to develop new concepts of appropriate educational forms and practice. Certainly, important, even unique, changes have been made in terms of nationalizing the content of education, and making it more relevant to the background from which students come and the life to which they will go. For example, great strides have been made in localizing the teaching force, in developing texts with a Tanzanian rather than a British frame of reference, and so forth. Yet with the notable exception of developments at Tabora School—where an effort is being made to train a leadership cadre —and in the field of adult studies, there seems to have been very little thought given to devising and testing new concepts and structures of education that might serve Tanzania's social policies more precisely than present practice. Until very recently, *Education for Self-Reliance* has been treated as a final blueprint rather than a tentative, albeit lucid, diagnosis calling for imaginative developmental experimentation and extension. In consequence, and despite some attempts at clarification and definition, there remains much uncertainty in the minds of pupils and teachers about what this oft-invoked document is really all about.

In one of the rare empirical studies of Tanzanian schools, Ruth Besha draws a picture of *Education for Self-Reliance* in action in primary schools in the Bagamoyo and Rufiji districts of Tanzania.[19] Her overwhelming conclusion is that the ostensible attempt to implement self-reliance contributes very little to developing among students a collective sense of social obligation, attachment to cooperative forms of action, or even a common political consciousness and commitment that are the bases of Tanzania's intended response to the problem of inequality. The two main pillars of this effort are agricultural work and political education. The study shows that the former is viewed by students mainly as a way of making money and reducing the cost of education to the government—which is certainly a part, albeit a subsidiary one, of the intention—and by parents as a waste of time. Few new skills are imparted by teachers untrained in agriculture, and there is little connection between these activities and the future capacity of students for contributing to new modes of production integrated into their rural setting. However, students do become used to the practice of working collectively, which could conceivably be the basis for future cooperative activity. The basic contradiction is that "as long as the economy of the rural areas is run on individual lines, the school effort at teaching children the advantages of cooperative work are doomed to failure."[20]

As a consequence of their political education, students are well versed in the rhetoric of Tanzanian socialism—the Arusha Declaration, the TANU Guidelines, and the concept that politics is agriculture (*siasa ni kilimo*); but in no measure do they internalize these as guidelines for their own lives, and in the oft-heard phrase *"hayo ni mambo ya siasa tu"* (Those are nothing but political matters) they disdainfully distinguish between things relevant and things political! At the same time, didactic styles of teaching, authoritarian and hierarchical relationships, and bureaucratic styles of work provide a standing contrast to the ideals of cooperation, participation, and democracy, which the students know are the ideals for decision making and organization within the schools. The ready recourse to corporal punishment, which is likely to instill fear and hostility rather than self-confidence and collective responsibility, highlights the gap between the ideal and the practice. In similar fashion the teachers themselves are subject to often-unexplained directives from the Ministry of Education that serve to sustain a sense of rigid hierarchy, in contrast with the egalitarian objectives implicit in official policy.

The essence of educational ideology in Tanzania has been the desire to reduce the extent to which formal education is a source of elitism and status differentiation that will impede the transformation to a socialist society. This policy rests on the expectation that the main consequence of primary education will be the commitment of pupils to a life of collective agriculture, and of postprimary students to a sense of social obligation to devote their skills to the service of the masses. It is clear from our brief overview of educational practice that, by and large, these objectives are not being met, and for two main reasons.

In the first place, it is evident that there are limits on the extent to which schools can instill values which are not yet reflected in the structures of the wider society and accepted by the populace. The limits may not be as absolute as those prophesied by early critics of the political objectives of Tanzanian educational policy;[21] but they exist, and as yet have neither been clearly identified nor taken into account in educational policy. Attainment of political goals is simply made more difficult by the fact that many of the teachers expected to lead in the propagation of socialist values, themselves the products of training in an earlier period, do not believe much of what they are required to teach.

Secondly, Tanzania has not yet created a system of selection that satisfactorily meets the combined economic and political objectives of educational policy.* In its absence, policy seems to fluctuate between two responses. On the one hand, there has been a tendency to reject altogether the need for technical specialization and to spread the view that socialism does not require differentiated roles. This kind of attitude probably accounts for the remarkable indifference in Tanzania to the impact on general efficiency that is created by frequent transfers of skilled workers, the relative lack of concern for matching an individual's training and potential to his actual job, and the lack of responsibility in the allocation of skilled manpower. On the other hand, to the extent that it is recognized that Tanzania requires professional and technical roles that will be inevitable sources of status differentiation, policy has tended to assume that the elitist consequences of this can be mitigated, and a social service outlook created, by means of political education. Yet the chances of this occurring have been reduced by the fact that the manpower-planning and vocationalization policies, to which formal education in Tanzania automatically relates, have remained buried in an inherited pattern of occupational categories. In this situation the Tanzanian ruling elite does not look much different from any other. Their social service function is tacked onto their occupational role, but not integrated into a wider socialist role, with the result that it is their rewards and life style that continue to be a source of aspiration for those still in the school system.

In sum it is clear that the policy summarized in *Education for Self-Reliance* is in some ways inconsistent with the goal of socialist transformation. It aims to fit students into a type of society that does not yet exist, and places excessive faith in changing student attitudes as a means of producing the desired reality.[22]

However, the experience of Cuba suggests that the transformation of the relationship between education and the social system cannot be accomplished overnight.[23] Rather, it is a process of grappling constantly with contradictions and searching for meaningful forms. For all the contradictions of educational policy that are apparent in Tanzania, the situation is not yet one for expressing despair about egalitarian education, but rather, it is one for being realistic in recognizing the magnitude of the task of implementing this particular ideal.

KENYA: SOCIAL MOBILITY AND SELECTION

The implicit ideology of educational policy in Kenya can also be viewed as a response to the problems of social inequality, but it differs strongly from that of Tanzania. Whereas, in Kenya, the prevailing social

---

*A new system of selection was introduced in 1976, and is designed to measure a variety of types of achievement and behavior. It is too early to assess the impact of the system.

philosophy permits sizable differences in individual rewards and status within society, the corresponding educational system must be part of a process that justifies the legitimacy of those differential rewards. Thus the catchwords of education ideology in Kenya are expansion, equality of opportunity, and advancement by merit.

The outstanding characteristic of the educational scene since independence has been the expansion of formal, and especially secondary, education. At first this was, and was presented as, a deliberate policy designed to meet urgent manpower needs. However, as the harambee impetus gathered steam, more and more schools were built with local finance on a self-help basis, were filled with students, and were presented for government support; as these established institutions developed a growth momentum of their own, it became increasingly difficult to justify this preemptive expansion in terms of preordained manpower priorities. At this point the policy justification began to give less emphasis to the manpower contribution of this expansion, and more to the extent to which it reflected a philosophy of expanded opportunity. In other words, a political rationale displaced the economic one.

The important point is that in Kenya, private demand for conventional types of education has been encouraged and accommodated to a much greater extent than in Tanzania. Hardly a day goes by without a major public official exhorting parents to send their children to school as a way of giving them a chance to benefit from the opportunities of independence. Expansion is accommodated because the alternative of reducing demand by altering the reward structure is politically unacceptable. To curtail expansion would be to admit—as Tanzania has had to do—that those deprived of any chance of education by such a decision would, at the same time, be deprived of any chance of qualifying for the higher rewards and privileges available in the society; and this in turn would tend to discredit the legitimacy of such rewards going to the elite.

As part of the broader objective of expansion, there has, secondly, been an attempt, akin to that of Tanzania, to direct resources to areas neglected in the colonial pattern of development.

Thirdly, accompanying the stress on access to educational opportunity is an emphasis on academic achievement as the criterion for advancement within the system, and this is the critical feature in the emerging rationale for Kenya's educational policy. If access to educational opportunity is to be truly equitable, it is essential that selection for each level of schooling be determined by criteria which apply in the same way to everyone, and which, at the same time, are seen and believed to be objective. Tested and certified academic achievement has been chosen as the measure of objectivity in Kenya. Every wage-earning job has a prerequisite minimum educational qualification. This is true not simply for the entry points to the formal system, but for every type of educational activity, including the university, with the sanctity of its degrees; adult education, where correspondence courses are geared almost entirely to formal examinations; technical education, with the remorseless domination of the London City and Guilds examination, and even the village polytechnics, which increasingly view success in trade tests as their raison d'etre.[24]

There has been little attempt to break away from the inherited pattern of academic credentials. Indeed, the pressure has been in the opposite direction, with a tightening of these relationships as employment opportunities become scarce; the minimum educational requirements have been raised, and research and reform efforts have been directed toward improving the efficiency of the examinations. Meanwhile, as this reform proceeds, the all-important factor is that the examinations are seen to be standard for all. The recurring nightmare of the Ministry of Education officials each year is that leakage or cheating might impair the aura of impartiality that is intended to pervade the content and administration of the examinations. The certificate of primary education (CPE) is printed in Britain and machine marked, and highly elaborate security arrangements accompany its preparation and distribution. Similarly, at the secondary level the concern for objectivity has led to relative tardiness in making a break with the Cambridge Overseas Examination Board, because the very name and distance of Cambridge are suggestive of impartiality.

This preoccupation with academic qualification as the touchstone of educational merit may be attacked on the educational grounds that examination results are a relatively poor predictor of employment performance, but it has a strong sociopolitical rationale. In a pluralistic society characterized by inequalities, it provides visible evidence against the charge of official discrimination. People can accept ultimate inequalities of wealth if they believe that they have a chance to enter the school system, will be judged by objective criteria within it, and will have an equal chance to enter employment outside it. To the extent that the ethos of equal opportunity and social mobility can be shown to coincide with reality, tensions arising from inequalities of wealth and status are correspondingly fewer.

The contradictions of Kenya's educational policy stem from the difficulty of fostering an ethos of equal opportunity where preexisting regional and ethnic inequalities in access to education within the population have developed a momentum of their own, in the context of a highly selective educational system monopolizing access to the highest rewards in society.

DILEMMAS OF KENYA'S EDUCATIONAL POLICY

The pattern of regional imbalance in the distribution of educational resources and opportunities that has taken root in Kenya since independence has been comprehensively documented by Kabiru Kinyanjui.[25] Originating, as in Tanzania, in the mode of colonial development, the direction of missionary activity, and the vigor or self-help efforts, this pattern of regional imbalance has been reinforced by the postindependence configurations of political power. There remain gross disparities between provinces and districts, along such dimensions as the proportion of the primary-age group actually in school, the distribution of secondary-school places, the opportunity to continue with further education, and so on. However, the purpose here is not to reiterate familiar facts, but rather, to analyze the nature and consequences of the official response.

It is quite clear that the Kenyan government has made substantial efforts to achieve a wider distribution of educational opportunity. The decree removing fees for the first four years of primary education, the partial allocation of resources on a regional basis, and special additional provision to previously deprived parts of the country are all evidence of the government's attempt to expand access to school facilities. At the provincial level, the number of state-aided secondary schools has increased relatively faster over the last ten years in provinces which previously had the smallest number, although this has made only slight inroads into the overall pattern of inherited educational provision.[26]

However, if this policy is viewed as a long-term response to mitigating problems of inequality, it contains a number of inherent contradictions. In the first place, marginal improvements in the pattern of distribution of government-aided schools have tended to be counteracted by the provision of self-help facilities; the wealthy and politically influential areas have been able to maintain their lead by the establishment of self-help harambee schools.[27] Similarly, as Kenneth King has shown, because attempts at redistribution of resources have not—in the Rift Valley, for example— been accompanied by strict ethnic quotas, they have served to intensify ethnic imbalance by providing additional opportunities to outsiders from areas which are already well endowed with educational facilities.[28] However, the Kenyan government has explicitly rejected the kind of quota system proposed in a 1972 study by the International Labour Office as a way of alleviating regional and ethnic inequalities of access.[29]

More important, perhaps, is the fact that while the wider distribution of educational facilities is a necessary first step in reducing regional imbalance, it cannot alone compensate for a history of relative deprivation, but must be accompanied by a substantial and sustained concern with the quality of those schools, measured particularly by the quality of teachers. Kenya, unlike Tanzania, has not been able or willing to allocate its best teachers to the most needy areas. The result is that the regional distribution of professionally qualified teachers tends to correspond to the pattern of school distribution, and within that the four main urban centers have an average of twice as many trained primary-school teachers as the rural areas.[30]

The pattern of regional and ethnic disparity in access to educational opportunity is similar to that of Tanzania. However, a distinctive difference is that no attempt has been made to produce a unified school system; Kenya has built into its system, at both the primary and secondary levels, different categories of schools derived from the colonial period. Primary schools in Nairobi, for example, are classified into three types, which correspond to the virtually segregated categories of the colonial period, and although racial exclusiveness no longer applies, the school types retain a differential quality in terms of teachers and resources.[31] A similar hierarchy prevails at the secondary level with the national catchment, locally maintained and harambee schools—while in Nairobi the former European schools—now designated "high cost" schools—serve to further differentiate the available categories. The relationship between type of school and subsequent mobility, with individual ability holding constant, has been well documented.[32] However, the existence of these subcategories in the hierarchy of the selective school system says nothing in itself about the nature of opportunity; for this we need to consider the criteria by which access to these schools is determined.

One aspect of the rationale for the emphasis on the provision of facilities—including high-cost and high-quality schools—is that it contributes to the notion of expanding opportunity, and this tangible demonstration of government concern, at the same time, places the burden of subsequent failure to advance upon the individual. However, to the extent that regional disparities in the provision of educational facilities continue to exist, and as long as access to higher-quality schools is visibly related to factors other than individual ability, it is correspondingly more difficult to diffuse acceptance of an ethos of equal opportunity.

Criteria of Access

Given the likely continuation of disparities of educational provision by region, a further dilemma for a policy based on spreading the notion of equal opportunity relates to the desire to use academic-achievement criteria as the determinant of future mobility. Although there are, almost certainly, undetected areas of cheating on the one hand, and blatant overriding of examination results on the other, by and large, there can be little doubt about the primacy of examination performance in determining access to further educational opportunity. The extent to which mobility from school to employment is governed by the same criteria is harder to assess, although Kinyanjui's data show a high correlation at least for the individual's first job.[33] At the same time, there is evidence to suggest that where examination performance for two individuals is similar, other, less universalized criteria have become second-order determinants of advancement in the long term, and these cases probably account for the frequently voiced charge of nepotism.[34] Nevertheless, by reference to the prevalence of standardized examinations, it is possible to proclaim that individual achievement is the criterion of advancement, and hence to foster a meritocratic ideology.

However, the fact that the examination system may advance the notion of meritocracy by its internal efficiency says nothing about the kind of merit that is being measured, and whether the criteria for its measurement are equally accessible for all individuals and groups from different backgrounds. Few examinations are very accurate predictors of subsequent performance, but evidence is now accumulating to suggest that Kenya's main examinations are also unable to comprehensively predict subsequent performance in the school system, except at the extremes of ability. More important than this for the argument, however, is the accumulating evidence that the content of the most important examinations is serving to compound the preexisting differential advantages of individuals and regions.

The critical examination for determining educational opportunity and subsequent mobility is the CPE, which is the selection device for secondary education. The range and subtlety of the ways by which the content of questions serve to predetermine performance is the subject of present research by H. C. A. Somerset that is likely to have a major impact on thinking in this area. Two general conclusions from this work serve by way of illustration.[35] In the first place, the examination, because it has required mastery of a vast corpus of abstract knowledge in anticipation of secondary-school requirements, has tended to be a test of teachers rather than students. The obvious effect of this is to reinforce the regional disparities that have already been noted. Secondly, to a large extent, the examinations have been a test of the English language. In the face of evidence regarding the unequal consequences created by the content of the CPE, the Ministry of Education is giving some attention to devising procedures which discriminate less than previously against those from rural and poor urban schools.

Analysis suggests that in certain subjects, it is possible to devise items which, by eliminating cultural bias and emphasizing inference rather than abstract content, serve to reduce the present wide margin of discrimination resulting simply from the content of the examination. However, there are limits to the extent to which the examination can be manipulated as a device to improve equity. To the extent that intelligence is a product of training, those from better-quality schools will be able to perform better on tests than their less-privileged compatriots, whatever the content. The most equitable type of examination would presumably be one which ruled out the need for a teacher by calling for material from a limited number of designated books; but to reduce the content to a lowest common denominator of this sort would obviously involve a high price in terms of the capacity of schools to produce imaginative and resourceful students.

A third related dilemma of Kenyan educational practice derives from its perpetual expansion. It was suggested that the constant expansion of formal education is necessary to preserve the impression of widening opportunity, but clearly there is a limit to the extent to which Kenya can absorb the cost of continuing at the present rate of expansion. The government spends approximately 33 percent of the total state budget on education, and dire predictions have been made about the damage to other forms of productive investment that is likely to be caused by a continuation of the present rate of growth of educational expenditures.[36] It is clear that there will be a slowing down in the rate of expansion of governmental expenditure on education, but the danger is that the effect of this will be to present the government as blocking the aspirations of those who had seen education as their salvation.

It should be clear from the foregoing that the problems of Kenyan educational policy, like those of Tanzania, center on the issue of selection. But whereas the selection function has been subordinated by TANU to that of socialization, in Kenya the opposite situation prevails: The political vulnerability of the government's educational policy lies in the extent to which opportunity is manifestly unequal. As educational opportunities are not equally available to all, and as present selection devices tend to reinforce initial regional and individual advantages, a critical question is whether the degrees of inequality pose an imminent threat to Kenya's much-vaunted social stability. Kenya, unlike Tanzania, has made little attempt to use schools for promoting a spirit of nationalism and self-sacrifice in favor of regional equalization. Instead, the appeal is to self-help and the meritocratic ideal, which tends to intensify regional inequalities as those best able to help themselves are those who already have resources to spare. Earlier evidence from a national sample of Kenyan secondary students suggests that, where an unequal distribution of resources is perceived, it is reflected in reduced enthusiasm for the central government, and it cannot be overridden by appeals to nationalism. If this is the case for students in school, one might expect a much greater degree of disaffection from the increasing ranks of the educated unemployed, the content of whose education has fitted them for little more than unemployment.[37]

It has been claimed that the alienation of those deprived of further education in China led them to become activists in the cultural revolution. In Kenya, however, the relative political quiescence of the educated unemployed suggests that, despite the anomalies and objective inequalities that have been identified, the government has been comparatively successful in promoting acceptance of the mobility ethos, and that the unemployed may have internalized norms which lead them to accept their position by seeing themselves as unfortunate, or personally derelict, losers in a basically just system.

CONCLUSION

This study has contrasted the condition of formal education in Kenya and Tanzania, and argued that the striking differences stem from a different ideological response to problems posed by conditions of inequality. In Kenya it is assumed that inequalities are an inevitable and necessary accompaniment to rapid economic growth; and, in consequence, educational policy has emphasized the meritocratic nature of selection procedures, and the ethos of equal opportunity, so as to secure the acquiescence of the nonselected. Tanzania's ideology has, by contrast, argued that the alienation of the masses in the face of inequality is the greatest danger to development, and that the minimization of inequalities and the development of mass consciousness are the necessary prerequisites for productive activity and economic growth. Hence its education policy has deemphasized the selective aspects of the education system and stressed political education, both of the few who proceed to secondary education and the many who do not.

Given that distributive inequalities and role differentiation are, in some measure, inevitable and in East Africa are deeply rooted in the colonial legacy, the growth of modern occupations, and the compounding of ethnic inequalities, education policy in both countries aims to secure a measure of popular acceptance of inequality by fostering one type of mass consciousness. In Tanzania it is the common consciousness of socialist citizenship and in Kenya it is the meritocratic ideal.

If the aim of educational policy in Kenya and in Tanzania is to contribute to the creation of a capitalist and a socialist society, respectively, it is clear that the Kenyan education systems fits more closely to its intention than that of Tanzania. The internal inconsistencies are less visible and less strong in Kenya than in Tanzania, which suffers from the eloquence and idealism of its stated goals. The gap between intention and implementation is glaring in Tanzania, in part because the aspirations have been more clearly and publicly stated than those of Kenya.

However, in the short run it is easier to continue an existing pattern, as Kenya has done, than to produce a radically different one, as Tanzania is trying to do. The fact that Kenya's education system conforms more closely to the country's dominant social ideology than Tanzania's does to its particular social philosophy may be accurate as a present generalization, but says little about the long-term viability of their respective modes of development. A recent comparison of the two on the basis of conventional educational criteria led to the conclusion that Kenya is relatively "stronger,"[38] but takes no account of the fact that social transformation is on the Tanzanian agenda. The more important comparison concerns how each is doing in relation to some of the fundamental political problems that both face. The broad question raised in this chapter concerns what an examination of their education systems suggests about their relative success at minimizing the destructive potential of inequality.

Implicit in Kenya's ideology of development is the assumption of a conflict between the goals of economic growth and those of distributive equality. Thus the concept of equality of opportunity is invoked as a means of achieving the political stability necessary to preserve a selective school system geared to the high-level manpower requirements believed to be necessary for economic growth. Explicit in Tanzanian ideology is a concept of equality that is viewed not simply as a means to political stability, but also as a basis for more efficient societal institutions and more rapid long-term economic development. From the perspective of the problem of inequality, the long-term test of Kenya's educational policy is whether the emphasis on high-level manpower selection can continue to be pursued without alienating, to the point of violent outrage, the mass of the population who are not selected. By contrast, one risk of Tanzania's alternative emphasis is that the cost, in short-term economic inefficiency, of transition to a more institutionalized egalitarianism might become the source of massive social discontent. Or, more fundamentally, the transition might be declared over before it is actually completed, with everyone designated as a worker, thus effectively castrating the demand for political equality.

The relative political quiescence of, first, primary-school leavers and, now, secondary-school leavers, which is a feature of the Kenyan scene, was earlier attributed to the fact that their experience had led them to internalize the meritocratic ideology in which their failure to advance was attributed to personal deficiency rather than systematic discrimination. That individual failure is not translated into collective action can be attributed to the fact that, despite the visible, not to mention the invisible, inequalities characteristic of the school system, it remains, in some measure, open, to the extent that every year enough children from impoverished homes, poor schools, and deprived areas join the academic mainstream to sustain the faith of the rest in "the Kenyan dream."

How open the school system is remains a matter of present controversy, and there is no space here to muster the still-fragmented empirical evidence on this question. Suffice it to say that the "ominous signs" of the emergence of a class-conscious elite that J. B. Olson documented in 1971 have intensified since then.[39] Nursery schools, the English language, and home facilities such as books and television, are the main means by which the elite is gaining a comparative advantage in using the education system for maintenance of its own status. Within the national system, the critical factor for mobility is the type of school to which one is able to gain admission.

Again, without further data, it is difficult to specify how far social stratification has crystallized, or is still able to expand, at the higher levels. In assessing the likelihood of ultimate popular protest, however, the actual reality is less important than what people believe is happening. Few who live in Kenya are unaware of the sentiment that a visible elite is manipulating the school system, as well as other instruments of the state, for its own advantage. At the point at which—if the process is continued—individuals cease to regard more education as a way out of their personal poverty, they may then view the school system, as well as other social structures, as something to be modified in their interest. At the moment, tolerance for the national lottery, which is Kenyan education, seems fairly elastic.

For the case of Tanzania, it was argued earlier that intolerance of economic hardship and inefficiency during the transformation to socialism posed the biggest threat to an educational and social policy that is stressing political socialization as a means for combating inequality. As with Kenya, tolerance for manifestations of the factors threatening policy has proved remarkably elastic among the elite and masses alike. When it was decided to base educational policy on the assumption that Tanzanian development had more to fear from social inequality than from economic poverty, Nyerere cannot have foreseen the degree of hardship that his people would in fact be called upon to face. If this tolerance is sustained and if the economic position improves, Tanzania will then have a chance to develop a socialist educational policy that takes account of some of the present contradictions.

While data on the extent of social stratification in Tanzania are even more fragmentary than those for Kenya, impressionistic evidence suggests that various aspects of educational policy contribute to minimizing the extent to which the Tanzanian elite is able to develop self-conscious class pretensions. The abolition of the English language in primary schools, the elimination of private primary schools, and a general ethos that discourages elitist manifestations all serve to reduce, albeit not remove, opportunities for self-interested class manipulation of the education system. The recent decision to end direct-admission to the university suggests that Tanzania is prepared to go to great lengths in its attempt to prevent a socially destructive elitism.

On the basis of the evidence adduced in this chapter, a definitive prognosis of any sort would be presumptuous. Yet as one surveys the continuing juxtaposition of the effect of inequality and the strength of popular egalitarianism in East Africa, it is hard not to conclude that lasting educational policy will have to break with its inherited structures. If this is so, we will have to find encouragement where we can—in the demonstrated resilience of Tanzania's ideals to sustained difficulties, rather than in the relatively efficient management of an exclusively hierarchical school and opportunity system in Kenya.

NOTES

1. Particularly useful in shaping a general approach to this topic has been Frank Parkin, *Class Inequality and Political Order* (London: Paladin, 1972). Other useful recent works which bear on this issue are Samuel Bowles and Herbert Gintis, "I.Q. in the U.S. Class Structure," *Social Policy* 3, no. 5 (January/February 1973): 65–96; Philip Foster, "Access to Schooling," in *Education in National Development*, ed. Don Adams (London: Routledge and Kegan Paul, 1971); and Albert Hirschman, "The Changing Tolerance for Income Inequality in the Course of Economic Development," *World Development* 1, no. 12 (December 1973): 29–36.

2. Some of the historical origins of regional inequality in access to education in Kenya are described in James R. Sheffield, *Education in Kenya: An Historical Study* (New York: Teachers College Press, 1973), and in John Anderson, *The Struggle for the School: The Interaction of Missionary, Colonial Government and Nationalist Enterprise in the Development of Formal Education in Kenya* (Nairobi: Longmans, 1970). Analysis of the colonial pattern and the trends it engendered in Tanzania is contained in Marjorie J. Mbilinyi, "African Education in the British Colonial Period, 1919–1961," mimeographed (Dar es Salaam: University of Dar es Salaam, 1975). For a comprehensive analysis of education in the first decade of Tanzania's independence, see David Morrison, *Education and Politics in Africa: The Tanzanian Case* (Nairobi: Heinemann, 1976). For recent changes, see T. L. Maliyamkono, "Educational Reform for Development," Dar es Salaam, mimeographed, 1977.

3. Details on patterns of present-day inequalities are presented in a number of documents. For Kenya, see particularly *Employment, Incomes and Equality* (Geneva: International Labour Office, 1972), and Kabiru Kinyanjui, "The Distribution of Educational Resources and Opportunities in Kenya," Discussion Paper no. 208, (Nairobi: Institute for Development Studies, University of Nairobi, 1974). For Tanzania, see Abel Ishumi, "The Educated Elite: A Survey of East African Students at Institutions of Higher Learning," mimeographed (Dar es Salaam: University of Dar es Salaam, Department of Education, 1974), and Marjorie J. Mbilinyi, "The Problem of Unequal Access to Primary Education in Tanzania" (Paper presented at the Annual Social Science Conference of the East African Universities, Dar es Salaam, 1973).

4. An excellent review and synthesis of this literature is given in Parkin, op. cit.

5. See, for example, H. T. Himmelweit and J. Wright, "The School System, Social Class and Attainment After School," University of London, 1967; H. C. A. Somerset, "Educational Aspirations of Fourth-Form Pupils in Kenya," in *Education, Society and Development: New Perspectives from Kenya*, ed. David Court and Dharam P. Ghai (Nairobi: Oxford University Press, 1974), pp. 67–101; Joel D. Barkan, *An African Dilemma: University Students, Development and Politics in Ghana, Tanzania and Uganda* (New York: Oxford University Press, 1975).

6. Most notably, in *The Arusha Declaration* (Dar es Salaam: Government Printer, 1967); "The TANU Guidelines (Mwongozo)," in *Mbioni* (Dar es Salaam) 6, no. 8 (1971); Julius K. Nyerere, *Decentralization* (Dar es Salaam, Government Printer, 1972).

7. Julius K. Nyerere, *Freedom and Unity/Uhuru na Umoja: A Selection from Writings and Speeches 1952–65* (Nairobi: Oxford University Press, 1966), pp. 16–17. For a discussion of Nyerere's views see Cranford Pratt, *The Critical Phase in Tanzania 1945–68* (London: Cambridge University Press, 1976), pp. 225–26.

8. Republic of Kenya, *Development Plan, 1974–78* (Nairobi: Government Printer, 1974), p. 3.

9. Republic of Kenya, *Report of the Commission of Inquiry (Public Service Structure and Remuneration Commission)* (Nairobi: Government Printer, 1971), and "The TANU Guidelines (Mwongozo)," loc. cit.

10. The argument that the Ndegwa Commission Report officially sanctioned the emerging functionalist ideology in Kenya is developed in Kenneth Prewitt, "The Functional Justification of Inequality and the Ndegwa Report: Shaping an Ideology" (Paper presented at the Annual Social Science Conference of the East African Universities, Nairobi, 1972).

11. See Julius K. Nyerere, "Progress Comes with Production," *The African Review* (Dar es Salaam) 3, no. 4 (1973): pp. 531–32.

12. See "Admission to University," in *Daily News* (Dar es Salaam), January 8, 1975.

13. For an evaluation of the campaign which preceded "Mru ni Afya," see Budd L. Hall, *Wakati wa Furaha, Research Report No. 13* (Uppsala: Scandinavian Institute of African Studies, 1973).

14. For an assessment of some of these efforts, see David Court, "The Social Function of Formal Schooling in Tanzania," *The African Review* 3, no. 4 (1973), pp. 577–96.

15. R. H. Sabot, "Education, Income Distribution and Rates of Urban Immigration in Tanzania," Paper 72.6 (University of Dar es Salaam, Economic Research Bureau, 1972), p. 36.

16. John Saul, "High Level Manpower for Socialism," in *Socialism in Tanzania,* vol. 2, ed. Lionel Cliffe and John Saul (Nairobi: East Africa Publishing House), 1973, p. 279.

17. K. F. Hirji, "School Education and Underdevelopment in Tanzania," *Maji Maji* (Dar es Salaam), September 12, 1973, p. 21.

18. Ibid, p. 20.

19. M. Ruth Booha, "Education for Self Reliance and Rural Development," mimeographed (Dar es Salaam: University of Dar es Salaam, Institute of Education, 1973).

20. Ibid., p. 33.

21. See, for example, Philip Foster, "Education for Self-Reliance: A Critical Evaluation," in *Education in Africa: Research and Action,* ed. Richard Jolly (Nairobi: East African Publishing House, 1969), pp. 81–101.

22. For an amplification of this general conclusion, see Hirji, loc. cit.

23. See Samuel Bowles, "Cuban Education and the Revolutionary Ideology," *Harvard Educational Review* 41, no. 4 (November 1971): 472–500.

24. For illustrations of the way in which the demand for credentials influences the nature of activity in different spheres of the educational enterprise, see the chapters by Court, by E. M. Godfrey and G. C. M. Mutiso, and by Peter Kinyanjui in *Education, Society and Development,* ed. Court and Ghai, op. cit.

25. Kabiru Kinyanjui, "The Distribution of Educational Resources and Opportunities in Kenya," op. cit.

26. Ibid., p. 29.

27. Ibid., p. 30.

28. Kenneth King, "Primary Schools in Kenya: Some Critical Constraints on Their Effectiveness," in *Education, Society and Development,* ed. Court and Ghai, op. cit., pp. 123–47.

29. Kenya, *Sessional Paper on Employment* (Nairobi: Government Printer, May 1973).

30. Kenya, Ministry of Education, *Annual Report, 1973* (Nairobi: Government Printer, 1974).

31. See Z. Ergas and Fred Chege, "Primary School Education in Kenya: An Attempt at Evaluation," *Journal of Eastern African Research and Development* (Nairobi) 3, no. 2 (1973).

32. Kabiru Kinyanjui, "Education, Training and Employment of Secondary School Leavers in Kenya," in *Education, Society and Development,* ed. Court and Ghai, op. cit., pp. 47–66, and Kabiru Kinyanjui, "The Distribution of Educational Resources and Opportunities in Kenya," op. cit., p. 36.

33. Kabiru Kinyanjui, "Education, Training and Employment of Secondary School Leavers in Kenya," loc. cit.

34. For some interesting data on these points, see Kenneth Prewitt, "Education and Social Equality in Kenya," in *Education, Society and Development,* ed. Court and Ghai, op. cit., pp. 199–216.

35. Some initial conclusions are in H. C. A. Somerset, "Who Goes to Secondary School? Relevance, Reliability and Equity in Secondary School Selection," in ibid., pp. 149–84.

36. Kenya, *Development Plan, 1974–78,* part 1 (Nairobi: Government Printer, 1974), p. 407.

37. David Court and Kenneth Prewitt, "Nation Versus Region in Kenya: A Note on Political Learning," *British Journal of Political Science* 4, no. 1 (1973).

38. Edmund O'Connor, "Contrasts in Educational Development in Kenya and Tanzania," *African Affairs* (London) 73, no. 290 (January 1974): 67–84.

39. J. B. Olson, "Secondary Schools and Elites in Kenya: A Comparative Study of Students in 1961 and 1968," *Comparative Education Review* 16, no. 1 (February 1972): 44–53.

10

FOREIGN RELATIONS: DILEMMAS OF INDEPENDENCE AND DEVELOPMENT

John J. Okumu

THE QUESTION OF THE NATIONAL INTEREST

ALL STATES STRIVE to create around them a climate of opinion favorable to the achievement of their own goals. Most debates on foreign policy issues therefore proceed on the understanding that they are basically oriented toward the national interest. They do not usually question whether or not there is one, but they do decide which interests are crucial and must be defended, and which can, if necessary, be sacrificed in a state's interacting with other states. Hence, the primary task for those responsible for the making of foreign policy is to first articulate their country's national interests in some logical order of importance. It is only by so doing, that it is possible to isolate the basic from the peripheral interests. Once this step is taken, it becomes less complicated to decide and to measure the amount of power or capability required to implement a foreign policy that is to the advantage of the state on whose behalf it is made.

It does not logically follow, however, that states which are capable of clearly articulating their foreign policy objectives and accurately assessing their capability to realize them always succeed in getting their way. Success in achieving objectives may depend on a country's weight or standing in the international community. Or, it may derive from the way the objectives are set in relation to those of other nations whose support may be deemed necessary for achieving them. Thus a foreign policy strategy may be directly or indirectly beneficial for new states, some of which find it difficult to chart an independent course on external affairs.

But there are always disagreements among various groups in the political system as to whose interests are to be served by a particular set of foreign policy goals. A foreign policy objective that advances the interest of primary commodity producers may be resisted by merchants who peddle foreign goods in the domestic market and who may be disinterested in seeing the growth of a viable domestic market. For instance, Tanzania's attempt to reorganize peasant production, and increase the workers' understanding of production relations, has not been liked by the small and rather unprogressive petite bourgeoisie whose interests collude with those of multinational capital. Occasionally, this petite bourgeoisie unwittingly creates artificial shortages that force the government to raise prices. At other times, it attempts to disrupt the distribution of basic commodities in the provinces, in such a way as to persuade the leadership to abandon the policy of socialism and self-reliance.

While domestic pressures do influence foreign policy objectives, they are more likely to overestimate the capability of the system to achieve them. There is therefore a frequent problem of stating one's foreign policy objectives without properly assessing the mechanism for realizing them. This is what often causes a disjunction between stated policy objectives and the actions taken to achieve them. This problem is common to most third-world countries and may be partly explained by the fact that significant social formations have not yet been fully articulated. This ambiguity frequently results in the leaders of new states entering into cooperative agreements with multinational corporations at the expense of what would appear to be the national interest. The most prevalent in this line are parasitic management and consultancy contracts, and concessions to multinationals for tax relief, which often include full repatriation of profits and invested capital. Thus in Kenya, the Foreign Investment Protection Act of 1964 seeks to attract private foreign investment by guaranteeing full repatriation of profits (in proportion to the foreign share of the equity), interest, and the repayment of foreign loan capital. Foreign companies are also given liberal depreciation allowances on their investments, which permits them to effectively escape taxation, and protected markets for the products they produce. Such policies are manifestations of the dependence and underdevelopment of most third-world states, and emphasize their powerlessness and the fact that these countries are a power vacuum that external interests may exploit.

The most effective uses of foreign policy should be directed to three main areas. First, foreign policy should provide a framework and an atmosphere of physical security against external aggression. The development of effective friendly relations with one's neighbors is conceivably the first step in this process. This can be realized by increasing the volume of transactions in other sectors, such as communications linkages, trade, exchange of research facilities and findings, and exchange of manpower and training facilities. Second, joint industrial, agricultural, and commercial ventures can be initiated in order to rationalize and facilitate effective uses of natural and human resources. Joint ventures between governments may also reduce the parasitic element prevalent in operations involving a multinational and a single underdeveloped country. Successful joint ventures may reduce the amount of reckless individual political opportunism that is so apparent in Africa today, because the leadership of one state involved in a joint venture would be subject to the scrutiny of the leadership of the other. Third, effective diversification of trade partners and aid donors can be emphasized to reduce the potential for the sabotage of the economy by external interests. Diversification can also be used as a way of practicing nonalignment. Finally, foreign policy can be geared toward maximizing technical cooperation among African countries, and between them and other third-world states. This would reduce heavy dependence on industrialized countries and increase mutual trust in each other, and make it possible for the third world to solve its problems without intervention from industrialized countries. In sum, developing countries can and should make use of foreign policy as an instrument of development. In the discussion that follows, we examine these points in relation to the foreign policies of Kenya and Tanzania.

THE POTENTIALS OF POWER

At independence, both Kenya and Tanzania recognized their poverty as surely as they acknowledged the ruthlessness with which the dominant powers often pursued their national interests by using their technological advantages. They were equally aware of the difficulties encountered by small and poor states that seek meaningful participation in international politics while possessing an insufficient amount of the major determinant of success in that arena, national power. Coupled with a background of dependence, they were aware that an assertive involvement in world affairs would be futile because there would be insufficient power to back it up.

The power potential of both countries leaves much to be desired. Tanzania, with an estimated population of 15.57 million in 1976,[1] had a per capita income of $170, compared to more than $6,000 for such richer states as the United States, West Germany, or Sweden.[2] It also lacks valuable materials, save some undeveloped iron ore and coal; and has no comparative strategic advantage that might be needed by other members of the international community. It had a GNP of $2.56 billion in 1975 and an average growth rate of only about 4.3 percent from 1970 through 1975.[3] Militarily, Tanzania had only 13,000 men in the army, 600 in the navy, 1,000 in the air force, and no paramilitary forces.[4] Its defense expenditure was also relatively small, amounting to about $70 million in 1975.[5] Comparatively, Kenya's power potential is hardly any better than Tanzania's. With a population of 13.86 million in 1976, Kenya had a GNP of $2.9 billion and a per capita income of $220.[6] Its growth rate from 1967 to 1970 was 6.7 percent, but dropped to 4.3 percent for the period of 1972 through 1976.[7] By 1975, its armed forces totaled 7,550 and consisted of 6,500 men in the army, 350 in the navy, and 700 in the air force, plus 1,800 paramilitary personnel.[8] Its defense expenditure in 1976 was $35 million.[9]

These figures compare very unfavorably with two principal adversaries of both countries—South Africa and Rhodesia. In 1976, Rhodesia's armed forces consisted of an army of 9,200 men, 10,000 territorial forces, and 35,000 reservists, supported by a defense expenditure of $130 million.[10] South Africa's defense expenditure for 1976–77 was more than ten times this amount, at $1.49 billion, which supported a regular army, air force, and navy of 51,500, plus 90,000 paramilitary personnel and police.[11]

This relatively weak power position of Kenya and Tanzania was further complicated by the fact that at the time of independence, the commanding heights of both economies were dominated by European firms and by Asian merchants who controlled retail trade as well as distribution. The links between metropolitan manufacturers and the Asians in East Africa became so strong that attempts by African traders to enter the trade sector in the interwar years, and especially after World War II, made only modest headway. The monopoly of available sources of finance by European and Asian banks further facilitated their dominance. This state of affairs was buttressed by the institutional dependence on Britain that characterized the East African monetary system, as part of the sterling zone centered in Britain. This situation continued until 1966 when the East African Currency Board was replaced by separate central banks in Tanzania, Kenya, and Uganda. It was only after this separation that Kenya and Tanzania were able to have some say on how to dispose of their domestic surplus.[12]

The significance of these institutional mechanisms is that they tied both Kenya and Tanzania to trading with Britain, and made their efforts to diversify their trading partners increasingly difficult. Thus, at the time of independence in 1961, more than a third of Tanzania's exports went to the United Kingdom, with another third going to the countries of the European Common Market, and the United States. A similar trend was evident in the import sector. In 1961, Tanzania imported 72 percent of its goods from advanced capitalist nations, of which more than half came from Britain. Less than 1 percent of the total imports at this time came from the socialist countries, though this figure began to rise by 1965, as indicated in Table 10.1.

By 1971, imports from China had exceeded those from Britain. This dramatic switch in the flow of trade was the result of an overall decline

TABLE 10.1: Tanzania's Trade with Principal Partners since Independence (percentages of total exports and of total imports)

Principal Partners	1961	1962	1963	1964	1965	1966	1967	1968	1969	1970	1971	1972	1973	1974	1975	1976	1977[a]
Exports																	
Western industrialized countries	74	72	67	70	63	61	59	54	54	54	44	40	41	43	44	54	66
United Kingdom	35	35	31	30	30	27	30	24	26	20	21	14	10	14	12	13	10
West Germany	8	8	7	8	8	7	5	5	4	4	4	5	6	5	8	14	20
Other EEC	13	13	13	14	11	9	11	8	36	30	28	23	21	27	25	25	26
United States and Canada	11	10	10	12	9	10	7	7	9	10	8	7	8	8	7	11	15
Japan	5	4	3	4	3	6	4	7	5	5	2	3	4	3	2	2	3
Socialist countries	—	—	—	5	8	6	6	5	5	5	5	7	7	5	5	5	5
China	—	—	—	3	7	4	4	3	5	3	4	6	4	3	4	3	3
Africa																	
Kenya	n.a.	n.a.	n.a.	n.a.	n.a.	n.a.	n.a.	n.a.	5	6	8	5	7	6	6	6	1
Value of total exports[b]	141	149	184	200	180	237	221	228	234	259	278	319	341	420	388	492	272
Imports																	
Western industrialized countries	72	72	73	77	76	70	73	70	67	56	50	52	50	49	55	54	64
United Kingdom	38	34	36	33	32	31	29	28	26	18	18	16	14	10	13	13	15
West Germany	5	5	6	6	8	9	6	8	8	8	7	7	8	8	7	9	9
Other EEC	12	11	12	11	17	13	20	16	41	32	29	30	26	20	24	26	32
United States and Canada	6	8	4	6	6	7	10	6	6	8	5	6	3	9	15	8	5
Japan	10	11	13	17	9	6	5	9	9	6	6	6	8	9	6	8	14
Socialist countries	.5	.5	—	2	5	8	6	8	8	13	24	19	22	12	11	7	3
China	—	—	—	1	4	6	5	6	5	12	22	17	20	11	9	6	3
Africa																	
Kenya	n.a.	n.a.	n.a.	n.a.	n.a.	n.a.	n.a.	n.a.	18	13	11	11	10	7	7	12	6
Oil-producing countries	7	7	7	4	2	3	7	8	.9	6	7	8	10	18	17	15	10
Value of total imports[b]	88	85	85	123	140	180	182	215	201	318	382	411	489	813	843	656	330

[a] First six months only.

[b] Total trade in millions of U.S. dollars.

Note: n.a. indicated data not available; dash indicates less than .5 percent.

Sources: International Monetary Fund, *Direction of Trade Annual* (Washington, D.C.: International Monetary Fund, 1961–75); *Direction of Trade Monthly*, December 1977.

in the United Kingdom's ability to maintain its share of world trade, combined with Tanzania's need to raise its imports from China in order to repay China's loan for the construction of the Tanzania-Zambia (Tanzam) railway. As indicated by the table, Britain's share of the Tanzanian market declined in the period from 1961 to 1977 by more than 60 percent, a decline which, as we shall see below, was almost duplicated in Kenya. In contrast, China's exports to Tanzania accounted for about a fifth of Tanzania's total imports from 1971 through 1973. Tanzania's imports from China were especially high during this period, when construction of the Tanzam occurred mainly in Tanzania, and Tanzania was able to pay for part of the local costs of the construction in its own currency by purchasing Chinese goods.* With the completion of the railroad in 1974, China's share of Tanzania's imports declined sharply. Nonetheless, the overall picture presented in Table 10.1 is that in the late 1960s and the first half of the 1970s, Tanzania started to effectively alter the traditional pattern of trade established during the colonial period.[13]

Equally noteworthy, is the extent to which Tanzania has succeeded in forging aid links with smaller European countries, and, in so doing, reducing her dependence on a few major donors. Such diversification is particularly significant because Tanzania depends on foreign assistance for more than half of its development budget. As indicated by Table 10.2, Britain, the former colonial power in Tanzania, has lost most of the influence it derived from being the major source of assistance at the time Tanzania became independent (in 1961). Having dropped to the twelfth position as a donor, and thus being the source of only 2.3 percent of the foreign assistance received by Tanzania between 1970 and 1974, Britain's influence has also been reduced through the nationalization of major British commercial interests, beginning with the banks and insurance companies in 1967. Yugoslavia, Sweden, Canada, Norway, and Denmark now occupy the top five positions after the International Bank for Reconstruction and Development/International Development Association (IBRD/IDA) and China. This demonstrates a shift away from the major powers, and particularly a shift away from the former colonial overlord, as important donors.

On the other hand, the pattern of foreign aid to Tanzania since 1970 cannot be described as a shift away from Western sources of assistance, nor a shift to the Eastern European countries of the Soviet bloc. Almost

---

*Most of these goods were of a consumer nature (for example, canned fruit, paper products), and were purchased at artificially high prices. Since most of these goods were brought by expatriates and members of Tanzania's middle class who could afford them, the importation and pricing of these items served as a clever device not only to pay for the railroad without placing an intolerable burden on Tanzania's foreign exchange position, but also to indirectly tax those who could most afford to pay for the project.

TABLE 10.2: Economic Aid to Tanzania, 1970–74

Donor	Amount (millions of U.S. dollars)	Percentage of Total
IBRD/IDA (World Bank group)	298.60	32.6
China	274.90	23.5
Yugoslavia	102.94	8.8
Sweden	79.21	6.8
Canada	69.63	6.0
Norway	66.66	5.7
Denmark	54.82	4.7
Finland	42.49	3.6
West Germany	37.59	3.2
United Nations Development Program/FAO	27.01	2.3
United States	26.82	2.3
United Kingdom	26.40	2.3
Netherlands	14.59	1.2
Italy	14.34	1.2
Japan	10.75	.9
Arab League's Oil Assistance Fund	7.50	.6
India	8.86	.6
Bulgaria	3.01	.3
UNICEF	2.38	.2
United Nations Capital Development Fund	1.47	.1
Commonwealth Development Corp.	.05	—
Total	1,168.02	100.0

Source: Susan A. Gitelson, "Policy Options for Small States: Kenya and Tanzania Reconsidered," *Studies in Comparative International Development* 12, no. 2 (Summer 1977): 48.

35 percent of Tanzania's assistance is in the form of bilateral aid from Western capitalist countries, while another third comes from the World Bank. What is significant about this aid is that most of it does not come from the major powers of the Western bloc. Sweden, Canada, Norway, Denmark, and Finland are nations whose foreign policies do not emphasize overt interest in specific spheres of influence, or in the usual power politics characteristic of U.S. and Soviet foreign policy. Together, Sweden, Canada, Norway, Denmark, and Finland aided Tanzania in the amount of $312.81 million in the 1970–74 period, a sum considerably larger than that given by China. Similarly, virtually all of the assistance Tanzania has received from socialist countries has come from China and Yugoslavia, which are not part of the Soviet bloc. Most of the assistance received from China, moreover, was for the construction of the Tanzam railroad. Since the completion of this project in 1974, the proportion of Tanzania's assistance

supplied by China has begun to fall, though China will continue to be a significant donor.

Thus, despite the fact that the bulk of Tanzania's aid still comes from the West, its diversification has neutralized the central position of the major powers and underlined Tanzania's policy of nonalignment. Tanzania's aid policy also illustrates President Julius Nyerere's contention that Tanzania's policy of nonalignment can only be delineated by a careful study of what Tanzania does, rather than by statements made by its leaders for public consumption.[14] It is therefore inaccurate to contend, as have some observers, that by 1970 Tanzania had become so dependent on China that it had virtually entered into an alliance with the People's Republic.[15] The inaccuracy of such conclusions is also underscored by the sharp reduction in the level of Chinese-Tanzanian trade since 1974.

In contrast to Tanzania, Kenya has maintained remarkable continuity in its relations with the West, both in trade and aid. The pattern of Kenya's international trade shows virtually no involvement with socialist countries. Although it too has diversified its trading partners since independence, diversification has taken place within the West, with Britain continuing as the main trading partner, as indicated by Table 10.3. As with Tanzania, Britain's share of Kenya's imports and exports has declined substantially since independence, but the decline has not been as pronounced as in the case of Tanzania. Part of both countries' diversification of trading practices has not been by choice. Since the sharp rises in the price of oil in late 1973 and 1974, a substantial share of both countries' imports is now tied to the importation of petroleum. Kenya, with its larger automobile-owning bourgeoisie and expatriate population, is particularly vulnerable in this regard, as oil now accounts for one-fifth of the country's imports.

In terms of aid, Kenya's record also demonstrates much less diversity than Tanzania's. As indicated by Table 10.4, approximately 99 percent of Kenya's aid has come from Western capitalist countries, and from international organizations such as the World Bank, which are dominated by these countries. In terms of bilateral aid, the largest single donor continues to be Britain, which accounted for 30.6 percent of the bilateral assistance to Kenya in the 1970–74 period, and a fifth of all assistance. West Germany was next, accounting for 16.2 percent of the bilateral aid, and 10.3 percent of all aid. Like Tanzania, Kenya has not allowed itself to become dependent on either the United States or the Soviet Union for development assistance. The U.S. presence in Kenya, however, has increased steadily since the mid-1970s as such U.S.-based multinationals as IBM, Firestone, and General Motors have entered the private sector along with several major U.S. banks. The United States is also in the process of becoming a significant, and perhaps ultimately the largest, foreign supplier of arms to

TABLE 10.3: Kenya's Trade with Principal Partners Since Independence (percentages of total exports and of total imports)

Principal Partners	1963	1964	1965	1966	1967	1968	1969	1970	1971	1972	1973	1974	1975	1976	1977a
Exports															
Western industrialized countries	64	64	61	64	58	58	40	40	37	43	44	40	38	46	65
United Kingdom	24	21	21	22	25	25	16	14	14	16	12	9	10	11	14
West Germany	13	14	14	13	8	9	8	6	6	7	8	8	9	13	23
Other EEC	11	9	9	10	9	10	22	22	20	26	23	22	18	23	31
United States and Canada	9	9	5	9	7	7	5	8	6	6	6	5	6	7	5
Japan	3	3	3	3	2	3	1	1	2	2	3	3	2	2	1
Socialist countries	.7	3	3	4	3	2	1	2	2	2	2	2	1	1	1
Africa															
Tanzania	n.a.	n.a.	n.a.	n.a.	n.a.	n.a.	13	14	13	13	10	9	9	10	3
Uganda	n.a.	n.a.	n.a.	n.a.	n.a.	n.a.	16	15	17	13	13	13	12	10	9
Value of total exports b	143	150	146	174	167	176	274	305	314	359	474	603	608	793	649
Imports															
Western industrialized countries	69	69	69	69	72	70	65	66	69	68	71	62	60	63	64
United Kingdom	31	31	28	34	33	32	28	26	28	25	24	18	20	19	17
West Germany	6	9	7	7	10	8	7	7	8	9	9	10	8	10	10
Other EEC	11	10	11	11	12	13	41	38	40	38	37	30	31	31	31
United States and Canada	5	7	10	8	8	8	7	8	9	7	9	6	9	7	5
Japan	13	9	10	6	6	7	7	10	10	9	12	11	11	11	13
Socialist countries	.4	3	2	4	2	3	3	3	3	2	2	4	1	2	2
Africa															
Tanzania	n.a.	n.a.	n.a.	n.a.	n.a.	n.a.	3	4	4	3	4	3	3	3	1
Uganda	n.a.	n.a.	n.a.	n.a.	n.a.	n.a.	6	6	4	4	2	1	1	—	—
Value of total imports b	270	214	249	315	299	321	362	442	560	539	616	1026	945	973	594

a First six months only.

b Total trade in millions of U.S. dollars.

Note: n.a. indicates data not available; dash indicates less than .4 percent.

Sources: International Monetary Fund, *Direction of Trade Annual* (Washington, D.C.: International Monetary Fund, 1961–75); *Direction of Trade Monthly,* December 1977.

TABLE 10.4: Economic Aid to Kenya, 1970–74

Donor	Amount (millions of U.S. dollars)	Percentage of Total
IBRD/IDA (World Bank group)	336.81	36.4
United Kingdom	180.29	19.5
West Germany	95.47	10.3
Sweden	90.79	9.8
United Nations Development Program	41.80	4.5
Canada	31.18	3.4
Japan	27.66	2.9
United States	26.78	2.9
Commonwealth Development Corporation	23.00	2.5
Netherlands	21.43	2.3
Norway	16.30	1.8
Denmark	15.30	1.7
African Development Bank	6.17	.7
European Economic Community	5.04	.5
Switzerland	3.64	.4
Soviet Union	2.43	.3
Yugoslavia	.78	.1
South Korea	.28	—
Total	925.15	100.0

Source: Susan A. Gitelson, "Policy Options for Small States: Kenya and Tanzania Reconsidered," *Studies in Comparative International Development* 12, no. 2 (Summer 1977): 43.

Kenya, having entered into an agreement in 1976 to supply the small Kenyan air force with modern jet interceptors.

Kenya's dependence on foreign, that is, Western, capital, is also far more pronounced than Tanzania's. As the most developed of the three East African territories, Kenya has historically attracted the largest share of foreign private investment into the region. And whereas Tanzania has, for the most part, discouraged such investment since the mid 1960s, in accordance with its policy of socialism and self-reliance, Kenya has actively sought to attract foreign private participation in its economy. In addition to the liberal Foreign Investment Protection Act noted above, the Kenyan government, via the state-owned Industrial and Commercial Development Corporation, actively pursues foreign private investment by entering into joint ventures with foreign firms. Kenya needs such investment to maintain the high growth rates (about 10 percent per annum) of the commercial/industrial sector of its economy, and to offset the regular deficits in its balance of trade. Foreign investment is particularly important for maintaining the viability of Kenya's tourist industry, the country's second largest earner (after coffee) of foreign exchange. Thus by 1967, 57 percent of the gross produce of Kenyan firms with more than 50 employees was derived from foreign-owned companies, and by 1972, the International Labour Office estimated that the figure had risen beyond 65 percent.[16] In sum, the pattern of external aid sources for Kenya, both public and private, suggests a definite Western and capitalist orientation, a point which raises doubt about Kenya's claims to a foreign policy of nonalignment.

However, figures on patterns of trade and aid may not be very reliable indicators of essential policy choices, or of ideological orientation. Nor do they explain why particular policy decisions to diversify or not diversify one's trade and aid relationships are made. Thus in Kenya, there is a close correlation between its sources of external aid and its open-door policy of encouraging foreign private investment. This open-door policy has operated in favor of capitalist countries whose multinational corporations now dominate the Kenyan economy.[17] As for Tanzania, the desirability of diversifying the country's trading partners and pattern of foreign assistance was dramatized by a number of incidents in the middle 1960s, soon after independence: Shortly after the union between Tanganyika and Zanzibar in 1964, East Germany opened consular offices in Zanzibar. West Germany took exception to this, and requested President Nyerere to prevail upon the Revolutionary Council on the island to close down the East German consulate or risk the withdrawal of aid. Nyerere refused and the aid was subsequently withdrawn. Two years later, when Britain showed a disinclination to take effective measures to end the illegal regime in Rhodesia, the Organization for African Unity passed a resolution calling upon member states to break diplomatic relations with Britain; as a matter of principle, and because of her commitment to the liberation of southern Africa, Tanzania was the first African state to sever relations. In retaliation, Britain terminated its economic assistance program in Tanzania. Occurring within a short period, these two incidents underlined Tanzania's vulnerability to the whims of the major powers, and forced the country's leadership to think seriously about how to avoid excessive dependence on a single donor.

Tanzania's trade-and-aid relationship with China can also be explained in terms of the special circumstances in the eastern and southern African politics of the early and middle 1960s. The Unilateral Declaration of Independence by the white minority in Rhodesia in 1965 complicated the handling of landlocked Zambia's imports and exports. The decision by Zambia and Tanzania to build a railway from Dar es Salaam to Kapiri Mposhi (in Zambia), so as to give Zambia an alternative outlet to the world, was universally opposed by Western countries and the World Bank —who had been approached to assist the project—as a white elephant. They refused to aid the project, which both Tanzania and Zambia regarded as an item of first priority. When China agreed to aid the project, and Tanzania began to trade with China, Western observers and the Western press vociferously denounced Tanzania's decision to do business with China as a move that gave Communist forces a foothold in eastern Africa. These same Western observers were unwilling to accept a very basic fact in the politics of aid giving: that it is normal practice for the recipient to import goods in one form or another from the donor as an important part of the package. Tanzania did just that—nothing out of the ordinary.

KENYA AND REGIONAL DIPLOMACY

Kenya's external relations have focused upon three principal issues: the ideological orientations of other states in the region, the security of its national boundaries, and the development of friendly and tranquil relations with its neighbors.

From an ideological standpoint, the year 1967 marked a watershed in eastern Africa. Tanzania announced its socialist program embodied in the Arusha Declaration and in the Tanganyika African National Union's policy on socialism and self-reliance. The promulgation of the Arusha Declaration had a significant demonstration effect not only on Kenya but throughout East Africa. No sooner had Tanzania embarked on a socialist policy than President Milton Obote of Uganda announced his intention to "move to the left." This culminated in the publication of the Common Man's Charter and related documents in 1969. As partners in the East African Community, these developments involving Tanzania and Uganda tended to isolate Kenya. In the same year, 1969, a military junta replaced the civilian government in Somalia and immediately announced its intention to develop Somalia as a socialist state. In addition, the military regime in the Sudan, which had seized power in the same year, resolved to move the Sudan slowly to the left. Consequently, Kenya found itself in a situation in which it was threatened by what it perceived as socialist encirclement, a development which moved it much closer to Ethiopia, and closer still to the West, especially to Britain,[18] its main source of military assistance. This situation continued until 1971 when Obote's government was overthrown by Idi Amin, who immediately abandoned Uganda's socialist pretensions.* Much to Kenya's relief, a Communist-engineered attempt to overthrow the military government in the Sudan in the same year was foiled. As a result, the Sudanese Communist Party was banned and the

---

*The coup d'etat in Uganda removed the specter of socialism but worsened relations between Kenya and Uganda on many other fronts, especially when Amin turned out to be an unreliable neighbor.

regime began an ideological shift toward the center.[19] As a result of these developments, Kenya succeeded in creating very cordial relations with the Sudan. With this done, the threat of socialist encirclement subsided and Kenya turned its attention to its historical problem in the North Eastern Province.

One of Kenya's main concerns in the region is the security of its northeastern territory, which is claimed by Somalia. When the military took power in Somalia in 1969, Kenya's reactions were twofold. First, it was unclear whether the military regime would revoke the terms of the detente that had been negotiated in 1967 following an earlier confrontation between the two countries. During the two years of detente, diplomatic and trade relations were established between the two countries. But when the new military government immediately established cordial relations with Tanzania, with which it shared a spirit of cooperation in socialist development, and subsequently with the Soviet Union, Kenya began to reassess its foreign policy and military preparedness. Second, this reassessment also led Kenya to reaffirm its mutual defense agreement with Ethiopia.[20] This agreement had been signed shortly after Kenya's independence when Somalia commenced military and propaganda activities in the Somali-inhabited territories of Ethiopia (Ogaden) and Kenya (North Eastern Province). The ideological instability of the region in 1969 provided the atmosphere that enabled Kenya to sign a second treaty with Ethiopia, establishing Kenya's permanent northern boundary.

These events occurred in quick succession at a time when Britain was Kenya's only dependable military ally. Since then, Kenya's relations with Britain, and later, with the United States, which has become a major source of Kenya's arms, have grown closer. This relationship has become tighter still as a result of the 1977–78 war in the Ogaden. The success of Somalia during the early stages of the conflict pushed Kenya deeper into the Western camp. This development may further weaken Kenya's relations with its neighbors, from whom it envisages some support in the event of an attack from Somalia. Somalia is fully aware that Kenya's relations with its East African neighbors are currently poor, and may not hesitate to take advantage of the situation. It is for this reason that Kenya has sought to maintain close relations with Ethiopia, and has supported Ethiopia during the conflict in the Ogaden, despite the Marxist orientation of the Ethiopian regime, and the presence of more that 17,000 Soviet advisors and Cuban troops on Ethiopian soil.

Kenya's relations with her two principal neighbors, Tanzania and Uganda, have had an element of suspicion that goes back to the colonial period, when a settler-dominated Kenya used Tanganyika and Uganda as captive markets for its agricultural products. When the East African High Commission was formed in 1948, both Tanganyika and Uganda opposed it because of the fear of settler domination at the political and economic levels. For almost three decades Kenya has been conscious of its vital and sensitive role as the main beneficiary in the East African interterritorial trade. Its neighbors, especially Tanzania, have never failed to make it clear that for a system of cooperation to survive in East Africa, it must be sensitive and responsive to the basic needs of the partner states. It was with this in mind that President Nyerere insisted in 1961, shortly after Tanzania became independent, that a new basis of cooperation be found that would better serve the interests of independent partner states.[21] As a result, the East African Common Services Organization was established in 1961, by substantially modifying the parent organization, the East African High Commission, to serve new needs. Although the reorganized commission's primary function was to coordinate common services such as transport, finance, social services, and economic relations, Tanzania's initiative had more far-reaching implications than its neighbors realized at that time. In essence, Tanzania wanted the reorganized commission to be responsive to its national interests, among which were the fair distribution of the benefits from the common services, and the creation of a viable domestic market. However, the East African Common Services Organization had come into being a year before Uganda's independence and almost two years before Kenya's. Little wonder, then, that Kenya and Tanzania were operating on different wavelengths. In Kenya, the nationalist struggle for independence was at its height at this time and was preoccupied with the single goal of winning independence. Issues regarding matters of cooperation in East Africa were taken for granted by most nationalist leaders, mainly because no operative foreign policy had been formulated. Besides, Kenya's leaders did not seem to have fully understood the basic reasons behind Nyerere's argument. Finally, Kenya's leaders had not crystallized or articulated their national interest on many other issues.

Despite Kenya's independence in 1963, the strains which the East African Common Services Organization was experiencing did not diminish. This led to the concluding of the Kampala Agreement, signed in 1964, which was an attempt to solve some of the problems confronting the less-developed partners, especially Tanzania. The agreement sought to reallocate

> certain strategic industries which had an interterritorial significance so as to balance industrialization and reduce deficits in Tanzania and Uganda in relation to Kenya. The arrangements were short-lived, however, largely because the industries that were allocated to some of the countries (e.g., electric light bulbs and radio assembly plants to Tanzania) became of interest to all of them and no country could actually be prevented from setting up an industry already allocated to her partners. Furthermore, there was no formal mechanism for implementing the agreement.[22]

By 1967, trade deficits experienced by Tanzania and Uganda from interterritorial trade necessitated a rethinking of the whole structure and function of the common-services organization. Trade figures for 1959 and 1966 effectively demonstrate the nature of the problem as it existed at the time. As indicated by Table 10.5, Kenya's dominance of the interterritorial trade had become more pronounced in the years immediately following independence, a condition which became a major source of tension between the three partner states.

In an attempt to overcome some of the major difficulties, a further stage in East African cooperation was reached with the signing of the Treaty for East African Cooperation in June 1967, which created the East African Community. The new treaty sought to "strengthen and regulate industrial, commercial and other relations of the partner states in order that there must be accelerated and sustained expansion of economic activities within East Africa, the benefit of which shall be equally distributed."[23] The treaty made provisions for a system of decentralization in the administrative structure of the community, which brought about the moving of the headquarters of two of the community's four statutory corporations from Nairobi to Dar es Salaam and Kampala; the Harbours Corporation went to Dar es Salaam, and the Posts and Telecommunications Corporation, to Kampala, while the headquarters of the community itself was moved to Arusha, Tanzania. Further, the East African Development Bank was set up in Kampala, with a constitution providing for 38.75 percent of its annual loans to be allocated to both Uganda and Tanzania, with Kenya getting the remaining 22.5 percent.

A system of "transfer taxes" was also established, whereby for a limited period, "Uganda and Tanzania could protect themselves against imports from Kenya of particular products in which they themselves had

TABLE 10.5: Shares of East African Interterritorial Trade, by Partner State (percentages)

Partner State	1959	1966	1970	1971	1972	1973	1974	1975	1976
Exports									
Kenya	61	65	61	64	69	75	76	80	83
Tanzania	13	11	15	19	14	16	18	15	16
Uganda	26	24	24	17	17	9	6	5	1
Value of total exports*	56	123	142	147	133	151	172	162	193
Imports									
Kenya	27	25	31	30	28	23	22	21	17
Tanzania	40	37	33	30	35	31	31	34	42
Uganda	33	38	36	40	37	46	47	45	41
Value of total imports*	56	123	142	147	133	151	172	162	193

*Total trade in millions of U.S. dollars.

Sources: International Monetary Fund, Surveys of African Economics, vol. 2 (Washington, D.C.: International Monetary Fund, 1969), p. 80; International Monetary Fund, Direction of Trade Annual 1969–75, and Direction of Trade Monthly, December 1977.

industries at an 'infantile stage.' "[24] Countries experiencing deficits in interterritorial trade were also allowed to impose quota restrictions on selected imports from countries enjoying trade surpluses in those goods. Tanzania, in particular, made immediate use of this provision to impose restrictions on a wide range of imports from Kenya. This slowed down the expansion of interterritorial trade, especially in 1966. Although Uganda used this provision to a lesser extent, it was, nevertheless, conscious of Kenya's dominant position in the common-market arrangements. As a landlocked country, Uganda also had fewer cards at its disposal because of its dependence on Kenya's port, Mombasa, for most of its imports and exports.

Despite these agreements, Kenya has continued to dominate interterritorial trade and commerce throughout the 1970s, as shown by the data in Table 10.5. Indeed, by the end of 1976, Kenya accounted for more than four-fifths of the total exports of the three partner states, up 34 percent from its share in 1970. During this same period, Kenya's share of interterritorial imports dropped from roughly one-third to one-sixth of the total, while the shares of both Tanzania and Uganda rose to more than two-fifths. Kenya's position in the common-market arrangements was maintained and strengthened by a series of other factors beyond the control of the other partner states. Its industrial structure was, and still remains, more diversified, especially in manufacturing, mining, construction, and services. While mining and construction contribute less to Kenya's gross domestic product, they are more developed in Kenya than in Tanzania or Uganda. Moreover, industry contributes more to Kenya's gross domestic product than it does to the economies of the partner states:

> What is most striking, however, is the variation in the degree of agriculture and services. Kenya has a highly developed service sector and, for a country in which the vast majority of the population is still rural, a surprisingly low dependence on agriculture. The contrast with Uganda is sharp. Half of monetary domestic product in Uganda originates in agriculture, while less than two-fifths is derived from services, whereas in Kenya nearly three-fifths of total monetary product is derived from services and little more than one-fifth from agriculture. Tanzania lies somewhere in between.[25]

Because of its dominant position in interterritorial trade, Kenya seemed to have developed a vested interest in the maintenance of the community. This argument was valid only to the extent that Kenya continued to dominate markets in the other partner states, and to experience large trade balances in its favor. Because of this favorable position, Kenya consistently opposed any arrangements that would reduce its interterritorial trade surplus. Such arrangements would have invariably meant the imposition of import restrictions by Tanzania to reduce its trade deficit and to protect its infant import-substitution industries. A conflict of interest thus developed that was allowed to intensify as workable arrangements to reduce Tanzania's unfavorable balance of trade with Kenya failed.

The irreconcilability of basic national economic interests between the partner states, and between Kenya and Tanzania in particular, was also exacerbated in the late 1960s and early 1970s by the pattern and flow of private foreign investments into the region. As the center of East African commerce, Kenya, and especially Nairobi, with its broad range of external economies, attracted private investment at a far higher rate than Tanzania or Uganda. This undermined the community's attempt to spread invest-ment in new industries throughout the region via the system of transfer taxes, and the activities of the East African Development Bank, and in-creased Kenya's dominance of the interterritorial trade.

It was the irreconcilability of these basic national economic interests, rather than the more publicized ideological and political differences, that led to the final breakup of the East African Community in 1977. Rather than saving the community, the decentralization of the administrative structure of the community contributed to its demise. By the mid-1970s the subdivisions of the community's four statutory corporations, located in each of the partner states, were well on their way to transforming themselves into independent national concerns. Staff recruited by each subdivision were increasingly limited to citizens of the country in which it was located, while staff who were citizens from partner states were steadily transferred home. Revenues collected by subdivisions were fre quently not remitted to corporation headquarters, or their remittance was delayed if the headquarters was located in a partner state. Conversely, disbursements from headquarters to subdivisions located in another state were often delayed.

The final breakdown of the community occurred in February 1977 when Kenya withdrew its financial support from the East African Airways Corporation, which was on the verge of bankruptcy, and launched its own national airline, Kenya Airways. Tanzania countered by sealing the border between the two countries, thereby bringing all trade and human traffic to a halt. Each state subsequently impounded the assets of the other that were located within its territory, and air traffic between the states was banned. Despite periodic negotiations to resume normal relations, the border be-tween Kenya and Tanzania remained closed as of November 1978.

The closing of the border between Kenya and Tanzania has, no doubt, had some adverse effects on the Kenyan economy. First, it has cost Kenya markets for approximately 13 percent of its total exports, including new markets in Zambia, which had become a significant importer of Kenyan goods.* Second, Kenya's textile industry, which has depended to a large extent on Tanzanian cotton, will have to find alternative sources of supply at relatively higher prices. Third, Kenya's tobacco and instant coffee industries, which have obtained the bulk of their supplies from Tanzania, have also been affected. Access to markets in Rwanda and Burundi have, likewise, become more difficult because of the risks involved in road transport through Uganda. Mombasa, Kenya's major seaport on the Indian Ocean, which has handled a large quantity of imports and exports for Zambia, Rwanda, and Burundi, is likely to lose substantial revenues because of reductions in this sector. Mombasa's loss will be gained by Tanzania's port of Dar es Salaam, to which a good portion of this traffic has now been directed. Trade figures for the first half of 1977 (see Table 10.3), however, suggest that Kenya will overcome these losses.†

Meanwhile, Tanzania's trade with its other neighbors, Zambia, Mozambique, Rwanda, and Burundi, has gained momentum. These markets are giving Tanzania a small but steady balance-of-trade surplus that may soon make up for losses incurred in trade with Kenya. As its communications system, especially railways and roads, is improved, Tanzania's trade with these neighbors is bound to become important. Thus, while both Kenya and Tanzania are likely to overcome the adverse effect of the closing of their mutual border, the burden of the closure will fall disproportionately on Kenya.

TANZANIA AND REGIONAL DIPLOMACY

Even before it formally adopted socialism and self-reliance as its model of domestic development in 1967, Tanzania embarked on a foreign policy that sought to break, or at least substantially modify, the relationships it had with other states at the time of its independence. We have already noted Tanzania's efforts to develop diplomatic and commercial relations with socialist countries, its break with Britain over the Unilateral Declaration of Independence in Rhodesia, its attempts to diversify its

---

*In 1976 Kenya shipped 10 percent of its total exports to Tanzania, and more than 3 percent to Zambia. Virtually all of these goods were shipped by road across the Kenyan-Tanzanian border.

†Kenya's favorable balance of trade for the first half of 1977, however, is largely the result of record high world coffee prices arising out of the 1975 frost in Brazil, which drastically cut the coffee exports of that country. The extent to which Kenya will be able to permanently overcome the loss of Tanzanian and Zambian markets for its goods will not be known until several years after coffee prices drift downward and stabilize at a level that reflects the current rise in world production.

dependence on donors of foreign assistance, and its attempts to assert its national interest in its relations with Kenya. In addition to these initiatives, and consistent with its ideological orientation, Tanzania became progressively more involved with the affairs of its neighbors to the south. As noted previously, the Rhodesian crisis, which began in late 1965, led Tanzania to develop close relations with Zambia, and to assist the latter to overcome its position of a landlocked state dependent on transportation routes through southern Africa to maintain its foreign trade. In addition to the construction of the Tanzam railway, the two countries arranged for the construction of an oil pipeline and an all-weather paved road between Dar es Salaam and Lusaka. This in turn has led to an expansion of the port of Dar es Salaam to deal with the increasing traffic between the two countries. Tanzania's friendly relations with Zambia were further strengthened in the early 1970s by President Kenneth Kaunda's declaration of "humanism" as the national ideology—a watered-down but, nonetheless, significant facsimile of Nyerere's Arusha Declaration.

The Rhodesian crisis, combined with the struggle in Mozambique between FRELIMO and the Portuguese, also led Tanzania to become, together with Zambia, one of the two most active independent African states involved in the liberation of southern Africa. Thus Tanzania has been the headquarters for the Liberation Committee of the Organization for African Unity, and over the past decade has provided a temporary or permanent base for a score of liberation groups including FRELIMO, the Zimbabwe African National Union, the Popular Movement for the Liberation of Angola (MPLA), and the South-West African Peoples Organization (SWAPO). Most significantly, Tanzania has provided diplomatic assistance, training facilities, and military bases for FRELIMO and the freedom fighters in Zimbabwe. As a rear base and haven from military attack, Tanzania played a critical role in FRELIMO's struggle against the Portuguese, without which the movement would not have been able to maintain its forces in the field. Tanzania also provided schools and other social services for Mozambican refugees.

Tanzania is currently providing similar support to various elements of the Zimbabwe Liberation Army, though Mozambique and Zambia, because of their common borders with Rhodesia, have assumed a greater role as a base and staging area, respectively, for the guerrillas of the Zimbabwe African National Union and the Zimbabwe African Peoples Union. Despite this shift, Tanzania remains the informal leader of the so-called frontline states that border on, or are located in close proximity to, Rhodesia and Namibia. As such, Tanzania has become a country with which the United States, Britain, and other outside powers must reckon when attempting to negotiate settlements to the Rhodesian and Namibian issues.

In the course of the 1970s, Tanzania has shifted the locus of its regional diplomacy away from its northern partners bequeathed from the colonial era, Kenya and Uganda, to its southern neighbors. This shift has been a result of Tanzania's domestic policies and ideological orientation, which have led Tanzania to become particularly sympathetic to the liberation struggles in the southern part of the continent, and to believe that the policies of its northern neighbors were inimical to its national interest. Tanzania sealed its border with Kenya, and withdrew from the East African Community, because it felt that it was no longer in its national economic interest to maintain a subordinate position to Kenya. As for Tanzania's relations with Uganda, the annual trade between the two countries had never been a major element in the East African equation except for the commerce across the common border west of Lake Victoria. And whereas relations between the two countries had been close during the presidency of Obote, and especially after his declaration of the Common Man's Charter in 1969, relations deteriorated rapidly after Amin's ascension to power in 1971. In 1972, Tanzania supported an abortive invasion of Uganda by followers of Obote, which ended in total failure, and which led to subsequent incursions of Tanzanian territory by the Ugandan army. As one of the few African leaders to speak out publicly against Amin's tyrannical rule, President Nyerere put Tanzania on record as wanting as little as possible to do with the military regime in Kampala. As a result, relations between the two former partner states in the East African Community have been virtually nonexistent for several years.

For Tanzania, the locus of regional diplomacy has shifted from eastern Africa to central and southern Africa. Given the imperatives of its domestic policy of socialism and self-reliance, it is unlikely that it will shift its attention back to its former partners in the East African Community within the foreseeable future.

THE FRONTIERS OF TECHNICAL COOPERATION

Technical cooperation between nations has been one of the most controversial subjects in recent years.[26] This is partly due to the fact that foreign assistance has often been viewed as an instrument of neocolonial domination of the countries which receive it. As African countries adopt a policy of self-reliance in domestic and foreign transactions, it is necessary to be sure that aid from any source does not compromise this policy. Kenya and Tanzania are fully aware of the asymmetrical connotation of the act of giving and receiving aid, especially where the donor is an industrialized country while the recipient is nonindustrialized. As Tanzania sees it, technical assistance, in its various forms, is an index of economic dependence.

This realization, however, has not reduced the amount of aid flow from industrialized countries to either Kenya or Tanzania, and continues to undermine the latter's commitment to a policy of self-reliance. Nevertheless, both countries generally agree that their economic development should be planned in such a way that continued growth is not dependent upon expatriate manpower and foreign technology. They are also determined to dispense with dependence on foreign technical assistance in the shortest possible time, and to build up substantial local competence in all the critical areas where technical assistance from outside is now heavily concentrated. The achievement of these goals will take some time. But it is important to state that effective and intensive technical cooperation among African countries in manpower training, exchange of personnel, research, and joint projects, to mention only a few areas, should be encouraged as a matter of diplomatic and practical priority. Despite their ideological differences, Kenya and Tanzania have the beginning stages of a new area of diplomatic initiative.

Kenya's Experience

Kenya's experience in technical cooperation with other African countries, and with the rest of the third world, has improved substantially since independence. However, the impact of this cooperation has been restricted to only a few sectors. According to available records, very few Kenyan professionals are officially seconded to other African governments except to the former High Commission territories of Botswana, Swaziland, and Lesotho. Because of a general shortage of trained personnel, secondment of technical officers to other African countries is limited by the fact that the donor does not usually wish to part with them for periods longer than six months to one year.

Manpower training is consequently one of the most active sectors of cooperation between Kenya and other African countries. It is made possible by the existence in Kenya of training institutions of some standing. Cooperation in training has taken two forms. The most common is one where Kenya provides training facilities and teachers, while the country that sends trainees provides maintenance for them—either from its own resources or through a third party, usually an international agency. In this case, the cost of training is shared by the parties to an agreement. Requests for places is usually made by the countries that need their people trained. The other form is through the direct offering of scholarships by the Kenyan government as a result of a standing agreement or through special and usually temporary arrangements. This form is less popular than the one previously described, which Kenya seems to prefer mainly because it is cheaper. Sharing training facilities is one way of articulating the spirit of self-reliance and of rationally utilizing limited resources.

Kenya has made training facilities available for senior and middle-grade public servants, agricultural and nutrition officers, and hotel and general management. The Sudan, Swaziland, Mozambique, Uganda, Tanzania, and, lately, Angola have standing agreements with Kenya for the training of senior and middle-grade public servants. A limited number of places is also provided for refugees from Zimbabwe, whose fees are partly paid by Kenya and partly by international bodies. The number of these places actually filled varies from year to year because Kenya's own training needs vary from year to year. Other governments also find it difficult to release a large number of officers at any one time to participate in such training programs.

Training of agricultural and nutrition officers seems to be one of the active areas of technical cooperation between Kenya and other African countries within and outside the region. The Egerton Agricultural College, in Njoro, Kenya, is the center of this activity. During 1977, students from 13 African countries were taking post-secondary-diploma courses in agriculture and home economics.[27] This program has been one of the most successful exercises in technical cooperation among English-speaking countries in eastern and southern Africa. Its value continues to grow as more accent is put on agricultural development.

Technical cooperation in research has been another active area. This is due to the existence of established research institutions, which served the settler economy in the colonial period but which have now been taken over by the Kenyan government. Kenya's improved maize and wheat seeds are used in Zambia, Ethiopia, Malawi, Tanzania, and Uganda. Because of the importance attached to this venture, a biannual meeting of these states has been established to review its future development and expansion. There is also a bilateral agreement between the Sudan and Kenya that enables the former to benefit from using the latter's improved potato varieties to improve their own, especially in the southern Sudan. In addition to potatoes, improved livestock varieties continue to be exchanged with the southern Sudan to improve livestock in that area. These experimental exercises are beginning to acquire lucrative commercial value. In cooperation with Morocco, Algeria, and Egypt, Kenya provides facilities at the Njoro Plant Breeding Station to enable these countries to germinate wheat seeds in the winter. The germinated seedlings are then transported to North Africa for planting at an appropriate time. Through bilateral arrangements, Kenya receives improved sorghum seeds from Ethiopia, with which it also exchanges research information on this crop.[28] Kenya also provides assistance to neighboring countries to raise the level of tea production among small-holder producers. The Kenya Tea Development Authority, with assistance from the World Bank, has provided seedlings, and extension services to Tanzania. Kenya and Tanzania also exchange important research documents on game research, especially between Serengeti (Tanzania) and the Tsavo Game Research Project (Kenya).

In addition to these bilateral efforts at technical cooperation between Kenya and other African countries, Kenya has become the international or regional headquarters for several international organizations concerned with technical cooperation. These include the United Nations Environmental Program (UNEP), the United Nations Development Program (UNDP), the International Institute for Research on Animal Diseases (IIRAD), and the Ford and Rockefeller Foundations. In seeking to become a base for such activities, Kenya has pursued a policy in the area of technical cooperation that is consistent with its policy of providing an open door to foreign private investment. Whether Kenya's willingness to be a regional center for such international organizations enhances or undermines its ability to engage in technical cooperation with other African states is an open question.

Tanzania's Experience

Tanzania's policy of socialism and self-reliance has greatly influenced its involvement in programs of technical cooperation. Since 1967, it has considerably increased its cooperation with African, Asian, and Latin American countries, especially those with which it has ideological sympathies. The data presented here are thin, but are nevertheless representative of an emerging pattern in the uses of foreign policy.

Tanzania, Mozambique, and Zambia have developed important channels of cooperation that exceed the purely political. Because of Tanzania's commitment to FRELIMO during its struggle with the Portuguese, its cooperation with Mozambique has been particularly close. Since Mozambique's independence, Tanzania has sent manpower and equipment worth several millions of dollars, at its own expense. Tanzania and Zambia are also cooperating in other projects besides the development of the extensive transportation infrastructure between the two countries. One is the initiation of integrated settlement schemes for the joint agricultural development of Zambia's Northern Province and Tanzania's contiguous Mbeya region. The agricultural potential of this region is vast and the success of the project is bound to open a new and important chapter in inter-African relations. Similar programs have also been started between Tanzania and Mozambique, through which an effective communication network is being established.

Since 1976, serious discussions and feasibility studies have been undertaken by Tanzania, Mozambique, and Zambia regarding the possibility of constructing a joint integrated steel mill by pooling their coal, iron ore deposits, and finances. Once operative, the project is bound to spill over into other sectors of economic cooperation. Beyond this level of cooperation, the three countries have recognized and, indeed, called for the need to develop new forms of bilateral and multilateral cooperation at subregional, regional, and the African regional levels. Many factors recommend this. First, Tanzania is firmly convinced that its problems are more similar to those of its neighbors than to those of industrialized countries. This is particularly true in respect to its neighbors to the south, with whom it shares a common ideological perspective, and with whom, in contrast to Kenya, it does not have an unfavorable economic relationship. Second, it is better to improve relations with other developing countries, because they have little interest in imposing their will upon other states. Third, effective mutual cooperation among equals creates a feeling of mutual self-confidence that is more likely, in the future, to enable developing countries to work out a common strategy for development. A common industrial strategy is also viewed here as a priority which cuts across ideological boundaries.

Yet it would, of course, be unwise to minimize the force of ideology as a divisive factor, because there are grounds to suppose that an ideological division within the region may be inevitable and may therefore reduce opportunities for effective cooperation of the type President Nyerere has in mind. Tanzania's links with Malawi, for example, are virtually nonexistent. Nevertheless, effective technical cooperation will surely develop among states which share the same ideological perspective. This is underlined by Tanzania's statement in 1976 that it intends to increase its cooperation with its southern neighbors, especially in trade, and in other fields. Once Zimbabwe becomes independent, Tanzania's relations with this part of Africa will have far-reaching economic implications, especially in terms of a larger market as well as vast natural resources. Tanzania has also greatly diversified and widened its scope in technical cooperation.

Technical assistance and cooperation with non-African third-world countries has not been limited to the well-known joint ventures with the People's Republic of China. Tanzania and India, for example, have actively cooperated in programs involving exchange of technical personnel and other forms of assistance. In 1974–75, approximately 121 technicians were recruited from India. Of this number, one-third were water engineers needed for various irrigation projects, while slightly more than half were science teachers for secondary schools. In addition, a number of technicians were recruited to assist in the expansion of the small-industries sector that the government began to emphasize early in the 1970s.[29] Under this agreement the Indian government becomes the appropriate staff, while Tanzania is responsible for all their emoluments. Besides cooperation in exchange of technical and professional staff, the two countries have set up a joint Economic Commission that meets regularly to discuss ongoing industrial projects and to survey new areas for future cooperation. In 1972, India gave Tanzania a loan worth $6.3 million for the development of the Kagera Sugar Scheme. The loan was used to purchase equipment and machinery from India. In 1975–76, a supplementary loan of $13 million was received from the Indian Development Bank for the same scheme. The later loan is guaranteed by the government of India. A third major Indian loan was negotiated to enable Tanzania to develop her natural-gas plant to be built at Songosongo. An agreement was also concluded under which Tanzania is to purchase Indian railway locomotives worth about $13 million. Finally, the two countries formed a joint shipping company as a commercial venture.[30]

Within Latin America, Tanzania has cooperated most effectively with Cuba, from whom it has received various forms of assistance. Cuba has constructed an artificial-insemination center in the Mara region, and has supplied all the necessary equipment for the project. Cuba has also embarked on a large-scale project intended to improve sugar production in Tanzania. The two countries have established a medical-training program under which Tanzania sends qualified doctors to Cuba for specialized training and further research. Although the program is specifically tailored to enable Tanzanian doctors to acquire techniques of organizing and managing mass-oriented medical programs, its research component is also important. Cooperation is also being explored in general educational sectors. Besides Cuba, Tanzania has forged cooperation links with Mexico, with which, for example, it has negotiated the setting up of a joint sisal-processing factory at Korogwe in the Tanga region.[31] Other agreements for technical cooperation with Latin-American countries include agreements with Guyana and Jamaica for the exchange of technical personnel.

As a poor country, Tanzania has done remarkably well in giving training facilities to other African countries. The role it has played in the training of freedom fighters for Mozambique, in particular, occupies an important chapter in the archives of the liberation of southern Africa. It has provided, and continues to provide, places for refugees from Zimbabwe, South Africa, and Namibia at the University of Dar es Salaam and at other specialized institutions. In 1976 more than 20 refugees were enrolled at the University of Dar es Salaam, taking courses in the arts, science, medicine, and law, and it was estimated that there were more than 200 undergoing training in various institutions in Tanzania. Other African countries have also provided training places for Tanzanians: Algeria (one), Ghana (four), Nigeria (five), the Sudan (nine), and Zambia (one).[32]

Contrary to popular belief, technical cooperation has become an important factor in the diplomacy of the poor. This trend is motivated partly by their desire to rely more on their own resources and by the fact that a few of the developing countries have already acquired substantial experience in some areas of scientific development that are still problematic in the others. Developing countries such as China and India have developed a respectable sophistication in intermediate technology that may be more relevant to other developing countries than technology from traditional industrialized centers of the West. So relevant is this expertise to general manpower training and adaptation of technology that developing countries would be well advised to increase such cooperation. While both Kenya and Tanzania have gotten off to a remarkably good start in this direction, the latter is ahead and provides a lead for the future.

CONCLUSION

Despite both Kenya and Tanzania having similar problems and characteristics of dependency, they differ significantly in the way they handle their foreign relations. Kenya's rather unbridled pragmatism in foreign affairs has paid some dividends in attracting large quantities of Western public and private capital. However, its overall effect has still to be fully assessed, especially in view of the dominant role of multinational firms in its economy. Kenya is the classic case where the former colonial power, despite the sharp decline of its neocolonial market, remains the main source of private foreign investment, the main donor of bilateral assistance, and until now, the main supplier of military assistance. This continuity of British influence, combined with an increasing German and U.S. presence, has limited Kenya's ability to take an independent course of action in international affairs. Although Kenya's pattern of foreign trade is remarkably similar to that of Tanzania, Kenya is far more dependent than its southern neighbor on the major Western powers for developmental and military assistance, and for the inflow of private investment on which the continued growth of its economy rests.

This situation in turn makes the Kenyan economy more vulnerable to sabotage, which could arise from the decision of a single donor to withdraw aid. Sabotage may also come from internal change that forces private foreign investors to hold back their capital. Thus a country such as Kenya, with an open-door investment policy, must constantly demonstrate to its donors that it is politically stable even when that political stability may be periodically maintained by artificial or covert means. This can go on for only a limited period before it is overcome by the forces of a crystallizing social formation. The recent political history of Kenya is strewn with good examples of this phenomenon.[33]

Attachment to Britain and to the World Bank has, nevertheless, given Kenya's ruling elite a false sense of the country's importance, especially in its relations with its immediate neighbors. This false self-image has often motivated its policy makers to behave in utter disregard for the national interests of its partner states in the former East African Community. In reference to Tanzania, Kenya's former foreign minister, Njoroge Mungai, has retorted: "Compared with a number of other developing countries where development is not matched by their exceedingly vociferous posture and extreme pronouncements, our record of development in all fields is praiseworthy and never exaggerated for political ends."[34] It really wasn't until after the breakup of the East African Community that Kenya began to appreciate the importance of its neighbors to its security and economic stability.

Tanzania, on the other hand, has had to diversify its markets and sources of aid as a strategy for demonstrating its nonaligned and self-reliant policy, and partly to avoid the possibility of new acts of sabotage —such as the withdrawal of aid by the British over the Unilateral Declaration of Independence in Rhodesia, and by West Germany over Tanzania's refusal to close East German consular offices in Zanzibar. Since 1967, Tanzania's external relations have been carefully managed so that its economy is no longer vulnerable to being sabotaged by a single donor. While Tanzania's policy of self-reliance has not enabled it to reduce its dependence on foreign aid (which, indeed, is greater than ever before), it has, nevertheless, enabled it to take very bold steps in respect to the liberation of southern Africa, and in the promotion of technical assistance among developing countries. Self-reliance has also made it possible for Tanzania to rationalize the internal reorganization of the economy by considerably reducing the volume of foreign ownership. Because vigorous diversification occurred in the post-Arusha Declaration period, it is perhaps fitting to assert that ideological clarity, political will, and commitment to principles have aided Tanzania in handling her foreign relations. From both long- and short-term uses of diplomacy, Tanzania has done remarkably well. This development may also give Tanzania some measure of freedom in choosing appropriate technology that best suits its level of development.

NOTES

1. International Institute for Strategic Studies, *The Military Balance 1976–77* (London: International Institute for Strategic Studies, 1976), p. 45.
2. Ibid., pp. 5, 22, 29.
3. "A Survey of Kenya and Tanzania," *The Economist* (March 11, 1978), p. S–4.
4. International Institute for Strategic Studies, op. cit., p. 45.
5. Ibid.
6. *The Economist,* op. cit., p. S–4.
7. Ibid.

8. International Institute for Strategic Studies, op. cit., p. 43.

9. Ibid.

10. Ibid., pp. 43–44.

11. Ibid., pp. 44–45.

12. See W. T. Newlyn and D. C. Rowan, *Money and Banking in British Colonial Africa* (Oxford: Clarendon Press, 1954).

13. For a summary of these transactions, see Susan A. Gitelson, "Policy Options for Small States: Kenya and Tanzania Reconsidered," *Studies in Comparative International Development* 12, no. 2 (Summer 1977).

14. Ibid., p. 34; and Julius K. Nyerere, *Freedom and Socialism* (Dar es Salaam: Oxford University Press, 1968), p. 195.

15. Gitelson, op. cit., p. 35.

16. International Labour Office, *Employment, Incomes and Equality: A Strategy for Increasing Productive Employment in Kenya* (Geneva: International Labour Office, 1972), pp. 442–43.

17. Colin Leys, *Underdevelopment in Kenya* (London: Heinemann, 1974), pp. 118–47. See also *International Labour Office*, op. cit., pp. 279–94, 437–58, 569–78.

18. John J. Okumu, "Some Thoughts on Kenya's Foreign Policy," *The African Review* 3, no. 2 (June 1973): 272–76. The reader should also recall that in 1969 Ethiopia was still ruled by Emperor Haile Selassie, who shared Kenya's fear of a socialist transformation of the region.

19. Okumu, op. cit., p. 273.

20. Ibid., pp. 273–74.

21. Ibid., pp. 276–79.

22. United Nations, *Survey of Economic Conditions in Africa, 1971,* part 1 (New York: United Nations, 1972), p. 197.

23. Ibid.

24. Ibid., p. 198.

25. See P. Robson and D. A. Lury, eds., *The Economies of Africa* (Evanston: Northwestern University Press, 1969), p. 329.

26. Material used in this section is drawn from my working paper (prepared for the United Nations Development and Advisory Team), "Technical Cooperation Among African Countries: The Experiences of Kenya and Tanzania," (Lusaka, 1976).

27. Information used here was provided by the Kenyan Ministry of Agriculture.

28. Ibid.

29. Figures cited here were made available by the Tanzanian Manpower Ministry.

30. Figures used here were provided by the Tanzanian Ministry of Finance and Planning. See also *New African Development,* October 1977, p. 993.

31. Information used here was provided by the Tanzanian Ministry of Agriculture.

32. Information used here was provided by the Tanzanian Ministry of Education.

33. Political assassinations, and detention of members of Parliament and other concerned Kenyans who wish to see the country's economy taken over by nationals are manifestations of stability maintained by fear. Even the so-called development emphasis in foreign policy dealings has not succeeded in reducing the skyrocketing unemployment rate that now threatens the country. See International Labour Office, op. cit., part 1.

34. See Colin Legum, ed., *African Contemporary Record 1971–72* (London: Rex Collings, 1973), pp. G35–38.

SELECTED BIBLIOGRAPHY
Prepared by Frank Holmquist

THIS BIBLIOGRAPHY follows the chapter organization of this volume, with some repetition of citations occurring when a work is relevant to more than one of the topics covered. There are also some citations for topics not covered. Most works of a historical nature have therefore been assigned to the section for Chapter 1, while most works that are primarily concerned with political parties or elections appear in the sections for Chapters 2 and 3 even though they contain much historical material of a general nature. Citations on ujamaa villages are mainly found in the section for Chapter 7 though many are also relevant to Chapter 6. Studies of industrialization, the working class, and employment are generally found in the section for Chapter 8. Materials on transnational corporations have been assigned to the section for Chapter 10. Only published sources are included, and no systematic attempt has been made to include publications appearing after 1977 though some works published in early 1978 are noted.

1. GENERAL

Kenya

Books and Monographs
Barnett, Donald L., and Karari Mjama. *Mau Mau From Within: An Analysis of Kenya's Peasant Revolt.* New York: Monthly Review Press, 1965.

Burrows, John. *Kenya: Into the Second Decade.* Baltimore: Johns Hopkins University Press, 1975.

Clayton, A., and D. C. Savage. *Government and Labour in Kenya, 1895–1963.* London: Frank Cass, 1975.

Gertzel, Cherry, Maurey Goldschmidt, and Don Rothchild, eds. *Government and Politics in Kenya.* Nairobi: East African Publishing House, 1969.

Ghai, Y. P., and J. P. W. B. McAuslan. *Public Law and Political Change in Kenya.* New York: Oxford University Press, 1970.

Kariuki, J. M. *Mau Mau Detainee* Nairobi: Oxford University Press, 1963.

Kenyatta, Jomo. *Suffering Without Bitterness.* Nairobi: East African Publishing House, 1968.

———. *Facing Mount Kenya.* New York: Vintage, 1962.

Leys, Colin. *Underdevelopment in Kenya: The Political Economy of Neo-Colonialism.* London: Heinemann, 1974.

Marris, Peter, and Anthony Somerset. *The African Entrepreneur and Development in Kenya.* New York: Africana Publishing, 1972.

Munro, Forbes. *Colonial Rule and the Kamba: Social Change in the Kenya Highlands, 1889–1939.* New York: Oxford University Press, 1975.

Murray-Brown, Jeremy. *Kenyatta.* London: George Allen and Unwin, 1972.

Mutiso, Gideon Cyrus. *Kenya: Politics, Policy and Society.* Nairobi: East African Literature Bureau, 1975.

Nyangira, N. *Relative Modernization and Public Resource Allocation in Kenya.* Nairobi: East African Literature Bureau, 1975.

Rosberg, Carl G., and John Nottingham. *The Myth of Mau Mau: Nationalism in Kenya.* New York: Praeger, 1966.

Rothchild, Donald. *Racial Bargaining in Independent Kenya: A Study of Minorities and Decolonization.* New York: Oxford University Press, 1973.

Tignor, Robert L. *The Colonial Transformation of Kenya: The Kamba, Kikuyu, and Masai from 1900 to 1939.* Princeton: Princeton University Press, 1976.

Van Zwanenberg, Roger. *Colonialism and Labour in Kenya: 1919–1939.* Nairobi: East African Literature Bureau, 1975.

Van Zwanenberg, Roger, with Anne King. *An Economic History of Kenya and Uganda 1800–1970.* Nairobi: East African Literature Bureau, 1975.

Wipper, Audrey. *Rural Rebels: A Study of Two Protest Movements in Kenya.* Nairobi: Oxford University Press, 1977.

Wolff, R. D. *The Economics of Colonialism: Britain and Kenya: 1919–1939.* New Haven: Yale University Press, 1974.

Articles

Amsden, Alice. "A Review of Kenya's Political Economy Since Independence." *Journal of African Studies* 1 (Winter 1974):417–40.

Godfrey, M., and S. Langdon. "Partners in Development? The Transnationalization Thesis in a Kenyan Context." *Journal of Commonwealth and Comparative Politics* 14 (March 1976):42–67.

Hazelwood, Arthur. "Kenya: Income Distribution and Poverty—An Unfashionable View." *Journal of Modern African Studies* 16, no. 1 (March 1978):81–95.

Hood, M. "Income Distribution in Kenya (1963–72)." *Journal of Development Studies* 12 (April 1976):221–28.

Kitching, Gavin. "Modes of Production and Kenyan Dependency." *Review of African Political Economy* 8 (January-April 1977):56–74.

Langdon, Steven. "The State and Capitalism in Kenya." *Review of African Political Economy* 8 (January-April 1977):90–98.

Martin, Denis. "The Crise Politique au Kenya, 1975–76." *Revue Francaise d'Etudes Politiques Africaines* 137 (May 1977):20–53.

Nellis, John. "Who Pays Tax in Kenya?" *African Review* 2 (1972):345–63.

O'Brien, J. "Bonapartism and Kenyatta's Regime." *Review of African Political Economy* 6 (1976):90–95.

Ogot, Bethwell A. *Hadith* (Proceedings of the Historical Society of Kenya), nos. 1–6 (Nairobi: East African Publishing House, nos. 1–4); (Nairobi: East African Literature Bureau, nos. 5–6).

Rana, K. A. A. "Class Formation and Social Conflict: A Case Study of Kenya." *Ufahamu* 7 (Los Angeles, 1977):17–72.

Steele, David. "The Theory of the Dual Economy and African Entrepreneurship in Kenya." *Journal of Development Studies* 12 (October 1975):18–38.
Stewart, F. "Kenya: Strategies for Development." In *Development Paths in Africa and China,* edited by U. G. Damachi et al., pp. 80–111. Boulder: Westview Press, 1976.
Swainson, Nicola. "The Rise of a National Bourgeoisie in Kenya." *Review of African Political Economy* 8 (January–April 1977):39–55.
Van Zwanenberg, Roger. "Neocolonialism and the Origin of the National Bourgeoisie in Kenya Between 1940 and 1973." *Journal of Eastern African Research and Development* 4 (1974):161–88.

Documents
Government of Kenya. *Development Plan 1974–1978* Nairobi: Government Printer, 1974.
———. *Development Plan 1970–1974.* Nairobi: Government Printer, 1969.
———. *African Socialism and Its Application to Planning in Kenya.* Sessional Paper no. 10. Nairobi: Government Printer, 1965.
International Bank for Reconstruction and Development. *Kenya: Into the Second Decade.* Baltimore: Johns Hopkins University Press, 1975.
International Labour Office. *Employment, Incomes and Equality: A Strategy for Increasing Productive Employment in Kenya.* Geneva: International Labour Office, 1972.

Tanzania

Books and Monographs
Cliffe, Lionel, and John Saul, eds. *Socialism in Tanzania.* Vol. 1, *Politics.* Vol. 2, *Policies.* Nairobi: East African Publishing House, 1972 and 1973.
Green, Reginald. *Toward Socialism and Self-Reliance.* Research Report no. 38. Uppsala: Scandinavian Institute of African Studies, 1977.
Ingle, Clyde. *From Village to State in Tanzania.* Ithaca: Cornell University Press, 1972.
Kimambo, I. N., and A. J. Temu, eds. *A History of Tanzania.* Nairobi: East African Publishing House, 1969.
Moore, S. F., and P. Puritt. *The Chagga and Meru of Tanzania.* London: International African Institute, 1977.
Nsekela, A. J., and A. M. Nhonoli. *Health Services and Society in Mainland Tanzania.* Nairobi: East African Literature Bureau, 1976.
Nyerere, Julius K. *Freedom and Unity: A Selection of Writings and Speeches, 1952–1965.* New York: Oxford University Press, 1967.
———. *Freedom and Socialism: A Selection from Writings and Speeches, 1965–1967.* New York: Oxford University Press, 1970.
———. *Freedom and Development—Uhuru Na Maendeleo.* New York: Oxford University Press, 1974.
O'Barr, W. M., and J. F. O'Barr, eds. *Language and Politics.* The Hague: Mouton, 1976.

Pratt, Cranford. *The Critical Phase in Tanzania 1945–68.* London: Cambridge University Press, 1976.

Ruhumbika, Gabriel, ed. *Towards Ujamaa: Twenty Years of TANU Leadership.* Nairobi: East African Literature Bureau, 1974.

Shivji, Issa. *Class Struggles in Tanzania.* New York: Monthly Review Press, 1976.

———. ed. *Tourism and Socialist Development.* Dar es Salaam: Tanzania Publishing House, 1973.

Smith, William Edgett. *Nyerere of Tanzania.* London: Victor Golanez, 1973.

Thomas, Clive. *Dependence and Transformation: The Economics of the Transition to Socialism.* New York: Monthly Review Press, 1974.

Tordoff, William. *Government and Politics in Tanzania.* Nairobi: East African Publishing House, 1967.

Uchumi Editorial Board, eds. *Towards Socialist Planning.* Dar es Salaam: Tanzania Publishing House, 1972.

Articles

Green, Reginald. "Redistribution with Growth—and/or Transition to Socialist Development." *IDS Bulletin* 7 (August 1975):22–28.

Helleiner, G. K. "Socialism and Economic Development in Tanzania." *Journal of Development Studies* 8 (1972):183–204.

Leys, Colin. "The 'Overdeveloped' Post-Colonial State: A Re-evaluation." *Review of African Political Economy* 5 (January–April 1976):40–48.

McCarthy, D. M. P. "Media as Ends: Money and the Underdevelopment of Tanganyika to 1940." *Journal of Economic History* 36 (September 1976):645–62.

Routh, Guy. "Development Paths in Tanzania." In *Development Paths in Africa and China,* edited by U. G. Damachi, pp. 10–38. Boulder: Westview Press, 1976.

Saul, John S. "African Socialism in One Country: Tanzania." In *Essays on the Political Economy of Africa,* edited by Giovanni Arrighi and John Saul, pp. 237–335. New York: Monthly Review Press, 1973.

———. "The State in Post-Colonial Societies—Tanzania." In *Socialist Register 1974,* edited by Ralph Miliband and John Saville, pp. 349–72. (London: Merlin Press, 1974).

Turshen, M. "The Impact of Colonialism on Health and Health Services in Tanzania." *International Journal of Health Services* 7 (1977):7–35.

Tschannerl, Gerhard. "Periphery Capitalist Development: The Tanzanian Economy." *Utafiti* 1 (1976):5–46.

Von Freyhold, Michaela. "The Post-Colonial State and Its Tanzanian Version." *Review of African Political Economy* 8 (January–April 1977):75–89.

Young, Crawford. "Tanzania and Uganda." In *The Politics of Cultural Pluralism,* pp. 216–73. Madison: University of Wisconsin, 1976.

Documents

Chama Cha Mapinduzi. *CCM Constitution.* Dar es Salaam: Government Printer, 1977.

Nyerere, Julius K. *The Arusha Declaration Ten Years After.* Dar es Salaam: Government Printer, 1977.

————. *The Arusha Declaration and TANU Policy on Socialism and Self-Reliance.* Dar es Salaam: Government Printer, 1967.

Tanganyika's Five-Year Plan for Economic and Social Development, 1964–1969. Dar es Salaam: Government Printer, 1964.

Tanzania Second Five-Year Plan for Economic and Social Development, 1st July 1969–30th June 1974. Dar es Salaam: Government Printer, 1969.

Kenya and Tanzania

Books and Monographs

Brett, E. A. *Colonialism and Underdevelopment in East Africa: The Politics of Economic Change 1919–39.* London: Heinemann, 1973.

Chambers, Robert. *Managing Rural Development: Ideas and Experience from East Africa.* Uppsala: Scandinavian Institute of African Studies, 1974.

Davey, K. J. *Taxing a Peasant Society: The Example of Graduated Taxes in East Africa.* London: Charles Knight, 1974.

Furley, O. W., and T. Watson. *A History of Education in East Africa.* New York: NOK Publishers, 1977.

Hutton, John, ed. *Urban Challenge in East Africa.* Nairobi: East African Publishing House, 1972.

Nanjira, Daniel. *The Status of Aliens in East Africa: Asians and Europeans in Tanzania, Uganda and Kenya.* New York: Praeger, 1976.

Seidman, Ann. *Comparative Development Strategies in East Africa.* Nairobi: East African Publishing House, 1972.

Articles

Berry, Leonard, and Robert Kates. "Views on Environmental Problems in East Africa." *African Review* 2 (1972):299–313.

Bienen, Henry. "Military and Society in East Africa." *Comparative Politics* 6 (1974):489–517.

Cliffe, Lionel. "Rural Class Formation in East Africa." *Journal of Peasant Studies* 4 (1977):195–224.

————. "Underdevelopment or Socialism: A Comparative Analysis of Kenya and Tanzania." In *The Political Economy of Africa,* edited by Richard Harris. Cambridge, Mass: Schenkman, 1975.

Davey, K. J. "Local Bureaucrats and Politicians in East Africa." *Journal of Administration Overseas* 10 (October 1971):268–79.

Elkan, Walter. "The Relation Between Tourism and Employment in Kenya and Tanzania." *Journal of Development Studies* 11 (January 1975):123–30.

Lonsdale, John. "Some Origins of Nationalism in East Africa." *Journal of African History* 11 (1969):119–46.

Moris, Jon R. "Administrative Authority and the Problem of Effective Agricultural Administration in East Africa." *African Review* 2 (June 1972):105–46.

Neher, W. W., and J. C. Condon. "The Mass Media and Nation-Building in Kenya and Tanzania." In *The Search for National Integration in Africa,* edited by D. R. Smock and A. Smock, pp. 220–39. New York: The Free Press, 1975.

Szentes, Tamas. "Socio-Economic Effects of Two Patterns of Foreign Capital Investments." In *The Political Economy of Contemporary Africa,* edited by Peter Gutkind and Immanuel Wallerstein, pp. 261–90. Beverly Hills: Sage Publications, 1976.

Vincent, Joan. "The Changing Role of Small Towns in the Agrarian Structure of East Africa." *Journal of Commonwealth and Comparative Politics* 12 (November 1974):261–75.

———. "Room for Maneuver: The Political Role of Small Towns in East Africa." In *Colonialism and Change: Essays Presented to Lucy Mair,* edited by Maxwell Owusu, pp. 115–44. The Hague: Mouton, 1975.

Documents

Institute for Development Research. *Dualism and Rural Development in East Africa.* Copenhagen: Institute for Development Research, 1973.

2. PARTY AND PARTY-STATE RELATIONS

Kenya

Books and Monographs

Bienen, Henry. *Kenya: The Politics of Participation and Control.* Princeton: Princeton University Press, 1974.

Gertzel, Cherry. *The Politics of Independent Kenya.* London: Heinemann, 1970.

Articles

Buytenhiujs, R. "KANU." *International Journal of Politics* 4 (1974):58–76.

Furedi, Frank. "The African Crowd in Nairobi: Popular Movements and Elite Politics." *The Journal of African History* 14 (1973):597–621.

Good, K. "Kenyatta and the Organization of KANU." *Canadian Journal of African Studies* 2 (1968):115–36.

Okumu, John. "Charisma and Politics in Kenya." *East Africa Journal,* (February 1968):9–16.

Tanzania

Books and Monographs

Bienen, Henry. *Tanzania: Party Transformation and Economic Development.* Princeton: Princeton University Press, 1970.

Howell, John B. *Tanganyika African National Union: A Guide to Publications by and about TANU.* Washington: Library of Congress, 1978.

Hyden, Goran. *Political Development in Rural Tanzania.* Nairobi: East African Publishing House, 1969.

Nduru, C. T., et al. *The Party: Essays on TANU.* Dar es Salaam: Tanzania Publishing House, 1976.

Proctor, J. H. *The Cell System of the Tanganyika African National Union.* Dar es Salaam: Tanzania Publishing House, 1971.

Articles

Ingle, Clyde. "The Ten House Cell System in Tanzania." *Journal of Developing Areas* 6 (January 1972):211–26.

McGowan, P. J., and H. K. M. Wacirah. "The Evolution of Tanzanian Political Leadership." *African Studies Review* 17 (1974):179–204.

McHenry, Dean E. "A Study of the Rise of TANU and the Demise of British Rule in Kigoma." *African Review* 3 (1973):403–21.

Miller, Norman N. "The Rural African Party: Political Participation in Tanzania." *American Political Science Review* 64 (June 1970):548–71.

Moderne, Franck. "Contribution à l'étude de l'Etat à parti unique: le modèle tanzanien." In *Annuaire des Pays le l'Océan Indien* 2, 1975, Aix-en-Provence: Presses Universitaires d'Aix-Marseille, 1977.

Pratt, R. Cranford. "The Cabinet and Presidential Leadership in Tanzania." In State of Nations: Constraints on Development in Independent Africa, edited by Michael Lofchie. Berkeley: University of California Press, 1973.

Samoff, Joel. "Cell Leaders in Tanzania: A Review of Recent Research." *Taamuli* 4 (December 1973):63–75.

Documents

Report of the Presidential Commission on the Establishment of a Democratic One-Party State. Dar es Salaam, Government Printer, 1965.

3. *LEGISLATORS AND ELECTORAL BEHAVIOR*

Kenya

Books and Monographs

Bennett, George, and Carl G. Rosberg. *The Kenyatta Election.* London: Oxford University Press, 1961.

Articles

Barkan, Joel D. "Comment: Further Reassessment of 'Conventional Wisdom': Political Knowledge and Voting Behavior in Rural Kenya." *American Political Science Review* 70 (June 1976):452–55.

Barkan, Joel D., with John J. Okumu. " 'Semi-Competitive' Elections, Clientelism, and Political Recruitment in Kenya." In *Elections Without Choice,* edited by Guy Hermet et al. London: Macmillan, 1978.

——. "Political Linkage in Kenya: Citizens, Local Elites, and Legislators." In *Political Parties and Linkage,* edited by Kay Lawson. New Haven: Yale University Press, forthcoming.

Hakes, Jay E., and John Helgerson. "Bargaining and Parliamentary Behavior in Africa: A Comparative Study of Zambia and Kenya." In *Legislatures in Comparative Perspective,* edited by Alan Kornberg, pp. 335–62. New York: David McKay, 1973.

Hopkins, Raymond F. "Th Kenyan Legislature: Political Functions and Citizen Perceptions." In *Legislative Systems in Developing Countries,* edited by G. R. Boynton and Chong Lim Kim, pp. 207–31. Durham, N.C.: Duke University Press, 1975.

Okumu, John. "The Bye-Election in Gem: An Assessment." *East Africa Journal* (June 1969).

Tanzania

Books and Monographs

Cliffe, Lionel, ed. *One Party Democracy: The 1965 Tanzania General Elections.* Nairobi: East African Publishing House, 1967.

Election Study Committee, eds. *Socialism and Participation: Tanzania's 1970 National Elections.* Dar es Salaam: Tanzania Publishing House, 1974.

Hopkins, Raymond R. *Political Roles in a New State: Tanzania's First Decade.* New Haven: Yale University Press, 1971.

Articles

Hopkins, Raymond F. "Constituency Ties and Deviant Expectations Among Tanzanian Legislators." *Comparative Political Studies* 4 (October 1971):321–38.

———. "The Role of the MP in Tanzania." *American Political Science Review* 64 (1970):754–71.

Kjekhus, Helge. "Parliament in a One-Party State: The Bunge of Tanzania, 1965–70." *Journal of Modern African Studies* 12 (March 1974):19–43.

Martin, Denis. "The 1975 Tanzanian Elections: The Disturbing Six Percent." In *Elections Without Choice,* edited by Guy Hermet, et al. London: Macmillan, 1978.

———. "La houe, la maison, l'urne et le maitre d'ecole. Les Elections en Tanzanie 1965–1970." *Review francaise de science politique* 25, no. 4 (1975).

Saul, J. S. "The Nature of Tanzania's Political System: Issues Raised by the 1965 and 1970 Elections." *Journal of Commonwealth Political Studies* 10, nos. 2 and 3 (1972).

Kenya and Tanzania

Articles

Barkan, Joel. "Bringing Home the Pork: Legislator Behavior, Rural Development and Political Change in East Africa." In *Legislators and Development,* edited by Lloyd Musolf and Joel Smith. Durham: Duke University Press, 1978.

Hopkins, Raymond F. "The Influence of the Legislature on Development Strategy: The Case of Kenya and Tanzania." In *Legislators and Development,* edited by Lloyd Musolf and Joel Smith. Durham: Duke University Press, 1978.

Hyden, Goran, and Colin Leys. "Elections and Politics in Single Party Systems: The Case of Kenya and Tanzania." *British Journal of Political Science* (October 1972):389–420.

4. ADMINISTRATION AND POLICY MAKING

Kenya

Books and Monographs

Hyden, Goran, Robert H. Jackson, and John J. Okumu, eds. *Development Administration: The Kenyan Experience.* Nairobi: Oxford University Press, 1970.

Leonard, David K. *Reaching the Peasant Farmer: Organization Theory and Practice in Kenya.* Chicago: University of Chicago Press, 1977.

————. ed. *Rural Administration in Kenya.* Management and Administration Series, no. 2. Nairobi: East African Literature Bureau, 1973.

Nellis, John R. *The Ethnic Composition of Leading Kenyan Government Positions.* Research Report no. 24. Uppsala: Scandinavian Institute of African Studies, 1974.

Trapman, C. *Change in Administrative Structures.* London: Overseas Development Institute, 1974.

Articles

Ashcroft, Joseph, et al. "Does Extension Create Poverty?" *East Africa Journal* 9 (1972):28–33.

Brokensha, David, and John Nellis. "Administration in Kenya: A Study of Rural Division of Mbere." *Journal of Administration Overseas* 13 and 14 (October 1974 and January 1975):510–23, and 17–29.

Dresang, Dennis, and Ira Sharkansky. "Public Corporations in a Single Country and Regional Settings: Kenya and the East African Community." *International Organization* 27 (1973):303–28.

————. "Sequences of Change and the Political Economy of Public Corporations: Kenya." *Journal of Politics* 37 (1975):163–86.

Gertzel, Cherry. "Administrative Reform in Kenya and Zambia." In *A Decade of Public Administration in Africa,* edited by A. H. Rweyemamu and Goran Hyden, pp. 185–207. Nairobi: East African Literature Bureau, 1975.

————. "The Provincial Administration in Kenya." *Journal of Commonwealth Political Studies* 4 (1966):201–15.

Hyden, Goran. "Social Structure, Bureaucracy and Development Administration in Kenya." *African Review* 1 (January 1972):118–29.

Leonard, David K. "The Social Structure of the Agricultural Extension Service in the Western Province of Kenya." *African Review* 2 (1972):323–43.

Parkin, David. "The Rhetoric of Responsibility: Bureaucratic Communication in a Kenya Farming Area." In *Political Language and Oratory in Traditional Society,* edited by M. Bloch, pp. 112–39. New York: Academic Press, 1975.

Documents

Ndegwa, D. N. (Chairman), Public Service Structure and Renumeration Commission. *Report of the Commission of Inquiry.* Nairobi: Government Printer, 1971.

Tanzania

Books and Monographs
Dryden, Stanley. *Local Administration in Tanzania.* Nairobi: East African Publishing House, 1968.
Etten, G. M. van. *Rural Health Development in Tanzania.* Essen: Van Gorcum, 1976.
Finucane, James R. *Rural Development and Bureaucracy in Tanzania: The Case of Mwanza Region.* Uppsala: Scandinavian Institute of African Studies, 1974.
Gish, Oscar. *Planning the Health Sector: The Tanzanian Experience.* London: Croom Helm, 1975.
Gottlieb, Manuel. *Health Care Financing in Mainland Tanzania.* Foreign and Comparative Studies/Eastern Africa, no. 20. Syracuse: Syracuse University, Maxwell School of Citizenship and Public Affairs, 1975.
Rweyemamu, A. H., and B. U. Mwansasu, eds. *Planning in Tanzania: Background to Decentralisation.* Nairobi: East African Literature Bureau, 1974.

Articles
Baer, K. L. "Administrative Structure: Situation and Culture in the Case of Urambo." In *The Administration of Change in Africa,* edited by E. P. Morgan, pp. 233–66. New York: Danellan Publishing, 1974.
Finucane, James R. "Hierarchy and Participation in Development: A Case Study of Regional Administration in Tanzania." *African Review* 2 (1972):573–98.
Green, R. H. "Relevance, Efficiency, Romanticism and Confusion in Tanzanian Planning and Management." *African Review* 5 (1975):209–34.
Hyden, Goran. "Policy-Making for Development: The Tanzanian Case." *African Quarterly* 15 (March 1976):5–24.
———. "Public Policy-Making and Public Enterprises in Tanzania." *African Review* 5 (1975):141–66.
Lawrence, P. R., et al. "Regional Planning in Tanzania: Some Institutional Problems." *East African Journal of Rural Development* 7 (1974):10–45.
Mcharu, F. J. "The Government and the Governed: The Tanzanian Model." In *A Decade of Public Administration in Africa,* edited by A. H. Rweyemamu and G. Hyden, pp. 75–85. Nairobi: East African Literature Bureau, 1975.
Mutahaba, Gelase. "The Effect of Changes in the Tanzanian Public Service System upon Administrative Productivity, 1961–72." *African Review* 5 (1975): 201–8.
Packard, Philip C. "Public Sector Control in Tanzania." *Quarterly Journal of Administration* 7 (April 1973):293–312.
Rweyemamu, A. H. "The Predicament of Managers of Public Enterprises in Tanzania." *African Review* 5 (1975):119–26.
Samoff, Joel. "The Bureaucracy and the Bourgeoisie: Decentralization and Class Struggle in Tanzania." *Comparative Studies in Society and History* (forthcoming).

Documents
Nyerere, Julius K. *Decentralization.* Dar es Salaam: Government Printer, 1972.

Kenya and Tanzania

Books and Monographs
Rweyemamu, A. H., and Goran Hyden, eds. *A Decade of Public Administration in Africa.* Nairobi: East African Literature Bureau, 1975.

5. IDEOLOGY

Kenya

Books and Monographs
Kaggia, Bildad. *Roots of Freedom 1921–1963: An Autobiography.* Nairobi: East African Publishing House, 1975.
Kenyatta, Jomo. *Suffering Without Bitterness.* Nairobi: East African Publishing House, 1968.
————. *Harambee!: The Prime Minister's Speeches, 1963–1964.* Nairobi: Oxford University Press, 1964.
Mboya, Tom. *Freedom and After.* London: Andre Deutsch, 1963.
————. *The Challenge of Nationhood.* London: Andre Deutsch, 1969.
Odinga, Oginga. *Not Yet Uhuru: An Autobiography.* London: Heinemann, 1967.

Documents
Government of Kenya. *African Socialism and Its Application to Planning in Kenya.* Sessional Paper no. 10. Nairobi: Government Printer, 1965.

Tanzania

Books and Monographs
Duggan, W. R., and J. R. Civille. *Tanzania and Nyerere: A Study of Ujamaa and Nationhood.* Maryknoll, N.Y.: Orbis Books, 1976.
Nellis, John R. *A Theory of Ideology: The Tanzanian Example.* Nairobi: Oxford University Press, 1972.
Nyerere, Julius K. *Freedom and Development.* Dar es Salaam: Oxford University Press, 1973.
————. *Freedom and Socialism.* Dar es Salaam: Oxford University Press, 1968.
————. *Freedom and Unity.* Dar es Salaam: Oxford University Press, 1967.

Articles
Damachi, U. G. "Julius Nyerere: Ujamaa—Socialism and Rural Development in Tanzania." In *Leadership Ideology in Africa: Attitudes Toward Socio-economic Development,* pp. 55–72. New York: Praeger, 1976.
Hyden, Goran. "Mao and Mwalimu: The Soldier and the Teacher as Revolutionary." *Transition,* no. 34 (1968), pp. 24–30.
Mazrui, Ali. "Tanzaphilia." *Transition,* no. 31 (1967), pp. 20–26.
Parker, Ian C. "Ideological and Economic Development in Tanzania." *African Studies Review* 15, no. 1 (1972):42–78.

Documents

Nyerere, Julius K. *The Arusha Declaration Ten Years After.* Dar es Salaam: Government Printer, 1977.

————. *The Arusha Declaration and TANU Policy on Socialism and Self-Reliance.* Dar es Salaam: Government Printer, 1967.

Tanganyika African National Union. *Mwangozo Wa TANU* [TANU party guidelines]. Dar es Salaam: Government Printer, 1971.

————. *Utaratibu No Maogozi Ya Chama Cha TANU* [TANU regulations on leadership]. Dar es Salaam: Government Printer, 1967.

6. PEASANTS AND PARTICIPATION

Kenya

Books and Monographs

Lamb, Geoff. *Peasant Politics: Conflict and Development in Muranga.* Sussex, England: Julian Friedman Publishing, 1974.

Parkin, David J. *Palms, Wine and Witnesses.* London: International Textbook, 1972.

Articles

Bolnick, Bruce R. "Collective Goods Provision Through Community Development." *Economic Development and Cultural Change* 25 (October 1976): 137–50.

Colebatch, H. K. "Access and the Study of Local Services: A Kenyan Case." *Development and Change* 6 (April 1975):107–18.

Godfrey, E. M., and G. C. M. Mutiso. "The Political Economy of Self-Help: Kenya's 'Harambee' Institutes of Technology." *Canadian Journal of African Studies* 8, no. 1 (1974):109–33.

Holmquist, Frank. "Toward a Political Theory of Rural Self-Help Development in Africa." *Rural Africana,* no. 18 (Fall 1972), pp. 69–80.

————. "Implementing Rural Development Projects." *Development Administration: The Kenyan Experience,* edited by Goran Hyden, Robert Jackson, and John Okumu, pp. 201–29. Nairobi: Oxford University Press, 1970.

Keller, E. J. "Harambee! Educational Policy, Inequality, and the Political Economy of Rural Community Self-Help in Kenya." *Journal of African Studies* 4 (Spring 1977):86–106.

Lamb, Geoff. "The Neocolonial Integration of Kenyan Peasants." *Development and Change* 8 (1977):45–49.

Leys, Colin. "Politics in Kenya: The Development of Peasant Society." *British Journal of Political Science* 2 (July 1971), pp. 307–37.

Steeves, Jeffrey S. "Class Analysis and Rural Africa: The Kenya Tea Development Authority." *Journal of Modern African Studies* 16, no. 1 (March 1978): 123–32.

Wallis, M. "Community Development in Kenya: Some Current Issues." *Community Development Journal* 11 (October 1976):192–98.

Winans, Edgar V., and Angelique Haugerud. "Rural Self-Help in Kenya: The Harambee Movement." *Human Organization* (Winter 1977), pp. 334–51.

Tanzania

Books and Monographs
Ingle, Clyde R. *From Village to State in Tanzania: The Politics of Rural Development.* Ithaca: Cornell University Press, 1972.

Maguire, Andrew G. *Toward 'Uhuru' in Tanzania: The Politics of Participation.* London: Cambridge University Press, 1969.

Liebenow, J. Gus. *Colonial Rule and Political Development in Tanzania: The Case of the Makonde.* Evanston: Northwestern University Press, 1971.

Samoff, Joel. *Tanzania: Local Politics and the Structure of Power.* Madison: University of Wisconsin Press, 1974.

Articles
Coulson, A. C. "Peasants and Bureaucrats." *Review of African Political Economy,* no. 3 (May–October 1975), pp. 53–58.

Feldman, Rayah. "Custom and Capitalism: Changes in the Basis of Land Tenure in Ismani." *Journal of Development Studies* 10 (1974):305–20.

———. "Ismani." In *Debate and Compromise,* edited by F. G. Bailey, pp. 280–308. New York: Oxford University Press, 1973.

———. "Rural Social Differentiation and Political Goals in Tanzania." In *Beyond the Sociology of Development,* edited by Ivar Oxaal et al., pp. 154–82. London: Routledge and Kegan Paul, 1975.

Kitching, Gavin. "Local Political Studies in Tanzania and the Wider Context." *African Affairs* (July 1972), pp. 282–92.

McHenry, Dean E. "The Underdevelopment Theory: A Case Study." *Journal of Modern African Studies* 14 (1976):621–36.

———. "Peasant Participation in Communal Farming: The Tanzanian Experience." *African Studies Review* 20, no. 3 (1977):43–59.

Mutahaba, Gelase. "Local Autonomy and National Planning: Complementary or Otherwise? Case Study from Tanzania." *African Review* 4 (1974):509–30.

O'Barr, Jean. "Pare Women: A Case of Political Involvement." *Rural Africana,* no. 29 (Winter 1975–76), pp. 121–34.

Rigby, Peter. "Local Participation in National Politics: Ugogo." *Africa* 47 (1977): 89–107.

Roth, W. J. "Traditional Social Structure and the Development of a Marketing Cooperative in Tanzania." In *Popular Participation in Social Change,* edited by J. Nash et al., pp. 45–53. The Hague: Mouton, 1976.

Samoff, Joel, and Rachel Samoff. "The Local Politics of Underdevelopment." *Politics and Society* 6 (1977):397–432.

Storgaard, B. "Women in Ujamaa Villages." *Rural Africana,* no. 29 (Winter 1975–76), pp. 135–55.

Tooker, P. D. "Sub-national Politics and the Advent of Dual Rule in Tanzania, 1961–65." *Quarterly Journal of Administration* 11 (January 1977): 43–62.

7. RURAL DEVELOPMENT POLICY

Kenya

Books and Monographs

Harbeson, John W. *Nation-Building in Kenya: The Role of Land Reform.* Evanston: Northwestern University Press, 1973.

Heyer, Judith, D. Ireri, and J. Moris. *Rural Development in Kenya.* Nairobi: East African Publishing House, 1971.

Heyer, Judith, and J. K. Maitha, eds. *Agricultural Development in Kenya.* Nairobi: Oxford University Press, 1976.

Mbithi, Philip. *Rural Sociology and Rural Development: Its Application in Kenya.* Nairobi: East African Literature Bureau, 1974.

Mbithi, Philip, and Carolyn Barnes. *The Spontaneous Settlement Problem in Kenya.* Nairobi: East African Literature Bureau, 1975.

O'Keefe, P. *Land Use and Development.* African Environment Special Report, no. 5. London: International African Institute, 1977.

Sorenson, M. P. K. *Land Reform in Kikuyu Country.* Nairobi: Oxford University Press, 1967.

Uchendu, Victor, and K. R. M. Anthony. *Agricultural Change in Kisii District, Kenya.* Nairobi: East African Literature Bureau, 1975.

Wasserman, Gary. *Politics of Decolonization: Kenya, Europeans and the Land Issue, 1960–1965.* London: Cambridge University Press, 1976.

Articles

Heyer, Judith. "The Origins of Regional Inequalities in Small-Holder Agriculture in Kenya, 1920–73." *East African Journal of Rural Development* 8 (1975):142–81.

Leitner, K. "The Situation of Agricultural Workers in Kenya." *Review of African Political Economy,* no. 6 (1976), pp. 34–50.

Livingstone, Ian. "An Evaluation of Kenya's Rural Industrial Programme." *Journal of Modern African Studies* 15, no. 3 (1977):494–504.

Ross, Marc H., and Thomas Weisner. "The Rural-Urban Migrant Network in Kenya: Some General Implications." *American Ethnologist* 4 (1977):359–75.

Staudt, K. A. "Women Farmers and Inequalities in Agricultural Services." *Rural Africana,* no. 29 (Winter 1975–76), pp. 81–94.

Wasserman, Gary. "Continuity and Counter-Insurgency: The Role of Land Reform in Decolonizing Kenya, 1962–1970." *Canadian Journal of African Studies* 7, no. 1 (1973):133–48.

Wilson, Rodney. "Land Control in Kenya's Small-holder Farming Areas." *East African Journal of Rural Development* 5, nos. 1/2 (1972):123–40.

Documents

International Labour Office. *Employment, Incomes and Equality,* chaps. 1, 10. Geneva: International Labour Office, 1972.

Swynnerton, R. T. M. *A Plan to Intensify the Development of African Agriculture in Kenya.* Nairobi: Government Printer, 1954.

The Royal East African Commission of 1952–1955 Report. Cmd. 9475. London: Her Majesty's Stationery Office, 1955.

Tanzania

Books and Monographs

Cliffe, Lionel, et al., eds. *Rural Cooperation in Tanzania.* Dar es Salaam: Tanzania Publishing House, 1975.

Hill, Francis. *Ujamaa: Mobilization and Participation in Tanzania.* London: Frank Cass, 1978.

Hyden, Goran. *Peasants and Underdevelopment in Africa: The Tanzanian Experience and Beyond.* Berkeley: University of California Press, forthcoming.

James, R. W. *Land Tenure and Policy in Tanzania.* Nairobi: East African Literature Bureau, 1971.

Jellicoe, M. *The Long Path: A Study of Social Change in Tanzania.* Nairobi: East African Publishing House, 1977.

Knight, C. G. *Ecology and Change: Rural Modernization in an African Community.* New York: Seminar Press, 1974.

Lundqvist, J. *Local-Central Impulses for Change and Development: Morogoro.* Bergen: Universitetsverlag, 1975.

Pipping, Knut. *Land Holding in the Usangu Plain: A Survey of Two Villages in the Southern Highlands of Tanzania.* Research Report no. 33. Uppsala: Scandinavian Institute of African Studies, 1976.

Proctor, J. H., ed. *Building Ujamaa Villages in Tanzania.* Dar es Salaam: Tanzania Publishing House, 1971.

Rald, Jorgen, and Karen Rald. *Rural Organization in Bukoba District, Tanzania.* Uppsala: Scandinavian Institute of African Studies, 1975.

Uchendu, Victor C., and K. R. M. Anthony. *Agricultural Change in Geita District, Tanzania.* Nairobi: East African Literature Bureau, 1975.

Vail, David J. *Technology for Ujamaa Village Development in Tanzania.* Foreign and Comparative Studies/Eastern Africa, no. 18. Syracuse: Syracuse University, Maxwell School of Citizenship and Public Affairs, 1975.

Van Hekken, P. M., and H. U. E. Thoden Van Velzen. *Land Scarcity and Rural Inequality in Tanzania: Some Case Studies from Rungwe District.* The Hague: Mouton, 1972.

Articles

Abrahams, R. G. "Time and Village Structure in Northern Unyamwezi: An Examination of Social and Ecological Factors Affecting the Development and Decline of Local Communities." *Africa* 47 (1977):372–85.

Aldington, T. J. "Tanzanian Agriculture: A Decade of Progress in Crop Production." *Tanzania Notes and Records* 76 (1975):57–66.

Awiti, A. "Economic Differentiation in Isami, Iringa Region." *African Review* 3 (1973):209–40.

Barker, Jonathan. "Ujamaa in Cash Crop Areas of Tanzania: Some Problems and Reflections." *Journal of African Studies* 1 (1974):441–63.

Bowles, B. D. "Export Crops and Underdevelopment in Tanzania." *Utafiti* 1 (1976):71–85.

Brain, J. L. "Is Transformation Possible? Styles of Settlement in Post-Independent Tanzania." *African Affairs* 76 (April 1977):231–45.

————. "Less than Second-Class: Women in Rural Settlement Schemes in Tanzania." In *Women in Africa: Studies in Social and Economic Change*, edited by Nancy J. Hafkin, pp. 265–82. Stanford: Stanford University Press, 1976.

DeVries, James. "Agricultural Extension and Development: Ujamaa Villages and the Problems of Institutional Change." *Community Development Journal* 13 (January 1978):11–19.

Feldman, David. "The Economics of Ideology: Some Problems of Achieving Socialism in Tanzania." In *Politics and Change in Developing Countries*, edited by Colin Leys, pp. 85–111. London: Cambridge University Press, 1969.

Gottlieb, Manuel. "The Extent and Character of Differentiation in Tanzanian Agricultural and Rural Society, 1967–1969." *African Review* 3 (1973):241–61.

Hill, Francis. "Ujamaa: African Socialist Productionism in Tanzania." In *Socialism in the Third World*, edited by Helen Desfosses and Jacques Lévesque, pp. 216–51. New York: Praeger, 1975.

Hyden, Goran. "Ujamaa, Villagization and Rural Development in Tanzania." *ODI Review* 1 (April 1975):53–72.

Lofchie, Michael. "Agrarian Socialism in the Third World: The Tanzanian Case." *Comparative Politics* 8, no. 3 (April 1976):479–99.

Mmapachu, Juma Volter. "Operation of Planned Villages in Rural Tanzania: A Revolutionary Strategy of Development." *African Review* 6 (1976):1–16.

Moderne, Franck. "Villages communautaive et socialisme tanzanien." *Development et Civilisations* (1970), pp. 147–67.

————. "Evolution et perspectives de la cooperations agricole en Tanzanie." *Revue Francaise d'Etudes Politiques Africaines*, no. 59 (November 1970).

Williams, Gavin. "Taking the Part of Peasants: Rural Development in Nigeria and Tanzania." In *The Political Economy of Contemporary Africa*, edited by Peter Gutkind and Immanuel Wallerstein, pp. 169–97. Beverly Hills: Sage Publications, 1976.

Raikes, P. L. "Ujamaa and Rural Socialism." *Review of African Political Economy* (May 1975), pp. 33–52.

Documents

Dumont, René, *Tanzanian Agriculture After the Arusha Declaration*. Dar es Salaam: Government Printer, 1969.

Kaplan, B. *New Settlement and Agricultural Development in Tanganyika*. Jerusalem: State of Israel, 1961.

Nyerere, Julius K. *Socialism and Rural Development*. Dar es Salaam: Government Printer, 1967.

Kenya and Tanzania

Books and Monographs

Hyden, Goran. *Efficiency Versus Distribution in East African Cooperatives*. Nairobi: East African Literature Bureau, 1973.

Articles

Inukai, Ichiro. "African Socialism and Agricultural Development Strategy: A Comparative Study of Kenya and Tanzania." *Developing Economies* 12 (March 1974):3–22.

8. URBAN POLICY

Kenya

Books and Monographs

Dutto, C. A. *Nyeri Townsmen, Kenya.* Nairobi: East African Literature Bureau, 1975.

Etherton, David. *Mathare Valley: A Case Study of Uncontrolled Housing in Nairobi.* Nairobi: University of Nairobi, Housing Research and Development Unit, 1971.

Housing Research and Development Unit. *Two Housing Schemes in Thika: User-Reaction Survey.* Nairobi: University of Nairobi, 1972.

King, K. J. *The African Artisan.* London: Heinemann, 1977.

Muller, M. S. *Social Relations on the Low-Income Housing Estate in Kitale.* Leiden: Afrikastudiecentrum, 1975.

Ross, Marc. *Grass Roots in an African City: Political Behavior in Nairobi.* Cambridge: MIT Press, 1975.

———. *The Political Integration of Urban Squatters.* Evanston: Northwestern University Press, 1973.

Sandbrook, Richard. *Proletarians and African Capitalism: The Kenyan Case 1960–72.* Cambridge: Cambridge University Press, 1975.

Stren, Richard E. *Housing and Urban Poor in Africa: Policy, Politics and Bureaucracy in Mombasa.* Berkeley: University of California, Institute of International Studies, 1977.

Werlin, Herbert. *Governing in an African City: A Study of Nairobi.* New York: Africana Publishing, 1974.

Articles

Avramovic, D. "Commodities in Nairobi." *Development and Change* 8 (April 1977):231–47.

Collier, Valerie C., and Henry Rempel. "The Divergence of Private from Social Costs in Rural-Urban Migration: A Case Study of Nairobi, Kenya." *Journal of Development Studies* 13 (April 1977): 199–216.

Elkan, Walter. "Is a Proletariat Emerging in Kenya?" *Economic Development and Cultural Change* 24 (1976):695–706.

House, W. J., and H. Rempel. "The Impact of Unionization on Negotiated Wages in the Manufacturing Sector." *Oxford Bulletin of Economics and Statistics* 38 (1976):111–23.

House, W. J., and T. S. Weisner. "Urban Migration and Urban-Rural Ties in Kenya." *Urban Anthropology* 5 (1976):199–223.

Harper, Malcolm. "Sugar and Maize Meal: Cases in Inappropriate Technology from Kenya." *Journal of Modern African Studies* 13 (September 1975):501–9.

Nigam, S. B. L., and H. W. Singer. "Labour Turnover and Employment: Some Evidence from Kenya." *International Labour Review* 110 (1974):479–94.

Pack, H. "Employment and Productivity in Kenyan Manufacturing." Discussion Paper no. 196. New Haven: Yale University, Economic Growth Center, 1974.

———. "The Substitution of Labour for Capital in Kenyan Manufacturing." *Economic Journal* 86 (March 1976):45–58.

———. "Unemployment and Income Distribution in Kenya." *Economic Development and Cultural Change* 26 (October 1977):157–68.

Ross, Marc. "Political Alienation, Participation and Ethnicity: An African Case." *American Journal of Political Science* 19 (1975):291–312.

———. "Community Formation in Urban Squatter Settlement." *Comparative Political Studies* 6 (1973):296–328.

Stichter, Sharon. "The Formation of a Working Class in Kenya." In *The Development of an African Working Class,* edited by Richard Sandbrook and Robin Cohen, pp. 21–48. Toronto: University of Toronto Press, 1975.

———. "Imperialism and the Rise of a 'Labour Aristocracy' in Kenya." *Berkeley Journal of Sociology* 21 (1976–77):157–78.

———. "Women and the Labor Force in Kenya, 1895–1964." *Rural Africana,* no. 29 (Winter 1975 76), pp. 45–67.

———. "Workers, Trade Unions, and the Mau Mau Rebellion." *Canadian Journal of African Studies* 9 (1975):259–75.

Tamarkin, M. "Tribal Associations, Tribal Solidarity, and Tribal Chauvinism in a Kenyan Town." *Journal of African History* 14 (1973):257–74.

Weeks, John. "Imbalance Between Center and Periphery and the 'Employment Crisis' in Kenya." In *Beyond the Sociology of Development,* edited by Ivar Oxaal et al., pp. 86–104. London: Routledge and Kegan Paul, 1975.

———. "Wage Policy and the Colonial Legacy—A Comparative Study." *The Journal of Modern African Studies* 9 (October 1971): 361–87.

Weisner, Thomas S. "The Structure of Sociability: Urban Migration and Urban-Rural Ties in Kenya." *Urban Anthropology* 5 (Summer 1976):199–223.

Documents

Bloomberg, Lawrence, and Charles Abrams. *Report of the United Nations Mission to Kenya on Housing.* Nairobi: Government Printer, 1965.

Government of Kenya, and International Bank for Reconstruction and Development. *Low Cost Housing and Squatter Upgrading Study.* Progress Report no. 7. Nairobi: Government Printer, 1976.

Government of Kenya. *Sessional Paper on Employment,* no. 10. Nairobi: Government Printer, 1973.

Tanzania

Books and Monographs

Barnum, H. N., and R. H. Sabot. *Migration, Education and Urban Surplus Labour: The Case of Tanzania.* Paris: OECD Development Center, 1976.

Friedland, William. *Vuta Kamba: The Development of Trade Unions in Tanganyika.* Stanford: Hoover Institution, 1969.

Mahiga, A., et al. *Labour in Tanzania.* Dar es Salaam: Tanzania Publishing House, 1976.

Mapolu, Henry, ed. *Workers and Management.* Dar es Salaam: Tanzania Publishing House, 1976.

Rweyemamu, Justinian. *Underdevelopment and Industrialization in Tanzania.* Nairobi: Oxford University Press, 1973.

Stren, Richard E. *Urban Inequality and Housing Policy in Tanzania: The Problems of Squatting.* Berkeley: University of California, Institute of International Studies, 1975.

Articles

Bienefeld, Manfred. "The Informal Sector and Peripheral Capitalism: The Case of Tanzania." *IDS Bulletin* 6 (February 1975):53–73.

Bienefeld, Manfred, and H. H. Binhammer. "Tanzania Housing Finance and Housing Policy." In *Urban Challenge in East Africa,* edited by John Hutton, pp. 179–99. Nairobi: East African Publishing House, 1972.

Coulson, A. C. "Tanzania's Fertilizer Factory." *Journal of Modern African Studies* 15 (March 1977):119–25.

Kunya, P. M. "Transfer of Technology: An Overview of the Tanzanian Case." *African Development* 2 (1977):47–72.

Loxley, John, and John Saul. "Multinationals, Workers and Parastatals in Tanzania." *Review of African Political Economy,* no. 2 (1975), pp. 54–88.

Roemer, Michael, et al. "The Range of Strategic Choice in Tanzanian Industry." *Journal of Development Economics* 3 (September 1976):257–75.

Sutton, J. E. G. ed. "Dar es Salaam: City, Port and Region." *Tanganyika Notes and Records,* (special issue), vol. 71 (1970).

Wangwe, S. M. "Factors Influencing Capacity Utilization in Tanzanian Manufacturing." *International Labour Review,* no. 115 (1977), pp. 65–78.

Documents

Tanzanian Ministry of Lands, Housing and Urban Development. *Urban Housing Needs, 1972–1976.* Dar es Salaam: Ardhi Planning Unit, 1971.

Kenya and Tanzania

Books and Monographs

John Hutton, ed. *Urban Challenge in East Africa.* Nairobi: East African Publishing House, 1972.

9. EDUCATION POLICY

Kenya

Books and Monographs

Anderson, John. *The Struggle for the School: The Interaction of Missionary, Colonial Government and Nationalist Enterprise in the Development of Formal Education in Kenya.* Nairobi: Longmans, 1970.

Brownstein, Lewis. *Education and Development in Rural Kenya: A Study of Primary School Graduates.* New York: Praeger, 1972.

Court, David, and Dharam P. Ghai, eds. *Education, Society and Development: New Perspectives from Kenya.* Nairobi: Oxford University Press, 1974.

Sheffield, James R. *Education, Employment and Rural Development in Kenya.* Nairobi: East African Publishing House, 1967.

————. *Education in Kenya: An Historical Study.* New York: Teachers College Press, 1973.

Articles

Court, David, and Kenneth C. Prewitt. "Nation Versus Region in Kenya: A Note on Political Learning." *British Journal of Political Science* 4 (January 1974): 109–15.

Ergas, Z., and Fred Chege. "Primary School Education in Kenya: An Attempt at Evaluation." *Journal of Eastern African Research and Development* 3, no. 2 (1973).

Evans, E. B. "Secondary Education, Unemployment and Crime in Kenya." *Journal of Modern African Studies* 13 (1975):55–66.

Keller, Edmond J. "The Political Socialization of Adolescents in Contemporary Africa: The Role of the School in Kenya." *Comparative Politics* 10 (January 1978):227–50.

McKown, R. E. "Kenya University Students and Politics." In *University Students and African Politics,* edited by William J. Hanna, pp. 211–55. New York: Africana Publishing, 1975.

Olson, J. B. "Secondary Schools and Elites in Kenya: A Comparative Study of Students in 1961 and 1968." *Comparative Education Review* 16, no. 1 (1972).

Tanzania

Books and Monographs

Barkan, Joel. *An African Dilemma: University Students, Development and Politics in Ghana, Tanzania and Uganda.* New York: Oxford University Press, 1975.

Gillette, Arthur L. *Beyond the Non-Formal Fashion: Towards Educational Revolution in Tanzania.* Amherst: University of Massachusetts, Center for International Education, 1977.

Hall, Budd L. *Adult Education and the Development of Socialism in Tanzania.* Nairobi: East African Literature Bureau, 1975.

Millonzi, J. C. *Citizenship in Africa: The Role of Adult Education in the Political Socialization of Tanganyikans, 1891–1961.* Foreign and Comparative Studies/ Eastern Africa, no. 19. Syracuse: Syracuse University, Maxwell School of Citizenship and Public Affairs, 1975.

Morrison, David. *Education and Politics in Africa: The Tanzanian Case.* Nairobi: Heinemann, 1976.

Resnick, Idrian, ed. *Tanzania: Revolution by Education.* Arusha, Tanzania: Longmans, 1968.

Articles

Barnum, H. N., and R. H. Sabot. "Education, Employment Probabilities and Rural-Urban Migration in Tanzania." *Oxford Bulletin of Economics and Statistics* (May 1977), pp. 109–26.

Court, David. "The Social Function of Formal Schooling in Tanzania." *African Review* 3 (1973):577–94.

Hirji, K. F. "School Education and Underdevelopment in Tanzania." *Maji Maji,* no. 12 (1973).

Mbiliyni, M. J. "Education, Stratification and Sexism in Tanzania." *African Review* 3 (1973):327–40.

Prewitt, Kenneth C., George Von der Muhll, and David Court. "Social Experiences and Political Socialization: A Study of Tanzanian Secondary School Students." *Comparative Political Studies* 3, no. 2 (1970):203–25.

Documents

Nyerere, Julius K. *Education and Self-Reliance.* Dar es Salaam: Government Printer, 1967.

Kenya and Tanzania

Books and Monographs

Prewitt, Kenneth C., ed. *Education and Political Values: An East African Case Study.* Nairobi: East African Publishing House, 1971.

Articles

Barkan, Joel D. "What Makes the East African Student Run?" *Transition,* no. 37 (1968), pp. 26–31.

Court, David. "East African Higher Education from the Community Standpoint." *Higher Education* 6 (1977):45–66.

Mbilinyi, M. J., ed. "Access to Education in East Africa." *Rural Africana* (special issue), no. 25 (1974).

O'Connor, Edmund. "Contrasts in Educational Development in Kenya and Tanzania." *African Affairs* 73 (1974):67–84.

Von der Muhll, George, and David Koff. "Political Socialization in Kenya and Tanzania: A Comparative Analysis." *Journal of Modern African Studies* 5, no. 1 (1967):13–51.

10. *FOREIGN POLICY*

Kenya

Books and Monographs

Amsden, Alice. *International Firms and Labour in Kenya, 1945–1970.* London: Frank Cass, 1971.

Holtham, G., and A. Hazelwood. *Aid and Inequality in Kenya: British Development Assistance to Kenya.* London: Croom Helm, 1976.

Kaplinsky, Raphael. *Readings on the Multinational Corporations in Kenya.* Nairobi: Oxford University Press, 1971.

Articles

Jorgensen, J. J. "Multinational Corporations and the Indigenization of the Kenyan Economy." *African Review* 5 (1975):429–50.

Langdon, Steven. "Multinational Firms and the State in Kenya." *IDS Bulletin* 9 (July 1977):36–41.

————. "Multinational Corporations, Tax Transfer and Underdevelopment: A Case Study from Kenya. *Review of African Political Economy,* no. 2 (1975) pp. 12–35.

————. "The Political Economy of Dependence: Note Toward Analysis of Multinational Corporations in Kenya." *Journal of Eastern African Research and Development* 4 (1974):123–59.

Martin, Denis. "L'Occident L'Ocean et le Kenya." *Annuaire des Pays de L'Ocean Indien* (1975), pp. 229–42.

National Christian Council of Kenya. *Who Controls Industry in Kenya?* Nairobi: East African Publishing House, 1968.

Okumu, John J. "Some Thoughts on Kenya's Foreign Policy." *The African Review* 3, no. 2 (1973): 272–76.

Documents

Who Controls Industry in Kenya: Report of a Working Party. Nairobi: East African Publishing House, 1968.

Tanzania

Books and Monographs

Bailey, Martin. *Freedom Railway.* London: Collings. 1976.

Gitelson, S. A. *Multilateral Aid for National Development and Self-Reliance: A Case Study of the UNDP in Uganda and Tanzania.* Nairobi: East African Literature Bureau, 1975.

Nnoli, O. *Self-Reliance and Foreign Policy in Tanzania.* New York: NOK Publishers, 1977.

Yu, George T. *China's African Policy: A Study of Tanzania.* New York: Praeger, 1975.

Articles

Bailey, Martin. "Zanzibar External Relations." *International Journal of Politics* 4 (1974):35–57.

Bienefeld, M. A. "Special Gains from Trade with Socialist Countries: The Case of Tanzania." *World Development* 3 (May 1975): 247–71.

Green, R. H. "Aspects of the World Monetary and Resource Transfer System in 1974: A View from the Extreme Periphery." In *A World Divided,* edited by G. K. Helleiner, pp. 251–73. Cambridge: Cambridge University Press, 1975.

Niblock, T. C. "Tanzania Foreign Policy: An Analysis." *African Review* (1971): 91–101.

Pratt, Cranford. "Foreign-policy Issues and the Emergence of Socialism in Tanzania 1961–68." *International Journal* 30 (Summer 1975):446–70.

Shaw, T. M. "African States and International Stratification: The Adaptive Foreign Policy of Tanzania." In *Foreign Relations of African States,* edited by K. Ingham, pp. 213–33. London: Butterworths, 1974.

Yu, George T. "Chinese Aid to Africa: The Tanzania-Zambia Railway." In *Chinese and Soviet Aid to Africa,* edited by W. Weinstein, pp. 29–55. New York: Praeger, 1975.

Documents

Nyerere, Julius K. "Policy on Foreign Affairs." Paper presented at biannual National Conference of TANU, October 16, 1967.

Kenya and Tanzania

Articles

Gitelson, Susan A. "Policy Options for Small States: Kenya and Tanzania Reconsidered." *Studies in Comparative International Development* 12, no. 2 (1977).

Stein, Leslie. "Export Trends in East Africa." *Development and Change* 8 (1977): 103–16.

INDEX

ABOUT THE EDITOR
AND CONTRIBUTORS

JOEL D. BARKAN is Associate Professor of Political Science at the University of Iowa, and was Senior Lecturer in Political Science at the University of Dar es Salaam in 1973 and 1974.

Professor Barkan is the author of *An African Dilemma: University Students, Development and Politics in Ghana, Tanzania and Uganda,* and has contributed to the *American Political Science Review, Western Political Quarterly,* and *Operations Research* as well as to several anthologies on various aspects of political behavior in the third world. He holds an A.B. from Cornell, and an M.A. and Ph.D. from UCLA.

JOHN J. OKUMU is Director of the East African Management Institute in Arusha, Tanzania, and was previously Professor of Political Science at the University of Khartoum. He has also been a member of the departments of political science at the University of Dar es Salaam, the University of Nairobi, Grinnell College, and Yale University.

Professor Okumu has published widely on various aspects of East African politics, and is the co-editor and co-author of *Development Administration: The Kenyan Experience.* He holds a B.A. from Grinnell, and obtained his M.A. and Ph.D. from UCLA.

CLAUDE AKE is a Nigerian and is presently Professor of Political Science at the University of Port Harcourt. Prior to returning to Nigeria in 1977 he taught at Carleton University, Columbia University, and the Universities of Dar es Salaam and Nairobi.

Professor Ake is the author of three books, the most recent of which is *Revolutionary Pressures in Africa.*

He holds a B.S. from the University College, Ibadan, and received his M.A. and Ph.D. from Columbia University.

DAVID COURT is Visiting Senior Research Fellow at the Institute for Development Studies at the University of Nairobi, and is the East African representative of the Rockefeller Foundation.

He is the co-editor and co-author of *Education, Society and Development: New Perspectives from Kenya,* and is the author of a variety of articles on education and educational policy in East Africa.

Dr. Court was born in Britain, and was educated at Cambridge, Makerere, and Stanford Universities.

FRANK HOLMQUIST is Assistant Professor of Political Science at Hampshire College, and was a member of the department of political science at the University of Dar es Salaam from 1973 to 1975.

Dr. Holmquist has contributed to *Development Administration: The Kenyan Experience,* and to *Rural Africana* and the *African Review.*

Dr. Holmquist was born in Madison, Wisconsin, and received his B.A. from Lawrence University. He holds an M.A. and Ph.D. from Indiana University.

GORAN HYDEN is presently the East African representative of the Ford Foundation for the social sciences, and has previously been a member of the departments of political science at the University of Dar es Salaam, the University of Nairobi, and Makerere University.

Dr. Hyden has published widely on the subject of rural development and administration in East Africa. He is the author of three books, the most recent of which is *Peasants and Underdevelopment in Africa: The Tanzanian Experience and Beyond.*

Dr. Hyden was born in Sweden. He received all of his university degrees from the University of Lund.

S. E. MIGOT-ADHOLLA is Senior Research Fellow at the Institute for Development Studies at the University of Nairobi.

A specialist on rural sociology, Dr. Migot has contributed articles on various aspects of rural development in East Africa to *Ufahamu* and to several anthologies.

Dr. Migot was born in Mombasa, Kenya. He received his B.A. from the University of Dar es Salaam, and his M.A. and Ph.D. from UCLA.

RICHARD E. STREN is Associate Professor of Political Economy at the University of Toronto. During 1972–73 he was in charge of the Planning Unit at the Ministry of Lands, Housing and Urban Development in Tanzania, and in 1973–74 he was a member of the Institute for Development Studies at the University of Nairobi.

Dr. Stren is the author of two monographs on housing policy in East Africa, and has contributed to the *African Studies Review,* the *Canadian Journal of African Studies,* and the *Journal of Modern African Studies.*

Dr. Stren was born in Toronto. He received his B.A. from the University of Toronto, and his M.A. and Ph.D. from the University of California, Berkeley.

RELATED TITLES

Published by
Praeger Special Studies

POLITICS IN THE SUDAN: Parliamentary and Military Rule in an Emerging African Nation

Peter K. Bechtold

THE STATUS OF ALIENS IN EAST AFRICA: Asians and Europeans in Tanzania, Uganda, and Kenya

Daniel D. C. Don Nanjira

AFRICAN URBAN SYSTEMS AND URBAN DEVELOPMENT

edited by R. A. Obudho and
Salah S. El-Shakhs

EQUITY, INCOME, AND POLICY: Comparative Studies in Three Worlds of Development

edited by
Irving Louis Horowitz